The Creation of Washington, D.C. The Idea and Location of The American Capital

Kenneth R. Bowling

GEORGE MASON UNIVERSITY PRESS
Fairfax, Virginia

Copyright © 1991 by

George Mason University Press
4400 University Drive
Fairfax, VA 22030

Distributed by arrangement with
University Publishing Associates, Inc.

4720 Boston Way
Lanham, MD 20706

3 Henrietta Street
London WC2E 8LU England

Library of Congress Cataloging-in-Publication Data

Bowling, Kenneth R.
The creation of Washington, D.C. : the idea and location
of the American capital / Kenneth R. Bowling.
p.   cm.
Includes bibliographical references.
1. Washington (D.C.)—History.   2. United States—
Capital and capitol.   3. United States—Politics and
government—1783-1809.   I. Title.
F197.B69   1990
975.3'01—dc20   90-39255 CIP

ISBN 0-913969-29-X (alk. paper)

 The paper used in this publication meets the minimum requirements of
American National Standard for Information Sciences—Permanence
of Paper for Printed Library Materials, ANSI Z39.48-1984.

To the staff of the
State Historical Society of Wisconsin
for their assistance over the years,
in particular,
Ellen Burke
Jerry Eggleston
Jim Danky
Sharon Mulak
John Peters
Wilma Thompson

Frontispiece: George Washington contemplating the plan of
the American Capital. *The Washington Family*, 1796, by Edward
Savage (The National Gallery of Art, Washington: Andrew W.
Mellon Collection).

Contents

Foreword vii

Preface ix

Acknowledgments xii

Introduction: A Capital for a Republican Empire 1

1. Chained to Philadelphia, 1774–1783 14

2. The Confederation Congress
   and the Federal Towns, 1783–1787 43

3. Exclusive Jurisdiction and the
   Constitutional Revolution, 1787–1789 74

4. Potomac Fever 106

5. The Rupture of the Federalist Consensus, 1789 127

6. The Crisis of the Union, 1789–1790 161

7. The Compromise of 1790 182

8. George Washington in Command, 1790–1799 208

Epilogue: Potomac Fever Revisited 235

Abbreviations Used in Notes 247

Notes 251

Index 280

Foreword

Article 1, § 8, Paragraph 17 of the Constitution of the United States provides for the establishment of a national capital. Its most important provisions specify "a seat of government" not to exceed ten miles square, exclusive legislation by Congress, and arrangements for the acquisition of related rights from the states involved. These were new and powerful ideas. A large Federal City, not just a few buildings, was to be created. In this district, Congress was to have exclusive jurisdiction, and the states ceding land were to yield jurisdiction. It was Congress, not the President or any other agency, that was to exercise these powers. Here was clearly a new kind of city. How should it be created? What rights would the residents of the capital city have—comparable to those rights given citizens in their state constitutions? Over two centuries have passed since the United States embarked upon this significant civic adventure, years in which this provision of the Constitution has been variously interpreted. Limited home rule now prevails in the District of Columbia, and the continuing campaign for statehood proceeds, a fight that will go on. One of the more recent issues is related to the Federal interest beyond the original "ten miles square" where most of the Federal establishment is located in a sprawling metropolitan city that has reduced "Washington" to the dimensions of a postage stamp on a regional letter.

Hardly an issue raised by this Constitutional provision and what Congress should do about it was not recognized and debated in the First Federal Congress that, in the end, located the Federal City on the Potomac. The same goes for the successive legislative bodies that in the last 200 years have kept it there and developed it into the magnificent city we see today and that is visited by tens of millions annually.

Kenneth Bowling's book is up-to-the-minute as the Capital Beltway or the 100 mile Metro transit system, the location of a new jail or airport, the quality of Potomac river water or the regulation of the drug traffic. It is a fully developed story from the time when James Madison first presented the capital's Constitutional language to Congress, fascinating in its details and its day-to-day language as if we were eye-witnesses to the action.

Dr. Bowling rightly takes the high ground and the long view, beginning with the wartime experiences of the peripatetic Congress. He is fully aware of the opportunities the founders and their designers saw in the clean slate offered by the Potomac location by contrast to the more pragmatic advantages of more fully developed Philadelphia, then the second largest city of the English–speaking world. But there were dozens of candidates in the competition for the capital location, each with its own list of qualifications. Not until the 1947 United Nations site selection competition was anything similar to be seen.

The heritage of this experience is the continuing debate on the kind of city Washington should be. No more searching, fundamental, or relevant contribution has been written than what you will discover in this book. May this volume find the readers it deserves as the capital city moves into its third century.

Frederick Gutheim

Preface

The debate over the nature of the American capital reflected, and can be seen as a metaphor for, the constitutional struggle over federalism which dominated politics throughout the thirty-year American Revolution. Some Americans, referred to here as centralists, sought a strong federal government supreme over the states and a capital to reflect its glory. Decentralists, on the other hand, supported state supremacy and a strictly limited federal government and capital.

The fight over the proper site for the American capital became a major issue in congressional politics during the Revolution. The documentation members of the revolutionary generation composed to report and justify their actions and opinions details the history of the location of the capital more completely than the history of such more familiar issues as the disposition of western lands and the acquisition of federal revenues. The time and energy they poured into the fight provide insight into the nature of the politics of compromise and the men who practiced it, as well as into the distinctions they made or failed to make among the good of the whole, the interests of their constituents and private gain.

More often than anything else between 1783 and 1791, the capital fight rent the deceptive veil behind which the North and South hid their differences. Congress devoted as much attention to the site of its temporary and permanent seat as it did to either the land or the revenue issues. The capital fight hobbled the Confederation Congress for more than a year, influenced the drafting and ratification of the Constitution, and dominated politics in the First Federal Congress between 1789 and 1791. It modified fundamentally the political image of George Washington as detached and magisterial, thus ending Federalist hopes of using him to construct an imperial presidency. The controversy also transformed James Madison from Federalist theoretician to leader of an emerging opposition party.

The fight over the location of the capital early on became caught up in a web of other questions facing the First Federal Congress. In 1790, the Federalist Party's new leader, Alexander Hamilton, proposed a relationship among private investors, banks, and the federal and state governments which gave congressional sanction to what became American financial capitalism. Southerners in

ix

particular balked at parts of the plan. Led by Madison, they proved most effective in blocking Hamilton's proposal that the federal government pay the revolutionary war debt of the states, arguing that the Constitution did not grant Congress the power to do so. The legislative process all but came to a stop. At the same time constituents, both in the North and the South, reported sentiment for a dissolution of the Union and even civil war.

Madison and Hamilton, with the backing of Thomas Jefferson and George Washington, struck a compromise by which the North secured southern acquiescence to both financial capitalism and the constitutional doctrine of implied powers. In exchange, the South—after seven frustrating years of defeat—at last gained passage of an act placing the United States capital on the Potomac River. Along with it came the strong implication that the North would not raise serious objections to the institution of slavery, for the North had consented to a capital located in two slave states. Although America's political leaders believed that the differences between North and South would long plague the Union, they hoped they had found an indissoluble bond: a republican empire, fueled by northern financial and commercial capitalism, the capital of which sat in the agrarian, slave South.

The Compromise of 1790 was the first of three great political compromises between the North and South which were to come with regularity every thirty years in continuing efforts to preserve the Union. It focused more directly on an issue which underlay the passionate debates of 1820 and 1850: the role of agrarianism in a capitalist economy. Appropriately, the outspoken agrarian democrat, Senator William Maclay of Pennsylvania, closed his diary account of the second session of the First Federal Congress in 1790 with the hope that the decision to go to the Potomac might give a preponderance to agriculture in the dire contest he foresaw between the two economic philosophies.

Maclay however failed to appreciate an important fact about Madison, Jefferson, and Washington. Although Virginians, particularly those associated with the economic promotion of the Potomac River, often spoke for the South in Congress, they were not typically southern. Strongly influenced by the commercial ethos of the Middle States, particularly the Chesapeake world, they did not oppose commercial capitalism. They opposed its profits going north. Consequently, they dreamt of a Potomac capital which would not only strengthen southern political power, but also establish Virginia as a commercial state perhaps without rival in the Union. The capital they envisioned would serve the American Empire as both its preeminent political and commercial center as it spread westward to the Pacific. For this dream of uniting The Hague and Amsterdam into one city, promoters of a Potomac capital abandoned agrarianism and even strict construction of the Constitution.

The 200-year old decision to seat the capital on the Potomac River has never been repealed despite the westward-moving center of both territory and population. The reason for this is the momentous nature of the 1790 decision, not the ever-increasing speed of communication and travel.

Acknowledgments

While doing research for a master's thesis on the first federal election, I puzzled over why the Federalists, after struggling so long for a more powerful federal government, allowed something as mundane as the meeting place of the First Federal Congress to stymie its implementation. In writing a dissertation on that Congress, I puzzled over why the same issue took up more time off the floor than any other, while on the floor the time spent in debate on it rivaled the time spent on Alexander Hamilton's plan for public credit. I decided to find out by looking at the issue in depth. Research time for this was made possible by a bicentennial fellowship from the National Endowment for the Humanities in 1971. While I taught at the Institute for Environmental Studies at the University of Wisconsin in the early 1970s, Associate Director John E. Ross provided me with enough research assistance to discover the vast amount of newspaper ink devoted to the issue of the American capital. Additional financial assistance came from the American Philosophical Society in 1977.

Dozens of people have contributed to this book during its many years in production. I will attempt to acknowledge them, regretting any omissions. Henry Young and Warren Gates of Dickinson College introduced me to the study of history. Merrill Jensen of the University of Wisconsin stimulated my interest in the politics of the American Revolution and a love for research. The staff of the State Historical Society of Wisconsin graciously assisted my exploration. My fellow seminarian Richard Kohn long has served as midwife for this book. Immediately after graduate school I searched American manuscript repositories for documents relating to the ratification of the Constitution, the first federal election, and the First Federal Congress. This brought me into contact with Leonard Rapport whose knowledge of manuscripts and the various routes they have taken from the hand of their authors to their late twentieth century locations expanded and enriched my graduate training. My fellow searcher Gaspare J. Saladino of the University of Wisconsin called many relevant manuscripts to my attention. At the same time I received support and encouragement from Julian Boyd, editor of the Papers of Thomas Jefferson. In 1974 Linda Grant DePauw made me an offer I could not refuse, and since then I have had the privilege of a research and documentary editing career. To these individuals and institutions I owe my greatest obligations.

Others who have assisted in a variety of ways include: Priscilla McNeil of Washington, D.C.; James Mooney, Arthur Breton, and Thomas Dunnings of The New-York Historical Society; Noble Cunningham of the University of Missouri; Edward Papenfuse of the Maryland Hall of Records; Jerry Nadelhaft of the University of Maine; Roy Merrens of York University, Toronto; William Appleman Williams of Oregon State University; George Billias of Clark University; Edwin Wolf, 2nd, then of the Library Company of Philadelphia; Margaret C.S. Christman and Roland White of the National Portrait Gallery; Peter Parker and the staff of the manuscript room of the Historical Society of Pennsylvania, particularly Conrad Wilson, Thomas Duncan and Vilma Halcombe; Carolyn Sung, Mary Wolfskill, Charles Cooney and Chuck Kelly of the Manuscript Division of the Library of Congress; Ron Grim of the Cartographic Division of the National Archives; George M. Curtis, III, of Hanover College; Tee Loftin of Washington D.C.; Betsy Abramson and Nancy Louther of Madison, Wisconsin; Carla Schmidt of Denver, Colorado; Linda Rodrigues of Newark, New Jersey; and Linda Newman and Richard Maxwell of the University of Wisconsin.

Particularly helpful have been those historians who have devoted at least part of their careers to documentary editing: foremost my colleague at the First Federal Congress Project, Charlene Bickford; Laurie Kittle and Karen Treeger, former colleagues there; John P. Kaminksi, Richard Leffler, Charlie Hagermann, Douglas Clanin, Gordon Den Boer, Lucy Brown, David E. Maas and Joseph L. Davis at the Ratification and First Federal Election projects; Paul Smith, editor of the Letters of Delegates to Congress, 1774–1789; Dorothy Twohig and Bill Abbot of the Papers of George Washington; Elizabeth Nuxoll, Mary Gallagher and Nelson Dearmont at the Papers of Robert Morris; Lyman C. Butterfield and Celeste Walker of the Adams Family Papers; Robert Rutland, Chuck Hobson and David Mattern of the Papers of James Madison; and Charles Cullen of the John Marshall Papers.

Various people have assisted with the publication process. The suggestions of Henry Tom of the Association for Documentary

Editing changed the book fundamentally. Jeffrey A. Kirsch of Tulane University critiqued the prose. My colleague Helen E. Veit, whose editing skills come with broad historical knowledge and a questioning mind, found numerous errors and made many useful suggestions. Avniel Ben-Israel lent his proofreader's eye. William diGiacomantonio assisted with indexing. Without the efforts of Jon Kukla of the Virginia State Library, Linda Lear of George Mason University and Allida Black of The George Washington University, I would not have discovered George Mason University Press. There Mark Carroll and Isabelle Gibb have a style of press–author relationship which is supportive and personal.

A heavily illustrated, different version of portions of this book, *Creating the Federal City, 1774–1800: Potomac Fever,* was published by The American Institute of Architects Press to accompany an exhibit at the Octagon Museum in 1988.

In quotations, spelling and occasionally capitalization has been modernized for the convenience of the reader. The extensive annotation which supports the text of this book is designed to assist interested individuals who wish to explore the topic in more depth and to act as a bibliography for what has previously been written on the subject.

Kenneth R. Bowling
First Federal Congress Project
The George Washington University
Washington, D.C.

Attempts to fix the seat of government, in every country where the people have the right of suffrage, are marked by the effects of passion and private interest.

> Former North Carolina Representative Hugh Williamson, *History of North Carolina* (2 volumes, New York, 1812), 2:56.

We should remember the question is not, what will be most convenient or best suit the interest of New England. But what does the interest of the Union require? How shall that be accommodated? But this last I suppose would be an odd question in Congress. There, it is the Southern interest, *or the* Northern; *and every man of them ranges himself upon one side or the other, and contends with as much earnestness and warmth as if at an Olympic Game.*

> Maine Newspaper Editor Thomas B. Wait to Congressman George Thatcher, 21 August 1788, FE 1:95.

If the Big Knife [Virginia and/or George Washington] would give up Potomac the matter would be easily settled. But that you will say is as unreasonable as it would be to expect a Pennsylvanian to surrender at discretion to New York. . . . It therefore amuses me to see the arguments our grave politicians bring forward when I know it will be determined by local interests which will not suffer intrigue and management to grow rusty from want of use.

> Former Congressman Richard Peters of Philadelphia to Secretary of State Thomas Jefferson, 20 June 1790, TJ 16:539.

Introduction

A Capital for a Republican Empire

THE HISTORICAL THESIS "WESTWARD THE COURSE OF empire takes its way"—from the Middle East to Greece, from Greece to Rome, from Rome to western Europe and soon to America—captivated mid-eighteenth century British intellectuals on both sides of the Atlantic.[1] Benjamin Franklin became one of the earliest and most articulate advocates of the idea in North America. In a pamphlet published twenty years before the Declaration of Independence, he vigorously advocated the agricultural expansion of Europeans westward across the wilderness continent. After reading Franklin's essay, twenty–year old John Adams speculated on a future when the seat of empire would cross the Atlantic. Even the British press occasionally commented on the spreading idea that America would be the future seat of empire and London merely a provincial seat of government. Belief in the westward course of empire and the collateral utopian idea of America as a beneficent or "good" empire, destined to conceive or revive a true republic for the benefit of all mankind, was central to the American revolutionary world view. "We have laid the foundations of a new empire, which promises to enlarge itself to vast dimensions, and to give happiness to a great continent," a South Carolinian revolutionary who had graduated from the College of New Jersey at Princeton proclaimed in 1778. "It is now our turn to figure on the face of the earth, and in the annals of the world."[2]

By 1789, when the First Federal Congress under the Constitution began to give force to the document's words, the idea that the United States would become the world's most powerful empire no longer belonged only to the well read few. That year Jedidiah

1

Morse justified publication of his popular *American Geography* on
the premise that it was "well known that empire has been travelling
from east to west. Probably her last and broadest seat will be America . . . we cannot but anticipate the period, as not far distant, when
the AMERICAN EMPIRE will comprehend millions of souls, west
of the Mississippi."³ Morse's belief that the United States might be
the final empire—that the rise and fall of empires might be reaching an end—reflected the impact of the idea of progress. This idea
underlay nineteenth–century American nationalism and the institutions which instilled it in the expanding vistas of American consciousness.

    Skepticism nevertheless existed about the feasibility of Ameri-
ca's ever becoming an empire. A French visitor to the United States
during the Revolutionary War considered Americans who espoused
the idea to be fanatics. An Englishman predicted that "when those
immense regions beyond the back settlements are taken into account . . . the Americans can never be united into one compact Empire under any species of government whatever." Americans had
hesitated during the war to confront the contradiction between republicanism, which they believed could thrive only in small homo-
geneous territories, and their vision of a vast continental empire
situated between two oceans and perhaps extending from the Canadian Arctic across the Caribbean to the Isthmus of Darien (Panama).⁴ In the "Tenth Federalist" in 1787, James Madison,
influenced at the College of New Jersey by the ideas of David
Hume, provided an argument for the survival of republicanism in a
large, heterogeneous empire: the more territory the Republic encompassed, the more diverse the competing interests; therefore,
no single interest, or any individual, could ever subvert liberty
throughout the land. This proved a captivating rationale and
quickly became American political dogma.

    Well versed in Ancient and European History, political leaders
of the revolutionary generation recognized many benefits
associated with capitals and their locations. They had fought over
the location of county seats and colonial and state capitals dozens of
times prior to the struggle over the site of the federal capital, just as
their descendants have continued to do.

From a political and economic standpoint, proximity to the seat of government meant access to federal officials and offices as well as the opportunity to take quick advantage of and influence information, legislation, contracts and jobs. Speculators in land and paper considered such access of special importance. Hard money would emanate from and circulate about the capital. The construction of buildings would offer employment and governmentally funded contracts for local residents. Property values in and about the site would rise. The federal government would pay for transportation improvements and military protection. Profits realized from serving the needs of federal officeholders portended to be as unlimited as the potential for government growth. Even farmers in the hinterland of proposed capital sites expected to reap some of the benefits.[5]

In 1783 congressmen estimated the annual value of the capital to a local economy at $100,000 to $150,000. Five years later the estimate ran as high as $250,000; in 1789 Madison set it at half a million. By 1790, when agreement on the location was finally achieved, Jefferson put its worth at approximately one million dollars per year.[6] If the capital became a commercial, manufacturing or financial, as well as political center, it would generate economic growth and additional wealth for the chosen locale.

Regional supremacy within the Union also stood at stake. Geopolitically aware Americans recognized two major sectional divisions within the United States. That between North and South was easiest to define because of the prevalence of slavery below the Mason–Dixon Line. That among the South, the Middle States, and the Eastern or New England States was more difficult. New York was sometimes included with the Middle States and sometimes with the Eastern States, but was considered distinct from the New England States. Connecticut, Maryland and Virginia were sometimes considered Middle States, and Pennsylvania sometimes a Southern State. There was not and cannot be agreement on precise boundaries.

Sectional consciousness, sectional power within the Union, and the threat of its dissolution influenced politics throughout the Revolution as much as they did in later years. Congress experienced frequent sectional disputes and members from each region knew keenly the value of residing close enough to the seat of government to arrive early and remain throughout the session. Such a sectionally divided society clearly understood that the power and prestige associated with the capital would provide political leverage to the section in which it was located.

The South, particularly sensitive to its identity, saw the advantages of a southern exposure for providing the proper hue to the government. Given the right location, southern views on any issue—including slavery—would be more readily heard than northern ones. During the 1780s the Southern States pictured themselves as a minority in the Union and their interests threatened by a combination of the Middle and New England States. On the other hand the South believed just as strongly that it would quickly become the dominant influence in the Union. It predicted that population would expand south and west and that new agriculturally based states in the West would ally themselves with the South. Southerners seized every opportunity to cite either their present minority status or their future majority status as reason for a more southern capital. America's ally France considered a southern location to be in its best interest.[7]

Despite predominant concern for the parts, the decision impacted the whole. Properly located, a capital would cement the North, South and West, thus insuring the survival of the Union and the prestige and respect Congress so desperately sought to establish for itself at home and abroad. It would reflect such American ideals as liberty, union and republican empire. By 1789 some Americans expected their capital to become a new Rome, "the mistress of the western world, the patroness of science and of arts, the dispenser of freedom, justice and peace to unborn millions," or a new Byzantium, "the seat of science, manufactures and commerce for ages yet to come." Six years later the author of an "Essay on the City of Washington" saw the capital as the means of confirming forever a union which would one day rule all of North America. To such a capital would flock those Americans who sought to participate in and witness the theater of American political, economic, and cultural life and had the wealth and concomitant leisure to reside there. The United States capital would, he predicted, outshine

Rome, London and all the capitals of ancient and modern civilization.[8]

The size of the capital and the amount of jurisdiction which the federal government would exercise there grew as the strength of the centralists increased. In 1783 the proposed sites ranged in area from one to twenty-five square miles, and Congress rejected a select committee proposal that it exercise exclusive jurisdiction over its seat. In 1787 the Federal Convention proposed, and the states ratified, a Constitution creating a district of one hundred square miles over which Congress exercised exclusive jurisdiction. The inclusion of exclusive jurisdiction expressed the fundamental change in the American attitude toward the federal government which took place between 1774 and 1788.

Prior to ratification of the Constitution in 1788 the term "capital" for Americans meant the seat of a state government. Even in jest or boast it was rarely used for the place at which the federal government conducted its affairs. During the war Americans usually referred to Philadelphia simply as the meetingplace of Congress. The idea that Congress should have its own territory was inconceivable to most of them. With the adoption of the Articles of Confederation and the sense of optimism which swept through the land after military victory had assured independence in 1781, different terms came into usage. "Residence of Congress," "seat of government" and "federal town" all became popular in the 1780s. With the emergence of a federal government dominant over the states at the end of the decade, grander terminology began to appear: "federal city," "capital" and even occasionally "imperial seat or city." The most common terms throughout the debate, "residence of Congress" and "seat of government," were often used interchangeably despite the fact that the latter implied greater permanency.[9]

Few Americans had specific notions about what cultural institutions should exist at their capital. As early as 1783 Rev. Jeremy Belknap of Boston proposed that Congress provide a room at "Columbia" to display trophies taken from the British during the War for Independence, since the sight of them would "fan the flame of liberty and independence." Various men made proposals during the First Federal Congress for a scientific society at the seat of government or an agricultural experimental farm outside of it. Charles

Willson Peale of Philadelphia hoped to settle near Congress and place his museum under its patronage. In the 1790s others suggested the creation of a botanical garden. Nevertheless, the only cultural institution which found any serious support, albeit minimal, was a national university. George Washington, who encouraged the idea, believed such an institution at the capital would allow young men from the North and South to mix, thereby breaking down sectional prejudices based on ignorance.[10]

Whatever institutions the capital might eventually house, at least one American knew they would not come quickly. No one gave more thought to the plan of an American capital than Pierre Charles L'Enfant, a French-born artist, architect and engineer, who had served in the Continental Army. In proposing an army corps of engineers to Congress in 1784, he observed that, considering the financial situation, it would take decades to build a town "in such a manner as to give an idea of the greatness of the empire as well as to engrave in every mind that sense of respect that is due to a place which is the seat of a supreme sovereignty." Five years later he enlarged on these thoughts to President George Washington: "No Nation perhaps had ever before the opportunity offered them of deliberately deciding on the spot where their Capital City should be fixed, or of combining every necessary consideration in the choice of the situation—and although the means now within the power of the country are not such as to pursue the design to any great extent it will be obvious that the plan should be drawn on such a scale as to leave room for that aggrandizement and embellishment which the increase of the wealth of the Nation will permit it to pursue at any period however remote."[11]

To those Americans who worried about the survival of republicanism, the dangers of a magnificent capital were immense, particularly if it became a commercial as well as a political city. Simply put, republicanism, as espoused by Americans at the time of the Declaration of Independence, was an institutionally expressed political and social philosophy which believed that people, while self-interested and power-seeking, were capable of uncorrupted self-government and industrious, frugal lives. Citizens delegated their sovereignty to popularly elected legislatures, supreme over executives. Representation was indirect, social distinctions but not aristocracy acceptable, and the interests of political minorities protected. Individual liberty, the good of the whole and the balance between them were its goals. Powerful social changes confronted republicanism in the late eighteenth century: urbanization, manufacturing, centralization, capitalism and the triumph of the economic rights of the individual over those of the community. As a result, the fulcrum of revolution bred intense debate and brought about a new definition of republicanism in the United States which accepted such previously anti–republican elements as the eighteenth century British fiscal system, "commerce," "luxury" (materialism), cities and even an urban capital.[12]

The threats which the capital posed to republicanism received their widest discussion during the struggle over the ratification of the Constitution in 1787 and 1788. But both before and after that great debate some Americans expressed concern. In 1785 the legislature of Massachusetts instructed its congressional delegation to appropriate money for a federal town built with that economy and plainness suitable to a young republic. Mercy Warren of Massachusetts feared mobs, the introduction of monarchical ideas, the parade and trappings of aristocratic courts and the arrival of European manners and the younger sons of European nobility. John Dickinson of Pennsylvania questioned the wisdom of locating the seat of government of a republic in that part of its territory in which slavery thrived. Patrick Henry of Virginia believed that the effect of proximity to the capital on a locality would be positive only if the federal government remained virtuous; if it evolved into a tyranny, a citizen would be better off living on the frontier, distant from its influence.[13] Thomas Jefferson of Virginia, blinded by his commitment to a commercial capital on the Potomac, was convinced that the Republic could remain virtuous and need not suffer from the intrigue, luxury, dissipation and vices of the body so inherent to Tom Jones's cosmopolitan London.

In 1786 the premier issue of the *Columbian Magazine* predicted that in 1850 the thirtieth state would join the Union and send delegates to the capital at Columbia. That the author ventured to estimate the number of states in the Union but not identify the location of Columbia reflects both a commitment to the westward course of empire and an absence of consensus as to where the seat of empire should be sited. Between 1782 and 1790 advocates of almost fifty sites between Newburgh, New York, Norfolk, Virginia, and the Ohio River spared neither superlative nor imagination as they competed for the capital. Environmental detail such as climate, relief, scenic grandeur, soil, drainage, healthiness and defensibility received attention. So too did economic base—accommodations, hinterland, transportation, labor, relationship to urban areas and the availability of energy sources and building materials. The preponderant considerations, however, were centrality and accessibility to both the West and the Atlantic Ocean. Nevertheless, it is well to remember that the "Ohioisms"—exaggerated claims on behalf of a site—as well as the statistics and reasoned geographical argument in favor of the various sites, had significant impact only when proponents had the political clout to back them up.[14]

The North and South disagreed on the definition of centrality, and politicians proved adept at portraying it in whatever manner best justified the particular place each supported. Northerners based it on population, arguing that equal access by the citizenry ranked paramount in a Republic. The 1790 census centered population southwest of the Susquehanna River in Maryland, at a point closer to the falls of the Potomac than to the falls of the Delaware. Before this was known, the North insisted that the point lay northeast of the Susquehanna in Pennsylvania, while the South believed it to be below that river and ever moving southwestward. Southerners considered centrality of territory on the Atlantic coast more important than centrality of population. Congress could more effectively apply the reins of government over the American Empire if no one part of it was more distant from the capital than any other. Centrality of territory did not appeal to the North because the midpoint between the St. Croix and St. Marys rivers—the northern and southern boundaries of the United States—was known to be on the Potomac River in the vicinity of Georgetown, Maryland, and Alexandria, Virginia. While a few northerners consequently dismissed geographic centrality altogether, others pointed out that the admission of Canada to the Union would shift that center northward, or that centrality of wealth should also be weighed.

The South's insistence that the future westward growth of the Union be taken into account in seating the capital fueled the sectional disagreement. By 1790 the American people, who seven years earlier had commenced a bitter dispute over which of several coastal communities should be selected as the seat of empire, were migrating west into and beyond the Appalachian Mountains. The western extremes of Virginia and North Carolina soon would have sufficient residents to qualify for admission to the Union as Kentucky and Tennessee. And five thousand American citizens lived north of the Ohio River. Concluded Rep. Elias Boudinot of New Jersey, "the western country blossoms like a rose and affords happy asylum for all the oppressed of the Earth. Plenty of the finest land in the Universe may be bought here."[15]

The speed of this westing and its geopolitical implications worried some northerners as much as it encouraged southerners, since they too believed the agricultural West would share more with the South than the North. At the Federal Convention in 1787, Gouverneur Morris and Elbridge Gerry, two northerners with antithetical ideas about the nature of federalism, had called for constitutional guarantees that the Atlantic States would always prevail in Congress.

George Clymer of Philadelphia, who warned the Federal Convention that encouragement of the West constituted suicide for the Atlantic States, preferred to populate the mountains and the lands east of them before settling on the western waters. When the First Federal Congress considered legislation to expedite westward migration, Rep. Clymer suggested to his friend Benjamin Rush that he prepare a pamphlet entitled "The Folly of Emigrating to the Western Lands Demonstrated." He proposed to prove with language comprehensible to the meanest intelligence that people who settled west of the mountains would never produce the surplus necessary to cast off their ragged clothes or to support the civilizing influences of schools and churches. Until such time as population within an "extending circle" had engendered a stable society, Americans should remain on the Atlantic seaboard.[16] Expecting the West eventually to secede from the Union, certain northerners were apathetic if not hostile toward western needs. Southerners resented this attitude. Consequently they exaggerated both it and the sentiment for separation from the United States spawned in the West by continued congressional neglect.[17] They made the possibility of the loss of the West a key argument in their strategy for establishing the capital on the Potomac.

The question whether the capital should have a tidewater harbor related closely to the criteria of centrality and accessibility to the West. Almost everyone believed in the necessity of access by water to the Atlantic, but many thought this could be achieved by an inland site above tidewater on a river with potential for navigational improvement. A Philadelphian, in a widely reprinted letter to a member of Congress in mid–1789, "had never heard of a nation who improved to any capital degree their navigation . . . if its court or capital was not near some principal harbor." He cited European history as proof, particularly the rise of Russian navigation after Peter the Great placed his capital on the Baltic. In the same vein, a New York newspaper piece recommended Sussex Courthouse in New Jersey for the capital, aiming its jocular barbs at the extravagant claims of those who promoted inland sites on potentially navigable rivers: any inconvenience to navigation caused by the fact that the adjacent creek had a depth of only two inches could be overcome by cutting an eighteen–mile canal to the Delaware River.

On the other side of the argument, a newspaper writer, citing centuries of waxing and waning empires, and pointing to Paris and Madrid, sought to prove that an empire could be influential on the sea even if it lacked a harbor at its capital. Successful empire depended on a genius for commerce: given such genius and the availability of able, virtuous civil servants, Congress could govern from the crest of the Appalachians. The United States must place its capital as near to the western country as convenience to the coastal states allowed, for in a few years the people of the mountains would be the right arm of the United States.[18]

Talk of locating the capital above tidewater close to the West raised another issue. Should it be placed at, or at least tied to, an already existing population center, or at an undeveloped site? Many Americans and their spokesmen in Congress believed that cities, with their commerce, local politics, luxury and mobs, were by definition anti–republican, and insisted that the United States should abandon the European precedent of placing capitals in large cities. The experience of Congress at Philadelphia during the War for Independence confirmed their opinion. Members of the First Federal Congress reported opposition, both within their body and from their constituencies, to fixing the capital at an existing commercial city. Such opposition ignored the reality that undeveloped sites would evolve into cities in time.[19]

A few Americans turned the old republican argument against cities on its head: a large city made the best place for the seat of a republican government because it provided the best protections for liberty. The larger the number of people and newspapers, the more closely government officials would be observed. A newspaper correspondent thought European precedent should be followed, not abandoned: had not London often saved the liberties of England? was not revolutionary Paris establishing the liberties of France? and was not the strength, safety and pride of European nations based in the largeness of their capitals? Another writer concluded that the American prejudice against great cities, and the resulting advocacy of a small town capital as a means of showing America's greatness in contrast to that of Europe, was nothing more than folly.[20]

To these Americans a preexisting population and economy were essential to the growth of an infant capital, and they condemned rural sites as utopian. This proved convincing to many New England republicans, who by 1789 had embraced the new definition of republicanism and come to fear the West even more than they feared urban centers like Philadelphia. By 1790 Vice President John Adams had come to believe that only a great city would do. Senator Tristram Dalton of Massachusetts insisted that locating the capital anywhere else would depress the United States for years to come. A Baltimorean reasoned that Congress must sit in a city where it could quickly obtain commercial information, financial resources, men for armies and news from Europe. The social amenities of a city would also serve to heighten the dignity, glory and importance of the capital in the eyes of both citizens and foreigners. Congress should go no farther from the Atlantic commercial cities than military defense required.[21]

The possibility that Congress might shun the Atlantic commercial cities stimulated ridicule as well as serious discussion, for those who supported a coastal city found it useful to equate undeveloped sites above tidewater with "wilderness" or waste land. "The idea of fixing their Residence in the Woods, can only be agreeable to *a Congress of hermits*," concluded a Baltimore newspaper. A Philadelphian pictured the idea of locating Congress in a rural village or "raising a new city out of the wilderness" as absurd.[22]

All of the undeveloped sites which Congress considered connected closely with existing towns or major transportation routes. It did not discuss any site truly adjacent to wilderness, although at least two men thought it should. In 1783 Rhode Island Congressman David Howell privately suggested that Congress temporarily sit at or near Pittsburgh, well west of any population center. He thought such a decision would raise the value of federal lands in the West and thereby rapidly pay off the public debt. In 1787 Manasseh Cutler, lobbyist for the land company that had settled Marietta in the Northwest Territory, argued publicly that the seat of empire belonged on the Ohio River. He urged Congress to postpone action until the claims of the Ohio could merit serious discussion. Facetious suggestions in 1789 and 1790 that the capital be placed at Marietta, or on the Wabash or Illinois rivers, indicated that at least some men made a distinction between the so-called Potomac wilderness and the real wilderness on the western waters. A Connecticut wit proposed as an Amendment to the Constitution that "the residence of Congress shall not be in an Indian wigwam nor in the howling wilderness."[23]

A final geopolitical argument stressed the importance of siting the capital in such a manner as to facilitate the economic development of the rising American Empire. At stake was which one of the great, mid-coastal rivers—the Hudson, the Delaware, the Susquehanna, or the Potomac—by the placement of the capital on its banks, would provide Americans with the best access to the wealth of the continent. The sites given the most serious consideration all lay on the latter three rivers, often at major obstacles to navigation. When these sites adjoined state boundaries they achieved stronger force of argument, for they tended to unite votes by offering to share benefits.

Concern about the idea of an American capital and the proper qualities of site were dwarfed by preoccupation among revolutionary leaders with the political means for achieving a location in the best interests of themselves and their constituents. Almost no one had the interest of the United States as their predominant concern, for the Union was too new to outweigh loyalty to section, state and locale. The widely revered Potomac River planter, developer and land speculator George Washington was no less political about the issue than the often vilified Philadelphia financier and congressman Robert Morris.

Washington more than anyone had the interest of the Union at heart, for if the American Revolution failed, so too did his ambition for immortality through history. His seeming personal disinterestedness in the decision was abetted by a geographic stroke of luck: Mount Vernon lay almost precisely at the north–south center of the United States. Nevertheless, Washington's acute appreciation of the interrelationship and use of economic and political power, his deep concern for his personal fortune and place in history, his sense of geographical place and his Potomac Fever profoundly influenced the location of the United States capital. His recorded comments on the subject before July 1790, when Congress selected the Potomac, were rare and discreet. John Adams once referred to this trait as Washington's gift of silence. Washington himself wrote that he always made it a "maxim rather to let my designs appear from my works rather than by my expressions." He once confessed to fellow Potomac River promoter Henry Lee that he always took pains to avoid the imputation of having interfered in an issue from improper or selfish motives, "for I hold it necessary that one should not only be conscious of the purest *intentions;* but that one should also have it in his power to demonstrate the disinterestedness of his *words* and actions at all times, and upon all occasions."[24]

1

Chained to Philadelphia, 1774–1783

BY 1774 MANY RESIDENTS OF GREAT BRITAIN'S SEMI-autonomous continental colonies in North America had concluded that a corrupt, decadent and power-hungry central government seated at a distant capital had launched a conspiracy against their political and economic republican liberties. Independence as a possible solution was a new concept, but discussion of an American Union was not.

During the seventeenth century, two temporary unions involving some of the northern colonies had been effected, although in each case disputes arose over the location of their seats of government. Many plans had been suggested during the eighteenth century. Those which envisioned a legislature often avoided the contentious question of its seat. William Penn's plan of 1696 recommended that it meet as near as convenient to the most central colony, which he conjectured as New York. An anonymous writer who disliked stationary seats of government argued at some length against Penn's plan. If the American deputies wished to acquaint themselves with all the colonies, they could observe it no better than by a transient legislature, which would also have the effect of spreading among them the money stimulated by such meetings. In 1751 one advocate of union proposed that commissioners from all the colonies meet yearly at Albany, or New York, New York. Three years later commissioners actually met at the former town and Benjamin Franklin proposed the so-called Albany Plan of Union. Neither the colonies nor the British favored the idea, which provided that a grand council sit at Philadelphia and thereafter at such places to which it adjourned. In 1765 the Stamp Act Congress, the first

14

intercolonial assembly to protest against Parliament, met at New York City.

When new plans for union emerged between 1774 and 1776, American leaders divided over the century-old question whether an intercolonial seat of government should be stationary, in the fashion of the southern colonial capitals, or transient, like most in New England. The Philadelphian Joseph Galloway favored a stationary seat, but for reasons of strategy refused to name a place. Franklin's plan proposed that Congress rotate perpetually among all the colonies, beginning with Annapolis, Maryland's capital. Thomas Paine made specific proposals for a union of independent states in *Common Sense,* but like Galloway, left an ominous blank in lieu of a place name.[1]

The colonies, which responded to Virginia's call in 1774 for an intercolonial Congress to meet "at such place annually as shall be thought most convenient," considered New York and Annapolis, but unanimously chose Philadelphia, capital of centrally located Pennsylvania. Nevertheless, a Fairfax County member of the Virginia Convention argued to his colleagues in favor of the second most important town in Pennsylvania, inland Lancaster. George Washington opposed meeting in the most populous city in the colonies since many of its inhabitants would be antagonistic to the American cause and its active port would provide easy entry and cover for British spies and other troublemakers. He also implied, and may actually have expressed, a fear that Congress could not maintain secrecy and autonomy in a wealthy and socially active commercial colonial capital, where influences of all sorts would affect even the most circumspect delegates.[2]

Philadelphia, William Penn's "greene countrie towne," with almost 40,000 residents and 6,000 buildings, figured among the most attractive, urbane, populous and religiously diverse cities in the English-speaking world. A transportation hub, the city boasted roads to all the rebellious colonies, and its ships sailed from Delaware River wharves to Europe, the West Indies and Africa. Its commercial hinterland encompassed all of Pennsylvania and Delaware, half of New Jersey and portions of Maryland and Virginia. Accommodations for visitors abounded in the pleasant cosmopolitan city, and many opportunities existed for those with the leisure to enjoy social and intellectual pursuits.

Delegates to the First Continental Congress in September and October 1774 generally liked their "place of meeting." One New England delegate described the city as the healthiest spot on the continent and more hospitable and frugal than New York. But no one could outdo the Philadelphians in praise for the city: "the almost universal topic of conversation among them" observed a visitor just prior to the war "is the superiority of Philadelphia over every other spot on the globe. All their geese are swans."

From the outset Congress had a powerful impact on the place where it met. The lawyers, planters and merchants who attended provided valuable connections for enterprising Philadelphians, one of whom urged James Madison, an ambitious young Virginian to come north to take advantage of the opportunities. Even before Congress convened, delegates were drawn—some quite willingly— into the partisan politics of the colony. Which building should Congress choose for its sessions: the State House, offered by the colonial Assembly, or Carpenter's Hall, proposed by a group of patriots? The delegates chose the latter and then elected the Philadelphia patriot leader Charles Thomson as their secretary. Winning the support of large, influential and centrally located Pennsylvania was vital to the revolutionary cause, and independence-oriented congressmen, such as Samuel and John Adams of Massachusetts, worked closely with Philadelphia's revolutionary committees.[3] Such involvement with local affairs would have occurred wherever Congress sat, but Philadelphia had not only more people but also more printers, social life and politics with which to become entangled. By the time the First Continental Congress adjourned, its members and the Philadelphians had begun to forge the links of a chain which would hold Congress to Philadelphia for most of the next eight years.

Congress agreed to reconvene at Philadelphia in 1775 if grievances against the government at London had not been redressed. Few if any objected to returning to the city despite the concern of the Rhode Island Assembly that smallpox and many other hazards made it an improper meetingplace. Nevertheless, immediately after the Second Continental Congress met at the State House in

May 1775, talk sprang up about moving closer to the Massachusetts battlefront. Connecticut's delegates, although recognizing the potential for southern opposition, took the lead in stressing the importance of a northerly move by Congress, or at least a large committee of its members. They suggested Hartford or New Haven in Connecticut. Although Commander in Chief of the Continental Army George Washington welcomed the possibility, southern delegates in general did not, and neither the threat of smallpox nor distaste for the foul city air moved enough delegates to support either a removal or a traveling committee. Nonetheless, talk of relocating to Hartford or Albany continued.

By the end of 1775, congressmen considered departure for reasons other than the protection of their health or the supervision of their army. One complained that certain Philadelphians constantly intrigued with the delegates for pensions, employment and contracts: "indeed I think we have been cooped up in this prison of a city long enough." Rumors of a removal spread during the winter and spring. Two weeks before Congress declared the colonies independent in July 1776, John Adams denied to his wife Abigail that Congress planned to move forty miles west of Philadelphia.[4]

In December 1776 British troops camped near Philadelphia. Within twenty-four hours of condemning as scandalous and malicious a rumor that it intended to flee its seat, Congress adjourned to Baltimore, Maryland, leaving behind a three-man executive committee. Although it had a population of 6,000, Baltimore was not yet the thriving commercial center the War for Independence would make it, and its crowded accommodations and muddy streets compared unfavorably with the spacious taverns and cobblestones of Philadelphia. Congressmen spent three months bemoaning exorbitant prices, dirt, weather-related illnesses and salty drinking water. While Sam Adams claimed that Congress accomplished more important business at Baltimore in three weeks that it had at Philadelphia in six months, and his Massachusetts colleague Elbridge Gerry hoped never to return to Philadelphia—"that Sepulchre of Genius and Enterprize"—most members considered their temporary seat an expensive, muddy hole.

Robert Morris of Philadelphia, who chaired the executive committee of Congress, compared Pennsylvania's relationship to the Union with that of the heart to the human body, and he and Congressman Benjamin Rush worked tirelessly for an adjournment back to their home city. When, by mid–January 1777, Philadelphia had not fallen to the British, other delegates talked of returning. Some thought Lancaster preferable. The opponents of Philadelphia, primarily southerners, argued that too much business pressed for Congress to suspend debate, that delegates would not assemble promptly and that the British might still take the city. The Virginians believed that leaving Philadelphia had stimulated the reluctant revolutionaries of Pennsylvania and other Middle States to a more aggressive posture and consequently hesitated to return. When the vote came at the end of February, it carried on a 6 to 5 North–South division which found all the states except New Hampshire and Georgia voting with their sections. "Congress has been so mad as to return," complained one of the Virginia congressmen. John Adams informed Abigail even before the delegates belatedly reconvened at Philadelphia that Congress might possibly move again, perhaps to Lancaster or Reading.[5]

The returning delegates encountered a different Philadelphia. Prices had doubled during their six–month absence and some complained about "the boundless avarice of the merchants, whose gain is . . . all the God they seem to know." A large body of tories in the city openly supported the British, and congressmen accused the Quakers of giving intelligence to the enemy. Congress and the state government established under the Pennsylvania Constitution of 1776 both met in the same building and clashed within a year.

Pennsylvania's Constitution and some Constitutionalists, as its supporters were known, aimed at democracy. The state Executive Council lacked power and looked to Congress for support. Some congressmen began to cooperate with Pennsylvania's Anti–Constitutionalists, just as others had previously worked with the colony's revolutionaries against its loyalists. In April 1777, with Pennsylvania again threatened by the British Army, Congress imposed itself on the executive affairs of the state with a resolution declaring Pennsylvania incapable of adequate response to the military crisis. This angered the Constitutionalists, and matters came to a head in August and September when ill feeling developed over congressional plans to imprison certain Quakers. The Pennsylvania Assembly reprimanded Congress. In addition, Philadelphians petitioned Congress on all sorts of matters and took sides in congressional disputes. Congressmen resented such intrusions of local and state politics into their affairs. "While we are situated in the Capital of such a State as Pennsylvania we shall never want ten thousand interruptions," lamented one delegate. Another concluded that "Congress seems to be chained to this place, and the longer they stay, the stronger a multitude of offices and officers are established and employed in this city."[6]

By early September 1777, another removal from Philadelphia became a serious topic of discussion among disgruntled congressmen, who described the city and its inhabitants as venal, cowardly and tory. A vote might have been attempted had not the British once again camped nearby. Many people considered the move to Baltimore premature if not improper, and Congress hesitated to depart too soon. As the British approached closer, however, Congress discussed moving to Reading, Lancaster, York, Easton, or Bethlehem, Pennsylvania. It agreed not to leave the state for fear of its defection to the British, and, in a rare Sunday emergency session, opted for Lancaster if flight proved necessary.

On the night of September 18, Washington's aide Alexander Hamilton brought word that the British could conceivably enter the city by morning. Taking a circuitous route as protection for the papers of Congress, seen by John Adams as more important than all the members combined, most congressmen arrived at Lancaster within a week. The town portended to be a crowded seat of government, since the Pennsylvania Assembly also convened there, and Congress remained only one day before adjourning to York, safely west of the wide Susquehanna River. The town served as the residence of Congress for the nine months in 1777–1778 during which the British held Philadelphia. York boasted about 500 houses and 1,800 residents, many of them Germans.[7]

Even if some delegates considered York more pleasant than Baltimore, housing proved scarce, the cost of living exorbitant, and the situation remote from the sea. In March 1778 New York's Gouverneur Morris considered proposing an adjournment to

Hartford. A month later Congress resolved to discuss leaving York for better accommodations, but the debate never took place. Although a Massachussetts delegate favored going "southward for the next ride if we make one in any other course than to the City of Philadelphia," and a South Carolina congressman predicted a struggle, the four–year old chain proved too strong. Philadelphia had become a symbol of the revolutionary cause in the popular mind and its financial and other resources made the transaction of congressional business easier and more enjoyable. Consequently when the British withdrew in June 1778, Congress returned triumphantly. It had not only refused to surrender when Philadelphia fell, but also had rejected as unsatisfactory a peace overture from the British. The thrill of the homecoming was nonetheless fleeting. Within a few weeks the old complaints against the city erupted again, and the chain almost broke a year later.[8]

Congress found itself in a hotbed. By 1778 the Constitutionalists had full control of the government of a state which more than any other was undergoing social revolution. The nearest equivalent in the United States to revolutionary Paris of the 1790s was Philadelphia from the fall of 1778 through the fall of 1779. Mobs, street brawls and threats against merchants accused of profiteering became almost routine. In addition to social upheaval, jurisdictional disputes arose. The state objected to interference in its internal affairs when Congress annulled a Pennsylvania court verdict in December 1778. The presence of a strong military influence at Philadelphia also annoyed the Constitutionalists. Sharp letters concerning the state's attempt to bring charges against Philadelphia's military commander, General Benedict Arnold, passed between Congress and the Pennsylvania Executive Council early in 1779. The situation became so aggravated by March that Secretary of Congress Charles Thomson asserted that the Council had determined to sink either Congress or itself. The Council adopted a series of resolutions calling the situation critical and demanding a conference. Congress agreed and the Council poured out a long list of grievances. After the conference both governments adopted resolutions declaring a restoration of mutual respect, but within a month Pennsylvania sent Congress an even stronger reprimand. In 1783, when Gouverneur Morris expressed the necessity of an exclusive jurisdiction for Congress over its seat, he cited the events of 1778–1779 as proof.

October 1779 witnessed the high–water mark of social revolution in Philadelphia. Angered by inflation and convinced of merchant profiteering, a heavily armed, militia–led mob attacked a house where prominent Anti–Constitutionalists, including Robert Morris, had gathered for protection. Three people died before the restoration of order. Two days later the mob attacked General Arnold, but he drew his pistols and escaped unharmed. Anti–Constitutionalists virtually went underground when Constitutionalists increased their power in the state elections which followed. The winners disliked cities as seats of government because of the influence of size and commerce on the functioning of republican government. Thus, the men Pennsylvania sent to Congress took the paradoxical position of opposing its remaining at Philadelphia.[9]

Congress had had enough. Early in December 1779 it resolved to leave Philadelphia in the spring. Members discussed moving to Bethlehem, but it lay within the jurisdiction of Pennsylvania, and its Moravians feared Congress would spoil both its markets and their morals. Other proposed locations included Hartford; Albany; Princeton and Burlington, New Jersey; or Fredericksburg, Virginia. The decision had to be postponed three times because a majority of states could not agree on a place.

In March 1780 southern delegates, in fear of being hauled northward, tried unsuccessfully to rescind the resolution for removal; they succeeded, however, with the aid of their old allies in Massachusetts and Rhode Island, in defeating adjournments to Trenton, New Jersey, and Hartford, Connecticut. The decision to remove having been made, the failure to select a site proved an embarrassment. At the end of the month Congress referred the matter to a committee of three Middle States delegates chaired by Robert R. Livingston of New York, mandating it to report the number of buildings needed, a place where they might be found and an estimate of the cost. Instead the committee buried the resolution. "However disgusting our stay here is to Congress and the inhabitants," all prospect for removing is at an end for some time to come, concluded a New York delegate. Although the reasons cited for not leaving Philadelphia in 1780 were the resistance of the South to

moving farther north, the general fear of inadequate accommodations elsewhere, and the need to supervise the upcoming military
campaign, the decision probably also related to the depressed state
of the war, the economy and citizen morale.[10]

The year 1780 marked the nadir of the Revolution. The restive
army condemned the United States for neglect. One of its generals
informed Congress that "our Army no longer consider themselves
as fighting the battles of *republics in principle* but for empire and liberty to a people whose object is property, and that the army expect
some of that property which the citizen seeks, and which the army
protects for him." Charleston, South Carolina, fell to the British in
May, giving them free rein in the Lower South. When supplies
failed to arrive at Washington's camp the same month, a mutiny occurred which nearly won the support of the officer corps. General
Arnold defected in September. Congress and the states were insolvent. Popular conventions met to protest inflation, trade restraints,
economic controls and government confiscation of property for the
war effort. A sense of despair seeped through the United States.
Some men abandoned hope and called for making terms with the
enemy or restricting civil liberty. Talk of a supreme head or dictator
(with vice–dictators in each state) and separate confederacies surfaced. Mutinies by the Pennsylvania and New Jersey lines early in
1781 climaxed the chaos. To some it appeared that the struggle for
independence had collapsed. The historic American response to
such a crisis has been dramatic change in the political makeup of
Congress. That response occurred for the first time in 1781.[11]

Since the Second Continental Congress convened in 1775, it
had been under the influence and then the control of political leaders who believed in decentralization and espoused the rights of the
states over those of the Union. Strongest in New England and the
South, the decentralists included Americans with such varied per-
spectives as John Adams, Mercy Warren, and Elbridge Gerry of
Massachusetts; David Howell of Rhode Island; and Arthur and
Richard Henry Lee, Patrick Henry, William Grayson, George Mason, and Thomas Jefferson of Virginia. Most advocated an essentially self–contained American Empire little involved with Europe:
wealth lay in the development of the North American continent,
not in intimate trans–Atlantic ties. They sought to expand the

empire and rapidly pay off the revolutionary debt by the sale of the western wilderness to farmers whom they considered the backbone of republicanism. Decentralists believed in a confederated empire in which the states were supreme and executives controlled by legislatures. Uncomfortable about the effect of new forms of social organization on the survival of republican liberty as they defined it, decentralists feared the social distinctions which they believed inherent in a commercial society, and sought to limit the growth of financial institutions. According to them cities posed the threats of political corruption, luxury, inequality of wealth, and a concentrated, landless population. Decentralists worried about maintaining republican forms of government if a powerful federal government was established for a territory so large as the United States portended to become.

The constitutional expression of the decentralist philosophy was the Articles of Confederation. Immediately upon declaring independence in July 1776, Congress considered a plan of union drafted primarily by the Pennsylvania centralist John Dickinson. His draft of an articles of confederation, which proposed that Congress remain at Philadelphia until otherwise ordered, reeked of too much centralism for the decentralist–controlled Congress, and fundamental changes were made before its submission to the states more than a year later. The final version contained no mention of a meetingplace for Congress, thereby leaving the door open for a transient one. "It is good to change place. It promotes health and spirits. . . . It does good to the place we remove from, as well as to that we remove to. And it does good to those who move," mused John Adams.

The Articles of Confederation, which was finally ratified by the necessary thirteenth state in February 1781, established a loose union of independent states and delegated to Congress little power other than to make war and peace, manage foreign affairs and resolve interstate disputes. Congress had no source of revenue except for unenforceable requisitions on the states, no supremacy, no control over commerce and certainly no power to establish a jurisdictionally independent residence for itself. Each state, regardless of its size, population, wealth or commitment to the Union, had one vote in Congress. Individual delegations, usually elected by state legislatures, varied in size depending on state policy and the willingness of delegates to attend a legislative body in a city distant and expensive for most of them. States with only one delegate attending, or with evenly split delegations, lost the right to have their votes counted. A quorum required seven states and the same number had to agree in order to take even the most routine action. Certain matters such as declarations of war, ratifications of treaties and appropriations of money required the concurrence of nine states. Amendment of the Articles required unanimity. Decentralists believed such a federal government was not likely to subvert state sovereignty.

The centralists, whose power was based in the commercial Middle States, believed the federal government must be structured in such a way as to preserve stability and to ensure economic growth. Most advocated supremacy for the federal government, a strong executive authority within it, and a long–term funding of the revolutionary debt as a means of guiding the economic development of the empire. Deeply wounded by the loss of support which they suffered when thousands of their natural allies opted against revolution and chose exile, centralist leaders included such men as Robert R. Livingston, Gouverneur Morris and Alexander Hamilton of New York; Elias Boudinot of New Jersey, Robert Morris, George Clymer, Thomas Fitzsimons, Richard Peters, Tench Coxe and Charles Thomson of Pennsylvania; and George Washington and— with an increasing ambivalence which made his role in the Revolution so important—James Madison of Virginia. They too recognized the vast potential of the American wilderness for development, but most preferred at first to emphasize cooperation and economic interdependence with Europe as a richer, stronger and more immediate resource. Most centralists saw urbanization, centralization and commerce, including the British fiscal system, as both exciting and essential to America's growth, and redefined republicanism accordingly. As the Revolution progressed they converted many New Englanders to their position, and at its conclusion had forged a strong bond between the New England and Middle States. More clearly than the decentralists, they recognized a national interest. Indeed, a few advocated a national or unitary government and the abolition of the states.[12]

In response to the crisis of 1780 and early 1781 Americans turned to the centralists. Commitment to a centralist solution, always strong in the Middle States, now flourished. A frightened South, a significant part of which the British controlled, allied itself with the Middle States. Even decentralist New England sent a few centralists to Congress, but these men, unlike their allies from the Middle and Southern States, did not approve of Philadelphia as the seat of government. Immediately after ratification of the Articles of Confederation, congressional centralists attempted to interpret and amend it in order to bolster the Revolution. They discussed among themselves methods for Congress to regulate commerce, to fund the debt and, in light of habitual poor attendance, to enact legislation by the agreement of five instead of seven states. Further discussion centered on the use of military force to compel the states to meet their congressional requisitions, the guarantee of a revenue independent of those requisitions, and the holding of congressional debates about finances in open session so that the public creditors of Philadelphia could better apply their influence. They succeeded only in the establishment of executive departments for Congress.[13]

Discussion of the divisive issue of an executive for Congress dated back to 1776. For Congress to succeed, Congressman Robert Morris observed then, it "must pay good executive men to do their business as it ought to be and not lavish millions away by their own mismanagement."[14] But the commitment to government by legislatures and the popular resentment of the king, royal governors, and their ministers proved so powerful that Morris and the slowly increasing number of congressmen who supported him could not prevail. In 1781 the centralists had enough power in Congress to institute three executive departments headed by non–delegates. Congress, however, supervised them carefully. The most significant was the department of finance under the secretaryship of Morris. Thus came even closer to the forefront the creative financial expert and planner who would seldom be far from the center of influence as the United States struggled to establish its seat of empire. Those who disliked him and believed him a profiteer nonetheless admitted his competence and even his brilliance.

As secretary of finance, Morris sought the creation of a federal government of "power, consequence, and grandeur" capable of encouraging domestic and foreign financial interests to develop the American Empire free from governmental restriction. He acted to restore the confidence of public creditors in the United States government, to direct money into the hands of those who could make it most productive, and to centralize the small federal bureaucracy. Impressive as a fiscal administrator, Morris's political and constitutional contributions to the Revolution proved even more important. Most centralists looked to him for leadership. By correcting defects in the constitution, he hoped to provide the hoop to the thirteen–staved barrel in order to draw by degrees "the bands of authority together, establishing the power of Government over a people impatient of control, and confirming the Federal Union." Morris saw the means to centralized empire in three measures: a federally chartered bank; a funded debt; and the establishment of permanent federal land, poll and liquor taxes and import duties. In particular, he implored the states to agree to a five percent import duty as an alternative to the unenforceable requisitions. Without a revenue Congress could not pay its creditors, be they foreign governments, banks, civilians or soldiers of the Continental Army. In 1781 Congress proposed such an import duty as an Amendment to the Articles of Confederation requiring ratification by all thirteen states.[15]

Opposition to the import duty Amendment revived the decentralists and by mid–1782 they began to send articulate leaders back to Congress. As an ally of long–time Morris antagonist Arthur Lee of Virginia came David Howell, a professor of natural philosophy at the College of Rhode Island, elected when his state repented its temporary alliance with the centralists. Once empowered to collect import duties, warned Howell, Congress would attempt to establish federal taxes. It would grow rich feeding on revenue until "the bond of the Union, to use the phrase of the advocates of these measures, would be complete. And we will add the yoke of tyranny fixed on all the States and the chains rivetted." Opposition also arose from those who feared that his program would draw specie from the states, to circulate only in the vortex of Philadelphia or wherever Congress sat. Rhode Island rejected the Amendment and the Lees helped persuade Virginia to rescind its ratification late in 1782.[16]

Despite this setback, Morris had become the most powerful man in the United States by 1783, save only for Washington. In essence, he administered the federal government. Decentralists viewed him and his centralist program as the very enemy combated by the Revolution: an overbearing federal government seated at a distant capital. They did not want to exchange the government at London for the government at Philadelphia, nor Lord North for Robert Morris. In particular they opposed the ultimate centralist goal, a new constitution which gave the federal government greater power if not supremacy. Centralist Congressman James Madison forecast in February 1783 that the next six months would determine whether the Revolution would end in prosperity and tranquility or in confusion and disunion. In April amid continued debate over a federal revenue, news of the unexpectedly favorable preliminary articles of peace reached the seat of government. Most centralists recognized foreign war—the "great friend to sovereign authority"—as fundamental to creating and maintaining the Union, and believed that it must be strengthened before the war ended. Unfortunately for the centralists, the coming of peace quickly pushed the terrible events of 1780 into the background and Americans, further reconsidering the mandate they had given the centralists three years earlier, continued to send decentralists to Congress.[17]

As news of peace and the recognition of American Independence spread, Margaret Beekman Livingston, grande dame of Hudson River society, dreamt of "America rising into a great Empire and being the land of liberty." Nevertheless, a clear sense of the constitutional dilemma which Madison had articulated existed at Philadelphia, particularly in the minds of the centralists. The crisis involved a host of issues and serious problems, but at its core burned the most critical question facing the United States: without a war to unite them, what would hold the autonomous states together in anything more than symbolic union? The United States had only a budding sense of itself as a Union, and many citizens and state governments hoped that sense never would flourish if it meant federal supremacy. Congress lacked both domestic authority and public respect, and some Americans even questioned its relevance. Its inability to solve problems and its threat to local control made popular hobby horses for state political leaders. Congressman Alexander Hamilton raged with anger and disgust when contrasting what he considered the constitutional imbecility of Congress with the popular attitude that it was a dangerous institution. He saw the source of the problem as people's blind disposition to arraign Congress for failing to act when they kept it powerless, yet simultaneously condemning it for lusting after power and encroaching on the rights of the states.[18]

According to Arthur Lee, the terror of a mutinous army was one of various engines employed by the centralists to gain support for permanent taxes. Indeed, army discontent as peace approached rekindled the hopes of some centralists that a revenue could be established and the debt funded. A delegation from army headquarters at Newburgh, New York, held conversations with Morris, several congressmen and other officeholders at Philadelphia early in 1783. Certain army officers later agreed to add their influence to that of other public creditors in an attempt to force through Congress and the states a program to fund the federal debt. Some of the most discontented officers went even further than most centralists desired with a March rebellion against Washington's moderate leadership. Although Washington delivered a coup de grace to the Newburgh Conspiracy, its Cromwellian overtones shook Congress badly.[19]

Washington fully supported the centralist program, even the desire for a "constitution that will give consistency, stability and dignity to the Union; and sufficient powers to the great Council of the Nation for general purposes." The officers' revolt nevertheless horrified him, for it threatened to "deluge our rising Empire in blood." The commander in chief was convinced that it had been planned and matured in Philadelphia. He blamed Robert Morris and, in particular, his assistant, Gouverneur Morris. Described by the decentralist William Gordon as "a downright Machiavellian politician," Gouverneur Morris believed that "nothing remained but vigor, organization, and promptitude to render this a considerable empire," and reflected two months after Newburgh that he was prepared *again to labor and to hazard.*"[20]

Gordon, a historian and commentator on revolutionary America, was deeply disturbed by the rise of the centralists, their vision for America and the continued residence of Congress at Philadelphia. He warned John Adams that America must "remain a collection of Republics and not become an Empire, for then freedom will languish and die. . . . If America becomes an Empire the seat of government will be to the southward, and the Northern States [will] be insignificant provinces." He appealed to Arthur Lee to keep Virginia vigilant, lest the scheming Philadelphia–based centralists happily make all the states into mere provinces of Pennsylvania. Gordon proposed a typically decentralist solution to the concentration of power at Philadelphia: let it remain the commercial and financial center, make Boston the military bastion and seat Congress at New York City.[21]

At the same time that Congress faced the difficult questions confronting a peacetime United States, it received an invitation from New York to establish its postwar seat at Kingston on the Hudson River. Soon thereafter Maryland offered Annapolis and its public buildings. Congress informed the states on 4 June of the two offers, invited other states to follow suit and set early October as the time to make a decision. Philadelphians did not see the threat as particularly serious. They believed that the seven states required by the Articles of Confederation were even less likely to agree on a place in 1783 than were a simple majority of the attending states when the matter had died with Robert R. Livingston's committee in 1780. Philadelphian George Clymer, embittered and discouraged by declining public support for the centralist program, jested that Congress might do well to retire to the small village offered by New York "for no where else will their grave authority be respected."

In June 1783 Philadelphia, the hub of the centralist–oriented Middle States, provided Congress with a sustaining environment from which to govern despite the fact that it had no jurisdiction over the city. Financial resources, commercial information and European news were readily available, and the Pennsylvania government, now controlled by the Anti–Constitutionalists, became increasingly supportive. Congressmen enjoyed spacious accommodations, hearty and exotic meals, stimulating intellectual dialogue and a varied, elegant social life. Philadelphia was, in addition, an

Elysian field for "susceptible hearts, persons of feelings, for men of large P_____ and women of wide ___t." Even a few centralists complained of the luxury, comparing the city to Roman Capua.[22]

For the decentralists Philadelphia had become synonymous with grasping federal government, wealth and corruption. One of them asserted that in that city, "plans for absolute government, for deceiving the lower classes of people, for introducing undue influence, for any kind of government, in which democracy has the least possible share, originate, are cherished, and [are] disseminated." In May 1783 Arthur Lee insisted that "Congress have set too long in a City where every man affects the politician, and having no system of his own, his zeal is made subservient to the designs of others, without his perceiving it. They must remove to some spot where they will have a better chance to act independently."[23] Lee was undoubtedly the happiest of congressmen when, within a month, Congress voted unanimously to sever the chain which had so long bound it to Philadelphia.

Warm winds carried the ominous drum rolls through the noonday streets of Philadelphia on 21 June 1783. Thirty well-ordered soldiers with fixed bayonets prepared to advance on the building in which the thirteen colonies had declared their independence from Great Britain. These troops were American, primarily of the Pennsylvania Line of the Continental Army. The soldiers came to demand redress from the state Executive Council, then meeting on the second floor of the State House, the capitol shared by Pennsylvania and the United States. What they wanted before they returned to their homes was half of the pay due them, interest–bearing certificates for the remainder and arrangements to settle their accounts and fulfill such enlistment promises as land patents.

The angry demonstrators had carefully chosen a Saturday because they knew that Congress recessed for the weekend. Knowing it to be insolvent, virtually impotent and dependent on the states for both money and authority, they bypassed it to make their demands on the state. Some of the soldiers had sought justice more peacefully from the United States several days earlier, but an indignant Congress had merely transmitted their demands to its secretary at war, whose compromise had failed. Just the previous day federal officials had fueled the discontent by making two decisions: no soldier was to receive further payroll certificates unless agreeing to return home prior to settlement of any claims for back pay against the United States, and rebellious troops who had marched on Philadelphia would not be paid until they returned to their barracks at Lancaster. That same evening Congressman Alexander Hamilton, Assistant Secretary of Finance Gouverneur Morris and Assistant Secretary at War William Jackson had gone to the barracks on a mission to calm the soldiers, some of whom by then had been mutinous for a week. Morris, perhaps seeing the opportunity he had been seeking since Newburgh, took the lead, and his patronizing remarks, interpreted as federal policy, inflamed the soldiers, who later blamed him for their demonstration.

As the troops assembled, Hamilton, chairman of a special congressional committee appointed to respond to the arrival of the troops from Lancaster, hurried to the home of his friend and political ally Elias Boudinot, president of Congress. Hamilton urged an emergency session of Congress on the grounds that the soldiers might rob the federally incorporated Bank of North America. Boudinot immediately convened Congress for a 1:00 p.m. session at the State House. The timing implied that Hamilton suspected where and when the troops planned to march.

In all probability, Hamilton and his centralist allies deemed it inappropriate that continental soldiers be allowed to settle their claims against Congress with a state government. With the British threat gone little existed to hold the Union together other than the jointly owed federal debt. Centralists could not afford the precedent of a state assuming upon itself part of that debt. Also, given the anti–military bias of Americans and the historical threat posed to republics by revolutionary armies, the incident might stimulate desperately needed public sympathy and support for Congress if it appeared to be the object of the soldiers' wrath. The political sparring match between Pennsylvania and the United States which Hamilton and Gouverneur Morris thereby brought about became a debate over the authority and dignity owed Congress by a state, an early contest over federalism. The soldiers served merely as the vehicle for which certain centralists had been waiting.

When the soldiers reached the State House, they formed in front of the building and submitted to the Pennsylvania Executive Council a crude note demanding authority to appoint new officers for the purpose of assuming command and redressing grievances with the state. While the Council considered and unanimously rejected the demand, about two hundred and fifty additional armed soldiers joined the demonstration. Council members expressed more surprise at the arrival of the congressmen who, Council President John Dickinson complained, were "upon the alarm . . . ~~hastily~~ specially summoned by their president, and at the place to which the soldiers were moving."

The soldiers allowed the congressmen to pass freely through their sentries, and the delegates waited impatiently inside the State House for a final member to form a quorum. *The necessary delegate never arrived and a quorum never formed.* Despite the forthcoming congressional protest to Pennsylvania and the routine legal and historical references to the event in the two centuries since, the body known as Congress was not surrounded by soldiers of the Continental Army. The congressmen nevertheless urged the Council to call up the Philadelphia militia to drive the soldiers away. Dickinson came downstairs to explain its refusal to do so. It doubted that the citizen militia would take up arms against the long–suffering men considered to have secured America's independence, at least not until an outrage against persons or property had been committed. To the Council the demonstration did not constitute such an outrage. The dilemma was classically American: what is the line between the right of protest and the maintenance of law and order?

Tension mounted as the cursing soldiers got drunk and pointed their muskets at the first floor windows behind which the congressman gathered. Supportive citizens cheered on the soldiers. Congressman James Madison did not expect premeditated violence from the soldiers, but feared hasty excesses from the liquor and the encouragement. Some congressmen, however, wondered if the mutiny related to others throughout the United States, and if that horror of republics—the takeover of civil government by a revolutionary army—was at hand. These questions remained when the armed demonstration broke up after the Council agreed to hold a conference with a committee of officers and to accept a petition from the soldiers. By then the congressmen, having given their blessing to the Council's solution, had safely left the building, ready to use the incident for their own political ends.

Boudinot called a second special session of Congress in the evening. This time a quorum of seven states formed and unanimously adopted secret resolutions, drafted in large part by Hamilton. They complained of gross insult to the authority of the United States, and carefully chose words to give the impression that Congress was in session ("Congress were assembled") during the demonstration. The resolutions instructed the Hamilton Committee to obtain prompt and adequate exertions from Pennsylvania to support the "dignity of the federal government" and ordered General George Washington to march a body of trustworthy troops to Philadelphia to suppress the mutiny. Finally, if no reason appeared to expect adequate and prompt protection from Pennsylvania, Boudinot, on the advice of the committee, should convene Congress at Trenton or Princeton, New Jersey, "in order that further and more effectual measures may be taken for suppressing the present revolt, and maintaining the dignity and authority of the United States."

The unanimity with which Congress acted arose from the uniqueness of the circumstance. Decentralists saw their opportunity to escape from a city they had long considered an unfit seat for a republican government. They succeeded finally because of the desire of the centralists, including the Pennsylvanians, to assert the authority and dignity of Congress at a moment when the very existence of a meaningful Union stood at stake. Most centralists nevertheless considered the removal temporary and intended to return to their stronghold as soon as their point had been made and order restored.

On Sunday and Monday Hamilton's committee held several meetings with Dickinson and the Council to discuss the situation. Pennsylvania was only four months away from a major election and Dickinson and his party did not want to give their opponents an issue. The political situation within the state thus reinforced Dickinson's caution, concern with public reputation and Quaker heritage. He considered the conference promised by the Council and approved by Boudinot preferable to force, especially as the mutinous soldiers had taken no action since their nonviolent demonstration on Saturday. Hamilton, who believed Pennsylvania's and Dickinson's conduct weak and disgusting, disagreed. He informed Boudinot that nothing could be expected from the state and drafted a proclamation which again implied that Congress had been the object of the demonstration, adjourned Congress to Princeton and placed the blame for the removal on Pennsylvania.[24]

The next morning the soldiers apologized to the Council for their conduct on Saturday, stating in their own defense that they had been inflamed by the three federal officials who had visited their barracks the night before the demonstration. Pennsylvania refused to consider the soldiers' grievances until they made a full submission to Congress. The leaders of the mutiny agreed to so inform the soldiers, expressing doubt that the men would be pleased, since their intention on Saturday had been only to involve the state. At that point the two instigators of the mutiny fled and the soldiers returned to their regular officers. The mutiny collapsed. Not a shot had been fired. No one had been injured nor had any property been destroyed. Dickinson informed Congress that order had been restored and that it could return to Philadelphia.[25]

The demonstration dramatically called attention to the overriding political issue of the American Revolution—federalism, the balance of power between the states and the federal government—and led for the first time to public proposals that Congress should exercise exclusive jurisdiction over the place where it met. Those Americans who sought a federal government dominant over the states deliberately distorted what had occurred and seized the incident as a vehicle which, while it would backfire at first, ultimately assisted them in attaining their goal.

Why had Congress unanimously agreed to reside in New Jersey rather than another Middle State? And why had Elias Boudinot selected Princeton over Trenton? With the British army stationed at New York City waiting to be evacuated, New York could not be considered. Delaware, with its uncertain accommodations, never received serious attention. Thus Congress had to choose between Maryland and New Jersey. Maryland lost for various reasons: it had only one delegate attending; the Maryland Line had participated in the Philadelphia Mutiny; and perhaps it lay too far south. Boudinot chose Princeton because he knew the village well. There he had grown up, attended college and married into the town's most prominent family. Madison, who had also graduated from college in Princeton, noted that it won simply for being the less unfit of the two places.

Healthy, elevated Princeton, soon to be known as the Montpelier of America, thus became the political metropolis of the United States. Princetonians enjoyed the excitement, notables, formal dinners and citrus fruit which suddenly became commonplace. Congressmen found the cost of living low, but the accommodations in its seventy-five houses and three inns crowded, the social life boring and the pleasures of Philadelphia not forgotten. Many relied on the "Flying Machine," which instituted one long day stagecoach service between New York and Philadelphia by way of Princeton. The cultural shock of village life often drove congressmen to that "Sweet Paradise" from which they had fled in order "to spout a little" and "enjoy asiatic dinners." Most of the men had left their female companions behind, and fantasies about the daughters of their landlords did not suffice. Secretary of Congress Charles Thomson arranged to meet his wife midway. Congressman James Madison, nursing a heart wounded when his sixteen-year old fiancee ended their engagement, generally devoted himself to intellectual pursuits at Philadelphia. Claims that congressmen frequented their old seat as often as their new one made but slight exaggeration. As a result, attendance during the summer of 1783 hovered just above the seven states necessary to transact business.[26]

To the shock of most centralists it quickly became evident that a majority of states opposed a return to Philadelphia. The summer air filled with charges between the partisans of Pennsylvania and Congress over the necessity of leaving Philadelphia, the degree of irresponsibility shown by the Council and the reasons for the ever more permanent nature of a supposedly temporary measure. Americans divided over the wisdom of Congress's insisting on respect for its dignity. Some considered the removal as "savoring more of childish petulance than dignified resentment" while others believed Congress "could not consistent with the Dignity of the United States" have acted otherwise.

Outside of Pennsylvania a majority appeared pleased that Congress no longer sat in Philadelphia. New Jersey residents,

organizations and towns took self-interested pains to welcome
Congress, to praise it for leaving Philadelphia and to condemn
Pennsylvania for its conduct. Robert R. Livingston congratulated
Madison on the escape, insisting that only armed force could have
freed Congress from that Capua. Virginia's governor reported general
satisfaction with the decision and concluded that nothing except
the advantages derived from the bank could have justified
staying in Philadelphia so long after the various insults Congress
had endured. Decentralists were exuberant. Although they expressed
regret at the event which had stimulated it, they agreed
that no true friend of the Union who had witnessed the baneful influence
of Philadelphia could regret the removal. "One great step
is already taken towards emerging from Morrisonian slavery," a
constituent thanked Arthur Lee, "and it is to men of your independent
principles and just sense of liberty that we must look up for the
rest."[27]

Pennsylvanians generally condemned Congress for its decision.
The Council's secretary suggested that many were not displeased
that "the grand Sanhedrin of the Nation, with all their
solemnity and emptiness, have removed to Princeton, and left a
state, where their wisdom has been long questioned, their virtue
suspected, and their dignity a jest." Hyperbolic Benjamin Rush
blamed Congress and compared its decision to march part of the
Continental Army to Philadelphia with the response of the British
Parliament to Boston in 1774. The Pennsylvania congressman to
whom Rush wrote declared that Congress would not stoop to return
to Philadelphia without an invitation. The Philadelphia press generally
sided against Congress. One writer stressed that Pennsylvania
had once again suffered from the interference of Congress in its
internal affairs, and suggested that "fear, jealousy, design, and perhaps
party precipitated a measure, which, on reflection, cannot be
justified." A newspaper parody likened Congress to an old ship
whose owners desired to move it to New York; perhaps, mused the
author, the time had arrived to build a new ship upon different principles
of construction.[28]

Many Philadelphians would have agreed with the pun of a Virginian
who urged Congress to investigate the mutiny because it
would uncover some "Capital movers." Hamilton complained to

Madison that an idea prevailed at Philadelphia that the actors in the removal, particularly himself, were influenced by the desire of getting Congress out of the city. That clearly motivated the decentralists; in addition, some Middle States' centralists saw the removal as an opportunity to affect the ultimate location of the postwar residence of Congress. The president of Congress figured foremost among these. Even before issuing his proclamation, Boudinot, who thought the removal might fix Congress in New Jersey, intimated to the state's governor the benefits New Jersey could anticipate from being the seat of government. James McHenry of Maryland was another, for he had tried to adjourn Congress to Annapolis, which he considered spacious and elegant.

It is impossible to determine the degree to which Hamilton's desire to move Congress to New York City influenced his behavior during the mutiny. He certainly wanted Congress to come to New York, yet the assertion of federal authority always weighed more with him than the location of the capital. The French minister reported to Versailles that Hamilton had soured the climate of compromise by spreading rumors in hopes of taking Congress to New York and that Dickinson's message to the Pennsylvania Assembly about the mutiny led the public to believe that the removal stemmed from Hamilton's machinations. Madison, who did not consider the allegation totally groundless, masked these feelings when Hamilton requested written proof against it.[29]

The refusal of Congress to return, even more than the removal itself, dismayed the proud Philadelphians, who fueled their engines of influence. Secretary Charles Thomson, less vociferous but as dedicated to bringing Congress home as was his friend Rush, claimed that Congress wished only for an invitation and an assurance of protection. He was pleased to learn that Thomas Paine had drafted such an invitation, that both Robert and Gouverneur Morris had approved the wording, and that the Address would be carried door to door for signatures. Thus began seven years of public and private activity aimed at returning Congress to Philadelphia.

The Address, cautiously worded so as not to offend either Congress or the Council, quickly became connected with the Pennsylvania Anti–Constitutionalist Party, though not with Dickinson, who refused to endorse it. Many Constitutionalists refused to sign what they considered an opposition party measure. So too did certain Quakers who sought a return to the quieter and less sumptuous Philadelphia of 1774. Some residents who wished Congress well believed it would fare better in a less cosmopolitan setting. Still others did not want Pennsylvania to beg. Only 873 people signed the Address, and rumor reached the willing ears of Boudinot that for each one of them, five would sign a petition asking Congress to stay away.

The Council refused to forward the Address to Congress on the grounds that the proclamation adjourning it to Princeton constituted an insult to the state. Additionally, as Dickinson insisted, Hamilton's official report on the mutiny grossly distorted truth. When Congress received the Address through unofficial channels, it honored it by submitting it to a committee of five members, but appointed three decentralists known to detest Philadelphia and one centralist known to prefer New York City. Nine-tenths of Congress "have a secret sigh after Philadelphia but some childish reasons or those less innocent prevail," observed Philadelphia congressmen Richard Peters. "From the complexion" of the committee, "I expect nothing. Possibly their answer may be very sweet but I will watch lest the Bee be drowned in the honey."[30]

No backlash of support for Congress arose from the public in response to the soldiers' demonstration. Indeed for many Americans and Europeans the removal provided a ready symbol of the incompetence of the federal government. For this situation Congress must assume responsibility, for it did nothing to bolster its dignity after asserting it by leaving Philadelphia. That it did not was due to the growing power of the decentralists and Hamilton's obsession with ruining Dickinson's political career. Hamilton became so filled with resentment that he never offered his promised motion for a committee to urge the states to take speedy and effectual measures on behalf of Congress. Charles Thomson wanted to use the demonstration and the removal to strengthen the Union, and expressed anger that private passion had allowed Hamilton and others to foresake the opportunity. When Hamilton finally took action it came in the form of a long resolution calling for a constitutional convention, a measure which he had to abandon for lack of support.[31]

The French minister correctly analyzed the political situation in the wake of the Philadelphia Mutiny when he concluded that while Hamilton had put the chestnuts into the fire to roast, someone else might eat them. Centralist power crumbled rapidly at Princeton. Congress granted Robert Morris's request to keep his department at Philadelphia where the vital papers of Congress remained, thereby establishing separate residences for itself and its executive offices. It had no secretary for foreign affairs and was not prepared either to elect a new one or reappoint Robert R. Livingston, who indicated his willingness to return, in part because Congress had left Philadelphia. The executive wing of Congress, which the centralists had struggled to establish, thus lost its influence.[32]

The crisis of the spring of 1783 abated with demobilization of the army, the removal from Philadelphia and the decline of Robert Morris and the centralists. They did not abandon their crisis mentality however. Thomson feared that the absence of common danger and the events surrounding the exodus from Philadelphia would allow local passions and prejudice to dissolve the Union and perhaps even lead to bloody internal convulsions. He could easily see separation into five confederations: the five Eastern States (New York and New England); the four Middle States (New Jersey, Pennsylvania, Delaware, and Maryland); the Carolinas and Georgia; the West; and large, haughty Virginia, which might establish a royal government. Most centralists did not paint the future in such stark terms as did the devoted secretary of Congress. Nevertheless, they recognized the need for a new strategy to achieve a stronger federal government. Most left Congress by the end of the year, taking their campaign into the press. By 1787 they had persuaded nearly all Americans that the Articles of Confederation must be strengthened.[33]

Congress at Princeton fell increasingly under the influence of the decentralists. They gradually became aware of their renewed power and its relationship to the removal from Philadelphia. One reported in August that congressmen acted with much more independence than they ever had or ever would at Philadelphia. Arthur Lee could hardly contain his delight at the decline of what he saw as Robert Morris's wicked influence. Rhode Island's David Howell noted decentralist gains in a debate concerning Morris's policies, and declared it an act of divine providence that Congress was driven out of a city unfriendly to liberty and into an uncorrupted village. "I cannot but hope the plan laid for *giving a tone to our federal government,* as gentlemen chose to express themselves, will be discomfitted. For my part, I like well the *tone* of Confederation, and hope the free tone of that important instrument may never be altered for the *tone of Tyranny.*"[34] The almost three-year dominance by centralists in Congress had ended. Ironically, they had spurred their defeat by using the military demonstration in an attempt to assert the dignity and authority of Congress and to motivate public support for it.

Peters had accurately predicted the report of the committee which considered Philadelphia's Address inviting Congress back. It took sweet pleasure in reviewing the past patriotic and spirited contributions of Pennsylvania to the revolutionary cause, but of the bee, the return of Congress, it took no notice. The decentralists opposed returning even if, as some Pennsylvanians suggested, the Assembly impeached Dickinson and the Council. According to Peters this was because certain delegates feared that if Congress returned, it would never again get away. Congressional fears on that account did not lack foundation. The Speaker of the Pennsylvania Assembly assured Peters that "it would be deemed the eighth wonder of the world" if ever again seven states would agree to leave Philadelphia should Congress come back. Rush pleaded with Boudinot, his wife's uncle, to return if indeed Congress had fled only for its safety, "but if you availed yourselves of an ostensible excuse only to detach Congress from their stronghold in Philadelphia, then stay where you are till you are duped and laughed at on Hudson's river."

When Congress failed to return to Philadelphia in response to the Address, Pennsylvania sought other means to reclaim it. Peters argued to Congress that, since the removal had been voted as a temporary measure, a continued absence gave the impression that Congress or some of its members had voted to leave for reasons other than those made public. He threatened that Pennsylvania might conduct an investigation of the mutiny which, if it arrived at different conclusions from Congress, might produce obstructions to strengthening Congress and a dangerous breach in the Union.[35]

Although Hamilton realized when Congress convened at Princeton that it would prove difficult to secure the votes, he had immediately offered a motion that Congress, "conformable to their said intention," return to Philadelphia. Instead, Congress adopted a substitute motion from the decentralists which declared that Congress must first be invited by the state and given satisfactory assurance of protection. In August, after much parliamentary maneuvering, the decentralists offered a motion for an immediate adjournment to Philadelphia, which they intended to vote against. Not even an assurance from Dickinson and Council that they sincerely desired Congress to return had sufficient impact. Attempts to leave Princeton for places other than Philadelphia also failed.[36]

Howell thought Congress at last had bid a final farewell to Philadelphia. His colleague from Rhode Island agreed on the grounds that "the political air of that state at present doth not suit northern constitutions." Rush dismissed the matter, asserting that Philadelphians could care less about what Congress did. The President of the Bank of North America found the refusal to return ridiculous, since the bank and the enterprising spirit of Pennsylvania would support Congress better than anywhere else it might choose to meet.[37]

Madison had lobbied hard for a return and the refusal of Congress to do so upset him, for he wished to show that its motive for leaving had been what it stated. He claimed that the majority's tactic of offering a motion to adjourn to Philadelphia so that it could be defeated would please no one except the executive of Pennsylvania, which believed that the removal rose from motives other than the dignity of Congress and the welfare of the Union. Equally important, Madison thought that not remaining away from Philadelphia would affect the upcoming October debate on the establishment of a permanent residence. It rendered Annapolis a prime contender. Such a move would enhance the political and economic power of Maryland at the expense of Virginia. He predicted that the poor accommodations at Princeton, combined with the difficulty of choosing among the rival offers, would guarantee New York City the temporary residence since it offered the best means of avoiding Philadelphia. This would be unfortunate, he concluded, not only because it removed Congress farther from the South, but also because it made a permanent seat of government in the South more difficult to achieve than if the vote were taken at Philadelphia.[38] This belief—that the route to a capital on the Potomac passed through Philadelphia—dominated Madison's thinking throughout the seven-year debate over the establishment of the seat of federal government.

2

The Confederation Congress and the Federal Towns, 1783–1787

ALL THE STATES EXCEPT NEW HAMPSHIRE AND GEORgia attended Congress in October 1783 for what portended to be a major sectional battle. On 6 October the Massachusetts decentralist Elbridge Gerry, who assumed a leadership role on the issue between 1783 and 1785, moved that Congress consider the offers for the postwar location of the seat of federal government received from New York, New Jersey, Pennsylvania, Maryland and Virginia.[1]

New York's offer was motivated by the wealthy centralist Robert R. Livingston, who had chaired the committee which buried Congress's 1779 resolution to leave Philadelphia. Early in 1782 he drafted a resolution for the New York legislature directing its congressional delegation to convince Congress to leave Philadelphia. Among the reasons for the necessity of a change, the resolution cited the stimulation such a removal would give a local economy elsewhere, the inflated costs of residing at Philadelphia which inhibited attendance, the impossibility of maintaining secrecy in a large commercial city crowded with strangers and the disaffected, and the threat of Philadelphia's dissipation diffusing via Congress throughout the continent, subverting the moderation and virtue so necessary to republican governments. The legislature failed to adopt the resolution, but discussed a bill granting Congress some jurisdictional prerogatives if it met in New York State.

At the end of the year, a few weeks after announcing his resignation as secretary for foreign affairs, Livingston pushed New York to grant Congress the picturesque town of Kingston, a dozen miles south of his Hudson River manor. New York responded with a limited jurisdiction over one square mile of land about the town. Displeased, Livingston castigated the legislature for its shortsightedness in allotting Congress less jurisdiction than it would a private corporation, especially considering that the grant would eventually be worth millions to the state. Congressman Alexander Hamilton expressed the same displeasure to his politically powerful father-in-law, New York State Senator Philip Schuyler, who admitted that the legislators had paid little attention to the matter since they believed Congress would not approve the location. If it ever seriously considered moving to the state, Schuyler concluded, the legislature would cede whatever jurisdiction Congress wished over any place except New York City or Albany. At the end of May 1783 a congressional committee declared New York's proposal unacceptable, but suggested that if the Kingston Corporation donated a three-mile square (nine square miles) and the state granted exclusive jurisdiction over all criminal matters, perhaps Congress might relocate there. The willingness of the United States to even consider such a secluded village stunned the French government, and its minister at Philadelphia had to explain at length the American prejudice against large cities.[2]

Fear of a move northward stimulated Virginia to action. Thomas Jefferson and Congressman James Madison crafted its response, thus beginning their seven-year effort to place the capital of the United States on the Potomac River. They believed Congress would prefer a site on the Potomac to Kingston, especially if the grant included ample jurisdiction. The two Maryland congressmen, Daniel Carroll and Thomas Sim Lee, both of whom lived along the Potomac, agreed. The Virginia and Maryland delegates proposed that their states should step forward with a tract of land in the neighborhood of Georgetown, Maryland. This pleased Jefferson, who believed that, if Virginia could not obtain a Potomac seat for the federal government, it should support a site north of the Chesapeake Bay, believing that any location on the bay threatened Virginia's interests "as it may attract the trade of that bay and make us with respect to Maryland what Delaware is to Pennsylvania."[3]

The political conflict between Maryland's Potomac and Upper Chesapeake Bay interests—which influenced its position throughout the fight over the establishment of the capital—prevented

Maryland from joining Virginia in an invitation. The Upper Bay Interest believed that a location on either bank of the Potomac would be dominated by Virginia and economically detrimental to the Upper Chesapeake. For several months its supporters, centered at Baltimore, had considered inviting Congress to Annapolis and moving the state capital to Baltimore.

As early as November 1782, a broadside signed "Aratus" (the Achaean League leader known for his devotion to the good of the state without self-interested motives) suggested that the Maryland legislature offer Annapolis to Congress. Its author, the well-to-do Baltimore merchant George Lux, Jr., proposed certain immunities for Congress, while allowing Maryland ultimate jurisdiction. Specifically, Congress should govern the town and determine who should reside there, so that Annapolis did not become an asylum for villains and traitors. Congressmen would of course be free from arrest. Referring to George Washington's opposition in 1774 to meeting at Philadelphia, Lux further urged that both the state and county governments and all merchants not necessary for provisioning the residents be removed, since everyone knew what Congress had suffered at the hands of Philadelphia politicians and merchants. In private letters enclosing copies of the broadside to influential friends, Lux added additional arguments for Annapolis: its centrality; its elegant but inexpensive housing; its famous wildfowl and seafood; and its location in a state whose constitution was stable and agreeable to all ranks of society, unlike the anarchy and democracy prevalent in Pennsylvania. He also named as the actual site he supported, approximately twenty square miles surrounding Annapolis between the Severn and South rivers.

In late May 1783 the "mightily cocked up" citizens of Annapolis offered the town's 300 acres to the United States. The legislature responded by promising the State House, the governor's mansion, $32,500 with which to build a hotel for each state delegation, and whatever jurisdiction over the town and its inhabitants Congress might find necessary for its "honor, dignity, convenience, and safety." The potential breadth of the promised jurisdiction constituted not only a reaction to New York's limited offer at Kingston but also to Lux's private advocacy of an exclusive jurisdiction for Congress.[4]

News of Maryland's action reached Virginia early in June and set back the governor and other influential politicians. They agreed with Jefferson and Madison that a joint offer on the Potomac from the two states must take precedence over any other unless Pennsylvania and New Jersey jointly proposed a site on the Delaware River. If Maryland preferred to compete, Virginia could match Annapolis. At the end of June Virginia granted Congress use of the Capitol, the governor's palace and all the other public buildings at Williamsburg, which it had vacated three years earlier after transferring its capital to Richmond. The offer included 300 acres adjacent to Williamsburg and up to $250,000 to build thirteen hotels for the state delegations. In addition, the state promised Congress as much jurisdiction over a five mile square (twenty-five square miles) district as the residents of the area would yield. Keeping its options open, the legislature promised similar terms if Maryland should someday agree to a joint cession on the Potomac. In that case, Virginia would make a grant directly across the Potomac from Maryland's cession; but, if Congress decided to place its buildings on the north bank of the river, Virginia would donate only $100,000, expecting Maryland to supply the other $150,000.

The residents of the five mile square about Williamsburg resolved to make the residence of Congress so agreeable that it would never regret its choice; but, since they had no idea what would satisfy Congress, they could agree only to "such jurisdiction as may be compatible with their political welfare, and worthy of generous minds either to demand or yield."[5] Disappointed by this circumlocution, Virginia's governor observed that it demonstrated only that Virginians still jealously guarded their liberty and feared that the presence of Congress would introduce too much luxury. The offer did not arrive in time for President Elias Boudinot to transmit it to the states with those of New York and Maryland, but news of it and Boudinot's letter stimulated discussion in New Jersey, Pennsylvania and Delaware.

The citizens of the western part of Nottingham Township in New Jersey asked the state legislature to grant Congress whatever jurisdiction over them it saw fit. Nottingham included the village of Lamberton and sat on what was then the southern boundary of Trenton. The offer encompassed about twelve and one-half square miles, including six miles of river frontage on the Delaware, and came in lieu of Trenton, New Jersey's part-time capital, which some suspected might be unacceptable to a Congress that had suffered so many jurisdictional disputes at Pennsylvania's capital. The federal government later learned that it would receive a $250 legacy from a Lamberton doctor if it located its seat there.[6]

In response to the governor's conviction that a majority in Congress would prefer New Jersey to either New York or Maryland, the legislature promised the federal government whatever jurisdiction it needed over a twenty-square mile district. In addition, New Jersey pledged $75,000 to purchase land and erect buildings and forwarded Nottingham's offer. The legislature asked other New Jersey towns to petition Congress directly if any wished to be chosen.

Responding to the legislature and the arrival of Congress in New Jersey, Newark proposed itself in July, and New Brunswick and Elizabethtown in August. Princeton never sent a formal invitation but figured in the competition by virtue of Congress residing there. Joseph Borden later claimed that he had written Congress suggesting Bordentown. President of Congress Elias Boudinot extolled Elizabethtown's merits, promising Congress that he would willingly rent his large house there as a residence for his successors. Secretary of Congress Thomson sarcastically observed that the spring and fall floods and summer mosquitoes were trifling by comparison to the increased value for the president's property.

Many expected Pennsylvania to make a magnificent overture, but instead it decided to wait until Congress specified the amount of jurisdiction it needed. Nevertheless, residents of Germantown suggested in the summer of 1783 that Congress move there. Many Americans viewed that village as merely another name for Philadelphia, seven miles to the southeast.

The Delaware congressmen launched a campaign to encourage their state not to pass up such a fine opportunity for aggrandizing itself, and proposed that it grant Congress 200 or 300 acres at Wilmington, with a generous jurisdiction over six or eight square miles between Christiana and Brandywine creeks, or perhaps south to include New Castle. Delaware failed to act.

By September New York's proposal of Kingston appeared so miserly compared to those of Maryland, Virginia and New Jersey that the village revised it to encompass more land and an absolute jurisdiction. New York's original offer especially chagrined Lewis Morris, a signer of the Declaration of Independence and the older half-brother of Gouverneur Morris. He wrote Congress directly at the end of September proposing that it choose Morrisania, his five-square mile manor on the Harlem and East Rivers just above Manhattan Island. Among a myriad of boastful arguments, Morris noted that the manor lay eight miles from fortified New York City, the best harbor in the United States. This was distance enough to protect Congress from the mobs and tumults associated with large cities, yet close enough for it to establish a federal arsenal and navy yard as well as transact its commercial business. Morris promised to donate 100 acres of land, to yield his extensive judicial and other manorial prerogatives and to see Morrisania entirely separated from New York State and placed under the absolute jurisdiction of Congress. The area involved, including the contiguous township of West Chester, encompassed twenty-five square miles. The want of suitable buildings caused only a temporary inconvenience, he argued, and should not be considered when making a decision of possible perpetual consequence. Morris immodestly suggested that Congress accept Morrisania on condition of New York's later concurring or postpone any choice until the legislature met.

George Washington visited Congress at Princeton just prior to the October 1783 debate. From Madison and others he quickly secured enough information for an accurate assessment of the situation and accepted the conclusion that seven states would never agree on a place. This led the commander in chief to predict that the issue would remain an irritant and prevent Congress from addressing other concerns.[7]

Attempts in Congress to postpone the decision on 6 October failed, and each delegation cast a vote for the state in which it believed the permanent residence should be located. Not surprisingly New Jersey and Maryland fared the best. The former received its own and the votes of three New England States, the latter its own and those of three Southern States. Both had made liberal offers to

Congress, and both needed the votes of New York, Pennsylvania and Delaware to be successful.

New Englanders favored New Jersey's claim to the "great prize" because of its convenience for them, its access to intelligence from Europe, its devotion to the revolutionary cause and its healthy climate. New Jersey's status as a small, rather than large, influential state constituted a special asset from their point of view, since additional power would accrue to the state in which Congress sat. Furthermore, "as New Jersey is not calculated for extensive trade or commerce," observed the Rhode Island delegates, "the probability is that she will the longer persevere in those economical manners, a departure from which so necessarily follows the excessive riches and luxury of commercial states." The area about Trenton at the lower falls of the Delaware River was the specific location New England supported, because of its centrality as to wealth, population and number of states. The site also provided access to the resources of Philadelphia while preserving the federal government from what New Englanders perceived as its dangerous influence.

Southerners supported Maryland, citing its geographic centrality, its access to the western country, and the stimulation it would provide for further land cessions from the three southernmost states. But the South could not unite on a place. Annapolis won strong support from many Marylanders, some North Carolinians and the South Carolinians. Baltimore also had a few advocates. Most Virginians, both in Congress and at home, agreed with the Potomac Interest of Maryland that a joint offer on the Potomac, rather than Williamsburg, remained their state's best hope. One praised safe, healthy, delightful and centrally located Georgetown, Maryland, which, if self-interest were laid aside, all America would deem the fittest place on navigable water. William Grayson called Kingston, New York, diabolical, any place in New Jersey, execrable, and Pittsburgh, Pennsylvania, infinitely preferable to either.

In Congress on 7 October Gerry moved that a federal town be established on the Delaware River near Trenton or on the Potomac near Georgetown. An attempt to add the Hudson River to the resolution, chiefly on the argument of its security from invasion, failed. When Congress struck the names of the towns from the resolution,

Maryland fruitlessly attempted to block further consideration. Although the delegation must have recognized that such Virginia Potomac River towns as Alexandria had suddenly become possibilities, its procedural maneuvers arose from the fact that towns in the states of Pennsylvania and Delaware had also become candidates. And that ensured a majority for the Delaware River.

Delaware moved for a site near Wilmington, but instead Congress agreed on the area about the falls near Trenton and delegated choice of the specific site to a committee consisting of Gerry and four other northerners. Lamberton was generally predicted as the spot that the committee would recommend. This would have placed the federal town at the head of tidewater thirty miles northeast of Philadelphia. The refusal to support Wilmington cost the North Delaware's vote, and the next day it joined the four Southern States in a call for reconsideration in order to fix on a place "more central, more favorable to the Union, and [which] shall approach nearer to that justice which is due to the southern states." But seven states had already decided the matter and, even if only six still supported the decision, five for reconsideration did not constitute a majority.[8]

The need for a temporary residence, an issue which would complicate the politics over the establishment of the seat of empire throughout the seven–year debate, now came to the floor for the first time. Several citizens of Trenton promised accommodations if Congress came there. Princetonians petitioned Congress to remain another year, or at least for the winter. The fact that Congress need not experience the inconvenience and expense of a removal favored remaining at Princeton. Its cramped facilities worked against it. Madison, for example, shared a narrow bed with a fellow Virginian in a room so small that one had to remain in bed while the other dressed. On 10 October only the three New England States voted to remain at Princeton, the village whose frugal image had become for them a symbol of republican virtue.

With the decision to leave Princeton, the likelihood that Congress would return to Philadelphia to await completion of the federal town near Trenton became greater than at any time since the supposedly temporary removal in June. Most Philadelphians, including Robert Morris and Congressman Thomas Fitzsimons, recognized the excellent opportunity despite the embittered contention of Benjamin Rush that a resolution respecting the residence of Congress held no more interest for Philadelphians than a resolution of Parliament. Its advocates made several arguments. No place matched Philadelphia for transacting the business of the federal government, for accommodating its members and the foreign ministers and for maintaining a vigil over the executive officers who remained there. Madison stressed again that a return to Pennsylvania's capital would alleviate the tensions between that state and Congress. In addition, he believed a temporary residence there would provide enough votes to reconsider the decision to place the federal town on the Delaware so that it could eventually be located on the Potomac.[9]

Hugh Williamson of North Carolina, Pennsylvanian by birth and urbane by temperament, made the motion for Philadelphia. Carefully crafted to unite New Jersey with the six states south of it, the resolution adjourned Congress to its former meetingplace at the end of October, to remain there until June 1784 when it would move to Trenton. The strategy failed because Maryland and South Carolina voted with the Eastern States. Although South Carolina's antipathy toward Philadelphia played a key role as it would for the next seven years, Madison blamed Congressman James McHenry of Maryland for the defeat.

Suffering from a severe headache brought on by the debate which he considered to be "long, renewed, continued, repeated, and more violent and acrimonious than any I have been witness to in Congress," McHenry supported a new motion to make Annapolis the temporary residence. The Maryland capital had in its favor the capacity to accommodate Congress and to soothe the Southern States in view of the decision to locate the federal town on the Delaware. Annapolis's distance from that site and the bypassing of superior comforts at Philadelphia militated against it, as did the opinion that such a decision would indicate continued resentment against Pennsylvania.

The motion was just as carefully worded as the earlier one for Philadelphia. Congress would remove to Annapolis until June 1784 and then go north to Trenton. The ensuing debate gave the decentralists another opportunity to condemn the influence Philadelphia had exerted over Congress when it met there. While other members denied the allegations, Arthur Lee named Robert Morris, and David Howell declared his preference for Williamsburg, Virginia, Charleston, South Carolina, or even Savannah, Georgia. The New England delegates voted for Annapolis to avoid Philadelphia, but the resolution failed because Virginia and South Carolina voted no. Congress adjourned in an ill humor. The Virginia delegates privately defended their vote against Annapolis on the grounds that such a move was anathema to Virginia commerce and the chances of the Potomac's later being chosen the permanent residence. Indeed, McHenry insisted that the motion, if successful, would have anchored Congress at Annapolis.

Secretary Charles Thomson took advantage of Sunday's recess and traveled to Trenton to consider the potential of the Pennsylvania side of the Delaware for a federal town. Despite his fear, after the bitter Saturday debate, that Congress would not meet again, it convened on Monday and Virginia proposed an adjournment to Williamsburg. Lacking both real conviction on the part of Virginia and support from any other state, the motion failed.[10]

The inability of seven states to agree on a temporary residence moved the debate from the floor to private meetings initiated by the frustrated and angry southerners, who feared that the North would use the influence of the Delaware location to maintain the South's minority political status in the Union. In hopes of securing a reconsideration, they presented several arguments to the New Englanders. The Articles of Confederation required nine states to agree on any appropriation. Nine would never agree to spend money for a federal town so far north. Centrality of territory bore greater importance than centrality of population. Future population growth would be to the south and west. The Delaware River choice would prove the allegation of the North's desire for hegemony. American dignity and the duration of the Union depended on justice and equality among the states. And "posterity would laugh at our federal buildings and desert them if we should unwisely for selfish purposes fix them on a corner of the Empire." What, in light of all this, did New England feel about the Potomac with its good climate and potential for binding the interior, western part of the Union to the coastal states? To influence the answer, the South threatened to

unite its votes with those of the Middle States for an immediate return to Philadelphia.[11]

In response New England proposed a bold solution: a second
federal town on the Potomac, a compromise with well known historical precedent in the confederacies of the Ancient World. Several informed sources credited Gerry with the proposal. It
rekindled the old debate whether an American capital should be
stationary or mobile.

New Englanders, whose state capitals tended to be the latter,
recognized republican as well as decentralist overtones in the proposal. In their view one federal town meant a concentration of
wealthy citizens, generally neither the most virtuous nor the most
patriotic of Americans, who would use their influence to establish
an aristocracy. Two residences meant greater obstacles to a consolidation of political and economic influence even if they led to delay
and difficulty in transacting business. As Gerry's decentralist ally
Howell expressed it, "a perambulatory Congress favors republicanism—a permanent one tends to concentrate power, aristocracy,
and monarchy." Howell had probably seen similar advantages in his
September suggestion that Congress reside at or near Pittsburgh.
Also, New Englanders feared that the Delaware location would so
upset the South that it might precipitate a change in the federal government which could cause greater calamities than the establishment of American independence. In more practical terms, the
South had to be accommodated for the necessary nine states to appropriate money for the Delaware federal town. Finally, New Englanders viewed the dual residence as the only way to avoid the
vortex of Philadelphia to which they feared Congress would become forever a mere appendage.[12]

The seven New England and Southern States agreed to support
the dual residence proposal despite New England's recognition
that the South's real motive lay in buying time for a single federal
town on the Potomac. Middle States congressmen quickly discovered that a deal had been struck. Boudinot could not help thinking
of Rome and Constantinople. While he described the coalition as
the most heterogeneous imaginable, it constituted the familiar alliance which had dominated the politics of Congress during the early
years of the Revolution. Above all, the dual residence realistically

reflected the sectional division of the Union and provided a bridge at a time when little existed to hold the states in anything other than symbolic union.[13]

Decentralists Gerry and Arthur Lee proposed on 17 October that buildings be erected at or near the lower falls of the Potomac or Georgetown under the same terms as the previous resolution for the federal town near the falls of the Delaware. The Middle States attempted unsuccessfully to postpone the question for six months, arguing that the states needed time to deliberate on the idea of two seats. During debate on 20 October it quickly became apparent that the dual residence coalition was not as united as first assumed. Howell, who worried that Congress might decide on Philadelphia as a temporary residence, insisted that question be determined first. Marylander Daniel Carroll proposed Annapolis. The Eastern members called for a second temporary residence closer to the Delaware River. Carroll then moved that Congress alternate between Annapolis and Trenton until the federal towns could be constructed. But the coalition could not agree on how long Congress should remain at each: a South Carolinian preferred twelve months and a Rhode Islander insisted on six. Adoption of the motion required both their votes and compromise failed.

Northerners and southerners immediately began to castigate each other, much to the silent delight of delegates from the Middle States. As the sun set and tempers rose, a Virginian laid open the details of the negotiations which had led to the proposal for a second federal town, condemning the New England members severely. With hope for agreement gone Congress adjourned. Southerners declared their intention to unite with the Middle States and return to Philadelphia. This frightened the New Englanders, who met and agreed to accept Gerry's compromise proposal for no less than six nor more than twelve months at each temporary residence.

On 21 October Congress adopted the Gerry–Lee resolution for a second federal town on the Potomac, alternate temporary residences at Annapolis and Trenton and adjournment of Congress to Annapolis at the end of November. Next, Congress appointed a committee consisting of Gerry and four southerners to visit the Potomac and report a proper district for the federal town. The

Maryland delegation urged its governor to take the necessary steps to assure adequate accommodations at Annapolis so as to impress Congress.

The dual residence compromise surprised the public. The French ambassador thought that it illustrated quite well the incongruity of a federal system of government where the satisfaction of conflicting interests always outweighed the public good. The cost and inconvenience of two seats could never be borne by Congress, he surmised, and, if the principle was true that dual residences would produce mutual confidence among the states, it followed logically that Congress had better move successively from state to state. The ambassador from the Netherlands complained that America's European creditors would never provide the money for its implementation.[14]

New Englanders generally saw the plan as republican and defended the expense of two federal towns as the price of union with the South, avoiding Philadelphia and stopping the Middle States' centralists. The dual residence "is considered by the patriots as a triumph," concluded a decentralist who claimed that Robert Morris had more influence at Philadelphia than a king. Some hoped the decision would extract his resignation. On the other hand, John Adams, who still believed in a transient seat for Congress, opposed the establishment of even one federal town, believing it constituted a fourteenth state where an independent army would be established.[15]

Residents of the Middle States found the plan utterly and completely preposterous. Robert R. Livingston, stunned that Congress had not adjourned to New York City upon the British withdrawal, predicted that, like a wounded comet, Congress would annually revolve around Philadelphia until sucked in and absorbed. The disappointed Philadelphians swelled their press with commentary. How could Congress seriously propose two federal towns costing half a million dollars when it could not pay its former soldiers? Two seats so far distant from each other bore a similarity to two powers and tended to divide rather than to unite, and, before long, to create in the United States a situation akin to the rivalry between the houses of York and Lancaster. The choice should have been made by a Congress with less prejudice against Pennsylvania.[16]

One Pennsylvanian however used the opportunity to suggest that the plan would guard Pennsylvanian republicanism from the expense, public amusements and federal jurisdiction associated with Congress. While Pennsylvania decentralists probably agreed with his analysis, most Philadelphia centralists did not. For them the undignified dual residence compromise symbolized the weakness of the federal government under the Articles of Confederation better than anything else the Confederation Congress ever did. "A pretty little history of the truly astonishing accidents" that led to it "might be wrote, and would certainly be highly pleasing to all lovers of romance, founded on real facts," concluded one. Robert Morris, examining the decision in the perspective of time, believed that the refusal to return to Philadelphia resulted from the nature of republican legislatures whose unwise decisions would be repealed as the members changed.[17]

Philadelphian Francis Hopkinson used his satirical pen to render the dual residence plan ridiculous in the public mind. He proposed to resolve the contradiction between Congress's earlier decision to erect an equestrian statue of Washington at its permanent residence with its present decision to have two. Let the statue be mobile too. Indeed, make it large enough to transport the congressmen from one federal town to the other. Such a trojan horse could even contain a little closet in its rectum for the secret papers of such an important body as Congress. Or, if Congress wished to avoid the expense of two sets of buildings as well as two statues, it might build but one "imperial city" and still have "*two* places of *alternate, permanent* residence" by placing the city on wheels.[18]

Maryland's Upper Chesapeake Interest saw danger in the decision to place even a part–time seat on the Potomac. It seized the opportunity of the public debate over the dual residence to propose the head of the Chesapeake Bay as a compromise site. Congress had situated itself like a lover between two mistresses. Instead it should ignore the state offers and select its own site so that all America might partake equally of that "national fountain of wisdom and protection." The head of the Chesapeake lay midway between the two proposed federal towns and held out so many advantages as to suggest its having been created for that purpose by the wise author of nature. Baltimoreans named Havre de Grace,

Maryland, and residents of economically depressed Charlestown on the eastern shore proposed their town.[19]

Aside from a few doctrinaire decentralists, most Virginians viewed the dual residence as nothing more than a temporary expedient to preserve the dream of a Potomac capital. Jefferson believed it turned a defeat into a draw and left the whole matter open for discussion. The governor saw the decision as assuaging Virginia's fears that a decided majority of the Union opposed southern interests, and expressed pleasure that Congress had been able to avoid Philadelphia, a vortex which swallowed Virginia's wealth.[20]

Soon after Congress left Princeton, the committee to view the Delaware, attended by Thomas Hutchins, geographer to the United States, studied the river banks from Howell's Ferry just below Washington Crossing down to Lamberton. It chose locations in both Pennsylvania and New Jersey. The Pennsylvania site, the highlands for a mile above Trenton Falls, provided healthy conditions, good springs, building materials and an extensive, pleasing view over New Jersey. The view from Lamberton, the New Jersey site, was delightful too, though less varied and without building materials. The committee recommended that Congress pick the state which secured title to the land on the best terms and complied with Congress's as yet unspecified needs respecting jurisdiction.[21]

In May 1784 the committee to view the Potomac toured both sides of the river from Georgetown to about four miles above Little Falls. They did not find a suitable spot for a federal town north of Georgetown and expressed regret that their instructions prevented them from looking at the level banks above Great Falls. The committee ordered Charles Beatty of Georgetown to survey two sites adjacent to the town, both of which it recommended to Congress. The first included about 600 acres of rising ground to the northwest. It encompassed all or portions of Frogland, Conjuror's Disappointment and Rock of Dumbarton land grants. The lines ran north from the river at about present-day 34th Street to about Davis Place, west to Glover Archbold Park, south to the Potomac and east to the starting point. Within the area today is Georgetown University. The second site, about 750 acres, was a tract below Georgetown. It included all or portions of the Vineyard, Widow's Mite and Little Prevention land grants as well as the platted but unsettled town of

Hamburg or Funkstown. Its approximate boundaries extended north from the Potomac up present-day 18th Street to Florida Avenue, southwest to Rock Creek, down the creek to the Potomac and back to the starting point. Within the area today are The George Washington University and Dupont Circle.[22]

Congress took no action on either committee report, and the maps which accompanied them have disappeared from federal records. Beatty's surveys arrived at Congress just as a fascinating piece of land biography began. Three residents of Chester County, Pennsylvania, and Wilmington, Delaware, set out to buy up as much land as possible north of the 600 acre Potomac River site. They eventually held most of the land from above Little Falls down to present-day Foxhall Road. In the first decade of the nineteenth century, Adjutant General of Maryland Henry Carbery, leader of the soldiers who surrounded the Pennsylvania State House in 1783, purchased a portion of the land.[23]

Congressmen, detained by smallpox vaccinations at Philadelphia and other matters, trickled into Annapolis in December. The Maryland legislature welcomed Congress and promised to take all measures necessary to make its permanent residence in the state as agreeable as possible once it had chosen a specific site, thus officially sanctioning for the first time the possibility of a Potomac capital. Jefferson, hoping to gain some real advantage out of the dual residence plan, seized the opportunity to renew negotiations for a joint Maryland-Virginia offer. He proposed that each state appoint three men to a commission which would superintend the purchase of land and the construction of buildings. In order to avoid delay, if the commissioners divided equally on a question, the matter would be resolved by a majority vote of the states' congressional delegations. Virginia, Jefferson knew, would benefit from such an arrangement since its larger delegation always attended Congress more faithfully. Nothing came of the initiative however, and Maryland's Upper Chesapeake Interest merely awaited another opportunity to assert the claims of the Chesapeake over those of the Potomac.[24]

Congress's six-month residence at Annapolis proved far more pleasant than its four months at Princeton. Annapolis, a picturesque town of about 1,300 inhabitants, several hundred of them slaves, had been Maryland's capital for almost a century. Oaks, chestnuts and walnuts shaded the streets while the formal gardens of many of its 300 houses enhanced the elegance. Although virtually surrounded by water, Annapolis lacked the usual marshes, salt meadows and stagnant waters. Much of the adjacent pine-studded countryside remained uncultivated: "the whole view resembling an asiatic picture, excites not those pleasing ideas which arise in the mind of a more northern inhabitant from the view of a country beautified by the hand of industry."

Congress met at the Maryland State House in one of the most impressive rooms in America, and the president resided at the governor's mansion. The members themselves found spacious accommodations at the twenty-three inns. The hospitable inhabitants of the town and the many wealthy planters who wintered there devoted themselves to the pursuit of pleasure. Entertainments included horse racing, fox hunting, balls, plays, concerts and general ogling. Hannah Thomson, first lady of the federal government in the absence of the president's wife, held conversations over tea each Saturday. Annapolis would outshine poor Philadelphia, beamed Arthur Lee, who joined in the festivities by courting one of the town's many attractive ladies, a seventeen-year old heiress. The New England decentralists, unlike their ally Lee, found the social calendar tedious and the dearth of churches symbolic. The effect of the social life on the business of Congress might have disturbed their republican sensibilities more had they not considered Annapolis' residents too devoted to pleasure to interfere with politics.[25]

Whereas congressional politics at Princeton had been in a transitory state with a considerable number of centralists still urging support for a stronger federal government, at Annapolis decentralists recognized that they once again controlled Congress. The most prominent centralist holdout was Secretary Thomson, whom decentralists failed to force out of office. Would, he moaned, that the preceding six months "could be obliterated from the annals of America and utterly effaced from my memory!" Thomson would be almost as displeased with the next twelve. The office of secretary of foreign affairs remained vacant. Robert Morris resigned and Congress replaced him with a three man Board of Treasury. No act more symbolized the decline of centralist influence. Localism and the related tensions among the states and sections became more pronounced as the New England–South coalition reforged at Princeton fell apart. Congress often lacked a quorum: at one point some members considered holding a special session at Philadelphia, where a sick delegate could complete the quorum of nine states required for ratification of the definitive peace treaty. This proved unnecessary, but the delay meant that the decision would not reach Europe by the day appointed for the official exchange of ratifications. A bitter Philadelphia delegate punned that blame belonged to the politicians who had so "cunningly removed Congress to the Lee Ward."[26]

Except for brief recesses when it moved from place to place, Congress had been in continuous session since 1775. Congressmen began discussing an adjournment early in 1784, soon after agreeing to the peace treaty. Business was less pressing than during the war, and some northerners did not hide their fear of spending a summer in a debilitating southern climate. In April Rhode Island called for Congress to adjourn for five months and reconvene at the end of October at Newport in their state. Congress refused, and also defeated adjournment to Philadelphia or Annapolis, before agreeing to adhere to its decision at Princeton to move to Trenton after Annapolis. For one Pennsylvania delegate the vote to leave that town was ample revenge against those who had carried Congress there. He took particular pleasure in the fact that it had been effected by reuniting New England and the Middle States against the South.[27]

Although Congress thus confirmed part of the dual residence agreement, the two permanent federal towns lived only as an idea. New England decentralists like Gerry, who still feared the centralist vision for the United States, wanted to keep at least that idea alive until such time as "we have effectually opposed the despotic system so warmly pursued to destroy the liberties of our country." If that could be done "they will have answered a great, and political purpose."

Jefferson reported to Madison that "the smile is hardly covered now when the federal towns are spoken of." He described chances for a Potomac residence as desperate, its only hope being the possibility of placing Congress temporarily north of the Chesapeake so that it could never consider itself fixed. For the Virginia delegation the decision to go to Trenton reaffirmed the South's minority status in the Union: "the votes in Congress as they stand at present are unfavorable to a Southern situation and until the admission of Western States into the Union, we apprehend it will be found impracticable to retain that body, any length of time, southward of the middle States."

The South nevertheless desired to turn the attention of Americans to Georgetown as the place the United States might ultimately choose for its seat of empire. Would Congress promise Maryland and Virginia credit against future federal requisitions for any monies the states spent to erect the necessary buildings at the site of the Potomac federal town? No. Would Congress postpone a final vote on the adjournment to Trenton until it had appropriated equal amounts of money for the construction of the two federal towns? Again no. A final effort admitted to the demise of the dual residence. Would Congress remain at Annapolis until erection of the necessary buildings at such single place of permanent residence as it later chose? No yet again.[28]

The Articles of Confederation allowed for the creation of a Committee of States, consisting of a member from each, to sit during an adjournment. Some delegates thought such a Committee unnecessary, but the view which prevailed held that an adjournment for even a few months without a Committee would accustom Americans to the absence of the federal government and perhaps lead to a collapse of the Union. After much debate Congress finally agreed on the Committee's powers and duties. At the insistence of the New England delegates, even routine business required the votes of nine states. This meant that the Committee would not adjourn itself to Philadelphia despite predictions to the contrary.[29]

When nine members of the Committee convened in June, they voted not to move to Philadelphia, but informed Pennsylvania that its action in response to an assault in the streets of that city upon an official of the French Embassy maintained the dignity of the United States. Charles Thomson, to whom the Committee granted permission to return to his Philadelphia–area home until Congress reassembled at Trenton, hoped that the arrival of additional states would provide the votes to adjourn the Committee to Philadelphia, thus ending the indignities and inconveniences occasioned by the ramblings of Congress since June 1783. Members from additional states did not arrive; consequently, the absence of a single member meant that the Committee could not function. The shaky quorum lasted a month. As July evaporated into August, the delegates of New Hampshire, Massachusetts and New Jersey failed to carry a motion to adjourn immediately to Trenton in order to prepare for the arrival of Congress. Asserting that they feared for their health at Annapolis and that the requirement for unanimity made any attempt to transact business futile, the three men left Annapolis for home. The New Englanders paid their respects to Secretary Thomson as they passed through Philadelphia and reportedly expressed fears of being robbed or assassinated in the city after dark.

The six powerless members sent the papers of Congress to Philadelphia until provision could be made for them at Trenton. Four of the six signed a letter to the states calling on them to send delegates as soon as possible to either Philadelphia or Trenton, if the papers had already gone there, so that the Committee could get back to business. Attempts to reassemble at Philadelphia, where Thomson kept the papers, proved unsuccessful during the next two and one-half months.

This left the United States without a federal government. America had sustained a rapid decline in its reputation since the peace both at home and abroad, complained Thomson, whom a friend described as a fish out of water during the adjournment. "Let the blame fall where it ought, on those whose attachment to State Views, State Interests and State Prejudices is so great as to render them eternally opposed to every measure that can be devised for the public good," one delegate complained to George Washington. "The evil is not however as yet entirely incurable. I hope and trust the next Congress will be more wise and be able to avert the mischiefs that appear to me to threaten the Union."[30]

Congress faced a critical situation when it met at Trenton, and its ability to revitalize the federal government stands as the significant result of its brief tenure there. Congressmen began arriving at the end of October 1784, but it took a full month before a quorum formed. This provided the delegates with time to reflect on the present and future situation of the Union. Even the decentralist

Richard Henry Lee complained about the lassitude in federal affairs, believing many subjects of great importance demanded the firm attention of Congress. Some of Lee's colleagues advocated the immediate convening of a constitutional convention as the best solution to the situation. Instead, a consensus formed to support several actions to revitalize the Union. These included the continued reorganization of the executive functions of Congress and the establishment of stronger diplomatic ties with Europe. Central to the consensus was the belief that Congress must remain stationary: a single federal town should be chosen and in the meantime Congress should sit in a large city where it would not suffer the inconveniences experienced in small towns.[31]

Although some people thought that Congress should endure almost any discomfort to avoid yet another move, and New Jersey appropriated $750 to help Congress procure buildings at Trenton, the town lacked adequate facilities. The situation worsened when the New Jersey legislature unexpectedly convened there. The Northern States were poorly represented when Congress, meeting in the elaborately redecorated Long Room of the French Arms Tavern, finally secured a quorum at the end of November. Consequently a report spread through the press that the South would probably draw Congress back across the Delaware to Philadelphia. Sarah Jay, shocked by the possibility of yet another change of residence, mused to her congressman husband John how fortunate it was for the reputation of females that none sat in Congress.

The Pennsylvania Assembly once again offered Congress space in the public buildings on State House Square in Philadelphia, along with the promise of laws to support its dignity. When Secretary Thomson sent off to Annapolis for the furnishings for the president's house left behind by the Committee of States, he ordered them to remain at Philadelphia pending a decision on where Congress would sit. That city, however, at last had acquired a rival which matched its merits in most respects except centrality and did not suffer from the stigma of eight years as the revolutionary seat of government. The New York legislature had just urged Congress to come to New York City.[32]

When the expected motion to leave Trenton came early in December, it failed because only the five states south of the Delaware supported it. The North desired to wait for enough votes to assure that Congress would adjourn to New York City rather than Philadelphia. By 20 December it had the votes, and Congress formally rescinded the dual residence resolutions of a year earlier. Three days later Gerry and Howell brought in an ordinance which provided for a single federal town on the Delaware. An amendment by the Virginians to locate the federal town on the Potomac at Georgetown failed because congressmen from the Lower South, who enjoyed the refreshing northern summers and the comparative ease of reaching the Delaware River on their coastal voyages between home and Congress, saw no likelihood of obtaining the necessary votes.

The question whether to choose New York City or Philadelphia for the temporary residence proved the most divisive issue in the debate, but even it was resolved with comparative ease. Trenton's inadequate accommodations proved an effective spur. In addition, a seemingly unrelated issue had an effect. Congress had finally selected a secretary for foreign affairs, and John Jay conditioned his acceptance on Congress becoming stationary, preferably at his home town, New York City. New England, except for Rhode Island, supported New York City out of its historic distaste for Philadelphia and a fear that once situated there, Pennsylvania, with southern assistance, would frustrate the completion of the federal town on the Delaware.

The South knew that it lacked the votes to remove to Philadelphia or to prevent a move to New York City. Southern congressmen took an uncharacteristically positive view of their situation, observing that placing the temporary residence at New York would bind together the interests of the South and the Middle States. Virginia members feared that sitting on the Hudson would stimulate the Mohawk rather than the Potomac route to the West, but Congress surely would leave New York before any real damage occurred. When a North Carolinian seconded a motion for New York City, the outcome became obvious. Only Pennsylvania voted no. Congress then dispensed with its rules and sped the ordinance to completion on 23 December. The next day it expressed its thanks to Trenton and New Jersey for their hospitality, informed

Pennsylvania how much it appreciated the offer of the public buildings at Philadelphia and adjourned to New York.[33]

The ordinance required three commissioners to locate, within eight miles of the falls of the Delaware at Trenton, a district for the federal town of not less than four nor more than nine square miles in area. Such a district could lie on either or both sides of the river approximately between Washington Crossing and Bordentown, New Jersey, but most observers expected the commissioners to choose a site in New Jersey south of Trenton toward Bordentown. In addition, the commissioners received authorization to purchase the land, to erect an elegant "federal house" for Congress, and to provide residences for the executive officials. Congress would move to, *and remain,* at New York City until the federal town had been completed.

The ordinance contained an appropriation of up to $100,000, thus requiring nine votes. Since only nine states attended, any one of them could have blocked it. Virginia's delegates took pride in their vote. "The great principles upon which we entered into the confederacy, a respect for the harmony and interests of the union, and a regard for the character and honor of our State" placed the general welfare ahead of the local interests of the Potomac. Yet, realism more than altruism lay behind its sacrifice. Maryland and Delaware were absent and the rest of the South did not support Virginia, and its lone dissent would have been overcome as soon as one of the absent New England States reached Trenton. Pennsylvania could have scuttled the ordinance too, but its delegates assented, arguing that the United States needed one stationary seat of government and that Pennsylvania should do everything in its power to promote the federal government. Besides, one argued, even if the federal town rose on the New Jersey side of the Delaware, much of the money spent there would flow to Pennsylvania.

The unanimity with which Congress, after months of bitter struggle, voted to appropriate up to $100,000 for a federal town on the Delaware and to reside in the meantime at New York City reflected both the consensus the congressmen had reached in October and the South's recognition that it lacked the votes to place the federal town on the Potomac. Rumor spread that Thomas

Jefferson, the new ambassador to France, would employ a French architect to design the federal town.[34]

Public reaction to the ordinance varied. The French charge d'affaires in the United States declared the matter settled until such time as the admission of new Western States led Congress to leave the Delaware, but he doubted the possibility, even then, of ever establishing an effective government over such a vast empire. In the meantime, the decision strengthened the federal government: having its own territory earned it a higher place in the American mind while its declared intention to remain at New York gave it immediate stability and order. The ordinance was, he concluded, one of the most fortunate actions Congress had ever taken. New Englanders credited Gerry for managing the maneuvers which defeated Philadelphia and removed the troublesome residence question from the congressional tapis. Nevertheless, they complained about the expense, particularly since no guarantee existed that a future Congress would not move the permanent seat elsewhere.[35]

Many Marylanders and Virginians disapproved of the decision to place the permanent seat of government on the Delaware. George Washington predicted to fellow Potomac River promoter Richard Henry Lee that by the time the federal buildings were ready on the Delaware, they would be considered very improperly situated for the seat of empire and a new location would have to be found. "If the union continues, and this is not the case, I will agree to be classed among the false prophets," he promised. Other Virginians raised the constitutional objection that Congress lacked the power under the Articles of Confederation to appropriate money for a federal town. Those Virginians who granted its power called for the payment of the revolutionary war debt first. As to the temporary residence at New York, many Virginians likely agreed with Jefferson who hoped Congress would continue there and not build the federal town. "When a sufficient number of Western states come in" Congress will move to Georgetown; "in the meantime it is our interest that it should remain where it is, and give no new pretensions to any other place," he instructed Congressman James Monroe.[36]

Landowners about Trenton filled the newspapers with advertisements for land in the vicinity of the proposed federal town.

Philadelphians, chagrined by the deflation of their hopes of erasing the stain of June 1783, took comfort only because their predictions then that Congress would move to New York City had proven true. As a result, the Philadelphia press considered New York City once again fair game in their old rivalry and initiated what became five years of mutual abuse, during which Philadelphia leapt at every opportunity to get Congress back.

New Yorkers were ecstatic. New York City, which they described as healthy and centrally located, would be restored to its pre-revolutionary war glory. "This pleasing event will undoubtedly be of an advantage of the first magnitude to New York; exclusive of the great name it will give us among nations, there cannot be a doubt entertained in the breast of the most fluctuating politician but what this city will be the first on the continent. Congress will every day increase in consequence . . . it being certain that the necessity of augmenting the power of that august body is acknowledged by every state in the union," predicted one newspaper.[37]

When Congress convened at New York in January 1785, the city and its 20,000 some residents had not yet recovered from a seven-year occupation by the British Army, two devastating fires and the loss of half its population and commerce. The arrival of Congress promised revitalization, and New Yorkers welcomed it accordingly. Whereas Congress had fit into Annapolis society, New York recreated its society around Congress. Delegates described the New Yorkers as the most hospitable people imaginable. Even the Philadelphia partisan Hannah Thomson admitted to New York's agreeableness. Sumptuous dinners, crowds of invitations and a frenzy of visits kept the members entertained. The delegates found ample accommodations and the city provided Congress with part of City Hall for its use. By the end of 1785 congressmen could attend fortnightly concerts and theater three nights a week. Rufus King, a freshman delegate from Massachusetts, married a New York lady. Several other delegates followed suit and Congressman William Grayson urged fellow Virginian James Madison to come to "Calypso's Island" and find a wife. Accustomed to criticizing Capuain Philadelphia, Spartan Princeton and Trenton, and even gay Annapolis, congressmen made few complaints, despite the cost of living.[38]

The residence of Congress at New York proved to be a revitalization for the federal government as well as the city, for Congress experienced both a rebirth of energy and increased public support throughout the Union. No long wait for a quorum occurred. New York's welcoming address lavished praise on Congress and called for augmenting its powers. The conflicts Congress had experienced with the governments of Philadelphia and Pennsylvania did not arise. The power struggle between centralists and decentralists which had bred paranoia and divided Congress for several years disappeared, particularly after the most vocal decentralists joined their centralist rivals in retirement at the end of 1785. New members and better attendance by the states also enhanced Congress. It decided to reunite its executive and legislative functions and ordered all of the executive officeholders to New York. Those who argued that they could better serve at Philadelphia were asked to resign. Thomson, the knowledgeable familiar pen of Congress, provided continuity. He decided to continue as secretary despite the fact that his old enemy Richard Henry Lee became president of Congress and that it resided at New York.[39]

Among its first actions at New York, Congress elected the three commissioners to locate and oversee construction of the federal town. Congress turned to the appointments in February, after postponements caused by several New England delegates, who enjoyed the convenience of New York and questioned the expense of the federal town, and by James McHenry of Maryland, who had not attended Congress at Trenton and now sought to repeal the ordinance because of the site chosen. McHenry offered a lengthy resolution which denied the authority of Congress to establish a federal town under the common defense and general welfare clause of the eighth Article of Confederation. He argued that it would be cheaper to reside at either New York or Philadelphia, pointed out the huge federal debt which should be paid first, and urged that delegates be allowed to consult their states for advice. The Virginians were furious, for had Maryland been represented in December, the result might have been different. The state's belated opposition would only throw contempt on the Union.[40]

Congress elected General Philip Schuyler of New York, General Philemon Dickinson of New Jersey and Robert Morris of

Pennsylvania as the commissioners. Each came from a state particularly concerned with the establishment of the federal town or the temporary residence, and each knew land values because of their own investments. Since two of the commissioners resided north of the Delaware River, predictions held that the town would be located on the New Jersey side. Other prominent Americans who sought the appointments included Jeremiah Wadsworth of Connecticut, Pierre L'Enfant and Baron Von Steuben of New York City, Francis Hopkinson of Philadelphia, Governor William Livingston of New Jersey and General Horatio Gates of Virginia.

Dickinson and Morris accepted immediately. Schuyler declined the appointment early in March. He gave poor health as his reason, but surely the conflict of interest between expediting construction of the federal town and retaining Congress at New York was another. The delighted McHenry tried to postpone selection of a replacement, but Congress chose John Brown, a merchant from Providence, Rhode Island. He too declined. David Howell withheld Brown's letter from Congress and pressured him to change his mind, for it was essential to Howell that the third commissioner be someone who would vote to place the federal town in New Jersey rather than Pennsylvania. Congress never replaced Brown after receiving his second letter of refusal in June. To make a selection seemed futile in light of its inability to appoint a committee to confer with Morris and Dickinson, who had come to New York for their instructions, and of a growing movement to block the first $30,000 appropriated for the federal town.[41]

Virginian William Grayson, who disliked the Delaware choice and wanted Congress at Philadelphia, led the appropriation fight. Like McHenry, he had not been in Congress when it had agreed to place the federal town on the Delaware and he vowed to do everything in his power to frustrate implementation of the ordinance, even though he lacked the support of most southern delegates. Building on the votes of Maryland and Delaware, which opposed the location, and New Hampshire, which opposed the expense, Grayson kept working. He received encouragement from George Washington, whose aide he had been during the war. "Fixing the Seat of Empire at any spot on the Delaware, is in my humble opinion, demonstrably wrong," Washington wrote Grayson. "To incur an expense for what may be called the *permanent* seat of Congress, at this time, is I conceive evidently impolitic; for without the gift of prophecy, I will venture to predict that under any circumstances of confederation, it will not remain so far to the Eastward long; and that until the public is in better circumstances, it ought not to be built at all. Time, too powerful for sophistry, will point out the place and disarm localities of their power."

By August Grayson expressed optimism to Madison. The Virginia delegates had begun to support him. The South Carolinians had been instructed by their legislature to oppose the appropriation. Even some Massachusetts delegates who had been instructed to support the appropriation privately agreed with him. Congress considered the federal budget at the end of September 1785. Gerry and Howell, soon to retire and hoping to keep Congress out of Philadelphia, moved that the appropriation be increased from $30,000 to the full $100,000. Only New Jersey supported that. Soon thereafter Congress killed the appropriation. The ordinance remained federal law, but only that part which carried Congress to New York would ever be implemented. The thrill of victory which Grayson experienced must have been felt also at Mount Vernon where Washington kept watch over the interests of the Potomac River.[42]

In early 1787 Thomas Jefferson still believed that keeping Congress at New York would buy time during which new Western States would provide votes for a permanent residence at Georgetown. But this long-range view ignored the immediate costs to the South. The ease of attendance for northern delegates sometimes affected the outcome of votes. Northern views, such as yielding to Spain's demand that the Mississippi River be closed to American trade for twenty-five years, had greater influence in Congress. Distance also created problems for southerners who sought to purchase western lands, secure appointments or redress grievances at the seat of federal government.

The situation forced itself on Madison's attention when he returned to Congress in the spring of 1787 after a three-year absence. "The eccentricity of this place as well with regard to the East and West as to North and South has I find been for a considerable time a thorn in the minds of many of the Southern members," he reported to Washington; "the Eastern members will never concur in any substantial provision or movement for a proper permanent seat for the national government whilst they remain so much gratified in its temporary residence." Unlike Jefferson and the Lees, Madison saw a return to Philadelphia as the best means for effecting a permanent residence on the Potomac. In addition, many southerners believed that leaving New York would elicit Jay's resignation and remove the threat of his agreeing with Spain to close the Mississippi to American commerce. Jay however threatened to follow Congress rather than resign, a tactic similar to his 1784 refusal to serve unless Congress became stationary. Finally, as more and more Americans accepted the idea of federal regulation of interstate commerce, southerners worried about its economic impact on the South if Congress resided so far north of the center of the Union.[43]

By the spring of 1787 the Southern States had become convinced by these concerns that Congress must return to Philadelphia despite the jurisdictional, political and social comforts of New York City. To the jubilant Philadelphians it seemed only a matter of months before the "Athens of America" would be once again the political as well as the intellectual and commercial capital of the United States. They invented two timely new arguments to support their contention that Congress should adjourn there. New York City did not deserve the honor since the state had just given the death blow to the 1783 Amendment to the Articles of Confederation allowing the federal government to collect import duties. And Congress had called the Federal Convention to meet at Philadelphia in May 1787, a choice almost no one complained about, although one delegate resigned rather than face the threat of smallpox. Many Philadelphia supporters argued that Congress should be there at the same time. This concerned Madison, who feared that Congress would limit the Convention's freedom if both met there, perhaps even in the same building. Thus he and his allies wanted any resolution for the removal of the seat of government to take effect with the new federal year in November 1787.[44]

After waiting several weeks for a seven–state majority willing to vote for an adjournment to Philadelphia, the South had the votes by early April. Despite Madison's concern, the southern motion called for Congress to recess at the end of the month and reconvene at Philadelphia early in June. Rhode Island proposed Newport instead, but that failed overwhelmingly as it had in 1784. Rufus King of Massachusetts, floor leader for keeping Congress at New York, moved to strike Philadelphia. His motion lost when, to his utter astonishment, Rhode Island voted with New Jersey and the five represented states south of it in favor of Philadelphia. A brilliant tactician, King proposed a minor amendment, and then Massachusetts exercised its right under the rules of Congress to postpone consideration until the next day. That night New York City's advocates changed the mind of one of Rhode Island's delegates.

The coalition for Philadelphia had to postpone the question until 10 May. This time King declared the motion out of order because the ordinance of December 1784 called for Congress to remain at New York until completion of the federal buildings on the Delaware River. The South renewed its motion, merely adding, "anything in the ordinance of the 23rd of December 1784 to the contrary notwithstanding." Heated debate continued the next day until someone suddenly noticed New Jersey's absence from the floor. Indeed, James Schureman, a resident of northern New Jersey and among the least committed members of the Philadelphia coalition, had gone home. Without Schureman, New Jersey lost its vote and the coalition for Philadelphia its campaign. Congress would remain at New York City. In early 1788 the Pennsylvanians pondered raising the issue once again, but decided against it.[45]

Philadelphia had been closer to regaining Congress in 1787 than at any time since it left in June 1783. Credit for its defeat in some part belongs to Henry Lee who, like his cousins Richard Henry and Arthur Lee, and Thomas Jefferson, believed the route to the Potomac ran through New York City, not Philadelphia. Henry Lee knew Schureman was anxious to leave and found a way to eat up enough time so that the New Jersian left. On the argument that a proper administration of the federal government required a centrally located seat, he attempted to substitute a motion which empowered the Board of Treasury to erect buildings for a federal town at Georgetown on the Potomac, allowed Maryland and Virginia credit against federal requisitions for furnishing money for the purpose and kept Congress at New York until completion of the new town. Maryland, represented by men of its Upper Chesapeake

Interest, refused Lee its vote. In its place Lee had the support of both New York and Massachusetts, whose motive was to keep Congress at New York. Lee's motion failed, but the potential for the renewal of a North–South coalition was apparent for all to see. The Eastern States, clearly aware of the sudden tenuousness of the temporary residence at New York, even suggested privately to the southern members that, when the opportunity next arose, they join the South in fixing "the capital of the federal Empire" at Georgetown. In return, they asked the South to agree to keep the temporary residence at New York until construction of the federal buildings on the Potomac.[46]

The Confederation Congress had not been able to construct a federal town. Nevertheless, both the dual residence resolutions and the 1784 ordinance had significant side effects. The expeditious 1783 compromise maintained the Union at a critical point in the Revolution and bought time for a Potomac site. The 1784 decision led to the revitalization of the federal government. Congress would not discuss the location of the American capital again until 1789. By then the adoption of the new constitution advocated by the centralists had complicated the legislative process and removed the ideological issues which had prevented the 1783–1785 debate from being just a power struggle between the North and South. When the fight renewed, it produced pure sectional alignments and the new government reeled from the impact.

3

Exclusive Jurisdiction and the Constitutional Revolution, 1787–1789

IN MAY 1787 THE CONVENTION TO REVISE THE AR-
ticles of Confederation, which centralists had sought since 1780,
convened at Philadelphia. Americans know little about the thirty-
year Revolution which resulted not only in independence, but also
in a federal government with a capital over which it exercised jurisdiction exclusive from the states which composed it. An exception is
the Federal Convention which Americans have been encouraged to
deify. Actually the Convention originated very little aside from the
institution of the presidency and the concept of balance of powers
as superior to separation of powers. Otherwise it drew upon two
centuries of political thought seeking a practical expression, more
than a century of colonial and state experience with "self-
government," a twenty–year public debate over the nature of
American federalism and especially the experience of a decade of
federal government. Much of the detailed implementation and interpretation of the new Constitution it left to the First Federal
Congress, the body which breathed life into the piece of paper
about which Americans expressed such strong opinions in 1787 and
1788. The most remarkable achievement of the Federal Convention was finding the means by which the constitution it proposed
could evolve over time: the original intent was that the document
be flexible and amendable enough to adapt to significant changes in
American society.

The necessity of ratification of its decisions prevented the Convention from including certain things in the Constitution. Thus the
document did not state the manner in which Congress should pay
the federal debt or explicitly grant it the power to charter a bank or

to assume the revolutionary war debts of the states. Inclusion of such elements of the British fiscal system as debt funding and banks would have disturbed Americans, for a majority of them had not yet accepted the new definition of republicanism. Similar political considerations kept the Convention from selecting a location for the American capital. Had the delegates somehow been able to agree on a site, they would thereby have threatened the possibilities for ratification of the Constitution in those Middle States which lost the great prize.

Convention delegate Robert Morris had some difficulty persuading his colleague Gouverneur Morris from proposing that the Constitution establish the capital at Newburgh and New Windsor on the Hudson, sixty miles above New York City. Like all promoters, Gouverneur Morris believed the site perfect: a readily defensible, ice–free naval base tied to the West once a canal from the Hudson tapped Lake Erie. Outside the Convention, Virginia Congressman William Grayson told James Monroe that the Constitution should have fixed the seat of government in the center of the empire at Georgetown, Maryland. Had it done so, both men would surely have been supporters of the Constitution rather than opponents.

The issue of the location of the capital briefly came to the Convention floor twice. George Mason of Virginia proposed that the Constitution forbid the selection of any state capital. Gerry supported Mason and suggested that large commercial cities also be prohibited as potential choices. Hugh Williamson of North Carolina understood how agitated people became over the choice of seats of government and agreed with Gouverneur Morris that inclusion of any prohibition might be strategically unwise, especially considering the potential for alienating residents of New York City and Philadelphia, both commercial cities and state capitals. Mason consequently withdrew his motion.

The issue arose again indirectly when the Convention discussed empowering Congress to adjourn to a different place of residence without passing a law, thus avoiding the necessity of executive approval of where the legislature chose to meet. Rufus King of Massachusetts argued that this would create a transient Congress, reminiscent of what had occurred during 1783 and 1784.

Madison agreed, and the two men moved to require a law to change the residence of Congress. Opponents complained that meant fixing Congress forever at the place where the First Congress convened. Madison disagreed. He believed that the United States would have greater need for a centrally located seat under the new Constitution because of the federal government's more extensive powers. Consequently, public opinion and the apportionment of the House of Representatives would force a removal from an eccentric location, even if a president was partial to it. Nevertheless, he proposed to empower the First Congress to adjourn to a place of its choice, but afterwards to require an act signed by the president. When that failed, the Convention recognized the right of Congress to adjourn to a different residence without the consent of the president. That decision would become the basis for the first public debate on the constitutionality of an act of Congress.

The Convention devoted even less debate to the idea of the capital. This was because the issues, other than size, had been resolved during the four preceding years in favor of one permanent residence over which Congress would exercise exclusive jurisdiction. Madison came prepared to discuss the nature of mobile capitals in ancient confederacies, but no one proposed such a plan for the United States even though the idea still had some currency as late as 1790.[1]

Exclusive jurisdiction—the concept that a federal government should have power over a territory of its own, independent from the states which composed it—was born out of the American Revolution, and has been adopted by younger nations throughout the world. Prior to 1783, only a few Americans supported exclusive jurisdiction, and always privately, for the concept was alien to the nature of the decentralist Revolution. They were probably limited to those familiar with the difficulties Parliament had experienced from time to time with the authorities and residents of London and which Congress had experienced during its tenure at Philadelphia.

In 1779 when Congress first debated the creation of a federal town, some members talked privately about purchasing a few square miles of territory at Princeton, New Jersey, on which to erect buildings. This suggestion is the earliest known mention of a district for Congress. The amount of jurisdiction Congress would exercise was not specified. Such discussion continued among congressman. In September 1782 the French ambassador reported that frustration with the problems Congress encountered at Philadelphia had convinced some members of the necessity of removing to an isolated district where Congress would be sheltered from such influences and independent of the states. He doubted however that such a plan could ever be accomplished.[2]

The Baltimorean, George Lux, Jr., while privately recommending Annapolis for the seat of federal government to several prominent friends in November 1782, advocated exclusive jurisdiction. He stated his conviction that the place chosen should become "a distinct independent territory totally under the government of Congress," but recognized that "so narrow in that respect are the prejudices of most of the States" that he doubted such a measure would meet with approval. It was probably also he who leapt on the opportunity of the 21 June 1783 military demonstration at Philadelphia to bring the issue out of the closet for public debate. In mid-July Philadelphia newspapers printed a "letter from Baltimore dated 3rd July," which stated "that the late confusion in your city evinces the absolute and indispensable necessity of Congress's possessing ample and supreme local jurisdiction in the spot where they sit." The concept gained support quickly during the competition over the location of the federal town in the summer of 1783 as states escalated their offers of jurisdiction in attempts to outdo each other. In addition, the peregrination of Congress during the year and a half between its leaving Philadelphia and its arrival at New York City bolstered the concept.

Soon after reaching Princeton in 1783, Congress had appointed a committee to recommend the degree of jurisdiction it should exercise over its seat, having discussed the matter only briefly when it received the offers from New York and Maryland in the spring. Committee members included three formidable centralists, whose contributions to American constitutional thought during the 1780s had few rivals: James Madison, James Wilson and Oliver Ellsworth. The issue facing them involved two questions. What should be the line between the authority of Congress and that of a locality or state over the seat of federal government? And what should be the relationship between the federal government and the residents of its seat?

Congress had no precedents to follow and only its experience at Philadelphia for guidance. Secretary at War Benjamin Lincoln turned to his lawyer son for advice, reporting in late July that talk about jurisdiction for Congress over a few miles about its seat had become common and that many people considered it a necessity. The major question he raised was, simply, did Congress have power under the Articles of Confederation to exercise such jurisdiction. Lincoln thought not and neither did his son whose reply delved into the legal ramifications at some length. The complexities of the issues proved puzzling even to Madison, who sought advice from Virginians. His request prompted Jefferson to draft a series of proposed congressional resolutions, rejecting both ownership of the land by the United States and the idea of an exclusive jurisdiction for Congress, on the grounds that both would cause unnecessary and time–consuming problems. He proposed instead that Congress rely on the honor and affection of the states to guarantee the privileges and immunities of congressmen and foreign ministers.[3]

Some Americans viewed the idea of exclusive jurisdiction more suspiciously than did Jefferson. One feared that it would create a hiding place for "all the scoundrels upon the continent and like the churches of Italy, a refuge from justice." Most public comment, often referring to the military demonstration at Philadelphia, supported the concept of a "supreme local jurisdiction in the spot" where Congress sat. "As we have made our way to empire solely by our union . . . ought not, then, the representatives of that union be so securely and commodiously placed, that the business of the continent may not, by local circumstances, be interrupted," observed a widely reprinted newspaper editorial.[4]

Emboldened by the increasingly generous offers Congress received from the states during the summer of 1783 and by the public discussion of the issue in the aftermath of the demonstration at Philadelphia, congressional centralists openly advocated an exclusive jurisdiction over an independent territory. President of Congress Elias Boudinot believed it indispensable. When his home town of Elizabethtown, New Jersey, offered to live under the absolute authority of Congress if it were made the seat of federal government, a subcommittee of the jurisdiction committee thanked the inhabitants for offering thereby to support "the honor, dignity, independence and constitutional authority of the supreme head of the American Union." But the decentralists would not hear of such a sweeping declaration of supremacy and magnificence for the federal government, and Congress struck the phrase from the resolution.

The jurisdiction committee reported in September 1783 that Congress should have exclusive jurisdiction over a district not more than six miles square (thirty-six square miles) nor less than three miles square (nine square miles). The report mentioned nothing of the rights of the inhabitants of the district, but Madison expected them to share with Congress the powers the federal government would exercise over them. Unlike the New England decentralists, Arthur Lee supported an exclusive jurisdiction for Congress. But he went further than Madison in attempting to secure the rights of the residents of the seat of government: they should be governed by their own elected representatives. Not surprisingly the decentralist David Howell disagreed. He predicted that the debate over jurisdiction would prove entertaining and bemoaned the prospect that a confederation of republics would follow the precedent of tyrants and make a small circle about themselves for their own protection.[5]

In light of the growing strength of the decentralists in Congress, that body took no action on the committee report and never discussed the issue again. The dual residence compromise of October 1783 handled the unresolved question by declaring that Congress should own the land and exercise an exclusive or such other jurisdiction as it determined in the future. The very mention of the concept in the resolutions, however, reflected how rapidly it had gained political credibility. The Ordinance of December 1784 ignored the issue, implying that the states retained jurisdiction.

Several members of the 1783 congressional committee on jurisdiction attended the Federal Convention and heard James Madison offer the proposition that became Article I, § 8, Paragraph 17 of the Constitution of the United States. He proposed that Congress have "exclusive legislation"—a less politically sensitive phrase than "exclusive jurisdiction," but no different in meaning—

over a stationary seat of government and a district surrounding it. Decentralists George Mason and Elbridge Gerry questioned the necessity but lacked the support to prevent it. The committee which worked on Madison's proposal strengthened the "exclusive legislation" provision, eliminated the explicit distinction between the seat of government and the district surrounding it, and determined the size of the district. The final wording authorized Congress "to exercise exclusive legislation in all cases whatsoever, over such district (not exceeding ten miles square) as may, by cession of particular states, and the acceptances of Congress, become the seat of government of the United States."

In a letter transmitting the document to Congress, the Convention recommended that, as soon as the required nine states had ratified it, Congress choose the place for commencing proceedings under the new government. It was a smart political move, but it would cause problems in implementing the Constitution.[6]

Opposition to the Constitution arose immediately. This was no revision of the Articles of Confederation, which most Americans understood as the purpose of the Convention, but rather a totally new constitution which, when ratified by nine states, created a supreme federal government. The Constitution endowed that government with both the power of the purse and the power of the sword and did not check it with a bill of rights to guarantee, among other things, that it would not also assume the powers of the press and the cloth. In addition, that government included a judiciary, independent of the legislature and able to enforce federal law in the states, and a semi-independent executive. Stunned, Richard Henry Lee and his allies prevented a congressional endorsement. Instead the Confederation Congress merely sent the Constitution to the states so that they could submit it to their citizens for ratification.

In the months ahead Americans divided as they had not since 1774-1776. Federalists (centralists) favored the new Constitution as essential for the modern empire they envisioned. Antifederalists (decentralists) opposed it as an over-reaction to the problems experienced under the Articles of Confederation and as dangerous to their brand of republicanism. Both groups understood the proposed Constitution as amounting to a second revolution, but they differed over whether it overturned or fulfilled the principles and promises of the first. Antifederalists viewed it as counter to the first while Federalists argued the fulfillment thesis.[7] Their division continued the debate between centralists and decentralists over the nature of federalism and cemented the foundations for the political parties which evolved in the United States during and after the First Federal Congress.

Beginning in the press in November 1787 and climaxing in the New York Ratification Convention in June 1788, Antifederalist leaders such as Mercy Warren of Massachusetts, George Clinton of New York and George Mason of Virginia publicly attacked what they saw as the inexorable result of a one hundred square mile district under the exclusive jurisdiction of Congress and distant from the eyes of the people. Both the lessons of history and their fears for republicanism provided a dangerous scenario which they did not consider exaggerated. Indeed, their attack on Article I, § 8, Paragraph 17 of the Constitution can be seen as a microcosm for many of their concerns about the document.

"It has cost me many a sleepless night to find out the most obnoxious part of the proposed plan," Board of Treasury member Samuel Osgood complained, "and I have finally fixed upon the exclusive legislation in the Ten Miles Square. . . . What an inexhaustible fountain of corruption are we opening?" Among several solutions to the problem, he proposed voting representation in the House for federal district residents. "How dangerous this city may be, and what its operation on the general liberties of this country, time alone must discover," warned one member of the New York Ratification Convention, "but I pray God, it may not prove to this western world what the city of Rome, enjoying a similar constitution, did to the eastern."[8]

Antifederalists envisioned a *city* larger and potentially more corrupt than Philadelphia or even London. Indeed, they, not the Federalists, gave currency to the new term, "federal city." One hundred square miles was an enormous area to an agrarian people whose largest city, thirty–six square mile Philadelphia, had a settled area of less than two square miles, and whose second largest city, New York, lay more than a mile south of Greenwich Village.

Antifederalists projected a population at the federal city of perhaps two or even four million people, either directly attendant on the federal government as employees or lobbyists, or indirectly dependent on it as family members of the attendants. These residents would be subject to a government with absolute authority over them but in which they were unrepresented. Since the Constitution had no bill of rights, residents of the district would be guaranteed none of the traditional English and American civil liberties protected by most state constitutions. Nor would the residents have common law rights. Antifederalists believed that the lack of state taxes in the federal district would not compensate for the absence of basic republican liberties and protections of the law. How easy it would be, they thought, for the federal government to corrupt a population so dependent upon it. Such people would make up a readily motivated mass of support for federal programs and for pressure on Congress. On the other hand, residents annoyed at the federal government might take matters into their own hands and subject Congress to mob action.

Mason recognized few clauses in the Constitution so dangerous as the one granting exclusive jurisdiction. Because the Constitution provided for extradition only between states, he and others saw the federal city as a refuge from justice for the state criminal, the debtor and the escaped slave. The judiciary centered there would try Americans without the benefit of juries or with juries composed of men dependent upon the federal government. Only the rich would be able to travel there for justice. Antifederalists saw exclusive control over its residence as a way for Congress to exercise powers which were implicitly or explicitly denied it in the states. Congress might order the state militias to the district and thus deny the states their only means of self-defense. Congress could naturalize whomever it wished there. It might hold all federal elections there, or haul political dissenters there to try them for treason. And Congress could reroute into its coffers at the federal city all the wealth of the states, for it would surely find the ways and means to spend as much money as could be raised by taxes throughout the United States.

Some Antifederalists viewed the president, with a large military establishment under his command, as a virtual monarch, and envisioned an aristocracy of political and commercial wealth rising about him. The federal city would become the cultural, social and fashion-setting seat of the United States. To it would flock those Americans who adulated people of fortune and power, and it would soon be home to the great and mighty of the earth. The base, idle, avaricious and ambitious would turn the federal city into a "happy place, where men are to live, without labor, upon the fruit of the labors of others," or into a "political hive, where all the drones in the society are to be collected to feed on the honey of the land." The American people would be taxed to pay for all of this.

Many Antifederalists predicted that the federal district would become a commercial as well as political center, attracting to it those who looked to finance and business as a route to wealth. It would be in the interest of the federal government to concentrate commerce there, at the expense of the Union's extremities, and all circulating money would be quickly pulled into the seat of empire to be spent in its immediate environs. Furthermore, the Antifederalists saw nothing to prevent Congress from exercising its exclusive control over the federal district to establish commercial monopolies. Such a grab at the power of incorporation—a power not explicitly granted Congress—might work in time to center the entire commerce of the United States at the federal city.[9]

For Federalists, the exclusive jurisdiction of Congress over its residence played an important role in the constitutional revolution of 1787–1790. It symbolized the kind of government they hoped to establish for the American Empire, and they employed their superior journalistic and financial resources to respond to the Antifederal attack. Ridicule served as a ready weapon. Many Federalist newspapers reported that the Antifederalists imagined a city walled like Jericho. Another popular reprint of a Federalist piece mockingly compared ancient Babylon to the Antifederal description of the federal city.[10] Ridicule, however, wielded minimal effect against such a seriously perceived issue, and Federalists such as James Wilson, Alexander Hamilton and particularly James Madison attempted to counter major Antifederal charges in the press and in several ratification conventions. Federalists, however, recognized that empires were symbolized by the grandeur of their capitals, and they did not deny the Antifederal claim that the ten mile square might become the focus of American politics, wealth and society.

To justify the necessity of exclusive federal jurisdiction, Federalists commonly pointed to the Pennsylvania State House demonstration in 1783 as evidence that Congress must be totally independent of any state jurisdiction in order to protect its members and its dignity from insult and violence. Also Congress could more easily prevent foreign corruption of the government if it did not share jurisdiction. Madison used future scenarios to defend the breadth of the provision. The federal government and its archives could not be allowed to become the creature of any one state, a condition which could anger other states and destroy the Union. The public improvements at the federal capital would make it difficult enough to change location without compounding the problem with shared jurisdiction.

Federalists denied that the liberties of the residents of the federal city would be infringed. No state would injure its citizens; consequently, any act of cession would protect the liberties, common law rights, and other interests of people who thereby became district residents. James Wilson supported a federal Bill of Rights for the district, but insisted that its content had to be determined by the residents of a particular district not yet chosen. Madison assumed that Congress would provide for a popularly elected legislature for the district. James Monroe sided with the Federalists on this issue. He pointed out to fellow Antifederalists that if Congress chose an unsettled area for the district, it would have to provide a mild government in order to attract residents. He predicted that Americans would be delighted to live in a city flourishing in population and wealth and under the government of an enlightened Congress.

Hamilton and Madison spoke to another Antifederal concern: the remoteness of the seat of government from most constituents. Hamilton argued that letters from congressmen and others, as well as the press, would keep people everywhere informed of events at the seat of the federal government. Even more significant, he thought, would be the rivalry between the state and federal governments, by which the states would become vigilant sentinels and balance the effects of distance. Rather than gaining special benefits over Americans remote from the federal city, those nearest it would have the same interests and would be the first to sound the alarm to distant fellow citizens if the federal government over-reached its authority. Madison concurred with Hamilton.

Finally, the Federalists insisted that the federal district would not become a place of exclusive privilege. It was absurd, argued Madison, to think that congressmen would provide exclusive advantages over commerce to one small area of the United States at the expense of the communities which had elected them. Edmund Pendleton of Virginia pointed out that, since the exclusive power of Congress extended only to the district, any enactment of such privileges would be nugatory elsewhere. He believed Congress could use its exclusive legislative power only to adopt laws to guarantee good government and an effective police. He also argued that Congress would never degrade the federal government by allowing the district to become an asylum for villains or other disreputable types.[11]

Not convinced by the Federalist arguments, Antifederalists sought protection from the evils they foresaw. In Danville, Kentucky, they redrafted the Constitution, omitting provision for a seat of government. A New Hampshire Antifederalist thought it a great mistake that the amendments proposed by his state did not curtail the federal city. But other state conventions did take action. Virginia, and later North Carolina, proposed an amendment to limit the exclusive legislation of Congress to "such regulations as respect the police and good government thereof," a phrase which one Federalist considered so broad as to be no limitation at all. A New York amendment went further. It specified that Congress could not exempt residents of the district from taxes and duties levied by the state in which the district lay, and that persons inside the district could not be free from arrest for crimes committed or debts contracted outside of it. A guarantee to inhabitants of the district of the essential rights enjoyed by all Americans was removed when the state proposed a separate bill of rights to the Constitution. Pennsylvania Antifederalists, meeting almost a year after their state's ratification convention, adopted a reworded version of the Virginia amendment.

No state suggested restricting the district to three miles square or to limit federal jurisdiction only to federal buildings, as some Antifederalists had suggested. Nor did any seek an amendment to give district residents representation in the House, although Hamilton introduced one at New York's convention. He proposed that, until population in the district reached a certain number, it would remain part of the state which gave the land to the federal government. When the required population level was reached, the district would cease to be part of that state and "provision shall be made by Congress for their having a District Representation in the Body."

Certain other of the one hundred ideas put forth by the states as amendments would have had the effect of preventing some of the dangers which Antifederalists saw as inherent to the concept of a district under the exclusive jurisdiction of Congress. Under those amendments, Congress would have been forbidden to grant titles of nobility, to create hereditary offices, to establish a standing army, to incorporate monopolies, to call a militia out of its state without the state's consent, to establish a national religion and to interfere with the freedom of speech, press, assembly or petition. A year after the ratification debate, the First Federal Congress easily defeated an Antifederal proposal to ensure the operation of state law within the federal district. At that time, a newspaper commentator argued that Congress needed exclusive jurisdiction particularly because of the foreign community and other special interests at the seat of federal government. He nonetheless recognized the problem of disenfranchisement in the district. His solution was to amend the Constitution to allow district residents congressional representation once their population reached forty or fifty thousand.[12]

Philadelphia held a great parade to celebrate ratification of the Constitution. On one float, printers ran off copies of an ode composed for the occasion by the parade's chairman, Francis Hopkinson. In it, "Columbia" called out, "Behold! behold! an empire rise! ... *Wisdom* and *Valour* shall my rights defend, And o'er my vast domain those rights extend." Many of the parading tradesmen carried banners and flags expressing federal sentiments in the idiom of their trade. The bricklayer's flag portrayed "the federal city rising out of a forest, workmen building it, and the sun illuminating it." "Both Buildings and Rulers are the works of our Hands" aptly proclaimed its motto.[13]

In June 1788 George Washington took special pleasure in the fact that Alexandria, his home town, was the first place in the United States to celebrate ratification by ten states, one more than necessary to render it effective. Pondering the implications of ratification, an Alexandrian concluded that it had been "a considerable and important revolution in our government." Other Federalists who believed a revolution had occurred preferred to see how the First Federal Congress fleshed out the Constitution before expressing their judgment.[14]

News of Virginia's ratification reached New York City well before dawn on 2 July 1788, the fourteenth anniversary of the day that Congress had declared the American colonies to be independent states. At 5:00 a.m. a ten cannon salute blasted many residents awake. Bells rang for four hours. Two days later Antifederalists burned a copy of the Constitution in a ceremony at the Battery. Congress began the process for organizing the new government on 2 July, even though New York, North Carolina and Rhode Island remained out of the new Union. A week later a committee reported dates for the First Federal Congress to assemble and for the presidential electors to be chosen and to vote. It left a blank for the place where Congress would meet. Despite some opposition from Pennsylvania, Congress postponed debate on that blank, hoping that the New York Ratification Convention would soon complete its proceedings, thereby giving Congress the option of calling the new Congress to New York City. The postponement had the effect of a bribe to the convention.[15]

Congressman Madison reported to Washington that New York's ratification had suddenly became of special interest to New York City. The strongly Federalist city raged at Governor George Clinton and the Antifederalists, since defeat for the Constitution meant Congress, with all its attendant benefits, would be forced to leave. Talk circulated about the six southern counties seceding from New York in order to form a new state. Samuel Osgood informed fellow Antifederalists at the convention that the universal opinion at New York City was that the Convention's vote on the Constitution and where the First Federal Congress would meet were intimately connected. Fear of losing Congress provided common ground for the leading spokesmen on both sides at the convention, all of whom except Clinton represented that part of New York lying east of the Hudson and south of Poughkeepsie. New York City's friends arranged a compromise. Downstate Antifederalists delivered enough votes to ratify the Constitution and Federalists endorsed a circular letter to the states calling for a second federal convention to amend it. New York ratified on 26 July. The news reached the City at 9:00 p.m. Bells rang. Cannons fired. People drank in the streets. After midnight a mob attacked the office of the influential Antifederal *New York Journal* and wrecked the press. Shocked at the role of Federalists in the deal that resulted in New York's ratification, Madison complained to Washington that a rejection would have been less harmful than the circular letter. He could account for it only on the grounds that New Yorkers would do anything to retain the seat of federal government.[16]

Congress immediately began to discuss the resolution for calling the new government into existence. All thirteen states attended for the first time since 1776. This reflected the significance of the decision Congress faced. The place of residence chosen for the First Federal Congress would affect its deliberations in general and the location of its permanent seat in particular. Philadelphians, counting on a continuation of the support they had received from the South since early 1787, once again began to count the benefits likely to accrue to them if Congress returned to its place of nativity. Congressmen expected a major fight, but not one that would last six weeks. The debate dragged on longer than the 1783 and 1784 residence debates combined, and resulted in more bitterness, more sectional divisiveness and more commentary by participants.[17]

Wishing to appease southern Federalists leery of a supreme federal government seated so far north, both New Hampshire and Connecticut voted for Philadelphia on 28 July. Nevertheless, it lost by one vote. Philadelphians blamed their native son Dyre Kearney, who cost them Delaware's support by splitting its vote in hopes that Wilmington might be chosen instead. But the situation was more complex. William Few of Georgia refused to vote for Philadelphia because of the undue influence it had had on congressional politics prior to 1783 and the fertile soil it offered for "the growth of that aristocracy or monarchy, so hateful to Americans, and to which there is too much reason to apprehend the new government will have a tendency" no matter where it sat. More importantly, the entire South Carolina delegation opposed Philadelphia. Although the French legation attributed this to the appetite of at least one of its members for New York women, South Carolina's opposition had other causes. South Carolinians could reach the ice-free port of New York more easily from Charleston because no river voyage was required and they feared the influence of Philadelphia and its vocal anti-slavery Quakers. The reluctance of Georgia and South Carolina to see Congress in Philadelphia continued to complicate the politics of the decision making process until 1790. Realizing that Philadelphia no longer had the unanimous backing of the South, New Hampshire and Connecticut switched their support to New York.[18]

The motion to convene the new government at New York came on 30 July. An unsuccessful amendment attempted to substitute Lancaster, which, as in 1774, appeared an ideal compromise to those who wanted a Pennsylvania site other than Philadelphia. To the surprise of most delegates, a motion for Baltimore carried on a strict sectional vote of seven states to six. Few and South Carolina willingly supported that rising town as a central location outside Pennsylvania's jurisdiction. Pennsylvania supported it on the gamble that it would so upset New England and perhaps New Jersey, whose chance for the permanent residence it would probably kill, that some of those states would switch their support from New York to Philadelphia. Baltimore? New Englanders considered it too far south. For Virginians it endangered the true object, a permanent residence on the Potomac.

New York City's Hamilton, once again a member of Congress, refused to consider the decision final. By persuading South Carolina that Baltimore was only a circuitous route to Philadelphia, cynically exploited by Pennsylvania, he secured reconsideration. A South Carolinian moved for New York on the grounds that the choice of a proper central situation should be left to the new government. Hugh Williamson of North Carolina, who argued that the new government must sit in a more central position at its first meeting, tried to block the motion. He moved that Congress convene somewhere south of New York, but South Carolina would not be had twice. Another motion—Philadelphia in lieu of New York—

also failed because of Few and the South Carolinians. At that point the original motion for New York secured the votes of all six states north of the Delaware River plus South Carolina.

The decision, nevertheless, was overturned the next day when Rhode Island, because it had not ratified the Constitution, declared its intention to abstain. This cost New York its crucial seventh state and reopened the entire matter. Frantic, Hamilton solicited the little whore, a nickname frustrated congressmen sometimes used for the independent minded state. He proposed the adoption of a resolution stating that Rhode Island had the right to vote on the ordinance by virtue of its membership in the Confederation, and that its vote in no way implied consent to the new Constitution. The motion might well have been adopted had it not included a dispensation for the other non-ratifying state, North Carolina. Supporting Philadelphia and not wishing to be connected in any way with Rhode Island, North Carolina's delegates offered an amendment disassociating their state from the motion. Hamilton then withdrew his resolution and the Rhode Island delegates left for home. An attempt to get them back to vote for New York failed, despite a promise by Hamilton to finance the trip if necessary.

On the same day North Carolina had demanded that it not be associated with Rhode Island, news reached New York that North Carolina had postponed ratification of the Constitution. Although North Carolina's delegates remained at New York, they did not thereafter participate in the debate. On 13 August Hamilton's ordinance for New York met with defeat. An attempt to introduce a new one with a blank in lieu of the place where Congress should meet failed the same day, and the question had to be put aside for two weeks.

New York City had the support of New Hampshire, Massachusetts, Connecticut, New York, New Jersey, South Carolina and Few of Georgia, almost the necessary seven states. Led by Hamilton, other spokesmen were Theodore Sedgwick of Massachusetts, Abraham Clark of New Jersey and Thomas Tudor Tucker of South Carolina. It also had the voice of Henry Lee, but his vote was not enough to divide the Virginia delegation. According to one observer, Lee would do anything to keep Congress from getting caught in the "net of the Philadelphians" where Robert Morris "was

burning with impatience again to attend to all financial operations." The fear of Philadelphia which remained so strong with Lee,
Few and the South Carolinians was also shared by the other end of
the old revolutionary axis, Massachusetts. Sedgwick spoke for several prominent constituents when he insisted that Congress should
not sit in a large commercial city, especially one whose influence
had proven inimical to the public good and whose legislature would
freely interfere in federal concerns. As a final argument, both
Hamilton and Sedgwick insisted that any temporary residence at
Philadelphia would be molded into a permanent one by the grasping Philadelphians.

In addition to the familiar negative argument in favor of New
York—keeping Congress out of Philadelphia—the North had more
positive ones. Congress, by postponing the enabling resolution
while the New York Convention sat, had implied its intention to remain if the state ratified. Hamilton allegedly informed Congress
that the New York delegation had assured the Ratification Convention that this would be the case. Furthermore, six states wanted
New York and the minority should concede to the majority so that
the new government, having survived the perils of a long ratification contest, could function. Less frequently, the North mentioned
the cost of transferring federal functions to Philadelphia and the
appearance this would give of a return to the instability which had
plagued Congress during 1783 and 1784. Finally, the North argued
that a more impartial choice of a permanent residence could be
made from New York than anywhere else since New York could not
be a contender; a move now to Philadelphia, whose suburbs wished
to become the permanent seat of government, would undermine a
decision which should be left to the First Federal Congress.

Philadelphia had the support of Pennsylvania, Delaware,
Maryland, Virginia and Abraham Baldwin of Georgia. The main
spokesman for the southern argument was William Bingham, a
wealthy Philadelphia financier and land speculator. He knew that a
victory for his city would not come easily since as many places desired the advantage as contended for the honor of Homer's birth.
Nevertheless, he met the challenge, expressing the case against
New York on the floor of Congress, in private letters, in the press,
and, most eloquently, in a resolution which he drafted but never

submitted to Congress. Despite the fact that two serious riots and a dispute between the City of New York and the Dutch minister had occurred, no one complained that New York provided an unfit environment for Congress. Instead, the South argued that keeping Congress at eccentric New York threatened the continuation of the Union.[19]

Bingham argued that the strongest southern objections to the Constitution had arisen from the belief that the South would relinquish its means of self-preservation—the powers of the purse and the sword—and become the weaker partner in the new Union. Indeed, Bingham continued, "the dangers that the Union has most to apprehend arise from the unequal portion of strength possessed by the Northern and Southern states." To add to this imbalance by retaining the residence of Congress in the North would severely aggravate the problem and cause the new system to "commence in distrust, proceed with jealousy, and possibly terminate in discord." Pennsylvania had half the states and members of the First Federal Congress to each side of it. By strengthening the center of the Union with the presence of Congress, the benefits and power of the new system would be proportionally felt even at the extremities of the empire. As the most southern of the commercial states, Pennsylvania enjoyed the resources necessary to ensure success to the commercial and financial arrangements of the new system so crucial to the North. The Congress of 1774 and the Federal Convention had met there and most Americans expected that the new government would begin its life there. Finally, Pennsylvania had offered Congress an entire city square with sufficient buildings for its needs and an elegant garden as an appendage.[20]

Bingham had assistance from Madison, who repeated most of Bingham's arguments in letters to Washington, Jefferson and other prominent Virginians. It was crucial to Madison that the new government be centrally located from the start because its early operations "may fix its tone for a long time" and because of "the catholic spirit professed by the Constitution." He stressed that choosing New York City discriminated against the West, where alienation from the federal government was even stronger than in the South.

In sharing his fears with Washington, Madison admitted "that I am much influenced by a view to the final residence." In contrast to

Jefferson and Henry Lee, Madison always believed that a temporary residence at Philadelphia better served the Potomac's interest than one at New York. If Congress remained at New York, he argued, southern dissatisfaction would prevent the delay Lee wanted and force an early decision before additional population could strengthen the South and West. Without a two- or three-year delay, he feared, the permanent residence would move no farther south than the Delaware River, most likely the New Jersey side. If Congress went to Philadelphia in 1788, it would prove difficult to reach agreement on the permanent site, "and it is from that difficulty alone, and the delay incident to it, that I derive my hope in favor of the banks of the Potomac." A fight in the First Federal Congress over the subject of the capital—guaranteed if Congress remained at New York—would destroy the harmony necessary to launch the new system. Madison considered that fact alone reason enough to go to Philadelphia.[21]

The two-week break in the congressional debate after 13 August turned the focus away from Congress to the newspapers. Philadelphia's press described that city as central, aggressively Federalist, resourceful and connected with the original splendor and fame of Congress. Encouraged by Bingham, who mailed articles home for publication, it was probably Tench Coxe who argued that six times more commercial connections existed between Philadelphia and the South than between New York and the South; consequently, federal revenues drawn to Philadelphia from the South would have a far better chance of returning than if Congress remained at New York. The Philadelphia press also mocked New York's pretensions: New York was eccentric both as to territory and population, its public buildings inadequate and badly situated and its population indefensible except by a large fleet. Was not New York State removing its capital elsewhere?

Annoyed by the self-importance rampant in the Philadelphia press, New York City's supporters responded. "Our brethren of the type in Philadelphia," observed one, have magnified and praised their city as the *metropolis of America* to such an excess, that it appears the honor will be conferred on Congress (by permitting them to reside there) instead of Congress conferring it upon them." "We have had Philadelphia represented to us as the center of

population, the mistress of arts and sciences, the emporium of commerce, and the *arbitress* of America," noted another. New York had
no need to extol its own advantages, claimed one writer, who nevertheless outlined several: the port of Philadelphia was generally
closed by ice three or four months each year; New York needed
Congress because it had suffered during the war more than any
other city; and a removal from New York would be expensive. Besides, a majority of the states wanted New York for the temporary
residence now as well as when they had adopted the residence ordinance of 1784. That majority ought to prevail. If only one delegate—an allusion to Baldwin of Georgia—switched his vote, the
matter would be settled. On an investigation of the American press,
the writer concluded, only Pennsylvania's political writers called
for a removal.

Meanwhile, several Pennsylvania and New Jersey delegates
had taken advantage of the break in the debate to return home to
discuss strategy. When one of the Pennsylvanians returned to Congress late in August he "found them nearly as I had left them, with
wounds still smarting and the *cicatrice* unformed, and indeed at present they have the appearance of two fortified camps within view of
each other, neither of whom wish to come out of their stronghold."
Madison found sentiment for New York over any more central
place stronger than ever and the willingness to compromise less.

On 26 August a new ordinance for convening Congress at New
York surfaced. Motions for Wilmington and New York lost, and the
stalemate continued. On 2 September pro–New York congressmen
came up with a different approach. Instead of naming the place for
the First Congress to meet, another new ordinance stated that it
should meet wherever Congress sat in March 1789. This meant little more than naming New York, since its supporters could delay
renewed discussion of the issue or simply desert Congress and leave
it without a quorum until the new government met. Consequently
still another new ordinance came to the floor; it included no mention of where Congress should meet, and motions for Lancaster and
Annapolis failed. Two days later New York's supporters attempted
to introduce yet another ordinance, but Congress refused to accept
it. Although Few had voted with Baldwin and united the Georgia
delegation behind Philadelphia for the first time, the only hope for

Philadelphia was a switch by New Jersey, followed by a change of at least one other state. Congress again postponed debate.

Bingham rallied Philadelphia's fatigued supporters. He urged them to pressure the New Jersey legislature into instructing its congressional delegation to support a temporary residence more central than New York. The key argument with strongly Federalist New Jersey, he believed, was that further delay of the enabling resolution would create pernicious consequences for the Union. Hamilton and his East Jersey allies even more actively lobbied New Jersey. They argued that Congress must remain at New York City to avoid the charge of having deceived New York into ratifying the Constitution, and that an adjournment to Philadelphia would kill any chance of Congress's establishing its permanent residence near the falls of the Delaware River in New Jersey. No state in the Union should be more interested in having the temporary residence at New York than New Jersey. He agreed with Madison about the effect the residence of the First Congress would have on the choice of a permanent seat. New York City was too eccentric to retain Congress very long; an early decision on the permanent residence would place the federal city in New Jersey, whereas a move to Philadelphia in 1788 would postpone the question of the permanent residence until the balance of population had shifted enough to establish it south of New Jersey, perhaps even on the Potomac. Hamilton outmaneuvered Bingham and the legislature refused to instruct its delegates to switch their support away from New York.

By late August Federalists throughout the United States began to worry that the constitutional revolution was threatened. New York had called for a second convention. North Carolina had postponed consideration of the Constitution. Pennsylvania Antifederalists planned a precedent-setting statewide political convention. Antifederalists in many states expected to run as candidates in the first federal election. These factors, and the desire to choose Pennsylvania's first United States senators before a new, politically unknown Assembly was elected, convinced Philadelphia Federalists, other than Bingham, that they must give up the fight over where the First Federal Congress should meet. "If Congress permit the ordinance for the new government to sleep much longer," Robert Morris told a Pennsylvania congressman, "they will probably meet the reproaches of the major part of the people of America."

Letters from less influential constituents calling for a decision poured into Congress. Bingham went home to Philadelphia early in September and did not return. A last minute attempt by some of Philadelphia's supporters to push Princeton as a compromise temporary residence failed to gain momentum and with that, Philadelphia's supporters gave up. "Let the place of meeting be New York, Philadelphia, or Baltimore, nay, the banks of the Potomac, Ohio, or Mississippi, let it be anywhere; but for Heaven's sake, let the *vox populi* prevail, let the government be put in motion," declared a Philadelphia newspaper. "The citizens of Philadelphia wish their pretensions to the seat of federal government may be waived, and that even their rival, New York, may be the place of first meeting, rather than have one hour's delay of putting the government in motion, which is so necessary to the happiness and honor of the United States," asserted another.[22]

On 12 September Henry Lee introduced the seventh ordinance for implementing the new government. It proposed that the "present seat of Congress" be the place. Few men spoke against it, for the choice, as Madison told Washington, was either yielding to New York or strangling the government at its birth. The angry Delaware delegates employed their right to postpone the final question for a day and stalked out of Congress, just as the Marylanders had done a few days earlier. Congress called one of its rare Saturday sessions the next day and voted unanimously to call the new government together on 4 March 1789 at "the present Seat of Congress." Having voted the death warrant of the Confederation, Congress limped on until March, usually without a quorum.[23]

What did the debate mean for the new nation? The French Embassy at New York was not optimistic, having preferred Philadelphia to Anglophilic New York. In official correspondence, the consul declared it one of the most passionate debates in congressional history. To him both sides seemed disposed to jeopardize the new Constitution rather than to yield. The charge d'affaires saw it as proof that the states really were not disposed to form the consolidated empire which the new Constitution implied. He credited passage of the ordinance in part to the press, which had begun to ridicule Congress for obstructing the formation of the new government.[24]

Virginia Antifederalists taunted their counterparts in the state. Was not the decision the first instance of that northern domination of the new government which they had warned about during the ratification process? Nevertheless, the Lees, both the Federal and Antifederal branches of the family, supported the decision. Arthur Lee had explained their position in an appeal to Washington for support: Virginia's commercial cities "are struggling against the vast superiority which Philadelphia acquired during the war. So great an addition of money and influence as the residence of Congress" would "give them a decided control over our commerce . . . all the profits of our trade would center in Philadelphia."

Washington had observed the proceedings at New York during the summer of 1788 through the eyes of delegates Madison and Henry Lee. He had at first wavered as to whether New York or Philadelphia best served the interests of the Potomac. With the Lees, he believed that Philadelphia not only hurt Virginia commerce but also would appease the South sufficiently as a temporary residence to postpone a move to the Potomac for many years. Upon reflection however, he sided with Madison in favor of Philadelphia, since to stay at New York would hasten the question excessively, and at the cost of destroying harmony in the First Federal Congress.[25]

New Yorkers hired Pierre L'Enfant to convert their city hall into a "Federal Hall" for the First Federal Congress. New Yorkers and their supporters declared it the most elegant building in America. The speed with which L'Enfant remodeled and expanded the building during the winter stunned observers. The only criticism was that he hired foreign labor, a complaint that would continue to haunt the construction and embellishment of the American Capitol. Newspapers throughout the United States kept Americans informed of the progress of the renovation, and Federal Hall quickly became the symbol of the new government. Although referred to as the "Hall" rather than as the "Capitol," the building served the same function.[26]

Congressman George Thatcher from the Maine district of Massachusetts had a wife who enjoyed discussing politics with her women friends. Consequently he kept her informed. Having such an elegant building in which to meet, he wrote home, would act against any attempt at the first meeting of Congress to adjourn to Philadelphia or some place more central. Upon seeing the building, one Pennsylvania member of the first House of Representatives admitted its elegance; nevertheless, he considered it "a Trap—but I still hope, however well contrived, we shall find room to get out of it."[27] Indeed, Pennsylvanians had been at work on a strategy to persuade the First Congress to adjourn to Philadelphia as soon as it met.

Not to be outdone by New York's new docks, newly paved streets and much-trumpeted Federal Hall, Philadelphia undertook civic improvements. These included the re-incorporation of the city and the legalization of public theater. Pennsylvania had long been divided over these issues, but the argument that both measures served to attract Congress had the desired effect. The year 1789 saw the repair and repainting of the State House, the completion of a County Courthouse a few yards to the west and the beginning of a City Hall to the east.[28]

The Philadelphia press swelled with articles in the fall and winter of 1788–1789 exposing New York City's shortcomings. It was the capital of a state where Antifederalism, led by Governor George Clinton, reigned supreme. Congress, by remaining at New York, had provided an economic stimulus so that the state did not experience the distress felt elsewhere in the United States; thus, by remaining at New York, Congress encouraged the state to remain Antifederal. New York had been the sink of British politics during the war and still suffered from a British odor. The New York press responded in kind about contemptuous Philadelphia. It was less virtuous, less healthy, less well governed and less impressive in its natural setting than New York; and Americans should not forget its coolness and neglect for Congress in June 1783.

The campaign of mutual vilification climaxed a month before the First Federal Congress met. A fictitious letter from the City of Philadelphia to her sister, the City of New York, noted that she had no need to found libraries or build Federal Halls because she had long had both. Further, New Yorkers should not complain about her press. It allowed people to vent violence by name calling and obscenity, even if it meant printing some falsehoods. This she much preferred to being like New York, where crime in the streets abounded. New York soon replied. Philadelphia was envious that congressmen who came to New York married its women, women who, incidentally, never deceived men by wearing make-up. Perhaps, the article concluded, Philadelphia—be the city a brother, sister, or "heteroclite"—should try promoting brotherly love.[29]

Philadelphia's supporters knew that denigrating New York would not bring Congress home. Consequently they attempted to influence the outcome of the first federal elections. Although the only common issue of the election was whether the new Constitution should be amended, the question of the location of the seat of federal government played a role in the Middle States, just as it had during the ratification debate.

Pennsylvania elected two Federalists to the United States Senate: the nationally known Robert Morris of Philadelphia and William Maclay, a landed member of the state's executive council, who resided at Sunbury on the Susquehanna River. For the election of representatives, the Assembly, controlled by eastern Pennsylvania, did what it could to ignore state geography. Instead of establishing congressional districts, it passed a law allowing each resident to vote for any eight men. Such a procedure guaranteed that the election would be dominated by eastern Pennsylvania's more concentrated and Federalist population. Six of the eight Federalists elected lived in Philadelphia or within forty miles of it.[30]

While the delegation could be expected to vote as a bloc to place the temporary residence at Philadelphia, it disagreed over the proper place in Pennsylvania for the permanent residence. Henry Wynkoop from Bucks County, and George Clymer, Thomas Fitzsimons and Senator Morris from Philadelphia supported a site on the Delaware River. Rep. Thomas Hartley from York and Senator Maclay advocated the Susquehanna River. Thomas Scott from Washington County, southwest of Pittsburgh, supported the Susquehanna, but the economic interest of his constituents gave him considerable sympathy for the Potomac. Daniel Hiester and the brothers Frederick and Peter Muhlenberg from Montgomery County were swing votes.

In Maryland, the first congressional election resulted in a delegation dominated by the Potomac Interest: Senator Charles Carroll and Reps. Benjamin Contee, Michael Jenifer Stone and Daniel Carroll resided on the western shore of the Chesapeake Bay while Rep. George Gale had been the Potomac Interest's unsuccessful candidate for the United States Senate from the eastern shore. Supporting Baltimore were its representative, William Smith, and Senator John Henry, as well as Rep. Joshua Seney from the upper eastern shore. Both Smith and Seney had districts bordering the Susquehanna River, a factor which would complicate debate over the location of the capital during the First Congress.

Benjamin Rush and Tench Coxe failed to persuade John Dickinson, a partisan of Pennsylvania, to represent Delaware in the United States Senate. Both Delaware senators and its lone representative supported Philadelphia as the temporary residence. Although long considered an appendage of Pennsylvania, Delaware remained unpredictable on the permanent residence; it might support a site in Pennsylvania, or it might insist on one within its own borders.

New Jersey was historically split by its social and economic ties to Philadelphia and New York City. The southern part of the state, West Jersey, looked to Philadelphia while the northern half of the state, East Jersey, looked to New York City. The state chose one senator from West Jersey and one from East Jersey. The former could be expected to support Philadelphia as the temporary residence, the latter New York City.

Following Pennsylvania's lead, New Jersey passed an election law which allowed the entire state to vote for all four representatives. West Jerseians announced a ticket which supported Philadelphia as the best choice for the temporary residence. Although it contained two men from East Jersey, Elias Boudinot of Elizabethtown and James Schureman of New Brunswick, neither was wedded to New York. Schureman had been prepared to vote for a removal to Philadelphia in the spring of 1787. Boudinot had recently purchased an estate there and his daughter had married the attorney general of Pennsylvania, a Philadelphian; on the other hand, he had some bitter memories of his experience as president of Congress when it left Philadelphia in 1783. The two West Jersey men on the ticket supported Philadelphia. Salem merchant Thomas Sinnickson had commercial ties with the Quaker City. Lambert Cadwalader was the son of the prominent Philadelphian, Dr. Thomas Cadwalader, and Hannah Lambert, daughter of the founder of Lamberton, the first New Jersey site offered in 1783 for the residence of Congress. The younger Cadwalader had been actively committed to Philadelphia's cause during the summer of 1788. Several tickets appeared in opposition to the West Jersey ticket. On almost all of these, however, two East Jersey names stood out: Abraham Clark and Jonathan Dayton of Elizabethtown, the two congressmen who had supported New York during the summer of 1788.

The intense competition between the tickets split East and West Jersey as never before. Voters' minds were made up on the question of which temporary residence would best suit their political and economic interests. Getting out the vote, not a debate over the issues, was all that mattered and voters flocked to the polls in record numbers during what became almost a month of voting. In Burlington County, across the Delaware from Philadelphia, seventy–eight percent of the eligible voters went to the polls; in Essex County, across the Hudson from New York, ninety percent voted. The West Jersey ticket was declared elected, but the pro–New York forces charged corruption and petitioned the First Federal Congress to declare the election invalid.[31]

In New York, Antifederalists, widely described by Federalists as opposed to the residence of Congress at New York, controlled the lower house of the state legislature. Federalists controlled the upper house. The lower house insisted on a joint session of the legislature to elect senators, the procedure the state had followed in electing delegates to the Confederation Congress. The upper house insisted on a concurrent vote so that it could block the election of Antifederalists or at least elect one Federalist. Both sides remained adamant for weeks. After all of the skill and exertion exhibited by Hamilton and his New England allies in their effort to keep Congress at New York in the summer of 1788, the impasse especially galled the city's supporters. In April 1789 New Yorkers gave the Federalists a majority in both houses of the legislature. A special session in July elected as senators Hamilton's father-in-law, General Philip Schuyler, and former Massachusetts Congressman Rufus King, who had recently become a resident of New York City. A Pennsylvania representative saw King's surprising election as a bid for New England's support on the residence issue. John Adams saw it as a reward for King's past efforts on behalf of keeping Congress at New York, particularly his success in blocking removal to Philadelphia in 1787.

In the congressional district which included New York City, John Laurance, a New York City lawyer and former congressman, ran against John Broome, president of the city's chamber of commerce. Since both Federalists opposed amendments, the choice became which man could best help the city remain the residence of Congress. Newspaper pieces pushed Laurance as a good orator who could better defend the city, and asserted that Broome had refused to contribute any money toward preparing Federal Hall. With the aggressive backing of Hamilton and other prominent New Yorkers, Laurance won.[32]

Philadelphia stood a much better chance of capturing the temporary residence in the House of Representatives than in the Senate. Assuming South Carolina's propensity to remain at New York, the Senate would likely tie on the question of transferring the government from New York and perhaps even on the choice of a permanent residence, if the proposed site was in Pennsylvania. Consequently, it became vitally important to Pennsylvanians to elect a vice president who would break any tie by voting with their senators.

Benjamin Rush thought he knew just the person, his old friend John Adams, recently returned to Massachusetts after a decade-long diplomatic career. Always blunt, Rush informed Adams that Pennsylvania would concur joyfully in his election as vice president, especially if Congress should fix its seat on the Delaware River. A carefully orchestrated newspaper campaign ensued. "Doctor Rush and myself . . . puffed John Adams in the papers," Senator Maclay later explained, because "we knew his vanity, and hoped by laying hold of it to render him useful among the New England men in our scheme of bringing Congress to Pennsylvania." Rush and Tench

Coxe worked to earn Adams votes in Maryland, Delaware, New Jersey and Virginia; and Rush attributed Maryland's and Delaware's support for other candidates to a foolish desire to punish the Eastern States for having voted in the summer of 1788 to keep Congress at New York.[33]

When Adams was elected "Vice President of the western Empire," Rush reminded him of his debt to Pennsylvania. "There is an expectation here which I have humored that your influence will be exerted immediately in favor of a motion to bring Congress to Philadelphia," Rush observed while offering congratulations. A month later he sent a flattering letter detailing eight reasons—with a ninth in a postscript—as to why it was in New England's interest to make Philadelphia the temporary residence of Congress. "By *delaying* the removal of Congress to Philadelphia," Rush warned, "you will probably be dragged in a few years to the banks of the Potomac, where Negro slaves will be your servants by day, mosquitoes your sentinels by night, and bilious fevers your companions every summer and fall, and pleurisies every spring." Still later, Rush wrote to claim that Trenton on the Delaware, Annapolis and Chestertown on the Chesapeake or even the banks of the Ohio were preferable to remaining at New York. Adams finally responded to Rush, denying his power to influence the matter and insisting that he must remain neutral, but to soften the blow he admitted that he could never be a zealous advocate for New York and that he wished the First Congress had been called to Philadelphia.[34]

In January and February the Philadelphia press overflowed with propaganda, some of which it knew would be reprinted to the north and south. "A True Federalist," written either by Bingham or an ally such as Coxe or Rush, constituted its best effort. The writer alleged that the location of the capital was crucial to the survival of the Union and that the North should yield to the South. Except for one point, his analysis repeated arguments familiar to those who had followed the controversy during the preceding summer. The new thesis suggested that Congress must consider the increasing importance of the West when making decisions about the residence of Congress, exactly what Washington and Madison had been saying privately for several years.

In the two months between the publication of the piece and the meeting of Congress, the Philadelphia newspapers reprinted numerous accounts from the southern press expressing concern about the new government's meeting at New York. One of these argued the necessity for a centrally located capital in order to overcome southern fears about New England's control over commerce under the new government. Another claimed that there could be no real confidence in the Union until recognition of its principles and the necessity of its preservation led Congress to the conclusion that "the banks of the Potomac [*the birthplace of the immortal Washington*] are destined by nature for the seat of national government." The most threatening warned that the North had best consider western and southern interests, "or we shall shortly, very shortly perhaps, have another Congress at Richmond."[35]

When the First Federal Congress met at Federal Hall on 4 March 1789, New England congressmen outnumbered their southern counterparts three to one. Despite Bingham's warnings that his successors should not get their hopes up for an early removal, half the Pennsylvania delegation was present. During the month–long wait for a quorum, the most talked about subject among the impatient congressmen was the residence of Congress.

New York belles, beaux and clergymen went from door to door among the congressmen soliciting support for New York. Led by Hamilton, who had urged New England congressmen to attend promptly, New Yorkers welcomed the new government splendidly. On the evening of 3 March thirteen guns fired from the battery to symbolize the death of the old government. Only eleven guns fired the next morning, but the absence of Rhode Island and North Carolina did not dampen the celebration. New York's advocates compared the welcome Congress received at New York with the treatment Pennsylvania had given it in June 1783. They played upon the old New England and southern prejudice against commercial Philadelphia and the danger of being fixed there permanently if a removal took place. They told the New Englanders that an adjournment to Philadelphia might place the permanent seat of government on the Potomac, and told the southerners that New York had a much better climate than Philadelphia, especially in the approaching summer season. How could the Union afford the expense, inconvenience and time lost by an immediate removal? Congress needed to levy import duties so that it could raise revenue from ships already in sail for American ports. And, of course, they stressed the elegance of Federal Hall.[36]

More concerned that eastern Pennsylvania have the permanent residence than that Philadelphia be the temporary residence, Senator Robert Morris nonetheless took the lead in lobbying for an immediate removal from New York, since a temporary residence at Philadelphia surely would dilute some of the popular prejudice against the city and its environs. He and other Philadelphia promoters raised various arguments with their fellow congressmen as to why Congress should leave New York as soon as it achieved a quorum: New York had shown its disinterest in the new government by not appointing presidential electors or senators; Federal Hall was too closed in for fresh air to circulate within the building; and Pennsylvania had once again offered the buildings on State House Square, the floor plans of which indicated that Congress would have more room. The Pennsylvania members urged friends at home to write any congressmen they knew, to wine and dine those who passed through Philadelphia en route to New York and to arrange for the publication of anti-New York propaganda which they sent for inclusion in the Philadelphia press.[37]

Pennsylvanians planned for either Senators Morris or Maclay to move that Congress reside at Philadelphia until the selection of a permanent seat. The motion would be made as soon as the votes for president had been officially counted, so that Washington and Adams could be summoned to Philadelphia instead of New York City. Despite Madison's six years of support for a return to Philadelphia, he and other less influential members of the Virginia delegation believed the sectionally divisive issue should not be allowed to disrupt the harmony of the new government while such fundamental matters as revenue, the organization of the executive and judicial branches and Amendments to the Constitution confronted Congress. Consequently, the Pennsylvania delegation agreed reluctantly to postpone raising the question until the end of the first session.[38]

4

Potomac Fever

WHILE STILL A YOUNG MAN, GEORGE WASHINGTON fell victim to Potomac Fever, a delusion–inducing obsession with the grandeur and commercial future of the Potomac River. It passed from generation to generation along with the property if not the genes of such families as the Washingtons and Lees of Virginia and the Johnsons and Carrolls of Maryland, whose land holdings on the Potomac and the Ohio to the west numbered in the tens of thousands of acres. This early strain of Potomac Fever culminated in the person of Washington. Through him it affected the role of the Upper South in federal politics as well as the location of the United States capital.

The Fever was endemic to the river long before Washington. In 1608 the English adventurer John Smith entered the inviting seven mile wide mouth of the river known to unrecorded generations of the Algonquin people as "Petomek." This name has been translated variously as trading place . . . a place to which something is brought . . . a place to which tribute is brought. The picturesque scene at the head of navigation 150 miles upriver captivated the men who soon followed Smith. Below impressive falls, the river passed through a narrow rocky gorge, rushed over rapids, and then spread out to flow more gently past creeks, woods and marshes teeming with life. Seven miles below the last falls, a river from the east widened the flow. Four miles farther on, a stream entered from the west. The former became known as the Eastern Branch of the Potomac, or Anacostia, and the latter as Great Hunting Creek. The area was the deepest penetration of tidewater on the eastern side of the continent. "This . . . is the most pleasant and healthful place in all this country, and most convenient for habitation, the air temperate in summer and not violent in winter," observed the Virginia fur trader Henry Fleete, who described the area twenty-four years after Smith. "It aboundeth with all manner of fish. . . . And as for deer, buffaloes, bears, turkeys, the woods do swarm with them; and the soil is exceedingly fertile." Amid this wealth of natural diversity for at least half a millennium, the sedentary Anacostians had built their wigwams among cornfields and gardens of squash, beans and potatoes.

Henry Fleete was trading for furs south of the Anacostia in 1634 when he heard word of a large ship sailing up the Potomac. Governor Leonard Calvert and his Maryland pilgrims were consequently confronted on their arrival by several hundred armed natives expecting Spaniards. Fleete willingly escorted his potential competitors down the Potomac to St. Mary's. There the colony's capital remained for sixty years until it became clear that the Chesapeake Bay, not the Potomac, would dominate Maryland's early development. Nevertheless, Marylanders thrust their land claims and tobacco plantations up the river, and, beginning early in the 1660s, the Calverts provided substantial speculative land grants about the Anacostia for such colorfully named tracts as Rome, New Troy, Scotland Yard, Widow's Mite and Cuckold's Delight.

In 1700, when the Maryland legislature debated the necessity of settling the area between the Anacostia and Little or Lower Falls, the colony's frontier rangers were stationed at the falls and a few people lived on Rock Creek three miles south. Settlement of the Virginia bank of the Potomac followed the same pattern as in Maryland: fur trade with resident and nomadic natives, large unsettled land grants, land sales and re-grants of expired patents, the first tenants, the gradual disappearance of the native population and, finally, the arrival of planter families. In 1669 John Alexander purchased six thousand acres beginning at Great Hunting Creek and running north along the Potomac shoreline to My Lord's (Roosevelt) Island. By 1700 a few frontiersmen living below the Arlington Hills could look across the river at the hearth smoke of their Maryland counterparts.

The ten mile stretch from the foot of Little Falls up to the spectacular Great Falls of the Potomac formed a natural if brief barrier

to European expansion. The hostile Iroquois soon agreed to remain
west of the Blue Ridge and thus sixty miles of new lands became
available between Little Falls and the Great Warpath which crossed
the Potomac at Conococheague Creek. The area was little known,
but offered access to the Indian trade of a continental interior not
yet comprehended. As early as 1699, the author of "Louisiana and
Virginia Improved" proposed reaching across the Virginia mountains to pull eastward the trade of the Great Lakes and the Ohio
Country.[1]

    The vision of a Potomac link between the Atlantic and the west-
ward flowing waters of the Ohio River found a more successful advocate in 1711 when Thomas Lee became resident agent for the
more than five million acres in northern Virginia owned by the Fair-
faxes. While thus employed young Lee succumbed to the Fever. He
envisioned the Potomac's ten mile drop onto the coastal plain as a
future emporium of commercial and political energy tying East to
West. There, he supposedly predicted, would rise a great Virginia
commercial city, the capital of a nation independent from Great
Britain. Moved by his dream, he purchased 20,000 acres of land,
stretching from Little Falls to above Great Falls. Lee thus tied the
destiny of the Potomac to Virginia's search for an urban center.[2]

    The many Virginians who believed in the necessity of towns for
defense, supply centers, and even modest economic self-
sufficiency had already been frustrated for a century when the Privy
Council at London vetoed the 1706 Virginia act for establishing
ports and towns. But British opposition to Virginia's town acts was
not as detrimental to the rise of towns as were the environmental
and economic realities. Tobacco required little attention after dry-
ing other than the rolling of the hogsheads to a ship. The work could
be done from plantations on any of Virginia's many tidewater rivers. In the mid–eighteenth century, with the food shortage in
Europe and the subsequent rise of the wheat and flour trade on the
Potomac, this situation changed dramatically. Extensive milling,
storage and transportation needs had to be met, and several Fall
Zone and Piedmont towns rapidly sprang up to provide these facilities. Nevertheless, none of these towns, not even the fifth largest
city in the colonies, the ice–free port of Norfolk, had been able to

overcome Philadelphia's domination of the colony's economic life. Virginia needed its own commercial city to preserve its wealth.[3]

By 1747 Thomas Lee was one of the most powerful men in the colony, soon to be president of the Virginia Council. In that year he, George Mason, Lawrence Washington and other Potomac promoters formed the Ohio Company as a means of establishing a Potomac link to the western fur trade. In a very short time the company blazed a path through the mountains from the Potomac to the Monongahela on the waters of the Ohio. When Lee died three years later, leadership of company affairs passed to a new president, Lawrence Washington.[4] Although Lee's sons, Arthur and Richard Henry, and his grand-nephews, the brothers Richard Bland and Henry Lee, inherited Potomac Fever, after 1750 it was spread primarily by the Washingtons of Fairfax County.

Lawrence Washington lived on a plantation above the Potomac which he had named after British Admiral Edward Vernon under whom he had served. Mount Vernon consisted of half the original patent of 5,000 acres between Dogue and Little Hunting creeks granted to his great-grandfather and a partner eighty years earlier. Like Thomas Lee, he understood Virginia's need for a commercial city, but, he opposed its rising on Lee family land at the Falls. Lawrence Washington became one of the first Virginians to consider the possibility of dominating western commerce from a city built on tidewater, for, if the Falls could be bypassed, there would be no need to transfer goods. Consequently he looked to the mile wide, eighteen foot deep tidewater harbor at the mouth of Great Hunting Creek, ten miles upriver from Mount Vernon. The Virginia Assembly had established a tobacco inspection station at the site in 1732. The settlement which grew around the station attracted Scottish merchants who recognized the location as providing easy access to the infant agricultural wealth of northern Virginia. Unsuccessful at first, Lawrence Washington and other prominent Fairfax County residents, convinced the legislature to charter the sixty acre site as Alexandria in 1749, naming it after the Alexander family. Three years later it became the county seat. Alexandria grew rapidly, becoming by the 1760s the preeminent Potomac River port town. It imported wares and building materials from England and rum and molasses from Barbados, while exporting wheat.[5]

Lawrence Washington did not live to witness the rise of Alexandria. His death in 1752 released twenty–year old George Washington from the chains of primogeniture. George inherited Mount Vernon and with it a commitment to the success of the Ohio Company and Alexandria. Thomas Lee and Lawrence Washington's vision matured during the half century of George Washington's stewardship; and at his death in 1799, Washington left a Potomac River on the verge of political, and anticipated commercial, emporium.

In 1755 five colonial governors met with British General Edward Braddock at Alexandria for consultations concerning French penetration of the Upper Ohio country. For Washington this happy omen confirmed the commodious and pleasant situation of the town and presaged a growth in population and trade. That Braddock chose a Potomac route to the Ohio did not please certain interests at Philadelphia who already saw the Potomac River and the Ohio Company as powerful competitors for access to the West. Three years later, despite Washington's repeated arguments for the road blazed by Braddock, the French were driven from their stronghold at the forks of the Ohio River by a military force which marched west on an all–Pennsylvania route. This competition between Virginia and Pennsylvania over the best route to the Ohio spread awareness of the Potomac link beyond Maryland and Virginia.[6]

By the end of the French and Indian War in 1763, with British claims to the Ohio Country secured, Virginians and Marylanders had settled both banks of the Potomac as far as Conococheague Creek. Potomac land speculators once again looked to lands in the Ohio River watershed for investment, convinced that the Potomac would provide the link. Most saw less success than Washington, who, by the 1780s, had acquired at Mount Vernon the alienated half of the original 5,000 acre grant and had added to it 3,500 additional acres.

Washington loved Mount Vernon and believed that its ten miles of Potomac River frontage, combined with its backwaters, marshes, wooded hills and elevation above the river, made it the most pleasantly situated estate in the United States. The five autonomous farms along with the mansion house, the home manufactures (including a mill), the meticulous landscaping, the deer yard and the largest group of slaves in Fairfax County enhanced the natural grandeur. The many visitors who came to Mount Vernon considered the plantation and its vista delightful. Yet Washington refused to limit his land hunger to the expansion and cultivation of his estate. Inheritances, adept investment of military bounties and his own funds and those of his wife, the wealthy widow Martha Dandridge Custis, had garnered him over 60,000 other acres stretching from Norfolk and the Dismal Swamp in the south, to the Mohawk Valley of New York in the north, and to the Kentucky wilderness in the west. Virgin land along the Potomac–Ohio–Great Kanawha river system made up over two–thirds of this acreage.[7]

To increase the value of his holdings and further his vision of the Potomac as the best access to the West, Washington early became the prime advocate of opening the river to navigation by clearing its channel of rocks and by building canals to bypass its several falls. In 1754 he canoed the river from near the site of present–day Cumberland, Maryland, to Great Falls and reported the Potomac to be the most convenient and least expensive route to the West, in spite of a scarcity of water during much of the year, a drawback he quickly and conveniently repressed.

Washington soon found an influential ally in Thomas Johnson of Frederick County, Maryland. The two men corresponded about the project during the 1760s. In 1770 Washington assured his friend that no person had more ardor for the opening of the Potomac than he himself and expressed fears that if the Potomac was not soon developed, other rivers would become "the channel of conveyance of the extensive and valuable trade of a rising Empire." That year Washington and Richard Henry Lee failed to get a Potomac navigation bill through the Virginia legislature, but two years later it did adopt a bill drafted by a committee on which Washington served. Such success led one enthusiastic promoter to proclaim that the Potomac would soon become the route for all the commerce between Great Falls and a point 300 miles up the Missouri River.[8]

Maryland held exclusive jurisdiction over the Potomac, but its legislature repeatedly refused to join Virginia in the effort to clear the river despite a letter from Washington to the governor of Maryland, visits to Annapolis by Washington and George Mason, and a bill carefully drafted by Mason, approved by Washington and sent to Johnson at Annapolis. Maryland opposition to the plan was led by the Baltimore merchants and their political spokesmen of the Upper Chesapeake Interest, who worried that opening the Potomac would destroy their dream of Baltimore's becoming the eastern terminus of western commerce. Even if the profits could be diverted from Alexandria to Georgetown, Maryland, they remained opposed.

Georgetown at Rock Creek on the Potomac, seven miles above Alexandria and three miles below Little Falls, was a potential competitor for both Alexandria and Baltimore. Maryland had authorized a road to the creek in 1720, a tobacco inspection station in 1745 and finally a sixty acre town in 1751. Georgetown also served as a ferry crossing. Like Alexandria, Georgetown had attracted Scottish merchants who envisioned a great future in its location at the head of Potomac navigation, but, unlike Alexandria, its shallow port suffered from shifting sand bars, flooding and ice floes. Regardless of such severe handicaps, its promoters predicted for it the same glorious future that Virginians dreamt for Alexandria.

Popular opinion that the head of tidewater on the Potomac was destined for commercial greatness stimulated landowners to plan towns and sell lots. In 1768 Jacob Funk platted Hamburg (Funkstown) just southeast of Georgetown at the mouth of the creek known variously as Tiber, Goose, or Duck. Two years later Daniel Carroll of Duddington laid out Carrollsburg at the mouth of the Anacostia.[9]

Just after the First Continental Congress in the fall of 1774, amid continued frustration caused by Maryland's refusal to cooperate with Virginia, Washington and Thomas Johnson met at Georgetown to discuss plans for the Potomac. Besides Washington and Johnson, Daniel Carroll of Duddington and George Mason figured among the subscribers appointed as trustees for a navigation company. Soon thereafter, at the Second Continental Congress, Johnson nominated Washington as commander in chief of the Continental Army, and the dream of a commercial emporium on the Potomac languished for a decade until 1783, when Washington returned to Mount Vernon and the British acknowledged American sovereignty over the entire Ohio River watershed.

The first step which Virginia's Potomac promoters took was the development of an Alexandria virtually untouched by the fighting and commercially stimulated by the war. Alexandrians predicted an economic boom. They found a powerful supporter in Washington, whose adult life had been intimately linked with the rise of his home town. He inherited and purchased lots there, represented its citizens as a town trustee and colonial legislator, presided over the meeting which adopted the Fairfax County Resolves in 1774 and served as an officer and benefactor for various of its civic organizations. Alexandria provided Washington, like other Fairfax planters, access to the benefits of urban life. There he traded, voted, celebrated and worshipped. A week after his return to Mount Vernon from the war, he rode to Alexandria to receive the salutations of its citizens. Proclaiming "your residence in our neighborhood will have a happy influence . . . on the growth and prosperity of this infant town," they welcomed home their first citizen. Washington responded, "that the circumstances are most favorable to the growth and prosperity of your rising town affords sensations of a very pleasing nature. May the agreeable prospects be soon realized!"[10]

The establishment of a commercial city within the state remained a paramount goal of postwar Virginia. Many of its leaders had long acknowledged such a city as essential for economic prosperity and self–sufficiency and justified the concomitant social costs by the wealth produced. Washington, Henry Lee, Thomas Jefferson and James Madison were the most prominent of many Virginians who hoped for such a city in order to protect their state's commerce not only from Philadelphia but also from rapacious Baltimore, which had invaded Virginia's economy.

By sponsoring a port bill in the Virginia legislature in 1784, Madison sought to use the power of the state to stimulate the growth of such a city and to avoid the colonial experience of having an excessive number of ports. His plan, endorsed by Jefferson, was to limit all foreign–owned vessels trading in Virginia east of the Appalachians to war–torn Norfolk. The political power of northern Virginia forced Madison to include Alexandria, situated in "the very bosom of Baltimore," as the only legal port of foreign entry on the Potomac. Other pressure groups increased the total number of ports to six, and James Monroe condemned the act as an invitation for Baltimore to pull Virginia's decentralized commerce into its vortex. The act benefited Alexandria, but Virginia's commercial duties diverted some Potomac trade to Georgetown. The French traveler Brissot de Warville visited Alexandria in 1788 and described it as still stagnant despite the postwar belief that it would rise "to an equality at least, with the first commercial cities in the United States." Washington agreed with Brissot, but predicted "that Phoenix like, it will again, from its own ashes, grow into consequence." Help was expected to come from the Constitution of 1787 with its uniform commercial duties.[11]

Washington knew that western resources and produce would have to travel eastward as long as the Spanish controlled the mouth of the Mississippi River. Four water routes from the West to the Atlantic existed: The Great Lakes–Mohawk–Hudson route to New York City; the Ohio–Allegheny–Susquehanna to Baltimore or Philadelphia, depending on which of the rival cities gained control of it; the Ohio–Monongahela–Potomac to Georgetown and Alexandria; and the Ohio–Great Kanawha–James to Richmond. Washington had land investments on all but the Susquehanna route. British control of the Great Lakes and the commitment of little more than words to the James–Great Kanawha route pointed to the Potomac and the Susquehanna as offering the most immediate access to the West.

Residents of Baltimore and the Upper Chesapeake retained their prewar opposition to the development of a Potomac route west, envisioning Baltimore as the future emporium of North America. Its growth as a result of the stimulus of war had made the port prominent on the commercial map of the United States. "Baltimore is a most thriving place," a visitor observed in 1783, "trade flourishes and the spirit of building exceeds belief. . . . The inhabitants are men of business." Marylanders of the Upper Chesapeake Interest were already at work on the navigation of the Susquehanna by 1784, despite the fact that its boulder–strewn channel led more north than west.[12]

Thomas Jefferson knew well the need for commercial penetration of the Appalachians, if the United States was to retain the West. He also understood Virginia's need for a commercial city and the benefits to the state if the Potomac or James rather than the Hudson or Susquehanna became the link. In February 1784 he proposed to Madison that the Virginia legislature levy an annual tax of about $25,000 until the Potomac–Ohio route opened, and that the revenue then be used to clear other Virginia rivers, beginning with the James. Madison doubted that the commercial genius of his state had matured sufficiently to challenge the effort on the Susquehanna, and believed that the Upper Chesapeake Interest would continue to block Maryland's participation in any Potomac project.[13]

As he wrote Madison, Jefferson cagily whetted Washington's appetite on the subject: "The present hurry forbids me to write to you on a subject I have much at heart, the approaching and opening of the navigation of the Ohio and the Potomac." Soon after, he served Washington a gourmet vision of Virginia's Potomac–based future, calling the river the true door to western commerce. "I am sure its value and practicality are both well known to you," Jefferson claimed. As a matter of fact, Jefferson, knowing that opening the river was an idea close to Washington's heart, had told Madison that the retired general would be willing to direct the effort, and that the resulting monument to his name would endure as long as the Potomac's waters. "This is the moment however for seizing it if ever we mean to have it. All the world is becoming commercial. Was it practicable to keep our new empire separated from them we might indulge ourselves in speculating whether commerce contributes to the happiness of mankind," Jefferson continued to Washington. "But we cannot separate ourselves from them. Our citizens have had too full a taste of the comforts furnished by the arts and manufactures to be debarred the use of them. We must then in our own defense endeavor to share as large a portion as we can of this modern source of wealth and power."

The commerce of the Ohio River would flow down the Potomac to Alexandria, but, beyond this, the enthusiastic Jefferson believed that the trade of the Great Lakes and the upper Mississippi would flow south to Alexandria even more naturally than east to New

York City. "Nature then has declared in favor of the Potomac, and through that channel offers to pour into our lap the whole commerce of the Western world." Jefferson counseled immediate action. He summarized to Washington the public project he had suggested to a reluctant Madison, stressing that he had provided for the James–Great Kanawha route to be opened only after the Potomac corridor. Jefferson noted, however, an even more powerful objection to his proposal than the opposition of Patrick Henry's James River Interest: the familiar argument that "public undertakings are carelessly managed and much money spent to little purpose." Only Washington could overcome this. Would he, alone or in conjunction with any persons he chose, superintend such a public project? "What a monument of your retirement would it be!" Jefferson proposed, before concluding with an assurance that his own zeal for the business was public and pure because he owned not one inch of land on the Potomac, the Ohio, or any of their tributaries.

"My opinion coincides perfectly with yours" respecting the Potomac–Ohio route to the West "and the preference it has over *all* others," Washington responded. "I am made very happy to find a man of discernment and liberality (who has no particular interest in the plan) thinks as I do, who have lands in that country the value of which would be enhanced by the adoption of such a scheme." He agreed that not a moment should be lost because the New Yorkers would waste no time in opening communications with the Great Lakes once the British surrendered the forts.

Washington also emphasized his commitment to commercial development: "from trade our citizens *will not* be restrained, and therefore it behooves us to place it in the most convenient channels, under proper regulation, freed, *as much as possible,* from those vices which luxury, the consequence of wealth and power, naturally introduce." He assured Jefferson that he too had been obliged to support the navigation of the James as the price for defeating opposition to his prewar proposal for opening the Potomac. Nevertheless, on the central question Washington hedged. He doubted public funding feasible in 1784 and would wait to see its terms before agreeing to superintend. "The immense advantages which this Country [Virginia] would derive from the measure would be no small stimulus to the undertaking," he encouraged Jefferson.[14]

What Jefferson and others failed to achieve by pen was accomplished by Washington's trip to the West in September 1784, his first in fourteen years. His primary motive was to visit some of his vast land holdings, although he also hoped to investigate the length and difficulty of the various portages between the Potomac and the Monongahela. Hostile activities by the native population prevented Washington from seeing his Ohio and Great Kanawha river lands, and he became much more concerned with Potomac navigation than he had at first intended. His diary overflowed with praise for the Potomac corridor, and he returned to Mount Vernon prepared to lead a revived campaign to open the river to commerce.

Washington's first salvo, a magnificent 3,000–word letter to Virginia Governor Benjamin Harrison, suggested that the governor's support for the project would engrave his name on Virginia history. Washington cited mapmakers Lewis Evans and Thomas Hutchins as authorities for the belief that navigation across the Appalachians could be accomplished most easily and inexpensively by way of one (or both) of the great rivers of Virginia. He believed, in spite of the jealousy between northern and southern Virginians, that the time had come to push the plan since other routes involved foreign entanglements. If Virginia did not wish to assume the expense of the project, he suggested that the legislature pass an act to incorporate any private company that applied to the state to develop the Potomac (or the James). Washington dismissed the problem of Pennsylvania's jurisdiction over the connections between the Potomac and the Ohio, claiming western Pennsylvanians favored a Potomac route to the ocean over the more difficult land route to Philadelphia. With uncharacteristic indiscretion, he asserted that, if Pennsylvania refused to cooperate, its western citizens would secede from it.

Washington journeyed to Richmond in mid–November to talk with Madison and other influential legislators. Upon returning to Mount Vernon he sent Madison a petition and a proposed bill for clearing the Potomac, drafted by a meeting of Marylanders and Virginians at Alexandria. The same documents went to the Maryland legislature. Following the Alexandria meeting, the town's newspaper discussed the political importance of opening the Potomac corridor as a means of tying the West to the East, concluding that the human mind lacked the ability to comprehend all the implications. At the end of the month Washington traveled to Annapolis, where he found Maryland's legislative leaders more receptive than they had been a decade earlier. He consequently proposed to Madison that Virginia appoint a group of legislators to join their counterparts in Maryland in drafting a Potomac navigation bill more acceptable to both states than the one drawn at Alexandria.

Instead of sending members of the legislature, Virginia sent Washington back to Annapolis as one of its negotiators. At the end of the year he spent a week at the Maryland capital chairing a joint committee of the Maryland legislature and lobbying for a Potomac navigation bill. His influence finally overcame twenty-five years of Maryland opposition, but this interference in its politics did not pass without comment. A member of the joint committee warned a relative in Congress about the dangers of a certain "Person from the Southward." Almost a year later the incumbent delegate from Baltimore had to defend himself against election charges that he had voted for the bill because he lacked the firmness to *withstand the great personage from Virginia.*" Washington urged the Virginia General Assembly to adopt the Maryland act verbatim. Led by Madison and William Grayson, it did just that. To assure passage, a separate act provided incorporation for any company applying to clear the James.

Washington, who arranged to have the Potomac act printed at Alexandria and distributed widely throughout northern Virginia and western Maryland, espoused the undertaking with earnestness. Madison informed Jefferson that Washington could have chosen no occupation more worthy of following upon that of establishing the political rights of his country than this one, which would double the value of half the lands in Virginia, extend its commerce, and link it to the interests of the Western States. Thomas Lee's son, President of Congress Richard Henry Lee, also praised Washington for his role.[15]

The Potomac Navigation Company chartered by Maryland and Virginia issued 500 shares of stock valued at $220,000. Each state purchased fifty shares. Virginia bought an additional fifty shares in Washington's name as a sign of appreciation and as a means of conserving his private funds. The gesture proved an embarrassment, but Washington did not refuse the offer, as he had all other postwar grants from public bodies. Thus, almost a third of the Potomac Company's stock was purchased with public funds. In May 1785 Potomac area residents—from Alexandria to Shepherdstown in Virginia and from Georgetown to Williamsport in Maryland—attended the first meeting of the Company. Washington was elected president and Thomas Johnson to the board of directors.[16]

Between 1785 and 1789 the clearing of the Upper Potomac for navigation—the promised key to Alexandria's prosperity–progressed steadily, if not as rapidly as its promoters dreamed. The Potomac Company's hired slaves and laborers cleared rocks from the river channel, deepened shallows, and dug narrow canals past Shenandoah, Seneca and Great Falls. By the end of the 1789 building season most of the work above Great Falls had been completed and the unusually high water of that summer had borne many boats of ten tons burden from Cumberland, Maryland, to Great Falls. Completion of the locks at Great Falls, as well as the locks and canal around Little Falls, still lay ahead. Much of this activity was known throughout the United States since American newspapers frequently reprinted the many news articles which originated at Alexandria and Georgetown.[17]

The success of the efforts on the Potomac led to other related schemes for economic development. Residents of the Great Valley of Virginia organized to clear the Shenandoah's channel north to the Potomac. Other Virginians began to ponder the navigability of the North Branch of the Potomac. The Virginia legislature appropriated money to cut a road from Morgantown, (West) Virginia, to Marietta on the Ohio.

The grandest developmental dream of all was Henry Lee's vision for his 500 acres at Great Falls through which the Potomac Company canal ran. His intention to develop a manufacturing town on the site was the re–awakened dream of his great–uncle Thomas Lee. He had massive water power at hand, and abundant timber and coal could easily be transported from the mountains on the waters of a now navigable Potomac. "The value of the spot is above present calculation," he stressed to Madison, and "no man more highly estimates it than General Washington who is one of the best judges of property and is intimately acquainted with the place." Late in 1788

Lee and Madison concluded an agreement by which each held two of eight shares of stock in the project. Instead of a large monetary commitment, Madison agreed to seek investors and to draw up a promotional statement. Although Washington lent his support to the project, the expected investors did not materialize. Lee admonished Madison that if he would give as much energy to their private interest as he had always devoted to the public, he could obtain the necessary funds in two days. Lee's enthusiasm for the project declined markedly after the death of his wife in the spring of 1790, and Madison, never as committed to the project, pulled out a year later.[18]

Washington's zeal for the Potomac Company did not cease with its organization. Throughout 1785 he attempted to interest non-Virginians in the plan, to the point of boring his guests. In March Washington played host to the Mount Vernon Conference at which commissioners from Maryland and Virginia discussed several problems related to the jurisdiction and navigation of the Potomac and Chesapeake. They adopted a mutually satisfactory compact which, among other provisions, declared the Potomac a highway for the citizens of both states. The commissioners also sent a letter to President John Dickinson of Pennsylvania requesting waiver of any Pennsylvania trade duties except those necessary to build and maintain a road between the waters of the Potomac and the Ohio. Two years later, when Pennylvania passed an act to authorize the construction and maintenance of such a road at the expense of its two neighbors, it also authorized another between the waters of the Susquehanna and the Allegheny.

Through Jefferson and LaFayette in France, Washington looked for European investment capital. The return on any investment would be greater than on "any speculation I know of in the world," Washington assured LaFayette with the hyberbole characteristic of victims of Potomac Fever. Washington made his most detailed argument to his wealthy friend Robert Morris, from whom he sought not only investment in the navigational scheme but also establishment of an Alexandria branch of his Philadelphia-based commercial firm. Washington claimed that the profits to be reaped on the Potomac were unequaled: "there is no place within my knowledge to which so much produce will, from the nature of

things, be brought, as to the highest shipping port on this river."
This he considered to be Alexandria not Georgetown. His comments, Washington concluded, were "not exaggerated in any instance intentionally. . . . I have no other objects in view, but to
promote a measure which I think is pregnant with great public utility, and which may at the same time, be made subservient to extensive private advantages."[19]

Washington had intimated to Morris that the navigation of the
Potomac involved important political as well as commercial consequences, and he frequently elaborated on this to others. In proposing the project to Governor Harrison, he had argued that the
political considerations outweighed the commercial. To his friend
General Henry Knox, he predicted that the western country would
populate faster than any area the world had ever known, and be settled primarily by foreigners who bore no particular predilection for
the United States. Commercial connections lead to connections of
other kinds and if those settlers made the former with the British in
the Northwest or the Spanish in the Southwest, "they will become a
distinct people from us, have different views, different interests,
and instead of adding strength to the Union, may in case of a rupture with either of those powers, be a formidible and dangerous
neighbor." To others Washington asserted the necessity of clearing
the Potomac route west before forcing Spain to open the Lower
Mississippi to American trade; for, if western commerce flowed to
New Orleans, the territory immediately west of the Appalachians
would mean no more to the United States than California.

Washington recognized that the states nearest to the center of
the Union would benefit most from a navigable Potomac because
the western country and the states carved out of it would share the
political interests of the seaboard states to which they were commercially tied. He also understood that Virginia could thereby retain its political influence in the West and guarantee itself future
political allies in Congress. Finally, he believed that a Potomac connection to the West could influence the choice of the permanent
seat of the federal government. Not only did his local newspaper
make this claim, but also did his old Maryland ally Thomas Johnson,
who predicted to him that the opening of the Potomac would draw
Congress to its waters because of the river's central location.[20]

While most of the energy behind the plan to center American
political and commercial emporium on the Potomac was Virginian,
Marylanders with economic and geographic ties on the Potomac
felt closer to the Virginians than they did to Baltimore and the Upper Chesapeake Interest. Despite the fact that the two states had
formed the Potomac Navigation Company, the division among
Marylanders remained at least as strong in 1789 as it had been in
1783, when Maryland refused to join Virginia in an offer of land on
the Potomac for the seat of Congress.

Just as the First Federal Congress convened in 1789, the rival
claims of Maryland's Potomac and Upper Chesapeake interests
were highlighted in "A Conference between the Patapsco and
Potomac Rivers," published in the Baltimore *Maryland Journal.*
Patapsco initiated the conversation by congratulating the Potomac
and all other American rivers on the successful formation of a powerful, energetic American Empire. Potomac replied that since the
election of George Washington as the first president, "I am become
so exceedingly vain, that I almost conceit myself no longer common
element, but the most refined nectar." Patapsco acknowledged
Potomac's vanity in presuming to dispute the location of the federal
seat of government with it. Both rivers agreed than an inland situation was not propitious as a site since the Union must be cemented
by one central emporium of commerce and manufacturing. "The
history of all former ages will readily show," Potomac observed,
"that it has been the invariable practice of all wise founders of Empires, Kingdoms and States, from Nimrod down to the immortal
Penn, to cement and support their dominions by one great Metropolis." Specifically, Potomac recommended the level, easily defensible land between Rock Creek and the Anacostia for a great
metropolitan capital city. Patapsco protested that Congress would
never choose such an undeveloped place when it could have the accommodations offered by Baltimore.[21]

Two months earlier "A Citizen of the World" had used the same
newspaper to first suggest the level situation between Rock Creek
at Georgetown and the Anacostia as the best place in America for
the capital. The man who chose as his signature the name of Oliver
Goldsmith's detached, aloof observer was the Georgetown merchant George Walker, who had come to America in the mid–1780s

as an agent for a Scottish tobacco exporting firm. A civic promoter, Walker advocated the creation of a sheltered, ice-free port on the west side of Mason's Island as a means of competing with Alexandria.[22] He argued that the area he proposed for the capital was safe from attack: warships required too much water to reach it and a few forts below the Anacostia would render the city impregnable. Placing the federal government there would stimulate the rise of a great commercial–political city, guarantee the swift completion of the navigational improvements on the Potomac, facilitate intercourse between East and West and prevent the secession of the latter from the Union. An inland site would not serve for the capital of a great nation since it would prove difficult to provide the necessities and luxuries demanded by cosmopolitan residents.[23]

The specific site for the federal city advocated by these two articles was primarily pasture and crop land, but it included the two undeveloped towns of Hamburg (Funkstown) and Carrollsburg. Some members of the First Federal Congress privately discussed the location but few made a distinction between it and adjoining Georgetown, which had flourished during the 1780s and soon would be the largest tobacco market in Maryland. The years 1788 and 1789 had witnessed the incorporation of the town, the laying of the cornerstone of Georgetown Academy (University) and the completion of a bridge across Rock Creek. Georgetown's residents petitioned Congress in September 1789 to make it the capital and sent a representation again in June 1790 as a reminder.[24]

Both newspaper articles pointed out another division of opinion within Maryland over the location of a Potomac capital: Should it be on tidewater or at a point above Great Falls? The first person to advocate an upriver Potomac capital was General Otho Holland Williams of Baltimore, a proprietor of Williamsport, Maryland, platted in 1787 at the mouth of Conococheague Creek. He had spent most of his youth on the Conococheague where his family had operated a major Potomac ferry before the Revolutionary War. In September 1788 he argued privately that Congress should not lay the foundation of its empire at a defenseless place. Even if all the seaports were perfect Gibraltars, fairness to the West required not fixing the capital in one corner of the continent. Congress should situate it west of South Mountain in the fertile, secure valley of the

Conococheague. It was probably Williams who, after reading "A Citizen of the World" six months later, put the site before the public. Convenient land on which to build a large city existed on both sides of the Potomac at the mouth of the Conococheague. The air was salubrious, the water abundant and pure, and the building materials inexhaustible. Finally, a Conococheague seat of government took into account the fact that within a few years the population of the United States would extend all the way up the Mississippi River to the shores of Lake Superior.[25]

Conococheague Creek, although it was west "a long way indeed" as its Algonquin name translated, had good reason to assert its claim to the capital. It coursed through the twenty mile wide Great Valley and had functioned as a major transport route long before the arrival of Europeans. The Ohio Company early established a storehouse there. White settlers came to the area late in the 1730s and it remained the western edge of settlement until the French and Indian War. During the 1760s thousands of emigrants on the Great Philadelphia Wagon Road from Pennsylvania crossed the Potomac on Williams Ferry. Both George Washington and Henry Lee recognized the importance of the Conococheague to the success of their dreams for the development of the Potomac, for they hoped to tap its resources almost as far north as Carlisle, Pennsylvania.[26]

Whether above tidewater or not, a Potomac capital also potentially involved land in Virginia. Indeed, Marylanders who opposed a Potomac site believed that, even if the entire ten mile square lay on their side of the river, such a capital would be dominated politically and economically by Virginia. When they debated the Constitution, Virginians considered its implications for both the state's commercial development and the location of the seat of federal government. In an anonymous public letter to the members of the ratifying convention, the Philadelphia publicist Tench Coxe urged them to consider the relationship between the Constitution and Virginia's dream of a commercial link to the West. If Virginia did not ratify, Pennsylvania could impose restrictive duties on Virginia's use of the indispensable Pennsylvania portion of the proposed Potomac route west. This would direct western trade away from the Potomac to the Susquehanna or the Hudson–Mohawk.

Convention delegates privately supported such Virginia locations for the federal district as Richmond, Williamsburg and Norfolk, but the only politically viable site remained some point on the Potomac. Most men favored its falls.[27]

Below the Great Falls of the Potomac lay Alexandria and its 2,700 residents. William Grayson had argued to the Virginia Ratification Convention that the Federal Convention had erred by not fixing the capital at Alexandria, the center of the Union. One Virginian predicted a great future for the Potomac if Congress chose the town, for it would soon exceed its Egyptian "namesake" in both wealth and grandeur. The Potomac below it would blossom like the ancient Nile and completion of navigational improvements above Great Falls would bring to it the resources of a country far more valuable than that which lay above the cataracts of the Nile.[28]

The frustrating decision in 1788 to keep Congress at New York caused Virginians such as Madison to fear that the Susquehanna was the best location that Virginia could expect for the capital. Consequently as an alternative they began to advocate an upriver capital nearer to Pennsylvania and the votes of its large congressional delegation. One suggested Shepherdstown, Virginia, as a potential site. It lay at the edge of the Great Valley midway between Williamsport, Maryland, and Harpers Ferry, Virginia. In 1789 Virginia congressmen told their colleagues from other states that they were willing to place the capital as far up the Potomac as the Conococheague and implied they favored an upriver location. Nevertheless, Virginia and Maryland congressmen who advocated the Potomac took care not to commit themselves to either an upriver or tidewater site.[29]

Upriver or not, those who advocated a Potomac capital had an advantage over other communities which sought to become the seat of empire. The aggressive development corporation known as the Potomac Navigation Company provided not only data and publicists, but also members who served in politically important positions. Marylanders Charles Carroll, Daniel Carroll and Michael Jenifer Stone, and Virginians Richard Henry Lee and Alexander White served in the First Federal Congress. Most importantly, the company's guiding influence and president until August 1789 was the developer George Washington. Potomac Fever, which infected these men and the corporation they founded, drove them to make passionate and unrealistic claims about the Potomac River. At the same time it sustained them as, year after year, they asserted the claim of the Potomac to the seat of empire.

In April 1789 Mount Vernon's 8,000 acres blossomed with the soft colors of a northern Virginia spring when Charles Thomson, having crossed the Hudson, the Delaware, the Susquehanna and the Potomac, rode up to the mansion door. The man who had been the pen of the Continental and Confederation Congress since 1774 carried important news from the First Federal Congress: the people of the United States had unanimously called their Cincinnatus from his plow to be their first president. Washington had prepared himself for the new undertaking by spending a week deeply engaged in political discussions with Madison at Mount Vernon. Surely these included the means of bringing the capital to the broad river which dominated the vista.[30]

Washington and Thomson soon left Mount Vernon for the seat of government. The adulation of a grateful citizenry, seeking to view the man above public criticism, embellished their route to New York. Even at Baltimore the president–elect received a grand welcome. En route to the Federal Convention in 1787, he had been allowed to pass through almost unnoticed because of anger about his role in the passage of Maryland's Potomac Company Act. Ten miles north of Mount Vernon, Washington met the first and most personal of the many celebrations. "I do not feel myself under the necessity of making public declarations, in order to convince you, Gentlemen, of my attachment to yourselves, and regard for your interests," Washington responded to Alexandria's welcome; "the whole tenor of my life has been open to your inspection; and my past actions, rather than my present declarations, must be the pledge of my future conduct." Publication of this speech at New York on the day before his inauguration might well have given pause to advocates of a capital located north of the Potomac.[31] When Washington returned to Alexandria almost two years later, he brought with him the American capital. But, as a result, neither he nor the institution of the presidency would ever again be above public criticism.

5

The Rupture of the Federalist Consensus in 1789

AS MEMBERS OF THE FIRST FEDERAL CONGRESS arrived at New York in March 1789, a widely reprinted newspaper editorial commented on the zeal with which so many contenders urged their claims to be chosen as the capital of the United States: "It is evident that the sooner that great question is determined the better—otherwise it will prove the cause not only of disputes, but of such jealousies, as many lay the foundation of *dissentions* that may prove fatal to the union."[1] The Constitution had been ratified by the narrowest of margins, particularly in the large, politically influential states. Less than a year later, a prediction of the possible dissolution of the Union did not appear so exaggerated an analysis to Americans as it does to their descendants.

Between April and August 1789 the Federalist consensus of 1787–1788 proved strong enough to withstand the pull of sectionalism. Although congressmen speculated privately over the possibility of dividing the Union on some north–south or east–west line, they agreed unanimously that the troublesome division between North and South which had played so prominent a role throughout the course of the American Revolution had not manifested itself inside Federal Hall.[2] This rare opportunity allowed Federalists to establish a federal revenue and an independent executive, defeat amendments altering the essence of the Constitution and produce a bill creating a powerful federal judiciary.

In September 1789, however, the familiar struggle between North and South reached a new level of intensity when Congress took up the question of the location of the American capital. The issue split the Federalist consensus along sectional lines and fired the opening volley in the battles that led to the Compromise of 1790 and the two nascent sectional political parties that had developed by the time Congress adjourned early in 1791. One of the great debates of the First Federal Congress and by far the most intense and explosive of the first session, it touched upon such classic themes of American history as immigration, internal improvements, slavery, sectionalism, states' rights, the rights of the minority, disdain for wilderness, the power of the executive branch, the durability and expansion of the Union and the American mission. During it, several months before the introduction of Alexander Hamilton's report on the public credit, James Madison used publicly for the first time the argument that overly powerful states were no longer the problem with American federalism. The length and intensity of the debate meant that the House had little time to devote to the Senate bill creating the federal judiciary. Southerners understood the importance of that bill, but most probably agreed with Arthur Lee that the location of the federal seat of government was more so.

Forcing the Pennsylvania delegation in April 1789 to postpone the question of an adjournment to Philadelphia until the end of the first session relegated the disruptive issue to conversation, the press and private letters.[3] By late July the delegation realized that its plan had to be scrapped, for neither the Eastern States nor the South would support a change of temporary residence unless that decision came in conjunction with the establishment of the permanent seat of government. In reality neither wished to consider the matter at all. The South, led by Virginia, saw benefit in delaying a decision until population in the South and West increased. The Eastern States saw no reason to debate the question as long as they could retain the temporary residence at New York. To bring Congress back to Philadelphia, Pennsylvania would have to make a deal. The delegation caucused twice at City Tavern as July turned to August in order to decide which section to approach. Meanwhile Philadelphians reportedly showed an "almost childish anxiety for the removal of the Congress" to their city and treated "the idea of fixing the permanent Seat of Government on Potomac within a century to come as too ridiculous to merit consideration."[4]

A deal with the South meant an immediate removal to Philadelphia at the price of a Potomac capital. A deal with the Eastern

States meant a capital in Pennsylvania at the price of remaining at New York for a few years more. The delegation reached a consensus that a capital in Pennsylvania was more desirable than the temporary residence at Philadelphia. But the delegation divided hopelessly over the proper place in Pennsylvania. A few advocated the Susquehanna River watershed. Others supported a situation near Philadelphia. Aware of the prejudice against the Susquehanna in eastern Pennsylvania and against Philadelphia throughout much of the Union, a majority, led by Robert Morris, favored the Delaware River opposite Trenton. In order to circumvent its division over the site, the delegation agreed to vote as a bloc for whatever location the Eastern States chose.

To encourage the Eastern States to cooperate seriously in a bargain, instead of working for the postponement they desired, the Pennsylvanians also made overtures to the South. By 21 August the Eastern States, while skeptical of the wisdom of debating the divisive question, had given Pennsylvania reason to believe that they would support a permanent seat in Pennsylvania in exchange for staying a few more years at New York. The falls of the Delaware was the rumored spot. Everything appeared settled and Thomas Scott of western Pennsylvania gave notice to the House that he would bring the question to the floor the following week.[5]

In response to Scott's announcement, members of both houses presented petitions from constituent communities seeking to become the federal capital.[6] By 1790, when Congress finally made its choice, sixteen sites—on the Delaware and its tributary the Schuylkill, on or near the Susquehanna and the Upper Chesapeake Bay and on the Potomac—either had petitioned the First Federal Congress to name them the capital or had been proposed during its debates. In addition, Havre de Grace, Elkton, Charlestown, Annapolis, Frederick, Ft. Frederick and Cumberland, Maryland, were mentioned off the floor. All the sites proposed for the seat of Congress in 1783 had either hugged tidewater or lay inland in New Jersey. Only three of these now remained viable contenders. Trenton, New Jersey, and Germantown, Pennsylvania, however, lacked access to the West despite such claims; Georgetown, Maryland, on the other hand, sat strategically at the head of navigation on the westward–leading Potomac.

Despite contentions that New York City's lavish efforts to accommodate Congress in 1789 formed part of a strategy to make itself the permanent capital and despite private discussions about New York State ceding Brooklyn and part of Kings County so the United States could build an Athenian capital on Brooklyn Heights, no place in New York State figured as a competitor. New Yorkers would vote for any site in exchange for votes which gave New York City the longest temporary residence.

Antifederalists attributed the quick and early ratification of the Constitution by Delaware, New Jersey and Pennsylvania, to the lure of being the site of the federal city. Patrick Henry told the Virginia Convention that Delaware had been so anxious that it ratified without even reflecting on the document.[7] Indeed, in December 1787 Delaware became not only the first state to ratify but also the first to offer Congress jurisdiction over a ten mile square. No site in the state made an effort on its own behalf, and in 1789 and 1790 motions to make Wilmington either the temporary or permanent seats failed in both houses.

In September 1788 New Jersey, following the recommendation of its ratification convention, offered jurisdiction over any ten mile square. Being astute, promoters of the area from Bordentown up to Howell's Ferry near Washington Crossing joined in an offer with Pennsylvanians on the opposite side of the Delaware River. Their petition stimulated a promoter of the Potomac, probably a southern member of Congress, publicly to declare the falls of the Delaware an eccentric, inconvenient and disgusting spot which should be forgotten along with the Old Congress. Nevertheless, the site became a major contender in the first session of Congress because Senator Robert Morris, who had begun acquiring land there in 1787, lobbied for it. The names Morrisville, Pennsylvania, and Federal City Road, northeast of Trenton, exist as reminders of the effort to locate the Federal City at the falls of the Delaware.

Thirty miles below the falls of the Delaware lay Philadelphia. While recognizing New York's role as the political capital of the United States, Jedidiah Morse declared in his *American Geography* in 1789 that if one considered "the convenient local situation, the size, the beauty, the variety and utility of the improvements . . . and the abilities of the inhabitants," Philadelphia "merits to be viewed as the capital of the flourishing *Empire of United America*."[8]

The Pennsylvania Ratification Convention resolved that, when the new government began to function, the state should grant it jurisdiction over any place except the city of Philadelphia, the contiguous district of Southwark and a portion of the adjacent township of Northern Liberties (south of present–day Girard Avenue in Philadelphia). The exclusion retained state jurisdiction over Pennsylvania's only ocean port and worked to keep the state capital at Philadelphia, since Pennsylvanians attempting to move it west to Lancaster or Harrisburg would be unable to cite the federal government at Philadelphia as a reason for leaving. The convention also invited Congress to reside at Philadelphia or any other place in the state until it had established its permanent seat. The convention's exclusion was confirmed by the Pennsylvania Assembly in September 1789 despite a small minority who contended that residents of the district would be no more than slaves because of the exclusive jurisdiction of Congress over them. Thus, Philadelphia's advocates in the First Congress, like New York's, wielded their influence and votes to negotiate deals by which the city might become the temporary residence.

Nevertheless, a few Philadelphia boosters vainly hoped that the city could become the permanent seat. Their strategy suggested that, despite the language of the Constitution, Congress did not need exclusive jurisdiction over its capital. In a nationally circulated pamphlet published during the 1789 seat of government debate, Pelatiah Webster advocated that Congress should have all the power, authority and jurisdiction that it needed to preserve its dignity and respectability, but that these powers should be inherent in Congress and not in the place at which it met. Exclusive jurisdiction made for bad public policy because it required Congress to spend considerable time governing the district. All of this prefaced a litany of praise for Philadelphia. The only objection to the site which Webster recognized was the American prejudice against large cities. It was futile, he reminded his readers, to think that Congress would not spawn a large city wherever it sat. If urban allurements proved too diverting to its members, Congress could impose severe penalties for immoral or scandalous behavior.[9] The old prejudice among some congressmen against establishing the capital at Philadelphia extended to its suburbs as well. Nevertheless, two areas adjacent to the city proposed themselves to Congress.

The effort on behalf of Germantown stunned Board of Treasury member Samuel Osgood. He believed placing the federal seat so close to Philadelphia would devastate the city, for its residents, dazzled by the splendor of the capital, would be drawn to it like insects.[10] Germantown and parts of surrounding Chester, Bucks and Philadelphia counties became a major contender on the floor of Congress in 1789.

Another Philadelphia–area location for the capital lay to the northeast of the city. Residents of Philadelphia, Bucks and Montgomery counties asked Congress to choose Old Philadelphia on the Delaware River, the place originally designated for Penn's great city. This proposed district lay between Pennypack and Neshaminy creeks on the Delaware and extended west approximately to present–day Rushland and Neshaminy, Pennsylvania. Some of the area included by the petitioners was the same as that proposed by Germantown's advocates.

A fifth Delaware River watershed site also petitioned Congress. Reading, fifty miles up the Schuylkill from Philadelphia, based its claim to consideration on its position at the head of the Great Valley, which ran from Pennsylvania to the Carolinas, and at the mouth of Tulpehocken Creek, which some Pennsylvanians advocated as a transportation link to the Susquehanna and the West.

In addition to the sites in eastern Pennsylvania, Congress had knowledge of six other contenders for the capital in that state. All were in the Susquehanna River watershed. Placing the federal capital there held important political and economic implications for the state, where rapid population growth in the central and western counties increasingly threatened eastern Pennsylvania's hegemony. Some thought such a location would add power to the western-based Constitutionalist Party, while others predicted a welcome decline in that party's influence and an impetus to form a new state constitution. Consideration of a Susquehanna capital also intensified certain historic tensions between Pennsylvania and Maryland because the river flowed south toward the port of Baltimore on the Chesapeake Bay. Hydrologically, the bay and the river were one.

Interest in navigational improvements to enable the commerce of the vast Susquehanna watershed, the largest in the eastern United States, to be carried to Philadelphia dated back to the last quarter of the seventeenth century. One plan required clearing the rocky, rapids–infested lower Susquehanna from Conewago Falls at Swatara Creek to its mouth at the Chesapeake Bay in Maryland and then digging a canal between the Chesapeake and Delaware bays. William Penn, on the other hand, dreamed of a sister city to Philadelphia, situated on the Susquehanna, and connected to it by an all–Pennsylvania water route reaching eastward from Swatara Creek to the Tulpehocken, the Schuylkill and the Delaware.

After 1755 commerce could flow down the placid upper Susquehanna to Middletown at the Swatara, where a road ran to Lancaster and on to Philadelphia. But by 1770 eight roads led from the western side of the Susquehanna toward Baltimore, and Philadelphia had lost a significant portion of its inland commerce to that young competitor. Philadelphians realized that the Susquehanna had to be cleared from Conewago Falls south to Wright's Ferry in order to prevent the trade of York and its hinterland from going to Baltimore. Thus, in 1771 the Pennsylvania Assembly declared the Susquehanna a public highway above Wright's Ferry. This meant that both the Susquehanna and its tributaries—most prominently the westward reaching Juniata—could be cleared of all obstructions to navigation. In 1785 the Assembly declared the Susquehanna a public highway to the Maryland line in an effort to obtain Maryland's support for a Chesapeake and Delaware canal, but appropriated money to clear obstructions only above Wright's Ferry.

Maryland, on the other hand, had strongly supported opening the lower Susquehanna. In 1783 it incorporated the Susquehanna Canal Company, the first such venture in the United States, to clear the river south of the Pennsylvania line and to provide short canals around the major obstructions. Maryland dreamers of empire on the Chesapeake envisioned capturing much more than the trade of central Pennsylvania and western New York. While some Pennsylvanians harbored doubts that the Susquehanna could be connected to the Ohio, Marylanders seemed not to. A newspaper article, published at Baltimore and reprinted at Philadelphia during the

Federal Convention in 1787, predicted that the Susquehanna would be joined to the Mississippi, and that "if we go up the Missouri... to its source, there is a near communication with the River of the West, which empties into the Western Ocean." Baltimore could become the greatest commercial city in America, if not the universe, and could afford to abandon opposition to a Chesapeake and Delaware canal, concluded the piece.[11]

Three towns on creeks connected to the Susquehanna petitioned the First Federal Congress. York, on Cordorus Creek, lay twelve miles to the west of the river. When Thomas Hartley left York to assume his seat in the House of Representatives, he carried a manuscript. His *Observations on the Propriety of Fixing upon a Central and Inland Situation for the Permanent Residence of Congress,* published anonymously at New York shortly after his arrival, put his home town's claim before Americans.[12] Greater effort was made on behalf of Lancaster on Conestoga Creek, ten miles east of the river. Americans knew it as the most populous interior town in America. With support from Representatives Peter Muhlenberg, who hoped to buy land within ten miles of the town, his brother Frederick, and, if York could not be chosen, Thomas Hartley, the Lancastrians had great expectations. William Hamilton, the town's major landowner, traveled to New York City to lobby for Lancaster. He discovered every congressman committed to the place which best served his own interest and none committed to Lancaster. He quickly returned to his exotic gardens and extensive art and book collections at Philadelphia, convinced that the trip accomplished nothing except to satisfy his Lancaster tenants.

A third off-the-river Susquehanna site, Carlisle on Conodoquinet Creek, lay seventeen miles west of the river. In one respect it differed from every other place suggested for the capital except those on the Potomac above Harpers Ferry: it lay in the Great Valley west of South Mountain. Two residents actively promoted the town. Charles Nisbet, the president of Carlisle's Dickinson College, asserted that if Congress did not select Carlisle it would lose the West either to the British and the Spanish or to an indigenous independence movement. He had little hope, however, believing private gain weighed heavily with Americans and that congressmen would vote solely upon which location best enhanced their land

speculations. General John Armstrong, Sr., more effectively advocated his home town. The most crucial qualities of site for an
American capital, he contended to George Washington, were
defensibility and access to the West. Only two places met the criteria: Carlisle and the mouth of the Conococheague on the Potomac.
Both lay in the Great Valley, and of the two he dared to state his
preference for Carlisle.[13]

Although Congress received no petition on behalf of a location
on the Susquehanna itself, it discussed three such places in September 1789. Rep. Joshua Seney of Maryland proposed Peach Bottom,
site of the southern most Susquehanna River ferry in Pennsylvania,
just above his congressional district. Harrisburg, a new town surveyed in 1785 by William Maclay on land owned by his father–in–law
also had support. Rep. Daniel Hiester proposed that the capital be
located in a district encompassing Harrisburg and Middletown at
the mouth of the Swatara Creek, eastern terminus of the proposed
all–Pennsylvania water route to Philadelphia. Wright's Ferry,
forty–five miles above the mouth of the river, received the most serious attention. Midway between Lancaster and York, Wright's
Ferry had served for decades as the major Susquehanna crossing
and the gateway to the West. In 1788 Samuel Wright platted Columbia at the ferry in hopes of drawing Congress there, and Wright's
Ferry figured as the subject of a low–key promotional effort in 1789.
Its advocates emphasized its natural beauty: situated on a narrow
floodplain below a bluff, the town looked west across the wide
Susquehanna to another high, wooded bluff. The nature of the river
at the site, however, did not allow for a harbor.

The Susquehanna entered the Chesapeake Bay fifteen miles
below the Pennsylvania–Maryland border. Because of conflicts between Maryland's Potomac and Upper Chesapeake interests, its
December 1788 act offering to grant Congress jurisdiction over a
ten mile square had not favored either. Despite newspaper mention of several upper bay sites in the state, particularly Elkton, the
Upper Chesapeake Interest united behind Baltimore, a city of
13,000 residents, as the premier site in Maryland for the federal
capital.

Since mid–century when it had become a major milling center,
Baltimore had penetrated Philadelphia's hegemony over the

Delmarva Peninsula, central Pennsylvania and northern Virginia, and attracted several Philadelphia commercial firms. The old political and commercial rivalry between Annapolis and Baltimore had been replaced by one between Baltimore on the Chesapeake and Georgetown, Maryland, on the Potomac. In his *American Geography,* Jedidiah Morse described the rapidly growing city as the fourth largest in the nation and the most hospitable, and its inhabitants as people concerned with making their fortune in this world without concern for the next.[14]

Baltimore's newspapers launched an aggressive propaganda campaign in January and February 1789. Nothing matched their effort until the Potomac Interest sent out its missives after the 1789 seat of government debate. While indulging in self-praise, Baltimoreans discussed what buildings should be remodeled for Congress and which were spacious enough for the president and the department heads. Someone recommended that a plan be readied to be shown Washington and the southern congressmen when they passed through the city en route to the First Federal Congress. In February Baltimoreans began to subscribe to a loan for the purpose of erecting a hall for Congress and other federal buildings. By the end of the month $20,000 had been pledged.

When it looked as if the capital would be established on the Potomac, New Englanders, seeking to attach the Upper Chesapeake Interest to the North and wishing to see Congress reside in a commercial city rather than a rural area, swung their support to Baltimore. Baltimoreans responded in June 1790 by re-pledging money. Governor John Eager Howard promised to donate a square block of land with a vista over the town and its busy harbor. These propositions, along with detailed economic statistics, were submitted to Congress. By a stroke of geopolitical fate, Maryland, the first state to raise the issue of the permanent seat, found itself in 1790 providing the two major contenders for the United States capital: Baltimore and Georgetown on the Potomac River. During the Senate and House debates, members proposed Hancock and Williamsport, Maryland, and Alexandria, Virginia, on the Potomac.

When the representatives assembled in their chamber at Federal Hall on 27 August 1789, the day Thomas Scott introduced his resolution to establish a permanent seat, anxious New Yorkers and at least one presidential aide packed the public galleries. Scott proposed that the site chosen be convenient and "as near the center of wealth, population, and extent of territory, as may be consistent with convenience to the navigation of the Atlantic Ocean, and having due regard to the particular situation of the western country." Scott portrayed the capital as the grand link in the federal chain, and argued that the future tranquility and well being of the Union depended as much on its location as on any other question that ever had or ever could come before Congress. To postpone decision meant that the choice would be made when sectional and party contentions—thus far absent from Congress—had reasserted themselves. Such a choice would be improper, and, if not overturned, would dissolve the Union.

Convinced of the existence of an unbeatable northern coalition, the South urged postponement until the next session. It argued that completion of the judiciary bill took precedence, that the seat of government debate would produce dissension, and that, because the continuation of the Union depended on the location, the choice should not be rushed. One by one influential New Englanders rose in support of the southern call for postponement, arguing that Congress did not have the resources with which to build a capital, that the public needed time for comment, and that the decision should not be made in the absence of North Carolina and Rhode Island. Convinced that weeks of negotiation had led to betrayal, the stunned Pennsylvanians saw their hopes evaporating. Instantly recognizing the opportunity at hand, the South reversed its position and voted with Pennsylvania to take up the resolution the next week.[15]

Early the next morning, the Pennsylvania delegation caucused. Bitterness toward New England ran high and the majority agreed to discuss with the South a move to the Potomac by way of Philadelphia. The minority still supported Morris's view that Pennsylvania should seek a permanent seat at the falls of the Delaware, but it could not interest the majority in new proposals from New York and New England carried to Morris by Alexander Hamilton.[16]

Although Pennsylvania and the South arranged no formal deal, their discussions persuaded New Englanders otherwise.[17]

Recognizing postponement as no longer tenable, they met with Senator Rufus King and Rep. John Laurance of New York City to discuss which site in Pennsylvania to support for a permanent seat. A Susquehanna site had the advantage of picking up votes from Representatives William Smith and Joshua Seney, the two Marylanders who represented Susquehanna River districts, and of better meeting the complaints of those calling for a more western location. Consequently the Eastern States decided to offer Pennsylvania the permanent seat on the east bank of the Susquehanna in exchange for remaining at New York until construction of federal buildings at the site. Senator King and Massachusetts Rep. Benjamin Goodhue met with the Pennsylvania delegation, all of whom attended except Senator William Maclay. Bedridden by a violent attack of sciatica, he lay there almost three weeks, receiving and recording reports of the debate and bargaining from a variety of informants, each attempting to justify himself.

The meeting had not proceeded beyond pleasantries when James Madison, the Potomac's leading advocate, joined the group. Chagrined, Morris hustled Goodhue and King upstairs while Madison discussed the possibilities of a Philadelphia–Potomac arrangement with the Pennsylvania representatives. Apparently Madison proposed that Pennsylvania join the South in support of a bill locating the permanent seat on the Potomac and that, at the end of the session, the South would support an immediate removal to Philadelphia. Madison left. Morris, Goodhue and King returned. Most of the Pennsylvanians declared their intention to continue the evolving arrangement with the South. King replied that the Eastern States would not make a formal offer until Pennsylvania freed itself from any engagement with the South, but indicated that they supported the east bank of the Susquehanna.

Because Senator Morris believed those Pennsylvanians who supported a Philadelphia–Potomac arrangement would not dare vote against a permanent seat within Pennsylvania if one were proposed on the floor, he continued to negotiate with the Eastern States. In particular, he lobbied them to switch their support from the Susquehanna to the Delaware. He talked at length about this to such prominent New Yorkers as John Jay and Alexander Hamilton and to the previously neglected New Jersey delegation.[18]

A confused and divided Pennsylvania delegation caucused again on the morning of 3 September, the day ordered for opening debate on Scott's motion. As Morris suspected, the men found themselves uncomfortable about voting with the South for the Potomac in preference to a location within Pennsylvania. How would their constituents react? Could they count on the South Carolinians to vote for a temporary residence at Philadelphia despite their previous votes against the city? How quickly would the Potomac apostle George Washington prepare the new capital, thereby limiting the time Congress spent at Philadelphia? In the end, the delegation agreed to support the proposal of the Eastern States for New York City and the Susquehanna, despite the fact that the politically powerful press of eastern Pennsylvania had concluded that a Susquehanna site would not serve the state well.[19]

When the House, sitting as a committee of the whole, took up Scott's motion, Goodhue presented a resolution which called for Congress to remain at New York until the completion of suitable buildings at a permanent seat on the east bank of the Susquehanna River in Pennsylvania. He declared that motives of convenience drew the Eastern States to the Delaware River, but that they had abandoned localism in order to support a situation which they believed, by going further south, would give more lasting content. Goodhue described the location as considerably south of the center of population, a center not likely to shift since the manufacturing states would grow faster than the agricultural states.

The Potomac's most formidable rival had at last reached the floor of Congress, and the inflamed South rose to its defense with passion. Richard Bland Lee, brother of former Congressman Henry Lee and grandnephew of the great Potomac visionary, Thomas Lee, assumed the floor on behalf of his constituents who resided along the river from Harpers Ferry to well below Alexandria. He offered a new resolution as an alternative to Scott's. Lee's second was Daniel Carroll whose Maryland district extended from tidewater Georgetown up the Potomac to the western reaches of the state. The new resolution differed from the earlier one by not defining centrality and by stressing the importance of a convenient communication to the Atlantic and especially to the West. A lengthy preamble insisted that the question involved the duration of the Union and the public's expectation that the place determined upon be wise and just, and suggested that no steps for establishing the capital at the place selected should be taken until after the completion of the arrangements needed for carrying the Constitution into effect. The question involved both the present and future interests of the United States and would determine "whether this government is to exist for ages, or be dispersed among contending winds," Lee claimed in defense of his resolution. Failure to abide by the general principles of the Constitution, particularly the common good, would alarm the South and ratify the apprehensions of northern oppression which had swept through it in 1788 when Congress decided to remain at eccentric New York.

John Vining of Delaware, who favored a Delaware River site, supported the southern effort to sidetrack the Susquehanna. He agreed that it was vital to have the general principles of the Union before the House. It might be possible to ignore them with George Washington available to cement and guard the Union, "but when he should leave us, who would inherit his virtues, and possess his influence? Who would remain to embrace and draw to a centre, those hearts which the authority of his virtues alone kept in union?" Northerners opposed Lee's motion as a stalling tactic, involving unnecessary altercation over abstract principles. The House defeated it by a two–to–one margin.

Debate on Scott's resolution centered on the definition of centrality and the comparative qualities of the Potomac and Susquehanna. Thomas Tudor Tucker of South Carolina attacked the resolution's categories of centrality: the centers of territory and population would shift while the center of wealth probably should not be considered at all. Madison then moved to strike "center of wealth" because Americans of all ranks should have equal access to the seat of government, and because the location should perhaps lean toward those least able to afford the cost of travel to it and most in need of its protection. The motion failed and the House adopted Scott's resolution.

Consideration of Goodhue's resolution for the Susquehanna began immediately. James Jackson of Georgia complained that the Union had been endangered by Goodhue's admission on the floor that the location had been agreed to off the floor. Madison condemned the preconcerted measure as a sacrifice of half the territory and near half the citizens of the United States. Lee demanded proof that the Susquehanna met the principles of Scott's resolution, especially as to its navigability and connection with the West.

Theodore Sedgwick of western Massachusetts defended the means used to form a majority consensus and turned to political theory for argument in favor of the Susquehanna. Montesquieu had postulated that in a country divided into northern and southern interests with poor and productive soil respectively, the center and influence of the government ought to incline toward the section with the poorer soil because necessity stimulated industry and a surplus of labor. The Susquehanna, Sedgwick continued, lay southwest of the center of wealth, population and resources of every kind, particularly when one recalled that the South included three-fifths of its slaves in computing population. These people had no rights to protect; if they were considered in determining the proper center of population, why not include the black cattle of New England on the other side? Wealth and population would always lie north of the Susquehanna because of the unhealthy southern climate.

The task of defending the Susquehanna fell to Thomas Hartley who owned hundreds of acres on the river and its branches. He argued that the easily defended river lay midway between the Delaware and the Potomac and that navigational improvements would connect it to both the Delaware and the Ohio. Its luxuriantly cultivated hinterland contained the best soil in the world. When Hartley and other Susquehanna supporters began to argue over the best specific site on the river, Madison and others called for postponement of the debate. He needed time to prepare a defense of the Potomac, especially proof that it had better communication with the West than the Susquehanna. Madison pled for even one day to prepare his thoughts, but the House voted 27 to 23 to continue debate.

Michael Jenifer Stone, who represented a Potomac River district in southern Maryland, assumed the floor. He attacked the Susquehanna because its access to the West came too close to Britain's Canadian colonies and because Americans would always prefer to live in the South and the West rather than on less fertile soil in the severe northern climate. The West and the South shared more in common than the North and the South and the location of the capital should reflect their needs rather than those of the commercial North, already unfairly favored by the adoption of the Constitution.

Lee moved to strike "the east bank of the Susquehanna in Pennsylvania" from the Goodhue motion and to insert "the banks of the Potomac," describing it as the only logical location for perpetual union. Had it not been difficult to persuade Virginia to ratify the Constitution because of the fear of some of its citizens that the North would sacrifice the South on the altar of its own interest? The Susquehanna sacrificed both the South and the West to the North; consequently, a Susquehanna location would shake faith in the Union in everyone south of the Potomac. New York City's John Laurance denied northern oppression of the South and reminded the House that a Virginia member had declared during the revenue debate that Virginians would have objected less to the Constitution at their ratification convention if they had known how moderate the North would be on the revenue issue. Madison rose to acknowledge that the remark had been his, but "give me leave now to say, that if a prophet had risen in that body, and brought the declarations and proceedings of this day into their view, that I as firmly believe, Virginia might not have been a part of the union at this moment."

In the wake of Madison's strong language, a member moved for adjournment. Northerners again opposed. Fisher Ames of Massachusetts reminded the South of its earlier plea for an immediate decision on the grounds that the Union demanded it. Now, he professed, the Virginians had reversed their position only because they feared the Potomac—which they considered a Euphrates flowing through paradise—lacked the necessary votes. Jeremiah Wadsworth of Connecticut insisted that delay meant only continued bargaining off the floor. He would not dare consent to the Potomac, because New England would thereby consider the Union destroyed. Sedgwick argued that the majority favoring the Susquehanna had a right to govern. Madison agreed that the majority should govern, but complained about its silent and determined manner: it had no right to deprive the minority of a free debate in which to bring forth all of its arguments. One day was insufficient to determine such a momentous question. The four-hour debate, which the press described as ingenious and animated, had carried the House well beyond its usual time of adjournment. Consequently Madison got the extra day he wanted.[20]

On 4 September the House's two leading orators, the detailed and analytical Madison and the more general and imaginative Ames, dominated the debate. Both stressed three now familiar arguments: the role of the West in determining centrality, the contrast between the Potomac and the Susquehanna, and the relationship between the location of the capital and the duration of the Union.

Madison's long and widely reported speech marked the public debut of a fundamental shift in his political stance from architect of a strong federal government to defender of states' rights and from leader of the Federalists to spokesman for a new opposition party built on a foundation of decentralism. Calling the United States a "Confederacy of States," he argued that justice and equality formed the basis of republican governments, particularly of federal republics. Federalism involved local distinctions, and "local governments will ever possess a keener sense and capacity, to take advantage of those powers, on which the protection of local rights depend." "There is no one right," he asserted, "of which the people can judge with more ease and certainty, and of which they will judge with more jealousy, than of the establishment of the permanent seat of government." Madison noted that in several states the citizens had struggled to move state capitals westward from their anachronistic colonial coastal locations. Virginia, North Carolina and South Carolina had already done so; in Delaware, Pennsylvania, New York and Massachusetts similar efforts were in progress.

Madison turned next to the thesis that republican government cannot long survive in extensive territories. He had masterfully turned this argument around in "Federalist Ten." Now he claimed that the idea had some validity. Consequently, those who wished well to the Union should diminish its inconvenience as much as possible. The best remedy was to center the capital at the point least removed from every part of the Union so that the legislature and executive could obtain information and act promptly. In the operation of the judiciary, centrality might be less necessary because of district courts.

Madison stressed that the United States government must retire as far from the Atlantic as possible in order to accommodate the western country. The capital might well be located with a bias toward the West where for a long time the greatest dangers to the Union would exist. The West did not expect the United States to ignore its historic commercial tie to the Atlantic Ocean, and would cheerfully accept a location east of the Appalachians and the true east–west center of the nation. If Congress did not now consider the importance of the West and adapt to it, its residents might form a separate confederacy, jealous of and hostile to the United States.

Madison concluded with a lengthy comparison between the Potomac and the Susquehanna. No one could claim the Susquehanna more central than the Potomac in terms of territory. While the 1789 center of population lay nearer the Susquehanna, Americans would flow rapidly out of the more populated North toward the southwest. Thus, a Potomac capital would only temporarily inconvenience those north of the present center, and any location north of the Potomac would precipitate later attempts to move the capital farther west. Madison closed with a reminder that the Potomac Navigation Company already existed, and the assertion that a site on the Potomac would be farther above tidewater and therefore healthier than one on the Susquehanna.

Ames, already viewed as a rival to Madison in abilities, delivered a long response. He declared it romantic to consider the West in establishing centrality of territory because no one could calculate when that immeasurable wilderness between the Atlantic States and the Mississippi would be settled or how it would be governed. He had no objection to moving the capital westward in a century, but in the meantime commerce, manufacturing, agriculture, climate and the absence of slavery would act to increase population in the North. Ames doubted that the Potomac had adequate water in summer for navigation, and questioned whether commercial growth generated by the capital would affect more than the local area. He did not address himself to Madison's constitutional arguments, but delivered a decidedly different interpretation of the possibilities of a division of the Union. He considered a north–

south split far more likely than an east–west one. Locating the capital on the Potomac would encourage separate nations while a location on the Susquehanna would better secure the Union.

Lee's attempt to strike the Susquehanna and insert the Potomac lost, 29 to 21. The vote was not recorded but the minority probably included no one north of Maryland and Delaware. Madison then moved to add the words "or Potomac" after Susquehanna, but that failed too and the House adopted Goodhue's resolution.[21]

When debate opened the next day, the North had a new proposal to attach to the Scott and Goodhue resolutions. Thomas Fitzsimons of Pennsylvania moved that the president be authorized to appoint commissioners to choose the best site on the east bank of the Susquehanna in Pennsylvania and that Congress appropriate money to buy land and erect buildings within a number of years yet to be specified. Significantly, the resolution authorized the first presidential commission.

Northerners styled southern attacks on the proposal as mere obstructionism. An embittered Madison, annoyed by the insinuation, crabbed that the South only wished to know its destiny if it was to be disposed of by the North. Northerners rejected his contention, arguing that they had refused to join any bargain until convinced that one existed to haul them to the Potomac. Madison wished that everything that had passed on the subject could be reduced to writing; for the South had acted in self–defense, having listened to no proposition until it had reason to fear an improper decision.

Antifederalists Thomas Tudor Tucker and Thomas Sumter of South Carolina argued that the Fitzsimons resolution delegated enormous power to the president that should reside in Congress, and moved that the commissioners explore the banks of the river and report several choices to Congress. By this means the sites would bid against one another and Congress might be able to purchase the land at a moderate price. The House rejected the amendment and agreed upon three commissioners and an appropriation of $100,000. It failed to agree on the time the commissioners should have to erect the buildings because the New York delegation self–interestedly broke with the New Englanders in order to prevent a date being set for when New York City's tenure as the temporary residence would end. The committee of the whole then reported the resolutions to the House, which adjourned until Monday. They consisted of Scott's preamble defining centrality, Goodhue's for New York City and the east bank of the Susquehanna in Pennsylvania and Fitzsimons's enabling clause.[22]

The representatives welcomed the brief respite from the passionate debate which had for the first time publicly and repeatedly raised the possibility of a dissolution of the new Union. Hartley claimed never to have seen such intrigue. The debate had proved perplexing and unseasonable for one New Englander, most likely Goodhue, who knew that New England still wished to postpone the residence question if it could be done without uniting Pennsylvania and the South. Because a "permanent residential fever" prevailed in certain states, Congress would ever be "tormented with this contentious question until it is ultimately decided," he concluded. Constituents in New England agreed. One wrote Sedgwick that he feared "it will issue in that odious distinction between Northern and Southern interest which the present Congress have hitherto had the credit of *concealing at least,* however their feelings might be. Will it not create a party spirit which will be carried into all other measures...? There is no subject from the discussion of which I fear and expect more pernicious consequences."[23]

Madison's remarks had most conspicuously reflected southern frustrations. Fitzsimons, while acknowledging that Madison had some reason given Pennsylvania's turnabout, considered his reaction overwrought: "in no one instance has he lost so much reputation as on this business which has transported him far beyond his usual caution." From the opening of Congress in April well into August, Madison, a "leading man in the Cabinet Council" and a future presidential contender, as Rep. William L. Smith of South Carolina called him, had been the floor leader of the overwhelming Federalist majority. Indeed, because of his close working relationship with the president and the conscious aping of the British in 1789, Madison had operated like a prime minister. Americans have always been quick to criticize their political leaders, and Madison's colleagues, particularly his Massachusetts rivals, scrutinized him carefully. Sedgwick considered him as haunted by the

Antifederalism of Patrick Henry and too democratic to withstand popular clamors. Within a month of the opening of Congress, Ames described Madison as pro–French and too Virginian. Within two months he criticized "our first man" as addicted to political theory, overly idealistic and so subject to error as to create mischief. Looking back on the first session of Congress, Ames concluded that Madison was also too libertarian and southern.[24]

Madison's analysis about local rights opened him to public criticism in the North. A friend reported that his remarks had excited the apprehension and displeasure of some Philadelphians, and that some of his enemies at New York planned to injure him in the public's estimation. "They have asserted that all was peace [and] quiet on the subject of amendments [to the Constitution] until the business was stirred up by you; and however distant, have endeavored to connect your conduct on *that,* with what you have said on the late occasion."[25]

Among the most apprehensive Federalists at Philadelphia was the energetic Tench Coxe. His anxiety arose from the dissension among Federalists in Congress and the stimulus it might give opponents of the new system. "I read with considerable alarm a statement in one of your speeches," Coxe wrote Madison. "I fear too that a phalanx, that has been forming for two years by the states east of Jersey, has manifested itself in such a way as to make us tremble upon all great subjects." The Middle and Southern States "will become impatient and the Union itself may be in danger . . . when I remember any long continued and fixed opinions of your heart and head I feel most sensibly the language" of the speech.

In reply Madison blamed the press for misquoting him; nevertheless, he repeated his belief that Virginia might not have ratified if it could have foreseen the overbearing northern majority during the seat of government debate. Nor did he regret his remarks, except as part of a debate in its entirety inauspicious to the public repose. A Connecticut Federalist analyzing the course of congressional politics seven months later credited the seat of government debate of September 1789 as breaking down the unity which had to that point filled every mouth with praise for Congress. It was then that Madison's passion had rendered him ridiculous.[26]

On Monday, 7 September, the representatives were given some anonymous, if ironic, advice in the New York *Daily Advertiser* as the House prepared to take up the three resolutions:

> In absolute governments, the capital is generally established by accident or the whim or caprice of the despot. Constantine from the mere impulse of his own opinion, removed the seat of empire from Rome to Constantinople, and in modern times the Czar Peter, removed his government from Moscow to Petersburgh; . . . perhaps the glory of transmitting their names to posterity might have had no small operation in the respective removals. . . . The nature of republics where equality is the basis, does not admit of an eccentric position to gratify the ambition of a monarch and the avarice of individuals, or to promote the aggrandizement of a favorite city. . . . An illustrious character in this union [Washington], who views himself only as an American, . . . declared his opinion on the subject, by pointing to a map where the centre of the United States was delegated. He has never given bad advice to his country.

Since the debate had moved to the House from the committee of the whole, the entire subject was again open to debate and amendment, and the roll could be called and votes recorded. The House quickly adopted Scott's preamble and began debate on Goodhue's resolution. Lee moved to strike "the east bank of the Susquehanna in Pennsylvania" and to substitute "north bank of the Potomac in Maryland," but his motion failed as before, 29 to 21. The division left no doubt about the sectional character of the conflict. The representatives north of the Mason–Dixon line backed the Susquehanna unanimously. They also had the support of William Smith and Joshua Seney, the two Marylanders whose districts bordered the Susquehanna. The southern representatives supported the Potomac.

Suddenly, however, the northern coalition started to weaken because of the effect of Morris's continued lobbying against the

Susquehanna in favor of the Delaware. Elias Boudinot of New Jersey attacked the Susquehanna as subject to periodic flooding and as offering no feasible communication with the West. The Potomac was preferable to it and the Delaware preferable to both. He moved to strike the Susquehanna and to insert the "Potomac, Susquehanna, or Delaware." The motion lost. But New Jersey's representatives had deserted the Susquehanna coalition, and the gap between the majority and minority began to close. Morris had been effective with New Jersey because of its obvious bias for the Delaware. In addition, its pro–Philadelphia representatives resented the recent unsuccessful efforts of some New Yorkers and New Englanders to have New Jersey's seats in the House declared vacant on grounds of election irregularities.[27]

Stone then moved to amend the Goodhue resolution by replacing "east bank" of the Susquehanna with "banks." This united his Maryland delegation because it was in the interest of Smith and Seney that the capital lie on the west bank where it would be more influenced by Baltimore than Philadelphia. With the loss of those two votes following so quickly after the four from New Jersey, the Susquehanna coalition lost its majority for the first time and the House adopted the amendment by one vote. Riding on the success of a first victory, Lee tried to insert "or Maryland" after the "banks of the Susquehanna in Pennsylvania." This was merely a tactic to break the Pennsylvania–Eastern States alliance, for Virginia still feared the economic implications to Virginia of an Upper Chesapeake Bay capital. The motion failed by one vote.

Frustrated by its inability to separate Pennsylvania from the Eastern States by making it possible to locate the capital in Maryland, the South attacked the majority from a different direction. It attempted to remove all mention of the temporary residence from the resolution, and, failing in that, to knock out specific mention of New York and substitute Philadelphia. Success in either effort might cause New York to advocate postponement of the entire matter. The effort failed, however, because only one Pennsylvanian left the coalition; all the rest uncomfortably went on record as favoring New York for the temporary residence because of their agreement with the Eastern States. The House then adopted the Goodhue resolution as amended to include either bank of the Susquehanna.[28]

The only chance left the southern minority was an amendment to the Fitzsimons enabling resolution. The South found something which once again attracted the two Marylanders with Susquehanna River districts. George Gale of Maryland's lower eastern shore, a man with well established ties to the Potomac Interest, offered what became commonly known as "the proviso." This shrewd and critically important amendment stated simply that, before the purchase of any land for the capital, Pennsylvania and Maryland must satisfy the president that they had made provision for the removal of all obstructions to navigation between the site in Pennsylvania and the mouth of the Susquehanna in Maryland. Its implications were not so simple, and it affected profoundly the politics of the debate. If the southern Susquehanna were opened to navigation, Philadelphia might lose much of central Pennsylvania's commerce to Baltimore. The South gambled that the six Pennsylvania representatives who resided in or near Philadelphia would not take such a risk for a Susquehanna capital. Furthermore, the proviso made George Washington, widely known as the prime mover behind the navigational improvement of the Potomac, the man who must be convinced that the required measures had been taken. If the bill became law despite the efforts of the South, he might delay purchase of land for the capital as long as he held the presidency.[29]

As expected, Seney and Smith, the two Marylanders with Susquehanna River districts, voted for the proviso, but because two Virginians were away from the floor the motion failed. Everyone knew, however, that the South had the votes to adopt it when the resolutions returned to the floor as a bill. The select committee named to draft it — Ames of Boston, Laurance of New York City and George Clymer of Philadelphia — could have reported within minutes. Instead it sat on the bill for a week while the North recalled three absent members to compensate for its losses and the expected arrival of Alexander White of northern Virginia whom Madison had urged to return to Congress.[30]

The week provided time for public reaction as well as comment by members of Congress. The Philadelphia press disliked the rage for city building and money borrowing, while the New York papers condemned the debate as a waste of time and declared that the Susquehanna would be likely to remain the center of wealth and population forever, since Canada would join the Union and the West would probably leave it. Rep. Clymer observed that "the Virginia pride is at present much hurt and heaven and earth will be moved, but they will never be able to bring us to the Potomac." He discounted the threats of disunion, but warned prophetically that the South would continue to employ every strategy it could devise until "the chapter" closed. "We have a faint hope of frustrating the [Susquehanna] project," Rep. Lee observed, "but even if this should be the case I very much doubt the practicability for a long time to come of prevailing on the Eastern and Middle states to re-move to Potomac."[31]

When Robert Morris had the audacity to ask Washington for his opinion of the House debate, the "Great Personage" appeared more reticent than usual. He had reason to be. If the bill passed Congress, he would have to make a difficult decision. Rep. Lee hoped Washington would veto it as partial and unjust. Dr. David Stuart, Washington's confidant and business manager, wrote the president anxiously from Alexandria: "The people here say that their expectations of its being on the Potomac were always centered in you, and hope that as your opinion has been long known on the subject, it will never pass with your concurrence." Circumspectly, Stuart suggested procedural grounds for a veto: it should not have been discussed without previous notice, nor before Rhode Island and North Carolina rejoined the Union.[32]

The Pennsylvania delegation continued to face a quandary. Some members feared that the New Englanders might opt again for postponement. Furthermore, the delegation felt discomfort in urging a Susquehanna capital while at the same time seeking to defeat the proviso. Senator Maclay knew the Susquehanna better than any other member of Congress because he had lived on its banks for twenty–five years, had surveyed thousands of acres of land on its tributaries, and had acted as a commissioner for clearing it of obstruction above Wright's Ferry. Not satisfied that the Susquehanna had been adequately defended in the House, the bedridden Senator penned a lengthy piece to influence the House debate.[33]

On 17 September the House took up the select committee's bill. Only one New Englander had returned, and, with the arrival of White, the strength of the two sides remained unchanged. Gale took the floor. To no one's surprise he reintroduced the proviso requiring the Maryland and Pennsylvania legislatures to satisfy the president that they had taken measures to open the river to navigation between the capital and the Chesapeake Bay. Hartley knew of Washington's bias for the Potomac and did not like the position in which the proviso placed the president, but he chose to assail it on other grounds. He claimed it unnecessary because Pennsylvania had declared the entire Susquehanna a public highway open to navigational improvement in 1785. Both Madison and Stone replied that Pennsylvania therefore should have no objection to the proviso; in any case, the United States could not take the risk of a landlocked capital. The proviso carried by the tie breaking vote of the chair. Gale next called for an amendment which allowed the presidential commission to select a site in either Maryland or Pennsylvania, but it failed by one vote.[34]

The House did not return to the bill for four days as the Susquehanna forces sought a means to knock out the proviso. They pressured Smith and Seney, threatening to give up the Susquehanna altogether if the proviso was retained. The two Marylanders held firm. On 20 September it remained unclear as to what would happen, since no one knew how Philadelphians Fitzsimons and Clymer would vote on the proviso–laden bill. Both Goodhue and Maclay predicted postponement until the next session. New Englanders, however, persuaded the reluctant Philadelphians to accept the proviso in the expectation that the Senate would amend it out of the bill.[35]

As the bill passed to its third and final reading on 21 September, Madison scoured it for constitutional objections, a tactic he often resorted to when efforts at fending off adoption of a bill had failed. He found two, the first of which resulted from a point he had lost at the Federal Convention. The provision for the temporary residence at New York should be struck as unconstitutional because Congress alone held the power to decide where it should sit, whereas the bill required the consent of the president. Acknowledging Madison's contributions to the Constitution, Ames refused to defer to him in the exposition of it, declaring that the power of adjournment had nothing to do with the temporary seat of government—the residence of the executive, the judges, the foreign ministers and the archives determined that. When the motion failed, Madison made one final and equally futile attempt to split the Susquehanna coalition. He wanted the word "permanent" struck from the bill as a term unknown to the Constitution.

On 22 September, after a month of bargaining and debate, the House adopted the seat of government bill, 31 to 17. It had the support of all the representatives from New England, New York and Pennsylvania, as well as two Georgians and five Marylanders, the proviso guaranteeing a clear Susquehanna route to Baltimore making it difficult for the latter to oppose the bill. The minority consisted of New Jersey, Delaware, Virginia, South Carolina, one Marylander and a Georgian. The Marylander was Georgetown's Daniel Carroll, who informed the House that he would have voted with the rest of his delegation had it not been for the unconstitutional provision for the temporary residence. Both Ames and Madison saw dread of the Delaware and despair of ever going south of the Susquehanna as the reasons why the southern votes switched at the last minute.[36]

The bill which the House sent to the Senate provided for the location of a district up to ten miles square on the banks of the Susquehanna in Pennsylvania. It authorized the borrowing of as much as $100,000 for the purchase of land and the construction of buildings. Finally, it granted extraordinary powers to the president, who would appoint three commissioners—without the consent of the Senate—to report to him rather than to Congress the most eligible site for the capital. Under his direction, they would purchase and accept grants of land and construct within four years suitable buildings for the federal government. In the meantime Congress would remain at New York. None of the powers vested in the president could be carried into effect until the Maryland and Pennsylvania legislatures satisfied him that they had taken measures to open the Susquehanna to navigation from the capital to the Chesapeake Bay.

Morris assumed management of the bill when it reached the Senate floor. He told his wife he had been "exceedingly plagued and harassed, fretted, vexed, and pleased, alternatively" with the House debate, but expected more success in the Senate. To bring the capital to the Delaware, as close to Philadelphia as politically possible, remained his goal. He would try first for Germantown and a portion of the Northern Liberties. That could fail because of New Jersey. William Paterson of East Jersey might well be opposed. Supportive Jonathan Elmer of West Jersey was absent, a fact cited later as costing him reelection. Next Morris would try for the falls of the Delaware. He understood the significance of the moment. The southern and eastern members, angry at each other over broken bargains and the intensity of the debate, could not easily combine against Pennsylvania. When North Carolina or Kentucky came into the Union, the capital would be carried to the Potomac. If Rhode Island or Vermont came in first, the temporary residence would remain at New York. Consequently he promised to leave nothing undone to achieve victory. Maclay, aware of both Morris's commitment to the Delaware and the desire of the Eastern States and the South to postpone a decision, feared the result of Morris's machinations.[37]

On 22 September the Senate received the House bill. Pierce Butler of South Carolina moved to postpone until next session. His second was William Grayson, the Virginian who four years earlier had successfully blocked appropriations for the federal town on the Delaware River. Grayson argued that the decision should wait until North Carolina and Rhode Island re-entered the Union and the first census had determined the precise center of population. Furthermore Virginia had offered Congress $100,000 if it would locate the capital there and he wanted Pennsylvania to match the sum. Morris opposed postponement and promised that if his state did not provide the land free of cost and $100,000 toward the buildings, individual citizens of the state would do so. The motion for postponement failed.

On the 23rd the South delayed action briefly, but its rumored filibuster—which would have been the first in Senate history—never materialized. As the debate began, Hartley, Fitzsimons and Morris called Maclay out of the chamber. They tried to persuade him to join a majority of the Pennsylvania delegation which favored cutting the proviso from the bill and, if that proved unsuccessful, attempting to insert Germantown or the falls of the Delaware in place of the Susquehanna. Maclay refused. He believed the loss of the Susquehanna meant that Congress would be carried to the Potomac later, and, now that he had recovered his health, he wanted to give the river on which he lived its due.

Grayson and Richard Henry Lee assailed the Susquehanna because of the political and environmental obstacles to its navigation and because it would give Pennsylvania added influence in the Union. The United States, Grayson argued, was founding "a city which will be one of the first in the world" and, like Czar Peter, should deliberate carefully before choosing its site. Morris moved to postpone discussion of the location in order to consider the proviso. A lengthy and heated debate ensued between Morris and the Maryland, Virginia and South Carolina senators. Butler accused Morris of representing a local view: Pennsylvania would not let Congress sit on the Susquehanna because the proviso would hurt Philadelphia. Butler considered navigation of the river at the capital essential for obtaining the coal on its banks and for the progress of the arts and sciences. Charles Carroll of Maryland believed Congress should pay more attention to the West and the benefits of a Potomac capital for it.

Morris's motion carried despite the impassioned southerners, and he then moved that the proviso be struck. Navigation above the spot where the town would be fixed was already good, he argued, and Pennsylvania should not be forced to open the lower Susquehanna until Maryland had agreed to a canal connecting the Chesapeake and Delaware bays. Furthermore, what would be the fate of a Susquehanna capital under the proviso if a majority of the Maryland legislature favored a Potomac location and consequently blocked navigation of the Susquehanna within its borders?

Carroll, a proprietor of the Susquehanna Canal Company, insisted that his state had not only already met the terms of the proviso, but also had appointed commissioners to confer with Pennsylvania about the Chesapeake and Delaware canal. He reiterated his preference for the Potomac on the grounds that it connected the West to the Atlantic States but promised support for the Susquehanna if the Potomac could not be carried. Nevertheless, his support for the Susquehanna was contingent on the proviso. Without it he would vote against the bill.

Maclay had some difficulty in securing the floor in the midst of the southern defense of the proviso. Successful at last, he insisted Pennsylvania did not deserve the abuse heaped upon it. It had already met the conditions by declaring the Susquehanna a public highway to the Maryland line. Nevertheless, if more were demanded, he had no doubt that the state would do it. Nor did he fear all the authority given to Washington by the bill, for the president had his honor to support and would not traffic with his own character or the public expectation. Debate continued. When the question was finally put, only Morris, two New Englanders and the New Yorkers voted to strike the proviso.[38]

Having failed to strike the proviso, Morris promised the New York senators that if they would vote for Germantown, he, the Delaware senators and the Pennsylvania representatives would promise to vote against a removal from New York before January 1793 even if the federal buildings at Germantown were ready sooner. Morris and six of the Pennsylvania representatives actually signed such an engagement, pledging in it the agreement of their state delegation to the Second Congress. The Delaware senators separately gave King their word. The New York representatives advised New York Senators Rufus King and Philip Schuyler to vote for Germantown provided that the Senate struck out the Susquehanna first.[39]

Morris spent his time before the Senate convened on the 24th taking members to a nearby committee room to discuss the engagement. When the Senate took up the bill, Grayson moved to delete reference to Pennsylvania so that the capital might be located on the Susquehanna in Maryland. As in the case of a similar motion in the House, Virginia sought to separate Pennsylvania from its alliance with the Eastern States, not to create an Upper Chesapeake Bay capital. All the southern senators voted for the motion, but it failed. Morris moved to strike the Susquehanna and to leave a blank for the place so that any senator could move another location. Maclay objected to this because the Senate might thereby eliminate the Susquehanna even though it had more support than any other site. Vice President John Adams ruled the motion in order but it also lost, much to the surprise of Morris who immediately called for reconsideration. Again Maclay appealed to the chair on procedural grounds, for no motion for reconsideration was in order from a member of the minority. Adams ruled against Maclay a second time. Morris stated his preference for Germantown and repeated his offer of money and land from Pennsylvania. Maclay rose to the defense of his beloved Susquehanna, denying that Pennsylvania had appropriated money for any location and insisting that the general sense of the state favored the Susquehanna over Germantown. Morris pledged in response that if Pennsylvania did not supply the money, he would find it. A Delaware senator claimed he had not understood the intent of Morris's original motion and, on reconsideration, the Senate struck the Susquehanna from the bill.

The question of location once again lay open and the New Yorkers, who had voted with Maclay and the South against eliminating the Susquehanna, now considered themselves free of their original commitment. Maclay spoke at length in opposition when the Virginians moved unsuccessfully for the Potomac. Butler, who had voted to strike the Susquehanna in order to consider the Potomac, moved to reinsert the Susquehanna. Maclay seconded this. Morris moved to postpone the Butler–Maclay motion in order to fill the blank with a site in Chester, Bucks and Philadelphia counties including Germantown and such parts of the Northern Liberties as had not been excepted by the Pennsylvania offer. Grayson could not take the proposal seriously and Carroll declared it would result in a division of the Union. Nevertheless, the Senate postponed the Butler–Maclay motion.

Morris then made his promised motion for Germantown. He and eight senators from Delaware north to New Hampshire supported it. Against it voted the seven senators from Maryland south to Georgia, Maclay, and William S. Johnson of Connecticut, who would have to resign either his senatorship or the presidency of Columbia College if Congress left New York. Maclay's refusal to vote in favor of locating the capital in the eastern part of his own state divided the Senate evenly. The question had to be determined by Adams who spoke well of the Potomac, slightly of the Susquehanna and highly of both New York and Philadelphia before casting his vote with the North for Germantown. Years later he could still recall his torment.

Debate continued on 25 September. Carroll's motion to delete mention of the temporary residence at New York proved unsuccessful. Adams and several senators reminded Morris of his monetary pledge. Morris then offered, and the Senate accepted, a new proviso to the bill. This required that no powers vested in the president be carried into effect until Pennsylvania or its individual citizens gave satisfactory security to the secretary of the treasury to provide the $100,000. The next day a motion to postpone the bill failed and the Senate agreed to it as amended, ten to seven. The South— Maryland, Virginia, South Carolina and Georgia—stood alone in the minority, Maclay having prudently left the chamber.[40]

The House coalition which had pushed the Susquehanna bill believed it should adopt the bill as amended by the Senate. To many of them the precise location of the capital made little difference so long as it lay north of Maryland. Boudinot, however, expressed disappointment in the New Englanders' reaction, for he had hoped that their historic fear of Philadelphia would act to place the capital higher up the Delaware at Trenton Falls. The South, of course, saw postponement as the only way to save the Potomac. Its representatives argued that the bill had been altered so materially that its principles had not been discussed by the House, that the Senate which represented the states had overruled the House which represented the people and that the public needed time to react to a location which had never been considered seriously before. The inflamed Marylanders threatened a division of the Union if the bill passed. A motion for postponement failed 29 to 25. The minority included every representative from Maryland southward and Philadelphia's old antagonist, Elbridge Gerry of Massachusetts. Ames moved to concur with the bill. Madison moved to table it. Ames claimed his motion took precedence. A motion for adjournment carried and the House dropped the subject until Monday. "It was a hair breadth business," Ames noted, "for a vote in five minutes would probably have made it a law, except the *King's* signature."[41]

Madison spent all weekend in a desperate attempt to kill the bill. He argued that if it was postponed until the next session, no limit would exist on how long New York might remain the seat of government. Influential New York citizens listened. They did not have faith in the engagement between the Pennsylvania and New York delegations, and they feared that the federal buildings at Germantown might be prepared as fast as New York had readied Federal Hall. These New Yorkers threatened to hold Senators King and Schuyler responsible if Congress left. The latter, who had refused to serve as a commissioner for the federal town in 1785, probably in part because he did not want to be in the awkward situation of making decisions which would end New York's tenure as the seat of government, agreed to support a postponement if the bill returned to the Senate. King, who had been deeply involved in the September bargaining, agreed only reluctantly.[42]

When the House took up the bill on Monday, 28 September, its supporters claimed that the Germantown site had fine commercial facilities and access by water to every populated part of the Union, dismissing access to the West as unimportant because it would not be settled in the foreseeable future. Southerners decried the high cost of the land, the difficulty of defending the site, the remoteness from the West and the likelihood that it would be swallowed up by Philadelphia. Madison quietly pointed out a minor problem with the bill: once Congress assumed jurisdiction over the territory it would be without benefit of law. Consequently, he moved that the bill be amended to provide that the laws of Pennsylvania remain in effect until Congress provided otherwise. The House adopted the amendment without a roll call. All other amendments to the bill failed.

The House then voted 31 to 24 to accept the Senate version of the bill as amended by Madison. Again the vote was sectional: only Boudinot joined the representatives from Maryland southward in the minority. He defended his vote against Germantown on the grounds that residing so close to a large commercial city would produce clashes over jurisdiction, and that it would create jealousy throughout the Union because it increased the power and influence of one of the largest states. Why, he wondered, had the Eastern States lost their terror of Philadelphia.

Madison's amendment sent the bill back to the Senate which promptly voted to postpone it until the next session. Morris had suffered a stunning defeat and his attempt to secure reconsideration on the final day of the session fell on deaf ears. The South, as in 1783 and 1785, had prevented a northern capital and again bought time for the Potomac. Although many people assumed that Madison had tricked the northern representatives with his amendment, Ames indicated otherwise. The postponement of the question—often declared to be New England's goal—had been achieved without reuniting Pennsylvania and the South.[43]

Although Morris justified himself by dismissing the Susquehanna as a mere ploy of the North and never a serious contender, the people of central and western Pennsylvania execrated him with as little reserve as they had Lord North during the war. Their representatives in the state Assembly vowed opposition to the $100,000 appropriation to which Morris had all but committed Pennsylvania. Even many Philadelphians reprobated his conduct, believing the Germantown bill dead. Maclay considered the loss of the Susquehanna as the greatest misfortune that had ever befallen Pennsylvania, and predicted that, at the next session, Virginia would come forward with five new representatives from North Carolina, and, with the help of some Pennsylvanians, drag Congress to the Potomac.[44]

Washington
by George Isham Parkyns, c. 1795
(Library of Congress)

Trenton sur la Delaware, New Jersey
by Edouard–Charles–Victumien Colbert, 1798
(New Jersey Historical Society)

Susquehanna River Ferry
by William Strickland after J. L. Morton, c. 1810
(Library of Congress)

Senator William Grayson
by an unknown artist
(Library of Congress)

Rep. Thomas Hartley
by Edward Malbone, c. 1798
(Independence National Historical Park Collection)

Rep. George Gale
(Clarence Bowen,
The Centennial of Washington's Inauguration)

Rep. Daniel Carroll
by Joseph Sansom, 1790
(Historical Society of Pennsylvania)

View of Congress on the Road to Philadelphia, 1790
(Historical Society of Pennsylvania)

Robert Morris and Federal Hall, 1790
(American Antiquarian Society)

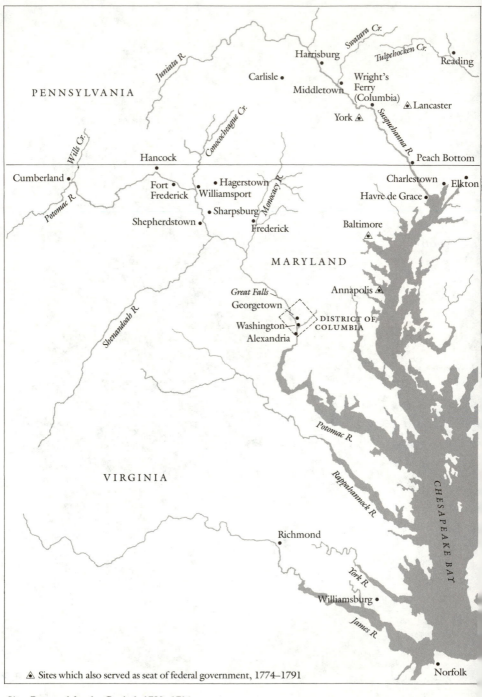

△ Sites which also served as seat of federal government, 1774–1791

Sites Proposed for the Capital, 1782–1791
(Graphics by Stephen Kraft)

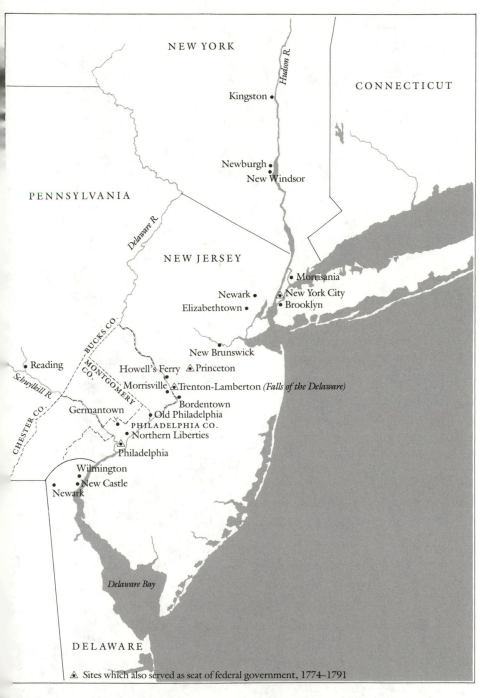

NEW YORK

Hudson R.

CONNECTICUT

Kingston •

Newburgh •
New Windsor

PENNSYLVANIA

Delaware R.

NEW JERSEY

• Morrisania

Newark •   ▲ New York City
Elizabethtown •   • Brooklyn

• New Brunswick

• Reading

BUCKS CO.

MONTGOMERY CO.

Howell's Ferry ▲ Princeton

Schuylkill R.

Morrisville ▲ Trenton-Lamberton *(Falls of the Delaware)*

CHESTER CO.

Germantown   • Bordentown
              • Old Philadelphia
      PHILADELPHIA CO.
       • Northern Liberties

▲ Philadelphia

• Wilmington
  • New Castle
Newark

Delaware Bay

DELAWARE

▲ Sites which also served as seat of federal government, 1774–1791

tes Proposed for the Capital, 1782–1791
*(*raphics by Stephen Kraft)

Congress Embarked on Board the Ship Constitution. . . , 1790

After the word [inserted: rejected] ⟨5th⟩ Line strike out & to the end of the clause and insert.

On the River Potowmack at some place between the mouths of the Eastern branch and Connogocheague be, and the same is hereby accepted for the permanent seat of the government of the United States, provided nevertheless that the operation of the laws of the state within such district shall not be affected by the acceptance, until the time fixed for the removal of the government thereto, and until Congress shall otherwise by law provide.

Charles Carroll's Amendment to Seat of Government Bill,
29 June 1790
(Record Group 46, National Archives)

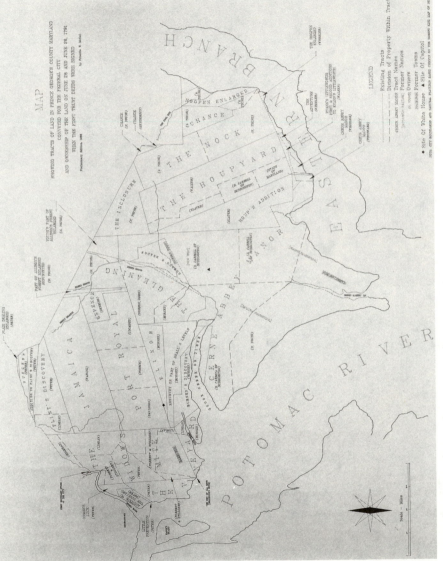

Tracts of Land Conveyed to the United States,
preliminary edition by Priscilla W. McNeil

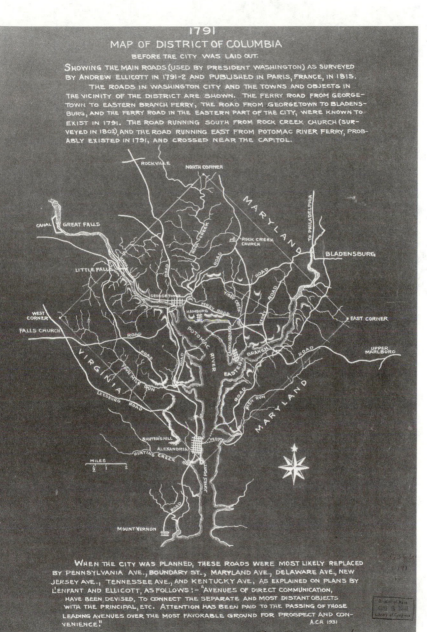

Map of the District of Columbia
by Artemas C. Harmon
(Library of Congress)

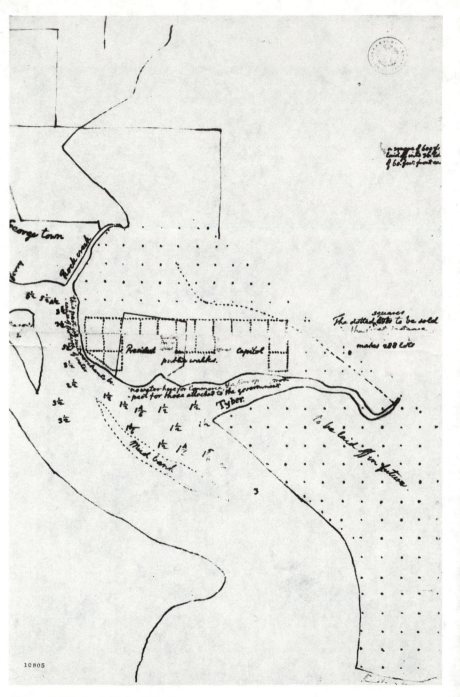

George town

The dotted squares to be sold
makes 288 Lots

President's
public walks.

Capitol

no water here for commerce or line of
pool for those attached to the government

Tyber.

Mud bank

To be laid off in future

10805

*Jefferson's Plan for the Federal City is a
dramatic contrast to that of Pierre L'Enfant, 1791*
(Jefferson Papers, Library of Congress)

Topographic Map of the District of Columbia
by Andrew Ellicott, showing L'Enfant's Plan for the Federal City, 1793
(Library of Congress)

Great Falls of the Potomac
by George Beck, 1802
(Library of Congress)

6

The Crisis of
the Union, 1789–1790

THE ACHIEVEMENTS OF THE FIRST SESSION OF THE First Federal Congress were monumental: a federal revenue system, the Amendments to the Constitution soon to be termed the Bill of Rights, and the organization of the executive and judicial branches of the federal government. Despite the fact that many of these issues had divided Americans throughout the Revolution, the session enjoyed unexpected harmony until the September seat of government debate.

Virginia Senator Grayson informed Patrick Henry that "the members would have parted [in] tolerable temper if the disagreeable altercations on the score of the seat of government had not left very sharp impressions on the minds of the Southern gentlemen." They "now begin to feel the observations of the Antis, when they informed them of the different interests in the Union and the probable consequences that would result therefrom [to] the Southern States who would be the milch cow out of whom the substance would be extracted." "The idea of a difference between carrying States and productive States and manufacturing States and slave States is not a mere phantom of the imagination," concluded Grayson.

Rep. Ames, who had complained earlier that the vile seat of government debate was "as fruitful of speeches, parties, and delays" as it had been in the Confederation Congress, concluded that only "the Lord knows what next session will produce in regard to that subject."[1] The Eastern States for whom Ames had become the primary spokesman would soon have reason to complain as loudly as the South about the implications of congressional decisions. Indeed, so much so that by the spring of 1790, prominent residents of New England began to suggest a familiar southern solution: disunion.

The Middle States, like the South, felt threatened by the seat of government debate. For the first time since the issue had come to the floor of Congress in 1783, the Eastern States had willingly supported a site south of the Delaware River. This generated arguments in the Middle States for an indefinite postponement of the question. Neither the Susquehanna nor the Potomac had a clear majority behind it and a hasty decision in favor of either could produce violence and destroy mutual confidence, if not the Union itself. Justice demanded that the public debt be funded before money was spent on the magnificent capital required by the dignity of the empire. Admission of new states would shift centrality. Only time would allow political passions to cool and the proper interior location to become evident. In the meantime, Philadelphia could serve as a central temporary residence.[2]

Some southerners welcomed the call for postponement. Several had expressed their dismay to Madison when the question first came to the floor in August. They considered a Potomac location the only cement strong enough to hold the Union together, and they would wait for the votes to become available. Madison, deeply affected by the intensity of the debate, was uncertain what course of action the South should follow. On the one hand, a long-term postponement had merit. Discussion of the issue would raise fresh objections in the Eastern States against expanding the Union westward and demands for a separation from the West. Pennsylvania would not readily support a capital to its south until such time as the election of its representatives by district brought in members from western Pennsylvania who recognized the importance of the Potomac to their constituencies.

On the other hand, when Madison considered the role that Vice President John Adams, heir apparent to the presidency, had played in the Senate, a long-term postponement appeared unwise. The implication of Adams's comments and votes was that the South should reach some agreement with Pennsylvania to place the capital on the Potomac while Washington remained in office. Immediately after the first session Madison received such a proposal from

Senator Morris. In summarizing the conversation for Washington, Madison doubted any arrangement could be made during the second session, considering Pennsylvania's bad faith during the first.

In the end, Madison concluded that an early decision was required in order to overcome sentiment for separation in the West as well as to maintain the harmony and even existence of the Union. This might mean that the Potomac would have to yield to the claims of the Susquehanna. He had implied as much to Washington in 1788 and the situation had only worsened. To prevent this the Eastern States and Pennsylvania would have to be persuaded that a Potomac capital was in their interest as well as the Union's. Senator Grayson of Virginia and Rep. Carroll of Maryland proposed a publicity campaign to Madison, and the next several months witnessed a significant propaganda effort by the Potomac Interest.[3]

In October 1789 appeared a lengthy pamphlet by the quixotic John O'Connor. A graduate of the University of Dublin, O'Connor had a checkered publishing career in the United States before moving to the Georgetown area in the late 1780s. There the enthusiastic man soon fell under the influence of Potomac Fever. He advertised his intention to edit a *Potomac Magazine,* and described one of his sources of information as a man so "well acquainted with the navigation of the Potomac, as if, probably, he claimed this knowledge a species of inheritance; though the doctrine of innate ideas . . . has been so long exploded." O'Connor's description of and praise for the river was more hyperbolic than anything written to support any location during the entire seven years of the debate. It even exceeded the prose of the English traveler who had written in 1784 that the Potomac was "certainly the most noble, excellent, and beautiful river . . . in the universe" where "every advantage, every elegance, every charm . . . is heaped with liberality and even profusion on the delightful banks of this most noble and superlatively grand river."

In *Political Opinions Particularly Respecting the Seat of the Federal Empire,* O'Connor implored Congress to center the great city on the Potomac. He called the Thames, the Seine and the Rhone rivulets compared with the Shenandoah, only one of many tributaries of the vast and luxuriant Potomac watershed. Its produce would soon "clothe and cherish the perishing sufferers in the wilds of

Siberia, as well as the pampered Alderman on the English Exchange." Providence had created a father to render the Potomac navigable, and "this *Father*—this instrument of Providence—this *chosen* secondary cause of every blessing to the human race," now served as president of the United States.

Like George Walker eight months earlier, O'Connor pointed to the flats between Georgetown and the Anacostia as the specific location for the capital. The climate was temperate and the place defensible enough to "shelter the Archives of the United States from the Invasions and Cannons of the Universe." The Potomac below the site, he claimed, could harbor 10,000 ships the size of Noah's Ark, and the Anacostia alone had room for all the ships on the Thames. John Carroll's arguments for establishing his academy at Georgetown served as an introduction for O'Connor's description of the town and its intelligent citizenry. A diversity of landscapes stimulated one's senses at Georgetown and the hills above the Anacostia provided ample space for the mansions of ambassadors. If this site—a center "without any parallel on the terraqueous globe"—was chosen for the capital, Americans would within a decade see a city more superb and powerful than London. It would be regarded with rapture by the children of future ages as the only imperial city ever founded on the principles of liberty and reason. On a more practical level, O'Connor reminded New England readers that Alexandria and Georgetown already had solid commercial ties with Massachusetts and Rhode Island.[4]

The most far-reaching effort of the Potomac Interest, and the most original of any promotional group, began in December. At a meeting called early that month to discuss strategy for a campaign to bring Congress to the Potomac, several leading citizens of Georgetown and Alexandria, most with ties to the Potomac Navigation Company, agreed to send a broadside appeal to the New Englanders. Signed by David Stuart, George Walker and other Georgetowners and Alexandrians, the broadside was mailed to the selectmen and other influential citizens of several New England towns. It quickly found its way into the press. The means employed—direct communication between the South and New England—was reminiscent of the politics of pre–Revolutionary War years.

Stuart crafted the final version. Educated at William and Mary and in Europe, Stuart, a Potomac Company investor, practiced both medicine and politics. He had represented Alexandria in the Virginia legislature and declined to represent it in the First Federal Congress despite the fact that he had been Washington's choice. Closely tied to the Washington family by marriage, he enjoyed an intimate relationship with the president. Stuart confessed to Washington that he expected the sagacious New Englanders would laugh at the "flaming" account by which southerners attempted to teach them their true economic interest.

Stuart began with the claim that the citizens of Georgetown and Alexandria believed the establishment of the capital carried greater importance for the present and future welfare of the country than any other issue except ratification of the Constitution. He dismissed arguments for placing it at the center of either population or wealth, since these fluctuated like the winds, and insisted that location at the center of territory paid greater attention to posterity and perpetual union. The Potomac would act to preserve the connection with the western country better than any other river, a consideration which required the utmost attention of the Atlantic States.

Next, Stuart described the navigation, extent and products of the Potomac, quoting Thomas Jefferson on the relationship between the Potomac and the western waters to show how the Potomac constituted a better route to the West than the Hudson, since it required a mere seventeen mile portage. The broadside noted the defensibility of the Potomac, the healthiness of the residents, the fertility of the soil, the salubrity of the climate, the fishing and the availability and abundance of building materials and coal.

A special appeal to New England's economic interests concluded the missive. Georgetown and Alexandria merchants lacked capital and owned few ships. This, Stuart suggested, provided an opportunity for New England investment which could not be expected if the seat of government were placed on the Susquehanna or the Delaware, where Baltimore and Philadelphia would engross the whole commerce to themselves. Finally, the agricultural and manufactured goods of the Eastern States would be in much greater demand on the Potomac than elsewhere.[5]

The Potomac Interest also sought the endorsement of the Virginia legislature, which early in December offered Congress jurisdiction over any ten mile square in the state. Authored by Henry Lee, the politically strategic bill stated that the best site for the capital lay far up the Potomac where the State of Pennsylvania as well as Maryland and Virginia could share the benefits. This appeal to Pennsylvania, however, did not mean that any part of the federal district need be in that state. The implication was nevertheless strong that the place Virginia had in mind lay between Williamsport and Cumberland, near Hancock, Maryland, four miles south of Pennsylvania.

Within a week after speedily adopting the act, the legislature passed two supporting resolutions despite some opposition by members from districts south of the James River. The first called on the governor to inform Congress of the state of Potomac navigation. The governor turned immediately to the Potomac Navigation Company for assistance and the data soon arrived. This, along with a map of the Potomac watershed and apparently a copy of Stuart's broadside, was sent to Congress. The second resolution called on the governor to transmit to Maryland a copy of the act of cession and to propose that it unite with Virginia in an offer of jurisdiction and money. If Congress accepted a cession on the Potomac from either or both states, Virginia would provide Congress $120,000 for erecting public buildings if Maryland would advance $72,000 for the same purpose. The resolution did not arrive at Annapolis in time for the Maryland legislature to act, or at least not in time for it to overcome internal divisions between the Potomac and Upper Chesapeake interests.[6]

In January 1790 "The Federal City Ought to be on the Potomac" appeared in the *Maryland Journal,* published at Baltimore. Its anonymous author, possibly George Walker, called the upcoming decision on the location of the capital the most important before the United States because it would determine whether the Union of North, South and West would survive or dissolve into the horrors of civil commotion. Providence had designated for the capital a site on the Potomac between Georgetown and Alexandria, the north-south center of the Union. Quoting at length from Stuart's broad-side, the author also directed his own special arguments to the New Englanders. The West contained the greatest treasure in the universe and in a century might become the most opulent and populated place on the globe. New Englanders already carried the trade of the Potomac and could be expected to dominate it when the new capital became the largest commercial city in America. Also, the Potomac offered New England the closest connection to its settlements on the Ohio River.[7]

The final effort of the Potomac Interest was *The Expostulations of Potomac,* a broadside widely reprinted in the New England press. Its author, General Adam Stephen of Martinsburg, Virginia, also relied heavily on Stuart's arguments. New York should support the Potomac, Stephen maintained, because it could thereby retain the temporary residence of Congress. If Congress placed its seat at Germantown, it would be drawn into the Philadelphia vortex. New Englanders, he hoped, were cognizant of the fact that if the seat of government moved to the Potomac, its "waters will groan under the pressure of New England manufactures" being conveyed west.[8]

Although Rep. Jeremiah Wadsworth expected Hartford, Connecticut, to reply to the broadside in a civil manner, most of New England's public response to the Potomac Interest's efforts came in the form of not so civil newspaper articles. One condemned those Virginians who threatened to leave the Union if Congress did not situate its seat of government in Virginia. Another jocularly advocated Newport, Rhode Island, the universally acknowledged garden of America, for the capital. The access of the Potomac to the West was unimportant, it claimed, compared with Newport's access to Canada, which would join the Union because of its proximity to the capital.[9]

The French attache clearly recognized the profound difference between the business of the first and second sessions of the First Federal Congress. The first, he explained to the French government, had as its aim the organization of the government while the second would be more important and more delicate because it would deal with finances and defense. He hoped the discussion would cause no schism. "A third object, much less interesting, may give a more perceptible shock to the new confederation. It is the eternal discussion about the residence. The champions of the two parties are more excited than ever." "It is pursued here very heatedly and . . . has already nearly broken up the confederation," he concluded.[10]

When the second session convened in January 1790, the two most active participants in the seat of government debate of the first session had not yet arrived at New York. Robert Morris remained at Philadelphia, allegedly to avoid a second defeat by calling for the postponed bill at the opening of the session as he had promised. James Madison lay sick with dysentery at Georgetown, under the care of Dr. David Stuart. Despite their absence Congress disposed of the bill immediately, if indirectly. The body lacked rules about the status of business unfinished at the end of a session. The Pennsylvanians, led by William Maclay and Thomas Hartley, the Susquehanna's strongest advocates, argued that matters should be resumed as if there had been no adjournment in order to save valuable time. The eastern and southern members insisted that everything be treated as new business, and they had the votes. Thus Congress established, and retained for half a century, a joint rule in order to kill a specific bill. Maclay concluded from this omen that no part of Pennsylvania would be considered as a site for the capital during the second session.[11] Officially, the residence question remained off the floor until it came up in the Senate late in May. Unofficially, the issue was ever–present.

From January through May the issue which dominated the attention of Congress, particularly the House, was the finances of the United States. In January Secretary of the Treasury Alexander Hamilton submitted a report on public credit which espoused that form of economic organization which has come to be known as financial capitalism. He proposed a long–term funding system to guarantee regular payment of the interest on the revolutionary war debt and the eventual payment of the principal. He argued that such a system would revive the credit of the United States and foster economic growth. In addition, Hamilton called on Congress to assume into the federal debt most of the war debt of the states, expecting that such an assumption would act to cement the Union more closely while tying state creditors to the success of the federal government. And he promised to submit a bill creating a national bank.

While some members favored paying off the debt rapidly through the sale of public lands or discriminating between original holders of the debt and those who had purchased it, Congress supported all of Hamilton's program except assumption. The political implications of assumption stirred up the old centralist-decentralist debate and exacerbated the sectional tensions left by the 1789 seat of government debate. Northerners, even many decentralists, welcomed the proposal as a means of escaping their state debt or as a force for political stability. Southerners (except for South Carolina) saw assumption as an unconstitutional seizure of state authority which might lead to a consolidation of the states in a unitary or national government. That the Northern States had larger debts than the southern ones (except for South Carolina), that northerners held much of the southern debt certificates and that southern records lay in disarray intensified the sectional division.[12]

All the Antifederalists in Congress should have opposed assumption as an unconstitutional invasion of states' rights. Instead, economic and sectional considerations proved more important determining factors. The two Massachusetts Antifederalists supported assumption as a means of bailing out their debt–ridden state. Gerry used antifederal arguments to defend his position: to leave the debt on the states would depress them and provide fuel to those who sought to abolish them. Both New York Antifederalists opposed assumption as did two of the three Virginia Antifederalists. The third was Theodorick Bland, whose position probably resulted from reluctance to support his long–time political enemy, Madison. Both North Carolina Antifederalists opposed it. South Carolina's three Antifederalists reluctantly obeyed the instructions of their state legislature and supported it, although Thomas Sumter waited until the last moment.[13]

Madison led the anti–assumptionists in the House. This publicly confirmed the change of mind which he had first intimated during the the seat of government debate in September: he would act more consciously as a decentralist, a southerner and a Virginian. Rep. Theodore Sedgwick of Massachusetts considered him an apostate, most likely a convert to antifederalism but perhaps preparing to assume leadership of a party of all the discontended. Other New Englanders also expressed their alarm. Support for Madison came from the Marylanders, all the Virginians save Bland, the Georgians and the North Carolinians, whose arrival at Congress in the spring guaranteed a majority against assumption. The representatives of Connecticut, Massachusetts, Delaware and South Carolinia favored assumption; a majority of the New Hampshire delegation supported it in the spring, but voted against it in the summer.

This sectional split left the evenly divided delegations of three Middle States, New York, New Jersey and Pennsylvania, open to lobbying by both sides. Week after week, despite every effort of the primarily northern forces supporting assumption, Madison prevented the House from including it in the funding bill. The critical vote came on 12 April when it lost in the committee of the whole, 31 to 29. Maclay, who saw assumption as the bedrock of a consolidated empire permanently seated at New York, witnessed the vote from the House gallery and heard the devastated northerners threaten a dissolution of the Union.[14]

Many congressmen saw Pennsylvania's large, eight-man delegation as the key to the fate of assumption. Thomas Hartley, Thomas Fitzsimons, George Clymer and Henry Wynkoop supported it. Peter Muhlenberg, Daniel Hiester, Thomas Scott and Speaker Frederick Muhlenberg opposed. The latter two and Hartley were not adamant, and this especially rendered Pennsylvania's votes subject to bargain. On 26 April the delegation joined the South in a vote not to reconsider the issue. Senator Philip Schuyler of New York condemned the three representatives from his state who opposed assumption, concluding that their support would have defused Pennsylvania's powerful position and guaranteed that Congress remain at New York City for many years.[15]

The long debate over assumption was not the only issue to intensify sectional divisions. In March the House devoted a week to a heated debate over petitions calling on Congress to discourage slavery, especially the slave trade. The Constitution implicitly reserved the power of emancipation to the states and expressly forbade Congress from outlawing the slave trade prior to 1808.

Nevertheless, one petition urged Congress to go to the limits of its powers to emancipate slaves, thus freeing the United States from an institution so inconsistent with the character of the American People. The impassioned South Carolinians and Georgians believed even consideration of the petitions fell beyond the ken of Congress, and they seized the occasion to attack the Eastern States and Pennsylvania. Thomas Tudor Tucker of South Carolina declared that the South would never submit to a federal grab for the power of emancipation without civil war.

The status of Rhode Island, the only state not to ratify the Constitution, had sectional implications too. John Adams believed it to be betraying the interests of New England, but southerners effectively opposed northern legislation designed to force it to ratify. When Rhode Island rejoined the Union late in May, Senator Schuyler considered the event pleasing to all who supported the interests of the Eastern States, and predicted, with the admission of Vermont, an ascendancy in the Union for the states north and east of the Delaware River.[16] Washington's potentially fatal illness in May gave Americans reason to ponder the feasibility of union without him.[17]

Southerners, particularly those who lived near the Potomac, confirmed the growth of sectional tensions. The 1789 seat of government debate had stirred up apprehensions in the minds of many of the warmest friends of the federal government in Virginia, confirming their opinion that the decision to remain at New York in 1788 had constituted only the first instance of northern oppression. One concluded after the 1789 debate that, if the conduct of the Eastern States continued, it would "teach us no longer to look upon the Union as 'the rock of our salvation,' nor to consider 'a whisper about separate confederacies as treason.'"

Henry Lee, among the more passionate in his reaction to political events, wondered whether the constitutional revolution of 1787–1788 would produce half the good predicted by its friends, and whether the seat of government debate had not proven beyond doubt the danger of associating with the Eastern States in a form of government in which the South was outnumbered. In response to the sectional tensions at Congress in the spring of 1790, Lee swamped Madison with letters. He concluded early in March that moving the seat of government nearer the center of territory would be one way to prevent the South from either being a slave to the North or having to cut the Gordian knot of union. In April he declared that Patrick Henry's prophecies during the ratification debate about northern domination of the Union had been proven without doubt and that civil war seemed inevitable. "To disunite is dreadful to my mind, but dreadful as it is, I consider it a lesser evil than union on the present conditions. I had rather myself submit to all the hazards of war and risk the loss of every thing dear to me in life, than to live under the rule of a fixed insolent northern majority." Madison held a more optimistic prospect for the Union, but cautioned Lee not to interpret this as meaning that he held much hope of Congress's moving to the Potomac.[18]

David Stuart reported directly to Washington about the rapidly growing dissatisfaction with the Union in Virginia. Like Madison, Washington attempted to calm the troubled Potomac waters. He regretted the situation, but, he argued to Stuart, everyone knew that certain matters particularly interested the Eastern States and that they pursued them steadily. The Southern States had interests of equal concern even though they failed to protect them as well. The success of the American Empire depended on a spirit of accommodation between the two sections. Would not Virginia and any other states which left the Union with her be the weaker party? Washington's rare candor did not mollify Stuart. While the assumption debate dragged on at New York, he informed the president that Antifederal fears that Congress would grasp power by unwarranted constructions of the Constitution would be verified, that Madison had gained great popularity because of his stand against Hamilton and that much advantage had been taken of the debate on slavery to disturb Virginian minds.[19]

The vote against assumption somewhat soothed southerners. Nevertheless, they reported continued discontent to the southern members of Congress, many of whom increasingly recognized the influence of section within Federal Hall and the need for stronger southern leadership in the Senate. Federalist Rep. Alexander White stressed "the necessity of supporting our State Governments in full vigor, if we to the South of the Potomac mean to appear in any other character than Colonies."[20]

Before the vote against assumption, most public discontent with the new government lay in the South. That vote raised fundamental questions in the North, particularly at Boston where the federal government's "best and most *substantial friends* are chagrined, mortified, and disappointed, and appear ready to say or do any thing to release themselves from a government that are not disposed to do them common justice." Another Bostonian cautioned that "unless some chain of more and stronger links than now binds the union" could be forged, at the death of President Washington "the American People cease to exist as a nation"; "and let me ask what other chain [is] so binding as that of involving the interests of the men of property in the prosperity of the Government." A newspaper in Hartford, Connecticut, predicted that a final rejection of assumption would shake the government to its center and turn the creditors to the states for redress, thus undermining the Constitution.[21]

One disgusted Connecticut assumptionist, incorrectly concluding that the slavery debate had caused southerners to oppose assumption, groused that Congress should "prefer the white People of this country to the Blacks. After they have taken care of the former they may amuse themselves with the other People." "People seem almost ripe for a national division of North and South," concluded one of Goodhue's constituents, who thought perhaps such action might be premature. "I really fear that some of my old friends both in Virginia and Massachusetts hold not in horror as much as I do a division of this Continent into two or three nations and have not an equal dread of civil war," rued Vice President John Adams even before the April vote.[22]

With talk of disunion and even civil war on the rise, especially at such proven seats of radical solution as Boston and the Potomac, with the South and Pennsylvania fuming over the continued residence of Congress so far north, and with the North angry over the refusal of Congress to assume the state debts, a fundamental compromise of almost constitutional magnitude appeared the only solution. From April to June various congressmen sought to resolve the assumption and seat of government issues by linking them in such a compromise between the North and South. For more than two months they succeeded only in complicating, frustrating and all but bringing the legislative process to a standstill as proposals for bargains were rumored, floated and attempted.

The Pennsylvanians, more concerned about immediate action on the residence question than other congressmen, naturally enough pursued the opportunity first. By March they had returned to their early 1789 plan to move Congress to Philadelphia without determining the permanent residence at the same time. To achieve this, some of the delegation advocated using its leverage on assumption by an agreement either with the South to vote against assumption or with the North to vote for it in exchange for moving to Philadelphia. Early in April, as the critical vote approached, the Pennsylvanians carried a proposal to the pro-assumption delegations from Massachusetts and South Carolina. Rep. Clymer discussed it at length with William Jackson, a Pennsylvanian serving as an aide to Washington. Senator Maclay, who considered it improper that a presidential aide be involved in congressional negotiations, argued to the delegation against any bargain. Since removal to Philadelphia had support from both assumptionists and anti-assumptionists, he thought it wisest to postpone the vote on assumption and take up the question of a move to Philadelphia while both groups still courted Pennsylvania. This became Pennsylvania's tactic, although not early enough to prevent the 12 April vote.[23]

On 11 April conflicting rumors about a residence–assumption bargain spread. New Englanders heard that Virginia and Maryland had promised their votes for an adjournment to Philadelphia in exchange for Pennsylvania's against assumption. Rep. George Thatcher of Massachusetts understood that the Pennsylvanians would vote against assumption the next day and then vote for it later in the session if Massachusetts would first vote for removal to Philadelphia. Since Pennsylvania would always hold the balance between the Northern and Southern States, Thatcher worried about furthering its influence by seating the federal government within its borders. He threatened to vote for a Potomac capital rather than submit to blackmail by the chauvinistic Pennsylvanians.[24]

The contrived appearance of votes against assumption by half of the Pennsylvania representatives on 12 April gave credence to a widespread belief among assumptionists that Pennsylvania withheld votes for assumption as a lever to carry Congress to

Philadelphia. "I clearly see," Rep. Goodhue warned a constituent, "that until we reside in a more central situation where attempts for removal should be trivial and ineffectual . . . we never shall be able to decide upon any great National concern in which the Northern and Southern States may be divided, simply upon its merits."[25]

When supporters of assumption attempted once again in mid-May to attach it to the House funding bill, both sides accused Pennsylvania of proposing bargains. South Carolina's Rep. William L. Smith complained that "the plain English is that the assumption must be kept back till the close of the session and then we shall be made to understand that unless we vote for Philadelphia, the State debts will not be provided for." New Yorkers feared South Carolina would make such a deal in order to get its debt assumed. Many New York City and Philadelphia residents believed Congress would adjourn to Philadelphia as a result of some sort of an agreement between its friends and those advocating assumption.[26]

Senator Morris cautioned his wife not to place confidence in reports circulating at Philadelphia about the expected arrival of Congress because none of the Pennsylvania delegation liked to discourage the hopes of constituents. Nevertheless, he expected that Philadelphia would succeed at last despite the attention New Yorkers lavished on the federal government. The delegation had decided to raise the question of a removal to Philadelphia in the Senate. Not even a proposal from the Eastern States to place the permanent residence at the falls of the Delaware, communicated to Senator Morris by Rep. Elias Boudinot, could sway Pennsylvania's resolve not to discuss the permanent seat. It fell to Senators Maclay and Morris to plan tactics. The two disagreed over whether to leave New York at the end of the session or at the close of the First Congress in March 1791. Presidential aide William Jackson and New Hampshire Senator John Langdon persuaded Morris to accept Maclay's position for removal at the end of the session. "Sleeping or waking for a week past, I have scarce thought of any thing but a removal of Congress," Maclay professed to Benjamin Rush; "to relate all our small difficulties and delays would be to write a volume."[27]

On 24 May Morris moved that Congress hold its next session at Philadelphia. He counted on the votes of a coalition composed of New Hampshire, which since 1787 had supported Philadelphia in most of its efforts to regain Congress; the three Delaware River States, which saw benefits from the location; and the two Potomac River States, which would have the satisfaction of moving Congress to a more central spot where their interests would be better served. Except for James Gunn of Georgia, the senators of the three Lower South States did not support Philadelphia. Their states had closer commercial and social ties with New York. Some of them disliked Philadelphia's political and anti-slavery climate, and they believed a temporary residence there would make it difficult to secure a capital south of the Delaware River. This coalition gave Philadelphia thirteen votes, a majority if Paterson, who spoke for that part of New Jersey tied to New York, and Gunn held firm.

Morris's motion came up for debate two days later. Advocates of New York City, led by Senators Rufus King of New York and Pierce Butler of South Carolina, argued that Philadelphia was not central enough and that Congress would be stuck once it went there. Maclay pointed out that historical precedent showed Philadelphia to be preferred for continental meetings and that Congress would have to leave Philadelphia eventually because Pennsylvania had refused to offer Congress jurisdiction over its only port. On a vote to postpone debate, both Paterson and Gunn abandoned the Philadelphia coalition and postponement carried 13 to 11.[28]

The next day it became clear why postponement had carried. Butler informed the Senate that he would bring in a bill to fix the permanent seat of government. Morris immediately withdrew his motion for a removal to Philadelphia, and Fitzsimons introduced it in the House, where the funding bill had just been ordered engrossed for its third and final reading without provision for assumption. On 31 May the House considered Fitzsimons's resolution. Supporters of New York attempted to attach a provision for the permanent seat on the Delaware. Its inclusion threatened to split the coalition committed only to a removal from New York. Arguing on behalf of deciding on the permanent and temporary residences in conjunction with each other, Gerry insisted that the dispute over the location of the capital retarded every great question and if a permanent seat were not chosen first, Congress would be dragged about from Williamsburg to Marietta on the Ohio River. The amendment failed and the House adopted the Fitzsimons resolution 38 to 22, with Massachusetts carefully dividing its votes in half in hopes of not alienating potential assumption supporters in the New York and Pennsylvania delegations.

While the House debated its resolve, in the Senate Butler introduced his bill to establish a temporary and permanent seat of government. The bill contained blanks instead of specific places, although rumors of an arrangement to place Congress on the Potomac after a few years at New York, the only effective strategy the North had against an immediate removal to Philadelphia, proved true. Maryland and Virginia remained committed to deciding only the temporary residence, but much to Madison's dismay the six Lower South senators all agreed to support a New York–Potomac seat of government bill.

Because of tie–breaking votes by Adams, both the bill and the House resolution for an adjournment to Philadelphia went to a committee chaired by Butler. The committee stalled for a week as it waited for the arrival of senators from Rhode Island, which had just ratified the Constitution. Reported to the Senate on 7 June, the bill proposed that the permanent seat be on the east bank of the Potomac in Maryland and that the Senate fill the blank for the temporary residence. Butler claimed that the key reason for the Potomac, in addition to its centrality, was that it acted to preserve the Union. Although Congress could name Georgetown as the specific place on the Potomac if a majority insisted upon a tidewater capital, he made clear his preference for an upriver location such as the rich, level and highly cultivated country near the mouth of Conococheague Creek where Pennsylvania, Maryland and Virginia could all share in the benefits. Butler claimed such a site would tie the coastal states to Fort Pitt and the western country. Surely, he concluded, "God and Nature intended this situation as the bond of our Union."[29]

That evening all eleven senators committed to an adjournment to Philadelphia without a decision on the permanent seat dined together. They agreed to call up the House resolution and to vote against any place proposed as a permanent seat, including the Potomac. The Senate proceedings the next day were fast, confusing and full of maneuvers by both sides. Philadelphia's advocates attempted to postpone Butler's bill in order to take up the House resolution. South Carolina moved to postpone the motion for post-ponement. The Senate tied and Adams voted against postponing postponement.

The Butler forces immediately sent for Senators Samuel Johnston of North Carolina and William Few of Georgia, who had been too ill to attend. Few came first. After Johnston arrived on the Senate floor, with his bed and two doctors, the House resolution lost 13 to 11. Next the Senate took up the Butler bill. Neither the east bank of the Potomac nor any other place could obtain the necessary votes to become the permanent seat because of the agreement of the evening before. Having made no progress, a motion to adjourn carried. Butler's bill, which Fitzsimons believed originated with Alexander Hamilton, had to be abandoned until the North could add the two Rhode Island votes.[30]

The Pennsylvanians refused to accept the Senate's defeat of the House resolution for Philadelphia as final and reintroduced the motion in the House. This, along with the lack of progress on But-ler's bill, led to an offer from New York to give Pennsylvania the permanent seat in exchange for two more years at New York. But Pennsylvania held firm in its alliance with Maryland and Virginia for a removal without mention of the permanent seat. The Phila-delphia forces attempted to rally on 10 June when, because of a storm, the ailing Johnston could not be carried to the Senate. If the motion for a removal to Philadelphia could be passed immediately and sent up to the Senate, it might be adopted. Representatives Gerry and William L. Smith however ate away the time with speeches which outlasted the storm. The next day the North, with the help of three Marylanders, amended the resolution so that the adjournment was to Baltimore rather than Philadelphia. But "we gain useless victories," Ames wrote home; "I would not find fault with Fort Pitt, if we could assume the debts, and proceed in peace and quietness. But this despicable grog-shop contest, whether the taverns of New York or Philadelphia shall get the custom of Con-gress keeps us in discord, and covers us all with disgrace."[31]

Unable to proceed with Butler's seat of government bill, the Senate took up the House funding bill. Northern senators over-whelmingly supported assumption while the South, except for South Carolina, opposed it just as vehemently. The division found the Senate evenly split. Led by Morris, those assumptionists who favored a removal to Philadelphia without determining the permanent seat made it known that they would not vote to attach assumption to the House bill, but implied that they would support a separate bill once the residence question had been decided. This tactic persuaded Rep. Thatcher that an agreement, or at least a good understanding, existed to make the assumption serve as a pack horse to transport Congress to Philadelphia.[32] It became clear to many congressmen that assumption could not pass the Senate until the residence question had been settled. Consideration of proposals to compromise on the two issues assumed a new seriousness.

On Friday evening, 11 June, Morris, newly appointed Assistant Secretary of the Treasury Tench Coxe and presidential aide William Jackson joined Representatives Clymer and Fitzsimons at their lodgings to discuss a bargain. These pro–assumption Philadelphians, having been blocked in the House and the Senate in attempts to carry the temporary residence to Philadelphia, stood ready to abandon their southern allies and promise Pennsylvania's votes for assumption in exchange for the permanent seat in their state. Morris knew Hamilton to be the key to northern votes on the residence question, and he requested that they feign an accidental meeting early the next morning at the Battery.

Morris found Hamilton waiting for him. Nearby was the newly laid cornerstone of the mansion which the State of New York was building for the president as an inducement to Congress to remain at New York, but this proved no deterrent. Hamilton asked Morris to secure one vote for assumption in the Senate and five in the House. If Morris got them, Hamilton promised that the permanent seat would go to Germantown or the falls of the Delaware. Interpreting his position to be strong, Morris insisted that the temporary residence move to Philadelphia as part of the deal. The two men parted.

The needed votes could be secured from Pennsylvania alone: five of its representatives—Hartley had switched sides—and Senator Maclay opposed assumption. But since Maclay refused to promise anything, Morris and Fitzsimons took Senator George Read of Delaware on a Sunday ride into the country and talked him into switching his vote. The assumptionists now had a majority in both houses. But Hamilton could not persuade New York and New England to give Pennsylvania both the temporary and permanent seats. Unable to meet Morris's terms, Hamilton apparently had Coxe sound out Maclay early Monday morning as to whether he and the Pennsylvania representatives would vote for assumption if Congress placed the permanent seat on the Susquehanna in Pennsylvania. Maclay refused the temptation.[33]

On 14 June the Senate debated a motion by Oliver Ellsworth of Connecticut that Congress assume the state debts. Assumptionists supporting a transfer of the government to Philadelphia held firm on their threat to block assumption until the residence question had been decided, and the motion was tabled. At any time during the next ten days, before the arrival of Rhode Island's anti–assumption senators, assumption could have passed if its pro–Philadelphia supporters had not blocked action. Next the Senate took up a motion to postpone the House resolution for an adjournment to Baltimore. Ellsworth considered postponement essential if the Senate were to make progress on other business, arguing that the residence question had "mixed itself with all our affairs" and complained of "a secret understanding, a bargaining, that ran through all our proceedings." Postponement carried by the now familiar 13 to 11 vote, a key defeat for those favoring Philadelphia. They had hoped to knock Baltimore out of the resolution and restore Philadelphia, thereby deciding the matter before the arrival of Rhode Island's senators, who favored New York City.[34]

By mid–June, after five months of intense debate and politicking, Congress had accomplished nothing in regard to assumption or the location of the United States capital. The coalition favoring a removal to Philadelphia without deciding on the permanent seat had been stopped in both houses. Butler's bill had been stalled because of the inability of a majority of the Senate to agree on the permanent seat. The House had refused to assume the state debts and the Senate had tabled discussion.

"Negotiations, cabals, meetings, plots and counterplots have prevailed for months past without yet ripening to any decision," Rep. William L. Smith complained. Thomas Jefferson, who had assumed his duties as secretary of state at the end of March, soon recognized how tensions between the North and South so crippled

Congress that, although it met every day, little or nothing could be done because of mutual distrust and antipathy. The situation had become so intolerable by the end of May that Madison reportedly considered forcing Congress to adjourn, a solution Massachusetts Rep. Sedgwick thought wise under the circumstances.[35] Congress had reached its first impasse under the new Constitution.

7

The Compromise of 1790

THREE POLITICALLY ASTUTE VIRGINIANS PONDERED the congressional impasse and the fact that the Pennsylvanians and the Eastern States were negotiating through Robert Morris and Alexander Hamilton about the terms of a residence–assumption bargain. The success of such a scheme would doom the dream of an American Empire centered on the Potomac River and dominated by Virginia. George Washington, Thomas Jefferson and James Madison, who had sought for seven years to place the United States capital on the Potomac recognized the moment at hand.

Washington's concern for discretion, and Madison's and Jefferson's willingness to honor it, mask his exact role. Several facts suggest that the two men worked closely with the president as the bargain evolved. Madison had kept Washington well informed about the politics of the residence debates in 1788 and 1789. The president's aides had been involved in various stages of the pre–June bargaining and showed their delight publicly when a Potomac seat of government bill finally passed Congress. Even more indicative were his central importance to the political process, his Potomac Fever and his almost fanatic attention to the development of the capital from July 1790 until his retirement.

On 15 June Jefferson proposed to Robert Morris that Pennsylvania and the South agree to support a fifteen–year temporary residence at Philadelphia and a permanent residence at Georgetown. Assumption was not involved. Morris called a meeting of the Pennsylvania delegation that evening and laid both the Hamilton and Jefferson proposals before it. The delegation rejected Hamilton's proposition for the permanent residence at Germantown or the

182

falls of the Delaware River, with the temporary residence remaining at New York, in exchange for Pennsylvania votes for assumption. Nor did it show much enthusiasm for Jefferson's proposal to reunite the removal from New York and the permanent residence, despite the attraction of the fifteen years at Philadelphia.[1]

Madison, at the same time, let the Massachusetts delegation know that the South would no longer block assumption, given modification of it and certain understandings about the residence of Congress. He told them he feared that Pennsylvania would soon cancel its agreement with Maryland and Virginia not to consider the permanent residence in 1790, and that, as a result, the bargain being discussed between the Eastern States and Pennsylvania to assume the state debts and place the capital in Pennsylvania would forever deprive the Potomac. Instead of dealing with the Pennsylvanians, he proposed that the Eastern States deal with Virginia. Madison offered to provide votes for a modified assumption if, instead of fixing the permanent residence in Pennsylvania, enough votes could be found to pass an act empowering Washington to adjourn Congress to Philadelphia in 1792. For the Massachusetts delegation, assumption suddenly and unexpectedly began to show signs of revival and their spirits lifted.[2]

The Pennsylvanians, probably having learned of Madison's proposal to Massachusetts, took a more serious look at Jefferson's offer. It came back to them through Rep. George Mathews of Georgia. The fact that he might persuade some of his colleagues from the Lower South to drop their opposition to Philadelphia had strong impact. On 17 June Peter Muhlenberg summarized Pennsylvania's choice:

> It is now established *beyond a doubt* that the Secretary of the Treasury guides the movements of the Eastern Phalanx. . . . They now offer a carte blanche for the Permanent Seat provided we will join in carrying the assumption, and permit the temporary residence to remain here two years longer . . . . The Southern Members have some suspicion that a measure of this kind is in agitation and in order to counteract it, propose to fix the temporary Seat in Philadelphia for 10,

15, or 20 years, provided the Permanent Seat shall
then be on the Potomac. The Southern Members
have hitherto acted with great candor on this occasion, and I am inclined to accede to their proposal, because no conditions are annexed that may be thought
dishonorable, and because in the course of 15 or 20
years, circumstances may alter cases.

The negotiations between Pennsylvania and the southerners which
continued over the weekend of 19–20 June seemed serious enough
to the New Englanders that they caucused on Sunday night to discuss strategy.[3] It proved to be the last of many times since 1783 that
they discussed how to block locating the capital on the Potomac.

At the end of the week which had seen the Senate postpone
both the residence and assumption questions, Jefferson ran into a
distraught Hamilton in front of Washington's Broadway mansion.
Hamilton raised the subject of assumption and its necessity, stressing that New England would make it a *sine qua non* for the continuation of the Union. He went on to suggest that his usefulness as
secretary of the treasury was over if he could not carry the measure
through Congress, and appealed to Jefferson to make common
cause with him and bring success to the Washington Administration's efforts to assume the state debts. Specifically, Hamilton
asked him to seek southern support. Hamilton knew from
Madison's proposal to Massachusetts that the votes might be procured, given the right agreement on the residence question. As secretary of state, an office with wide–ranging domestic functions in
1790, Jefferson might have considered the residence question his
official concern, and, like Hamilton, been ready to push for legislation of particular interest to his department. The two secretaries
parted with Jefferson promising to consider the matter.

Immediately upon reaching his lodgings, he invited Hamilton
and Madison to dine alone with him so that they might seek "some
temperament for the present fever." Over dinner the next day
Madison agreed to provide the necessary southern votes to adopt a
modified assumption. He would not vote for it himself nor completely withdraw his opposition, but he would not be strident. In return, Madison sought assurance that the capital would be placed on

the Potomac. *He did not need any votes for a Philadelphia–Potomac seat of government bill.* What he needed from Hamilton was his influence with the New Englanders to prevent them from interfering yet again with the negotiations between Pennsylvania and the South.[4]

Two representatives had switched sides since Hamilton's 12 June estimate that he lacked five votes for assumption in the House. And, despite the addition of George Read, another senator had to change his position in order to counter the opposition of the new Rhode Island senators. Thus Madison needed to find three representatives and one senator willing to vote for assumption. Naturally he looked to the Maryland and Virginia delegations.

The fabulously wealthy Senator Charles Carroll, whose ten thousand acre estate lay just off the Potomac south of Frederick, Maryland, had never violently opposed assumption. Presented with the bargain, he agreed to provide the necessary vote in the Senate. The easiest representative to convince was Richard Bland Lee. His opposition to assumption had not been adamant either. He had hoped it could be postponed until a later session, but had long been prepared to vote for it under two conditions: that Virginia did not lose in the settlement of accounts and that "the seat of government was so stationed [as] to diffuse the wealth of the Capital in equal measures to the extremes of the empire." Madison must have promised that the seat of government bill would be so drafted that Alexandria, the chief town of Lee's congressional district, would be included within the federal district, for Lee reported that information to a constituent on 26 June.

Madison also secured the vote of Alexander White, who represented Virginia from Harpers Ferry westward to the Ohio River. White had been more opposed to assumption than Lee and, according to Jefferson, participated in the bargain with revulsion. Years later, Jefferson apparently became revolted with his own role, and sought to downplay and justify it on the ground that it had been necessitated by the need to appease the North, which had threatened disunion as a result of congressional opposition to assumption.[5]

Madison went to the Maryland representatives for the final vote. Apparently he brought the details of the bargain to several who had gathered for the purpose at Daniel Carroll's lodgings, assuring them that the public buildings would be restricted to the Maryland side of the Potomac. Carroll, who represented a district which included Georgetown and all of western Maryland, agreed to shift his vote. He had joined White in parliamentary maneuvers aimed at killing or delaying assumption, but his position had been more moderate. Also, he probably knew that Georgetown would compose part of the federal district.

Although Madison had found the three votes Hamilton needed, he searched out a fourth for security. Michael Jenifer Stone, a staunch opponent of assumption who represented the three lower western shore counties between the Potomac and the Chesapeake, refused. Taking advantage of the information, however, he began to sell property at Baltimore because of its inflated value as a rival capital site. Madison found the fourth vote elsewhere: George Gale, the long–time Potomac supporter from the lower eastern shore who had introduced the controversial proviso regarding navigation of the Susquehanna River into the 1789 residence debate.[6]

Having fulfilled his part of the arrangement, Madison informed Hamilton and then concentrated on making certain that Virginia's financial accounts with the federal government stood in the best possible light. Hamilton assured several of his Massachusetts supporters on 22 June that assumption would be added to the funding bill if a Philadelphia–Potomac seat of government bill passed Congress first. What Hamilton wanted from the Massachusetts delegation was assurance that it would not, as in 1789, support efforts to block the Philadelphia–Potomac scheme with a counteroffer to Pennsylvania. In addition, the senators from Massachusetts might have to vote against New York as the temporary residence and in favor of Philadelphia, but only if too many of the Lower South senators held out for New York. The idea of a Potomac capital displeased Massachusetts, but with assumption as its primary goal, the delegation agreed to Hamilton's request.[7]

On 23 June Hamilton told Morris that he no longer opposed Philadelphia as the temporary residence. According to Jefferson, Hamilton also convinced Morris that Pennsylvania must accept a ten–year (rather than fifteen–year) residence at Philadelphia. This was the price the Lower South demanded for supporting

Philadelphia rather than New York as the temporary residence. The following evening the Pennsylvania delegation caucused with Jonathan Elmer of West Jersey and the senators from Delaware, and all agreed to vote for a bill providing a ten-year temporary residence at Philadelphia and a permanent residence on the Potomac. On 25 June Carroll and Lee moved to resume consideration of Butler's bill in the Senate, but with the votes of the finally arrived Rhode Island senators, the motion was postponed over the weekend. The New York interest thereby gained a few more days to come up with an alternative to the Philadelphia–Potomac plan.[8]

As in 1787 and 1789, Rufus King led the fight for New York City. He had a busy and unpleasant weekend. Senator King suggested a permanent residence at Baltimore after four or five more years at New York, with the votes for assumption in the Senate and House to come from Maryland. Baltimore's representative, William Smith, agreed to vote for assumption, but found little support from his Potomac oriented House colleagues. The six senators from the Lower South promised King their votes if the measure could be carried in the Senate. Connecticut and Rhode Island agreed to it.

Both Massachusetts senators were essential to turn King's twelve senate votes for Baltimore into a fourteen vote majority and King devoted considerable effort to winning their votes when they showed a surprising reluctance. Both refused, and Hamilton had the uncomfortable job of explaining why to fellow New Yorkers King and Rep. John Laurance. Hamilton told them that "the funding system including the assumption is the primary national object. All subordinate points which oppose it must be sacrificed. . . . Agreeing to New York and Baltimore will defeat it, so that in the present state of things nothing but Philadelphia or Philadelphia and Potomac will ensure it. Massachusetts therefore will not agree to New York and Baltimore, because her object is the assumption." King realized that "if a bargain existed between the southern States, who wishing for the Seat of Government on the Potomac, Pennsylvania who wished Congress in Philadelphia and the Massachusetts people who were anxious for the assumption—the measure would succeed." Hamilton thus fulfilled his part of the dinner bargain with Jefferson and Madison.[9]

Although few people knew the precise details of the bargain, word spread quickly that the sectional impasse at Federal Hall had broken. By Sunday, 27 June, the Federalist editor John Fenno expected the upcoming week to "bring light, order and decision." Representatives Fisher Ames and Theodore Sedgwick agreed. Rep. Lee knew as well that "this week will decide the fate of the Potomac forever" and that the "harmonious conclusion of our session" depended much on the arrangement agreed to. "If it fails I fear we shall break up abruptly in disgust and confusion."[10]

On 28 June the Senate took up Butler's bill. A motion to make Baltimore the permanent residence lost when both Massachusetts senators opposed it. Carroll, who had joined his colleague from Maryland in voting against Baltimore, then moved that the permanent residence be on the Potomac between the Anacostia River and Conococheague Creek. By not specifying the east bank of the river as Butler had, the new language allowed for the inclusion of land in Virginia. The 16 to 9 vote in favor of the motion reflected the fact that the Potomac had the support not only of the Philadelphia–Potomac coalition but also, now that Baltimore had lost, of all the senators of the three Lower South States.

The question of the temporary residence brought on impassioned debate. A motion from the Lower South to remain at New York City carried by a single vote. This threatened the entire compromise. The next day, with the help of the Massachusetts senators, a new majority knocked New York City out of the bill. Carroll then moved that Congress stay at Philadelphia until 1800. Attempts to divide the ten years between New York and Philadelphia failed. But when the Senate tied 13 to 13 on Carroll's motion, Adams voted against it. The next day, 30 June, Butler moved reconsideration, confirming that the leading southern spokesman for remaining at New York had joined the Philadelphia–Potomac coalition. The Senate then voted 14 to 12 to place the temporary residence at Philadelphia.

On 1 July the bill had its final reading. Connecticut's Oliver Ellsworth endeavored to split the coalition at the last minute. He moved to amend the bill so that the permanent residence on the Potomac had to be placed within thirty miles of Hancock, Maryland. This limitation included the mouth of the Conococheague but not

Georgetown. Hancock lay less than four miles south of the Pennsylvania border, and the amendment held out the possibility of placing a sizable portion of the federal district in Pennsylvania. Despite the temptation Morris and Maclay refused to support the bargain-breaking proposal.

King made one final attempt to buy a little more time for New York. Would the Senate give it six more months, until the beginning of May 1791 when current leases expired? Butler thought the request fair and the Senate tied again. This time Adams voted against the amendment. King became so enraged that he accused his colleagues of bargains that would sever the Union. Nevertheless, the Senate passed the seat of government bill, 14 to 12. The ten senators of the five states from Pennsylvania south to North Carolina, Butler of South Carolina, James Gunn of Georgia, Jonathan Elmer of New Jersey and John Langdon of New Hampshire voted for the bill.[11]

The Senate vote produced considerable comment among congressmen. Senator Maclay thought his state could have done no better, considering the fact that Washington wanted a Potomac capital. "He, by means of Jefferson, Madison, [Charles] Carroll and others, urges the business. And, if we had not closed with these terms, a bargain would have been made for the temporary residence in New York." Marylanders and Virginians expressed delight. Rep. Stone, convinced that the bill would pass the House if none of its members died first and that Pennsylvania would be cemented to the southern interest, approached ecstasy: "Joy! Joy to Myself! Joy to my Country [Maryland]! Joy to the United States! Joy to the Lovers of Mankind!" He predicted that the capital would remain on the Potomac long after it ceased to be central, and, even if the government never actually came there, the very idea would convert the river into a field enriched by speculation. Madison informed James Monroe that "if the Potomac succeeds . . . it will have resulted from a fortuitous coincidence of circumstances which might never happen again." Massachusetts Rep. Thatcher agreed that only "a very singular combination of circumstance" could have produced a southern capital. Otherwise New Englanders kept silent. New York's bitterness more than filled the vacuum. Senator Philip Schuyler considered the bill indecent in light of everything his state

had done to accommodate Congress, and he and Senator Morris ex-
changed hot words at a dinner party.[12]

On 2 July the House received the seat of government bill. It
provided that the capital be located in a district of territory not exceeding ten miles square at some point on the Potomac River between the mouths of the Anacostia and Conococheague, and, that
in the meantime, Congress would meet at Philadelphia. Also included was the language that Madison had used to postpone the
1789 seat of government bill: state law remained operative in the
district until Congress provided otherwise. Further, the bill created
a presidential commission modeled after the one proposed a year
earlier. The president could appoint and keep full a three-man
commission which, under his direction, would survey a district, purchase or accept as much land on the Maryland side of the Potomac
as the president deemed necessary for the federal city and supervise the construction of public buildings. Finally, the president
could accept money for purposes of the act, but Congress appropriated only the "sufficient sum" necessary to transfer the capital to
the Potomac in December 1800.

The House opened debate on 6 July. The ripe rhetoric, the dire
predictions and the personal attacks played to packed galleries. In
particular, Senator Richard Henry Lee noticed all the lovely
women whose very presence, he protested, said "as you vote, so will
we smile. A severe trial for susceptible minds. And a very unfair (if I
may say that Ladies can do any thing unfair) whilst the abundant
beauty of Philadelphia had not an equal opportunity of showing its
wishes." This time Madison led a majority: all the members from
West Jersey to Georgia, except most of the South Carolinians and
William Smith and Joshua Seney, the two Marylanders with
Susquehanna River districts. It insisted that the bill be adopted
without amendment. Under no circumstances could it return to the
Senate.

In opposing the bill, the minority followed closely the tactics
and arguments used by the Senate minority. Claiming that the
Potomac was too far South, Aedanus Burke of South Carolina seconded a motion to substitute Baltimore. He described most of the
area proposed for the permanent residence as desert and questioned whether Congress really preferred a place in the woods to a

populous city. Recalling the behavior of the Quakers when they brought their antislavery petition to New York, Burke could not help but expect more interference from them if Congress sat at Philadelphia, a city less comfortable for South Carolinians than a hornet's nest. Besides, Congress should not reside in a state whose representatives had agitated the continent at the last session with their unremitting efforts to relocate Congress. As proof of their abilities, he protested, they had now secured Madison, the man who had killed their 1789 seat of government bill, to ensure their hope of carrying Congress to Philadelphia.

New York City's John Laurance agreed with Burke that Congress would never remove to so remote a part of the Union as the Potomac and that Philadelphia would become the permanent residence. To him the bill threatened the existence of the Union. Frustrated by the minority's inability to win votes, and as bitter as Senator King, he intimated for the record that the fate of the funding bill was tied to the passage of the seat of government bill. Maryland's Seney complained that Pennsylvania and Virginia, but not his state, would reap benefit from a Potomac capital.

With one exception, the Massachusetts delegation made no serious effort to defeat the Potomac. Elbridge Gerry defended Baltimore and ridiculed the idea of going to the Conococheague. "Enquiries will be made, where in the name of common sense is Connogochque, and I do not believe that one person in a thousand in the United States knows that there is such a place on earth." What would happen once Congress had cut down the woods, laid out the streets and erected buildings? Would congressmen find the accommodations what they ought to be? Would markets and other conveniences follow the federal government? Would a society form? Or would not Congress soon sicken of its lonely seat at that "Indian place" and adjourn to Baltimore, Philadelphia or somewhere else? Various reasons occurred to him for postponing the bill. It had a pernicious influence on the funding plan and the continuance of the Union. New York had incurred great expense to accommodate Congress. Had not the Confederation Congress sanctioned a promise to that state to the effect that, if it ratified the Constitution without conditional amendments, it would retain the temporary residence?[13]

In response to all this, Richard Bland Lee updated his argument from the 1789 debate. The Union needed a centrally located capital more than ever because, as a result of Hamilton's funding program, wealth would concentrate there. Furthermore, a Potomac location offered the only opportunity to overcome the existing sectional imbalance in the Union, an imbalance which must be redressed to prevent the Eastern States from swallowing the South. He described disunion and civil war as terrible to contemplate and waxed optimistically about the Union as long as it paid attention to both northern (funding–assumption) and southern (the location of the capital) interests. Even though he had been led to believe that Alexandria would be included in the federal district, Lee insisted that the bill held out the possibility of a site on the Potomac north of Baltimore. Madison listed the Potomac's advantages over Baltimore and predicted that a commercial town would soon rise on the river. He urged southerners not to be seduced by Baltimore, for, if the bill returned to the Senate, Baltimore might be replaced with either the Delaware or Susquehanna rivers. If the Potomac did not succeed now, he warned, "the prospect of obtaining a Southern position [would] vanish for ever."

Debate on the motion for Baltimore continued on 7 July. Burke and Gerry denied charges that their remarks had encouraged New York City's residents to consider mob action against Congress. Thomas Hartley of Pennsylvania declared that New Yorkers should blame their senators for tabling the 1789 seat of government bill rather than the Pennsylvanians for the 1790 bill. Gerry complained that the Union had almost fallen apart when Congress resided at Annapolis in 1784 and predicted that many northerners would refuse to serve in a Congress situated at such an unhealthy place as the Potomac. He expected that the Virginians planned to include Alexandria within the ten mile square. Thus he moved that the House require its inclusion. He hoped by such an embarrassing motion to defeat the bill by denying it the support of those who expected that a Potomac site would be as far upriver as the Conococheague. The House rejected the amendment.

Alexander White defended his district and the land opposite it in Maryland from Gerry's ridicule, predicting rapid economic growth for the area as a result of the opening of the Potomac to navigation. South Carolina's Smith agreed with Madison on the need for a southern capital, but he wanted a guaranteed one. It was naive to think that Congress would leave Philadelphia in 1800, for congressmen would not choose to go to the wilderness and rusticate. The House defeated the Baltimore amendment, 37 to 23, thus crossing the last barrier to the Potomac. The majority may have included at least one Massachusetts representative, for Theodore Sedgwick had indicated that he would probably vote with the Philadelphia–Potomac coalition.

On 8 July the House debated an amendment from Burke that Congress remain at New York until 1792. Laurance argued that New York deserved the extension for various reasons, alluding to the means used to secure the state's ratification of the Constitution. Virginia's Page thought New York had been amply rewarded already. The Burke amendment lost.

The next day the House turned back a dozen amendments, including ones to place the capital at Germantown, at Baltimore, on the Delaware or somewhere between the Susquehanna and the Potomac. The minority also failed in its attempts to postpone the final vote and the House adopted the bill, 32 to 29. No representatives north of West Jersey voted for it, and only Seney and Smith of Maryland and Burke, Tucker and Smith of South Carolina voted with the northern minority. Recalling the debate months later, Smith described Madison as a general who marshalled his troops so well that not a single change was made to the Senate bill.[14]

The ecstatic Pennsylvanians quickly sent the news to Philadelphia, several members of the delegation expressing hope that Congress would never leave Philadelphia. Although pleased that Congress had escaped from New York, Maclay complained about the bargain that tied assumption to the residence and the influential role of the president: "Alas! That the affection, nay, almost adoration of the people should meet so unworthy a return. Here are their best interests sacrificed to the vain whim of fixing Congress and a great commercial town (so opposite to the genius of the southern planter) on the Potomac. And the President has become in the hands of Hamilton the dishcloth of every dirty speculation, as his name goes to wipe away blame and silence all murmuring."[15]

New England congressmen, several of whom expressed doubt that Congress would leave Philadelphia in 1800, might have complained more to constituents had they not known that passage of the seat of government bill ensured success for assumption.[16] The well-informed Massachusetts speculator Andrew Craigie, who lodged at New York with Senator Caleb Strong and Representatives Ames and Sedgwick, concluded upon "the *best information* that can be procured ... that an accommodation has been made (call it a bargain if you please) by which the residence, temporary and permanent, [and] the funding and assumption are secured. This is not publicly known although by some people suspected."[17]

On 12 July the bill went to the president for his signature. No one questioned Washington's support for a Potomac capital. Indeed, an anonymous newspaper writer reported "the rude behavior of certain gentlemen, who are near the person of the P_____t of the US" at the final House vote. "I mean their sneering conduct on that day to the virtuous minority." But the losers were not content with attacking presidential aides. Washington soon found himself confronted with an appeal to, and attacks upon, his honor. On 13 July, in a newspaper address to the president signed "Junius Americanus," Rep. Smith of South Carolina declared publicly for the first time that a bill on the president's desk was unconstitutional. That was so, he argued, because the Constitution gave Congress the sole power of adjournment while the bill, which adjourned Congress to Philadelphia, required the president's signature. Smith further reminded the president that Representatives Madison and Daniel Carroll had declared the seat of government bill of 1789 to be unconstitutional on the same grounds. "The Constitution is the rock of our political salvation . . . our only bond of Union; . . . every citizen who has taken an oath to support the Constitution, *violates that oath* if he silently suffers any law to pass which appears to him, in the smallest degree, repugnant to it," Smith stressed most pointedly to Washington.

Although some observers doubted that the argument of "Junius Americanus" would have much weight with a man as biased toward the Potomac as Washington, he could not ignore the public challenge. Immediately after reading the article, he turned to Jefferson for an opinion on the constitutional question. The secretary of state, with Madison's concurrence, assured the president that the bill was constitutional and politically safe to sign. "The majority (a Southern one) overruled the objection, as a majority (a Northern one) had overruled the same objection the last session on the Susquehanna residence bill . . . and may be fairly supposed to have declared the sense of the whole union." Further, the argument of "Junius Americanus" lacked validity because of its false assumption that Congress held the power of adjournment from the Constitution. On the contrary, Congress held it as a right from nature. The Constitution, however, in Article I, § 4, and elsewhere, had abridged that right by granting the president a say in the matter in certain instances.[18]

Others naively believed that Washington could be convinced to veto the bill, or thought that he would allow it to become law without his signature, a course of action at which Jefferson had hinted. On 16 July a New York newspaper described the president's situation as delicate, and observed that bets remained open as to what he would do. Washington stopped such speculation by signing the bill that day. New Yorkers, hurt in both their pocketbooks and their pride, attacked him immediately: "the Holy Name of the P_____t is not much respected in the mouths of the profane." One newspaper writer referred to him as formerly America's favorite guardian and deliverer. Several others criticized the mayor and city council for commissioning a portrait of Washington, suggesting that a Republic should not glorify its leaders until their deaths allowed their entire careers to be judged. Washington's ruling passion had been made clear by his signature, one of them asserted. "Truth" (probably Smith) concluded that local prejudices appeared to have had far more influence than proper.[19] Washington and the presidency no longer sat above public criticism.

While the House and the president considered the seat of government bill, the Senate had turned its attention to the funding bill. The day after passing the bill locating the capital on the Potomac, the Senate appointed a committee to consider assumption, choosing as its chair the recently converted Charles Carroll. Within a few hours after Washington informed the Senate that he had signed the seat of government bill, the Senate voted to add the assumption of state debts to the funding bill. The vote was 14 to 12 because Carroll voted aye. King, despite threats, voted with the assumptionists, and on 21 July the Senate sent the funding bill back to the House with several amendments, including one assuming $21,500,000 in state debt. The figure was higher than previously considered by the House mostly because of more liberal allowances for Virginia, North Carolina and Georgia. When the funding bill came before the House once again, "B.K." wrote a piece for the New York press predicting the outcome. "The true reason of the *removal* of *Congress* from this city will be explained to the people in the course of a very few days. . . . it will be seen, that the Pennsylvania and Potomac interests have been purchased with *twenty–one and an half millions of dollars*. . . even the powers of Mr. M[adiso]n are to be silent on the subject, but to preserve a consistency of character, he must vote against it."[20]

On 24 July the House defeated, 32 to 29, a motion to disagree to the Senate amendment attaching assumption to the bill. This was the first time that the House had voted in favor of assumption. Although there had been many reports that assumption would pass because of the Potomac capital, the names of the men who had agreed to shift their votes now became public. "We have gained Lee and White of Virginia and Gale and Carroll of Maryland—it seems there was an understanding between these gentlemen and some of the New England members that the latter would give no serious opposition to the seat of government bill if some of the Maryland and Virginia members would vote for the assumption. . . Some danger might have been expected from the New York members but Hamilton has kept them with us," Rep. Smith of South Carolina explained.[21]

At the last minute, before the final vote on the funding bill, Timothy Bloodworth of North Carolina attempted to suspend that part of the seat of government act which related to the ten years at Philadelphia. His intent was to defeat assumption by undermining the bargain which had assured its passage. When the House defeated consideration of the motion, the majority included several New England assumptionists.[22]

Despite Bloodworth's failure, much speculation arose as to whether the seat of government act would in fact be implemented. Rep. Thatcher expected that Washington would be replaced as president before 1800 by a Pennsylvanian or New Englander. Would Pennsylvania and the Eastern States go to the Potomac then? And if they refused, would the South insist that, since the Eastern States had violated one law, the South had a right to violate others, including the Constitution itself, and to establish a separate Republic? Maclay believed a disruption of the Union would be the consequence of a refusal to go to the Potomac in 1800. He predicted another danger: "fixed, as Congress will be, among men of other minds on the Potomac, a new influence will, in all probability, take place. And the men of New England, who have hitherto been held in check by the patronage, loaves and fishes of the president . . . may become refractory and endeavor to unhinge the government." The Susquehanna, he concluded of the river on which he lived, would have been a better location; "but, query, is not this selfish, too? Aye, but it may, nevertheless, be just."[23]

Although the establishment of the permanent residence on the Potomac and the assumption of the state debts highlighted the Compromise of 1790, it resolved other issues as well. First, the rules for settling accounts among the states were liberalized to benefit the South. Second, additional revenue had to be raised to fund the state debts. When Hamilton proposed an excise on domestic spirits during the third session, Madison joined with George Gale (he missed the final vote), Daniel Carroll, Richard Bland Lee and Alexander White as virtually the only southerners to vote for the measure.[24]

Ames, Sedgwick, Hamilton, Madison, Jefferson, Washington and other influential political leaders saw the Compromise of 1790 as the best means of preserving the Union. Executive branch officials exuded their delight. Washington always considered the federal debt and the residence of Congress as the most "delicate and interesting" issues "which could possibly be drawn into discussion. They were more in danger of having convulsed the government itself than any other points. I hope they are now settled in as satisfactory a manner as could have been expected; and that we have a prospect of enjoying peace abroad, with tranquility at home." Jefferson agreed: "assumption and residence . . . really threatened, at one time, a separation of the legislature *sine die.* They saw the necessity of suspending almost all business for some time; and, when

they resumed it, of some mutual sacrifices of opinion. It is not foreseen that any thing so generative of dissension can rise again."
Hamilton kept his own counsel.[25]

Northern leaders proclaimed assumption—and its legislative
acceptance of the constitutionality of implied powers—to be the final cementing of the Union and downplayed the implications of a
southern capital. Southern leaders heralded the decision to place
the capital on the Potomac and stressed the advantageous terms of
the assumption and settlement of accounts.

New Yorkers, of course, had the most reason to complain about
the deal. When the question of leaving New York City had first
come to the floor in June, they declared the debate a waste of time
and money, removal to Philadelphia an expense the United States
could ill afford and both as signs to Europe of the instability of the
new federal government. The New York press vented public frustration in attacks on Philadelphia. Although most of the New York
writers remain anonymous, Philip Freneau, the poet and later Jeffersonian newspaper editor, wrote several of them.[26] Most of the
arguments exaggerated familiar prejudices about the quality of life
at Philadelphia and its desirability as a seat of government. Its summers were excessively hot, its servants the worst on the continent,
its infant mortality high, its diseases epidemic, its drinking water
impotable and its much trumpeted Delaware River an open sewer.
Philadelphians would drown Congress with petitions and mobs
would attack members who opposed them. Pennsylvania had done
nothing to protect Congress when "enraged assassins" surrounded
it in 1783. And, once back at its old residence, Congress would never
escape. The New York writers tailored other arguments to 1790:
Pennsylvania was anti–slavery and Philadelphia a gloomy Quaker
dominated city which lacked the social life of New York.

Unlike 1788 and 1789, however, no journalistic war erupted between the two cities because most Philadelphians accepted the advice of their congressional delegation and remained silent. The
irrepressible Benjamin Rush merely pointed out that if Congress
sat at Philadelphia its members would gain a better understanding
of the country and its people since fewer members would arrive by
sea than at New York.[27]

New York's campaign of invective peaked at the end of July, but it did not cease until early the next year. The bitter prose and poetry touched on a variety of issues. The state ratification convention should not have fallen for the promise that New York would remain the temporary seat of federal government. Congress showed ingratitude for all that had been done to accommodate it, and the city deserved federal aid as compensation for the disaster. Virginia and Maryland deluded themselves if they believed the Potomac would ever have Congress on its shores. Bargaining was an improper means for conducting the business of the Union.[28]

New Yorkers found personal attacks on congressmen cathartic. The Pennsylvania delegation in particular felt the barbs during their last uncomfortable month at New York. Even the common citizens taunted them in the streets.[29] Although he played a role less crucial than the attacks implied, Robert Morris, because of his reputation as powerful and corrupt, made a ready target. By the fourth of July the abuse had become so threatening that he made a prudent visit to Philadelphia. Fitzsimons and Jefferson claimed that Morris had had a powerful influence in achieving victory for Pennsylvania, but others in the know downplayed his influence or attributed much of the success to Fitzsimons. There can be no question that Morris's role in 1790 was much less significant than it had been in 1789; not even the Pennsylvanians were as willing to trust him. Nevertheless, attempts to credit one man more than the other ignores the intimacy between the two Philadelphians. They had been political and business associates for years and the best way to influence Morris, as Maclay knew, was through Fitzsimons.[30]

The Maryland and, even more, the Virginia delegations did not escape criticism for their role in the bargain. The newspapers called Madison a debtor, a cloistered pedantic monk, a closet politician and the dupe of an insidious contract. Once the House assumed the state debts, the press printed the names of the representatives who had switched their votes.[31]

A final though relatively uncommon theme in the New York press was: "So what, who cared?" Most New Yorkers had not benefited from the residence; in fact, one asserted, it had sometimes been difficult to buy the necessities of life with all the federal officials in town. The civic improvements occasioned by the residence of Congress might not otherwise have occurred for half a century. Would New York once again become a wilderness inhabited by wolves? Would parties and the drama cease? Would no streets be paved? Would Federal Hall be empty? Nonsense. Unless Congress prevented the Hudson from flowing to the sea, no ultimate harm had been done. One writer urged his readers to think about New York City's bounteous future. He recommended efforts to open navigation along the Mohawk River in order to gain access to the vast wealth of the Great Lakes. Millions of Americans and great towns situated there would soon need a water route to the Atlantic. Far from not having a future, "the present comparatively small city of New York will, if we please, be the *great emporium* of the new world." He concluded that the advantages of being the seat of federal government paled when compared with such an endless source of wealth, grandeur and influence.[32]

Abusive newspaper articles were not new to the United States, although Congress and the president had never been treated so harshly. A novelty was the libelous, unsigned political cartoons hawked on New York streets as early as 3 July. At least four were engraved during the month. Political cartoons attacking Great Britain and the Americans who supported its position had been effective tools in urban centers prior to the War for Independence, but none had appeared during the momentous campaign for the ratification of the Constitution, and those of 1790 apparently were not again matched in number until the controversy over Vermont Rep. Matthew Lyon in 1798.

Among the first to be engraved bore the title "View of Con[gre]ss on the road to Philadelphia." One New York newspaper described it as the most villainous cartoon ever issued in America, in its implication that one of the senators had voted for the bill in exchange for money. It pictured a huge Robert Morris, money bag in hand, carrying the fourteen senators who had voted for the seat of government bill on a ladder of preferment and pulling the members of the minority along by strings through their noses.

Another of the early cartoons showed Morris, led by the devil, en route to Philadelphia with Federal Hall on his shoulders. A man in women's clothing introduced himself to a Philadelphia prostitute as procuress for Congress. A congressional chaplain promised to pray wherever he was paid. Multicolored and expertly accomplished, the cartoon circulated outside of New York City and received attention in the American press.[33] A different version (or versions), of which no copies exist, extended the satire to the judicial and executive branches. Chief Justice John Jay, Secretary of War Henry Knox and Secretary of the Treasury Hamilton rode in Morris's pockets while James Madison hung as a bauble on his watch chain. In place of a walking staff, Morris rested his right hand on Secretary of State Jefferson. The windows of Federal Hall revealed senators encouraging and abusing Morris. Several representatives stood in the background with Sedgwick at their head shouting, "Stop Robert you rascal and take my assumption with you."[34]

The most significant cartoon, and probably the last, appeared after Washington signed the residence bill. In it Congress had chosen to follow Morris and the southerners in the ship *Constitution* over a waterfall to Philadelphia. A member of the northern minority, being pulled behind in a small boat, suggested that the rope which tied it to the *Constitution* be cut as soon as the ship appeared in danger, while another declared it best to do so immediately since the *Constitution* was going to the devil. This cartoon, the first to attack a President of the United States for an action he had taken, accused him of signing the seat of government bill for reasons of "self–gratification."

The remarkable silence about the residence issue at Philadelphia during June carried over into July. Instead of celebration, comment focused on the importance of preventing a removal in 1800, for it was "abhorrent to common sense to suppose they are to have a place dug out of the rocky wilderness, for the use of Congress only four months in the year and all the rest of the time to be inhabited by wild beasts." This stimulated a newspaper correspondent to urge that no official of Pennsylvania ever stain the honor of the state by acting in any way to prevent removal to the Potomac in 1800.[35]

In New England, dissatisfaction with the federal government, which had centered during April and May on the inability of Congress to provide for the federal debt, mounted during the residence debate of June and early July. Congress wasted time and public money on a subject of little interest to the Union when it should fund the debt. It might be necessary in twenty or thirty years to place the capital on the Potomac—"that *River* of *Rivers,* whose salutary waters would wash out all our *political leprosy"*—but such a decision now was premature. "If the interest of the northern and southern states are so totally *opposite* and *incompatible* as will admit of no coalition, no compromise, where from *mutual concessions mutual benefits* will accrue to both parties; we had better separate at once." Individual New Englanders echoed the complaints of their press and decried as dishonorable rumors of a link between the residence and assumption issues.[36]

Continued reports that a funding–assumption act would follow in the wake of the seat of government act did not at first soothe the angry New Englanders. The idea of placing the seat of empire on a creek on the "wild and savage" Potomac—"that American Nile"—galled them and their press overflowed with ridicule. "The great, the *all important* question is, at length, brought to an issue *for the present,"* declared one article; "Happy times! Blessed era! Philadelphia 'who sits mistress of the world,' is to embosom the grand council of America, till the year 1800, and then. ... Conogocheague [will] exchange her wigwams for palaces, and her tawny inhabitants for the brilliant circle of a polished court." Readers learned that at Conococheague the deer sported seven–foot racks and that the men were of extraordinary size too. The pronunciation of "Conococheague" so offended New England women that they blushed. A friend later joked to John Adams that Noah Webster should provide a softer spelling for it, and that in the meantime General Josiah Harmar, recently defeated by Indians in the Northwest Territory, could "guard the future Wigwam of Empire."[37]

As it became apparent that Congress would assume the state debts, New England rhetoric changed dramatically. "For awhile, however, I was so vexed at the clashing of northern and southern politics, local interests, and the contentions of rival cities for the seat of government that I heartily wished the avenging angel would sever the continent in twain at the Hudson, Delaware or Potomac," observed a resident of Hartford, Connecticut. But by early August he believed that most people recognized that the decision on where to meet had "oiled the wheels of government" and ushered in assumption. An influential Federalist newspaper at Boston reported at the end of August that "it must give sincere pleasure to every one who wishes well to his country, to reflect on the happy issue of the late session of Congress. The business they had to accomplish was arduous—the obstacles to be removed almost insurmountable." Although most Rhode Islanders opposed assumption and therefore saw little advantage in the Compromise of 1790, one publicly approved the decision to move Congress to Philadelphia because it would help in the fight to regulate the slave trade.[38]

Southern dissatisfaction with Congress had deeper roots and proved more difficult to allay. Before they knew of the seat of government act, Virginians warned Madison and Jefferson that assumption in any form would prove unpopular at home and that not even placing the capital on the Potomac would compensate for its evils. Newspapers carried letters from the South asserting that southerners preferred a dissolution of the Union to assumption.

Although the seat of government act gave southerners reason to reconsider their fears about the viability of union with the North, they still doubted that the other part of the Compromise of 1790 would be acceptable to the South. James Monroe saw neither the wisdom nor the necessity of assumption, but agreed that it would be more palatable in Virginia because of the location of the capital. While some Virginia politicians considered assumption unjust and unconstitutional, others condemned the means of its passage. George Nicholas considered vote trading bad policy in a republic. In addition, he foresaw a possible constitutional crisis ahead. The Pennsylvanians would surely break their contract with the South and join the Eastern States in attempts to thwart implementation of the seat of government act. The only preventive would be a presidential veto for any act which interfered with it. This would place the president in opposition to a majority of Congress. Concluded Nicholas, "these two questions have called forth more of the spirit of party and intrigue than will ever again be exercised in Congress."[39]

Virginians had some opportunity to express themselves on assumption during the second congressional election, held within a few weeks of the adoption of the measure. Attention focused on the bitter contest between incumbent Richard Bland Lee and his cousin, Arthur Lee. Rep. Lee knew that his vote for assumption threatened his reelection, but he expressed willingness to fall victim to it if the federal government prospered. Rumor alleged that Arthur Lee, an architect of the dual residence plan of 1783, had opposed a Potomac seat of government in 1783 and 1784. Although all the incumbents who stood for election won, the vote did not indicate public acceptance of assumption, since only two Virginians had voted for it.[40]

The real contest over assumption in the South took place in the Virginia legislature at the end of the year. Long time political opponents Patrick Henry and Henry Lee joined forces to attack both its policy and constitutionality. Despite the efforts of the young John Marshall, its chief defender, the resulting memorial to Congress termed the funding act anti–agrarian, anti–republican, too much like the British fiscal system and likely to throw influence into the hands of the executive branch. Widely reprinted in the press, it marked the first time a state had taken such action and set a precedent for the 1798 Virginia and Kentucky resolutions denying the constitutionality of the alien and sedition acts. For Alexander Hamilton, Virginia's petition to Congress expressing its concerns was symptomatic of a spirit which must be extinguished before it destroyed the Constitution. Would other Southern States follow suit? South Carolina, of course, favored assumption, and Georgia believed the federal government's support for the indigenous Creek Indians more worthy of legislative condemnation. North Carolina's assembly devoted a great deal of time to assumption without coming to any resolution. Maryland adopted and then rescinded a resolution declaring assumption a threat to state sovereignty.[41]

Marylanders complained much more about the decision to locate the capital on the Potomac River. That issue dominated the state's second congressional election. Each voter cast ballots for six men, and all the incumbents except William Smith of Baltimore stood for reelection. Two tickets appeared. The Potomac Ticket included the names of all the incumbents except Joshua Seney, the only member of the delegation to consistently support either the Susquehanna or Baltimore. The Chesapeake Ticket recommended only Seney.

The Upper Chesapeake Interest was relentless, claiming that Maryland gained nothing by the Potomac location, which Virginia would dominate if Congress should ever escape from Philadelphia. Baltimore, the true gateway to inland navigation, would have been chosen had the Pennsylvanians not duped the Maryland congressmen into a bargain designed to enhance Philadelphia at Baltimore's expense. "A Marylander" suggested that Rep. Gale and Senator Henry voted for the Potomac because they owed money to its wealthy supporter Senator Charles Carroll, and urged the ouster of all three from public office. "A Citizen" pointed to Representatives Gale and Daniel Carroll as the men who had bound Maryland to pay the debts of the other states in exchange merely for the possibility of seeing the capital on the Potomac in a decade.[42]

The Potomac Interest had less access to the press but privately defended its ticket. One Georgetown leader observed that his fellow Potomac residents would never again deserve the exertions of any man if they allowed Gale's defeat. Rep. Stone complained about the naivete of the Baltimoreans for thinking that their city had ever stood a chance to become the capital without some sort of residence–assumption bargain. Senator Carroll, convinced that the seat of government act would greatly benefit Baltimore, predicted that within five years after Congress arrived on the Potomac, the Susquehanna would be opened; that Baltimore and Maryland would flourish economically; and that Maryland's influence in the Union would rise dramatically, perhaps even surpassing that of all the other states, but certainly equalling that of her politically powerful neighbors, Pennsylvania and Virginia.[43]

The voters of Maryland, dominated by populous Baltimore, repaid their delegation for bringing the federal government to the Potomac by reelecting Seney and defeating all four of the incumbents who had voted for the seat of government act. Washington immediately rewarded with federal jobs both Gale and Carroll, the two Marylanders who had voted for assumption. The Upper Chesapeake Interest however failed to oust Charles Carroll from the Senate.[44]

Americans residing abroad made particularly perceptive comments about the implications of the Compromise of 1790. Gouverneur Morris disliked the chosen site, but hoped nevertheless that Washington would live long enough to implement the decision since a poor location was superior to an ambulatory Congress. The always well–informed John Browne Cutting of Massachusetts, who lived near Morris at London, had predicted that several significant measures would result from the very animosity with which they had been agitated in Congress, and, although he regretted the bargaining, he considered it to have fixed the "two great pivots upon which our national union may turn." From Lisbon, Washington's former political aide David Humphreys expressed pleasure with the Compromise of 1790 because the "public debt and permanent residence were always . . . the rocks which most endangered the safety of the American Union."[45]

The adoption of the state debts turned the clairvoyant mind of the Frenchman Hector St. John de Crevocoeur once again to the future of the United States. Eight years earlier, as "An American Farmer," he had published one of the first analyses of the American character. To him, assumption meant that the Union had been consolidated, that the great revolution begun under the influence of American reason in 1787 had been completed, and that public confidence would now call forth all the hitherto hidden American advantages so that its industry, commerce and agriculture would grow with double speed on expanded wings.[46]

The Constitution survived its first major crisis because of the willingness of the American public to accept the Compromise worked out by the executive and legislative branches of the federal government in 1790 and reaffirmed early in 1791 with the passage of the bank, excise and supplemental seat of government acts. The first publicly fought out compromise in American history, it marked the end of the American Revolution, for it resolved the two most difficult and lingering issues: what to do about the war debt and where to establish the capital. Those leaders who condemned as dangerous to republican liberty the vote trading which made the Compromise of 1790 possible proved to be a minority.[47]

Nevertheless, the tranquility at home which Washington and others expected to result from the Compromise did not last. Americans realized that "southern and northern will often be the division of Congress. The thought is disagreeable, but the distinction is founded in nature, and will last as long as the Union."[48] Thirty years later, in 1820, and thirty years after that, in 1850, it again became necessary to resolve congressional impasses between the North and South by major compromises similar to that of 1790. The Compromise of 1850 did not last thirty years and the Civil War, which some political leaders of 1790 saw on the horizon, finally settled the debate over the divisibility of the Union. Henry Lee and other southerners had clearly stated the cause for which Lee's son Robert E. Lee would fight in 1860.

8

George Washington in Command, 1790–1799

ONCE GEORGE WASHINGTON SIGNED THE SEAT OF government bill in July 1790, he had complete authority over and responsibility for its execution. Congress had relinquished its oversight by not requiring senatorial consent to the commissioners Washington appointed for the federal city and by not appropriating any money for its construction. From 1791 until his death in 1799, Washington worked unceasingly to guarantee that the federal government would be seated on his beloved Potomac at the beginning of the nineteenth century. Foremost, he believed that this would strengthen the Union and consequently his reputation in its history. In addition, he expected the siting of the capital to ensure the Potomac's preeminent role in the political economy of the emerging American Empire as it, in the words of a publicist, advanced to "sovereignty of the globe."[1] *The Washington Family,* the large painting which Edward Savage completed at Philadelphia in 1796, aptly captured Washington's vision for the seat of empire. In it the family sits around a map of the federal city with the wide, majestic Potomac River behind them. Washington rests his arm on the shoulder of young George Washington Parke Custis. The boy, symbolic of the next generation, rests his hand on the globe.

Washington involved himself in the choice of a specific site on the Potomac for the federal district, the purchase of land for the federal city within it, the activities of Pierre L'Enfant, the details of the construction and financing of the city and the neutralization of political opposition.[2] Contemporaries recognized the development of the capital as the project which "more than anything else had his attention." His preeminent biographer states that had the District of Columbia been Washington's only responsibility, "he scarcely could have found the future seat of government more time-consuming." By 1795 the man and the capital were so entwined that Thomas Johnson told Washington that "the success of the City has now become important to your Reputation."[3]

At the end of August 1790 Washington asked Secretary of State Jefferson for advice on implementing the seat of government act. Jefferson sought assistance from Madison.[4] Both advisers knew where Washington planned to locate the federal district and that the act had been drafted to allow him to name that place without consulting the Commission. Until he suddenly recognized the indiscretion at the end of July, Jefferson had told his correspondents that the capital would be at Georgetown.[5] Madison recommended, and Jefferson agreed, that the president begin by locating only part of the ten mile square, so that places which "it may not be prudent now to accept" could be included later. Alexandria—Washington's home town, which lay below the southern limit of the district as specified by the act—was the place he meant.

Soon after the meeting Washington left for Mount Vernon, his first trip home since assuming the presidency. New Yorkers gave him a polite but restrained send off, while Philadelphians welcomed him as the hero of the Western World. He stopped at Georgetown for a meeting of the Potomac Company, and many of its prominent citizens, as well as several from Alexandria, welcomed him with great expectations, convinced he would select their locale for the federal district. Acting at Washington's direction, Jefferson and Madison toured the area between Little Falls and the Anacostia with a group of landowners. Jefferson stressed to them not to lose the opportunity at hand, for Congress would never give the Potomac a second chance. He explained the dangers of relying on public bodies for funds and suggested that they make a generous offer of land.

Jefferson and Madison next sounded out the independent and outspoken George Mason, who owned 2,000 acres on the Virginia side of the Potomac from a point opposite Georgetown up to Little Falls. With his report to Washington about the meeting with Mason, Jefferson enclosed a form for conveying to the United States lands for the federal city, which he had written for Daniel Carroll of

Duddington, the principal landowner along the Anacostia and a cousin of Rep. Daniel Carroll. Washington, without disclosing his involvement, approved the method and forwarded the document to Duddington as if it had come straight from Jefferson.[6]

Because of the rivalry between the proprietors of land south and east of Tiber Creek—the Anacostia or Carrollsburg Interest—and those north and west of it—the Georgetown Interest—the Maryland landowners did not join in a common offer to the federal government. In mid-October several Georgetown area landowners submitted an agreement to Washington, offering their lands for the federal city on whatever terms he deemed reasonable and just. With the agreement came an argument for Georgetown's merits over any other site in the immediate vicinity: placing the federal buildings adjacent to healthier and more defensible Georgetown, with its superior port, would act to guarantee the arrival of Congress in 1800 because investors would prefer to buy lots contiguous to an already thriving town; and the best way to facilitate the interests of the Anacostia proprietors was to expand the federal city in their direction from Georgetown. The timely document arrived just as Washington set out on a trip up the Potomac for the ostensible purpose of selecting a site for the federal district. Discretion required the trip and, he hoped, it would also keep the Georgetown proprietors from excessively inflating the value of their lands. Washington spent a day touring the area between the Anacostia and Little Falls and requested a map of landownership.[7]

Washington did not devote much attention to the other potential sites and his unannounced twelve-day journey caught advocates of an upriver location completely unprepared. Most of the land between Great Falls and the mouth of the Monocacy River below Frederick, Maryland, was gently rolling woods and farm land with easy access to the Potomac, but devoid of the concentration of capital available at the towns immediately below the falls. Landowners suggested the mouth of the Monocacy, including part of Senator Charles Carroll's 10,000 acre estate, as an ideal site. Just north of the Monocacy, the Potomac tumbled out of the Appalachian foothills. Within a few weeks of Washington's surprise arrival at Shepherdstown, Virginia, its principal citizens, in conjunction with their counterparts across the Potomac, raised pledges of land

and $25,000 for a federal district focused on Sharpsburg, Maryland, and Antietam Creek.[8]

Washington next went to Hagerstown, Maryland, the Great Valley town located just above the mouth of Conococheague Creek. He must have raised hopes by his claim to its residents that impartiality would continue to govern his execution of the public trust. From there, he rode down to Williamsport at the mouth of the Conococheague. Its major landowner, General Otho Holland Williams, rushed west from Baltimore upon hearing of Washington's trip, but did not arrive in time to present personally the case for the site which had been the subject of so much congressional and public ridicule. Williams and his supporters soon made a handsome offer of land. Continued land speculation in the vicinity of the Conococheague bore witness to the optimism of the residents.[9]

Wherever its location, the capital's success required more funds than the $120,000 promised by Virginia. Despite objections from the Upper Chesapeake Interest, Maryland appropriated $72,000 to Washington's use in November.[10] Everything seemed in readiness for the president to announce the location of the federal district when Congress opened its third session at Philadelphia in December 1790.

To no one's surprise, the political and social atmosphere surrounding the federal government changed dramatically with the transfer of the temporary residence from New York to Philadelphia. The 1790s would have been politically turbulent wherever Congress sat, but at Philadelphia, with its concentration of 42,000 people, tensions magnified. More cosmopolitan and politically conscious than New Yorkers, Philadelphians and Pennsylvanians once again involved themselves in federal affairs. Congressmen complained of insults based on their political stands and too many petitions from city and state residents. Congress found itself at one point in the uncomfortable position of debating an excise bill while the legislature of Pennsylvania sat next door condemning the debate as subversive of peace, liberty and the rights of its citizens. A newspaper writer warned that Congress would not remain in Philadelphia if subjected to such treatment.[11]

Society was more formal than at New York, and a republican court founded on social rank evolved. Entertainment during the first winter included a lecture series by James Wilson and a ballet entitled "The Congress' Return," as well as theater, dinners and drawing rooms. This rekindled in a few people the fear of luxury which had earned Philadelphia the reputation of a modern Capua during the war.

Philadelphia provided a special problem for southerners. Pennsylvania law stated that any slave who remained in the state six months became free. The Pennsylvania Society for the Abolition of Slavery had agreed not to insist on enforcement against members of Congress and federal officials, but nothing prevented individual citizens from informing slaves about their rights. Thus Washington, for example, made certain that his slaves left the state once every six months—if only for a few hours—so that he would not become embroiled with the state's judiciary.[12]

Pennsylvania made adequate preparations for a much larger federal government than the one that had left in 1783. Some men had supported lavish quarters, enhanced by gardens, west of Broad Street on one of the many quiet rural squares which William Penn had platted a century earlier. This resulted in part from a desire to provide enough space so as not to fuel the argument for moving the state capital westward. Instead, Philadelphia remodeled the recently completed Philadelphia County Courthouse. Renamed Congress Hall and fitted out to match Federal Hall as closely as possible, the building stood a few yards west of the State House where Congress had met during the war. The Common Council finally decided to rent Robert Morris's house, two blocks from Congress Hall, as a suitable mansion for President Washington and his family. Rep. Fisher Ames described the accommodations as good and Philadelphia as magnificent.[13]

To the surprise of many, Washington did not announce the location of the federal district when he addressed Congress in December 1790. Early in January he was still exploring the best way to run the lines so that the maximum amount of land could be included about Alexandria, allowing the town to grow westward as well as northward within the federal district. Finally, on 24 January, he issued a proclamation announcing the chosen site. Washington not only included Alexandria—four miles south of the lower limit specified in the seat of government act of 1790—but also named a point within the town as the starting place for the survey of the district's boundaries. The proclamation stated that only the area north of the lower limit specified by the act be accepted for the district at first. In a letter to Congress, Washington suggested that it pass a supplemental act to enable him to complete the full ten mile square to his liking, by taking in Alexandria and land south of the Anacostia in Maryland.[14]

By his placement of the district and his request for a supplemental act, Washington courted not only renewed sectional tensions and a confrontation between Congress and the president, but also attacks upon himself.[15] That the president had chosen the southern limit specified by their act did not surprise congressmen, despite the clear implication of the Virginia act of cession and the southern argument during the residence debate of 1789 that an upriver site was desired. Instead, the stunned congressmen complained of his proposal to include land in both Maryland and Virginia south of the limit established by Congress. Rep. Theodore Sedgwick's observation that Mount Vernon bordered Alexandria exaggerated only slightly. He had no way of knowing that Washington owned almost 1,200 acres along Four Mile Run within the proposed district or that George Washington Parke Custis, Martha Washington's grandson and the president's ward, owned the 950 acre plantation that became Arlington Cemetery. Rep. William Smith of Baltimore did not believe self-interest had the smallest conscious influence on Washington, but he knew nevertheless "that almost all men form their opinions by their interest without always knowing the governing principle of their motives or actions."[16]

A few Americans did attribute the choice to Washington's desire to enhance the value of his own property. Dickinson College President Charles Nisbet stated it privately in 1792. Others insinuated it publicly later in the decade. In fits of self–pity after his retirement, John Adams declared that the decision had raised the value of Washington and Custis property a thousand percent.[17] But to attribute the choice only to a desire to raise the value of Mount Vernon, or family lands within the district lines, belittles Washington's vision. He had more important reasons for his choice than lining his pockets.

To be sure, Washington clearly foresaw an immediate rise in the value of his land as a result of the location, for one of his most conspicuous traits was an open concern for his own economic interest. More than once during the 1790s he referred in business transactions to the increase in the value of Mount Vernon that followed from the establishment of the federal district nearby, using this to justify rent increases. That he did not site the capital primarily for that reason is suggested by the fate of Abingdon, a 950 acre river plantation adjacent to present–day National Airport. In 1789 Washington secured an act from the Virginia legislature allowing him to alter the will of Martha's son Jack Custis in order to return the plantation to its previous owner. The land had been a heavy burden on the Custis estate, but worth retaining if holdings within the federal district were his aim.[18]

What motivated a man so attuned to politics, public opinion and his own reputation in history to select the site he chose and to risk putting the issue before Congress again? By fortunate chance, the place happened to be the midpoint between Maine and Georgia. He considered it the best spot for the survival of the Union to which so much of his life and reputation had been devoted, and he had faith in the commitment of Congress to the Compromise of 1790 and in the secureness of his reputation with Americans. Potomac Fever and his commitment to the economic growth of Alexandria, however, outdistanced other factors in importance. Still as captivated by the Potomac as ever, and convinced that it would become the grand emporium of North America, Washington purchased paintings of Great Falls and Harpers Ferry by George Beck to hang in the presidential mansion at Philadelphia; to further American consciousness of the river's grandeur, he informed Congress that he had recommended its scenic vistas to another landscape artist. To David Stuart, Washington stressed the "intimate connection in political and pecuniary considerations between the federal district and the inland navigation of the Potomac." "No exertions," he continued, "should be dispensed with to accomplish the latter. For, in proportion as this advances, the City will be benefited."[19]

Other than the few congressmen who privately implied criticism of Washington's motives in 1791, few Americans reacted to the location. John Dickinson of Delaware considered a magnificent city on the Potomac distant from the people and surrounded by a large population of slaves to be dangerous to republican government. Further, he feared what would happen should the Eastern States consider the capital a commercial and manufacturing rival. Surely, Dickinson concluded, the improbable water connection between the Potomac and the Ohio did not justify the choice. The only concentration of interest in Washington's decision came from Marylanders and Virginians residing on the Potomac. They expected it to boost the Potomac Company and to open new fields for commercial and land investment. "The Potomac will soon redound with the din of industry, agriculture and commerce," predicted a Georgetown merchant, who sought to buy land near Tiber Creek where he assumed Washington would place the public buildings. At Alexandria people saw their fortunes ensured forever.[20]

At least one Potomac promoter did not consider the matter of imminent importance to anyone's fortune. George Mason told Jefferson that he did not believe Congress would escape from the "Whirlpool of Philadelphia . . . for half a century to come." Others agreed with Mason's assessment. Rep. Sedgwick reported he had heard that the Pennsylvania delegation had no intention of aiding in a removal in 1800 and that he had been cited as an ally. From a variety of circumstances, the French attache believed Philadelphia would become the permanent residence despite the president's machinations for the Potomac. Such a climate of opinion reinforced southern intentions not to let anything interfere with the implementation of the seat of government act. Three hundred thousand—not three hundred—Paxton Boys would march on Philadelphia in 1800 if its partisans attempted to keep Congress there, a Maryland newspaper warned.[21]

A week after Congress convened in December 1790, southerners saw what some believed to be the first legislative threat to a removal to the Potomac in 1800: Alexander Hamilton's plan for a national bank. Deep-seated prejudice against banks existed in the United States, above all in the South, where they were popularly considered to be monstrous, aristocratical creatures inconsistent with a republican social order. Southerners viewed the bank as an especially dangerous instrument in the hands of a northern-controlled federal government. Added to assumption and the proposed excise, the bank would heighten the imbalance of power not only between the states and the federal government, but also between the North and the South in the national economy.

Several weeks before Hamilton officially proposed the bank to Congress, the French attache reported an additional concern of the South. The federal government and the bank would quickly become so entwined that one would hardly be able to get along without the other; consequently, the bank, located at Philadelphia, the financial capital of the United States, would act to render that city the permanent seat of Congress. Rep. George Thatcher believed the South viewed the bank "as throwing a monstrous thick anchor in that harbor [Philadelphia], which no future Congress will ever be able to weigh."[22]

Southern fears intensified when a Senate committee reported the bank bill in January 1791. The bank would have a twenty–year charter. Under the terms of its incorporation, it would remain at Philadelphia after Congress left in 1800. Rep. Ames and Senator William Maclay attributed southern opposition to the bill solely to the belief that this fact threatened the seat of government act. Southern senators gave support to this contention when all of them voted in favor of an unsuccessful amendment to limit the bank's charter to 1801. Rep. William L. Smith later claimed that the Virginians had promised support for the bank if its charter expired after ten years.

Having passed the Senate by a substantial majority, the bank bill sailed smoothly through the House until the last minute. Only then did Madison come forth in a stunning two–hour speech with the constitutional argument that Congress had no power to charter a bank. But northerners recognized a smoke screen when they saw one. Rep. Ames considered the argument as merely one of several ploys to secure a shorter charter for the bank, and insisted that even southerners belittled the constitutional objection. Northerners saw confirmation of their opinion in the publication at Philadelphia in the midst of the bank debate of a letter from Rep. Daniel Carroll warning his constituents on the Potomac River of the potential threat to the seat of government act.[23]

In response to the issue Madison had raised, the House debated the bill for an additional week. Occasional references to the alleged relationship between the bill and the seat of government act elicited no confirmation from either Madison or other southerners, who insisted their opposition rose solely from constitutional objections. The bank bill passed the House on 8 February with a two-to-one majority, despite the opposition of all but four southerners, two of them being William Smith and Joshua Seney, the Potomac's enemies in the Maryland delegation. Senator Charles Carroll failed once again to limit the charter when Congress adopted a supplemental bank bill later in the session.[24]

The only hope for southerners was to persuade the president to inaugurate his veto power. As Rep. Ames suspected, they found a willing ear in Washington, whose obsession with protecting the federal city against any threat faced its first test. He received the bill on 14 February and turned immediately to his attorney general, the Virginian Edmund Randolph, for an opinion on the constitutional question. Randolph deemed the bill unconstitutional and Jefferson confirmed that view. Washington sent both opinions to Hamilton for his arguments in favor of its constitutionality.[25]

On the same day as Washington requested an opinion from Hamilton, Charles Carroll gave notice in the Senate that he would bring in a supplemental seat of government bill pursuant to the president's recommendation. Carroll's bill included within the federal district Alexandria and a few square miles of Maryland south of the Anacostia, but reaffirmed the provision that the federal buildings had to be situated on the Maryland side of the Potomac. "The President's heart is no doubt much set on" the Potomac "and there is as little doubt but that a majority of Congress are decidedly against it," observed Senator Paine Wingate of New Hampshire. "The question therefore is a very disagreeable one to decide, and it will try the feelings of some of the courtiers pretty much." The Senate began debate on 18 February. Maclay—courted by both Jefferson and Washington—determined to say nothing, but in the end could not restrain himself. No courtier, he complained that the expectations of the people had been disappointed by the president who should have allowed the Commission to choose the site.

On a motion to postpone the bill for one week, every senator north of Maryland voted yes. Rep. Alexander White, informing a prominent citizen of Alexandria about the postponement, refused to repeat any of the rumored reasons, "but only [to] state the Fact. I will mention another Fact; the President must within that period approve or disapprove the bill for establishing a bank."[26] The first confrontation between a congressional majority and a president over the possibility of a veto loomed, and Congress had strengthened its position by letting Washington know that passage of a favorite piece of presidential legislation first required his signature on the bank bill. Once again the residence question had established political precedent.

For Washington it proved the most politically uncomfortable event of the First Congress. While waiting for Hamilton's opinion, he experienced painful conflict. His discomfort did not arise from any fundamental doubts about the constitutionality of the bank. He knew that Congress had acknowledged the doctrine of implied legislative powers by assuming the state debts. What troubled Washington was the proposed bank's threat to the capital. He and Madison discussed the crisis several times, and Madison drafted a veto message at his request, arguing against the bill on grounds of both constitutionality and merit.

Tension mounted at Philadelphia when Washington had not returned the bill within a week. Word spread that his advisers were split. Public securities fell. The bank's partisans at New York charged him with selfish motives, probably recalling their feelings when the president had refused to veto the seat of government act in 1790. By 23 February, the day on which Washington received Hamilton's masterful defense of the doctrine of implied powers in support of the bank bill's constitutionality, the general opinion at Philadelphia held that Washington would veto the bill. Sedgwick prayed that he would be more discreet, for, if by some chance the veto stood, the congressional majority would be thrown into a violent flame.[27]

By the morning of the tenth day, "there was general uneasiness and the president stood on the brink of a pre[ci]pice from which had he fallen he would have brought down with him much of that glorious reputation he has so deservedly established." Washington signed the bill. Immediately thereafter the Senate took up the post-poned supplemental seat of government bill. Robert Morris, Philip Schuyler and John Langdon—the men who had spearheaded its postponement—and George Read—whose vote was needed to balance that of his colleague who had been absent the week before—joined with the southerners to defeat by one vote a motion for further postponement. The bill passed the next day and the House agreed to it without comment, 39 to 18, several northern delegations carefully dividing their votes in half.

Congress had Washington's signature on the bank bill and he had congressional approval for the inclusion of Alexandria within the federal district. But, in the process, Washington had been subjected to greater public criticism than at any previous time in his presidency. After the reaffirmation of the Compromise of 1790 by the adoption of the excise, bank and supplemental seat of government bills, the third session of the First Federal Congress closed. Rep. Ames thought it had passed with unusual good temper. "The last was a dreadful one. In public, as well as in private life, a calm comes after a storm."[28]

Washington had not waited for the supplemental act to begin developing the capital. His first action after selecting the site was the choice of the three commissioners to superintend the planning of the federal city within the district. Madison suggested the political wisdom of picking one man from Massachusetts, but Washington refused to take the risk. On 24 January he named David Stuart of Alexandria, Thomas Johnson of Frederick, Maryland, and Rep. Daniel Carroll of Montgomery County, Maryland. All were Potomac Company investors, victims of Potomac Fever, and, in the opinion of Jefferson, ready to do Washington's bidding. The president believed he could not have found three men more committed or better disposed to accommodate the conflicting interests.[29]

Few men had as intimate a relationship with Washington as Stuart. The two carried on a private correspondence about the affairs of the federal city as long as Stuart served, and through him Washington transmitted confidential information and personal opinions for the guidance of the commissioners. No one had been longer associated with Washington in the promotion of the Potomac than Thomas Johnson, the man who had nominated him to be commander in chief in 1775 and who had replaced him as president of the Potomac Company when he became president of the United States. Johnson had overseen construction of Maryland's magnificent Capitol, and Washington held a high opinion of his abilities. Carroll played a role in the political economy of Montgomery County, Maryland, similar to that of Washington in Fairfax County, Virginia. A large slaveholder, Carroll lived at Joseph's Park, a 4,000 acre plantation northeast of Georgetown, and owned thousands of other acres in the county. His appointment to the Commission held special importance, for, although tied economically to Georgetown, he was related by marriage to both Notley Young and Daniel Carroll of Duddington, who owned large plantations in the Carrollsburg area of the federal city. Washington hoped he could bridge differences between the two groups of proprietors.[30]

Washington had no intention of slowing progress by waiting for the Commission to meet. Early in February he dispatched Andrew Ellicott to Alexandria, where that surveyor, assisted by the free Black Benjamin Banneker, began to run the four boundary lines of the federal district as a preliminary step to a more exact survey to be made later. Even more important than the survey of the district was the plan for the federal city within it. Little attention had been given during the long debate over the establishment of the capital to the question of a plan. George Walker in January 1789 had called for a city based on the best models of ancient and modern times, particularly Babylon and Philadelphia, and clearly separated into political and commercial sectors. In order to discourage speculators, he had further suggested that each purchaser erect a house built to certain standards within a set number of years. With such a plan the city would be able to accommodate residents even before construction of the public buildings. "Potomac" in its March 1789 discussion with "Patapsco" had included such proposed details as the width and angle of the streets. "The genius of America will rise superior to the Gothic taste that has so long pervaded" urban design, "Potomac" hoped, "and will, in some measure, revive the elegance, regularity, and grandeur of the ancients."[31]

A variety of individuals suggested to Washington that they or their ideas be employed in designing the city. Nevertheless, he considered only one man, the French–born artist, architect and civil engineer, Pierre Charles L'Enfant. Washington considered L'Enfant a scientific man of taste and the best qualified person in the world likely to accept the job. L'Enfant's talents first came to Washington's attention during the War for Independence, when he served with the Continental Army. A variety of artistic and architectural endeavors drew public attention to L'Enfant during the 1780s, none more prominently than Federal Hall, symbol of the new government. Its elegance and the speed of its construction caused people to overlook the unexpected expense. Rep. Thomas Fitzsimons had recommended that L'Enfant prepare the public buildings at Philadelphia for the return of Congress in 1790. In addition to his talents, Fitzsimons praised him as a mild, unassuming person who would not expect too high a compensation and who worked well with common laborers.[32]

The planner reached the federal district early in March, and, supervised personally by Washington, began by studying the topography and surveying the land between Tiber Creek and the Anacostia. Washington's purpose in keeping L'Enfant south of the Tiber was to frighten the Georgetown landowners into selling their land at reasonable rates to two agents at Georgetown whom the president had secretly asked to purchase land for the public. Recent allegations that Washington was using the agents to buy land for his personal speculations is totally groundless. The money Washington intended to use, had any transactions actually occurred, was that previously appropriated by Maryland.[33]

The feint had to be abandoned when the enthusiastic L'Enfant violated his instructions. Washington then authorized a survey north from the Tiber to what eventually became Florida Avenue, so that he could have a rough plat of the entire area between Georgetown and the Anacostia. Such a plat, he hoped, would allow him to play the Georgetown area proprietors off against those on the Anacostia. The president tended to prefer the land along the Anacostia with its pronounced topographic features and commercial potential. Nevertheless, he was unsure, because he agreed with the Georgetown proprietors that a city located near an existing population center would grow more quickly. L'Enfant helped to convince Washington that the entire area was necessary to the vision they shared.[34]

At the end of March Washington called the rival proprietors together at Suter's Fountain Inn at Georgetown to impress upon them the past trials and future challenges to the Potomac capital. Their jealousies might deprive the federal government of the only means available to raise funds for buildings. They need not be rivals, for the lands of both groups were necessary to provide the United States with a capital equal to its importance. The proprietors reached an agreement with Washington on 30 March: they would deed to the public all the land which the president wished to include within the federal city and he would have complete control over its disposition. Once L'Enfant completed a city plan, the proprietors would receive half the lots platted on their former holdings as well as $66.67 an acre for as much land as Washington wanted for public buildings and reservations. The federal government would retain half the lots and all the land designated for streets. The United States thus acquired 10,136 lots and miles of streets at no cost to itself and over 500 acres of public reservations for $36,099. With the land acquired, Washington instructed L'Enfant to prepare a plan, stressing the importance of including as much of the proprietors' holdings as possible.

Washington had negotiated an advantageous deal for the United States. The outline of the acquisition arrangement had been that proposed by George Walker in January 1789. Walker believed his plan would eventually raise about ten and one–half million dollars, allowing the government to construct a great city with speed while not taxing the people. The United States had previously considered a variety of means for financing the purchase of land and construction of buildings for its capital. In 1783 it was content to rely on commitments from the states which made offers, and a year later was willing to appropriate $100,000. In 1789 Congress considered borrowing that sum, but concluded instead that the money should be provided by the states or citizens of the states in which the capital was fixed.[35]

Soon after meeting with the proprietors, Washington set off on a tour of the South where he hoped to stem growing opposition to federal measures by drawing attention to the location of the capital and the mutually beneficial agreement he had negotiated with the proprietors. Consequently, Washington worried when he received news from the commissioners that problems had arisen over the agreement. Several of the proprietors refused to convey their lands, complaining that Washington had deceived them. These men rightly recalled that the president had indicated the need for approximately 4,000 acres, while L'Enfant's plan covered 6,000. They feared that the city would be divided into so many lots that the value of each would be diminished. Other proprietors, generally investors who had purchased their land after the adoption of the seat of government act, supported the president. Led by George Walker, they believed Washington should not be bound by anything he might have said, but only by the agreement itself, which clearly gave him the power to include as much land as he saw fit. They urged the Commission not to concede to any demands that would mutilate the "Metropolis of America" or frustrate the desires of the president. It wisely decided to leave the situation unresolved so that Washington could handle it personally.[36]

Rep. William L. Smith passed through the federal district en route home from the First Congress. The widely traveled South Carolinian found the grand, romantic vistas enchanting, and believed they held more advantages for a capital than any place he had seen in America. "Nature has done much for it," the enraptured L'Enfant told Smith as they rode about the chosen area, "and with the aid of art it will become the wonder of the world." To his friend Alexander Hamilton, L'Enfant expressed equal enthusiasm. No place in America was more susceptible to improvement or more capable of promoting the rapid growth of a city destined to be the capital of an extensive empire. He hoped New Englanders would accept the site, and urged that they invest in lots and send their emigrants there rather than into the West. The location, he believed, would end the demarcation between North and South.[37]

L'Enfant took his plan to Mount Vernon soon after Washington returned from the South. Its key feature was a system of radial avenues imposed on a grid of streets. The resulting circles and squares provided numerous public reservations throughout the city. The Capitol, facing east toward the commercial and residential area of the city rather than west to the governmental sector, rose near the Anacostia on wooded Jenkins Hill. (Few if any of the citizens of the republican empire in 1790 knew that the first proprietor of Jenkins

Hill had called his plantation New Troy, or that John Pope had pat-
ented Rome on the banks of the Tiber just below the hill.) Not surprisingly, the presidential mansion looked straight down the
Potomac to Alexandria. The great distance between the Capitol
and presidential mansion came from the political necessity to provide something for both groups of proprietors. The decision to
name the great avenue connecting the two buildings after the State
of Pennsylvania surely also reflected political considerations.

Washington suggested few changes in L'Enfant's plan, but his
influence on it was significant, since he had chosen the ground within the district upon which L'Enfant imposed his design. Had Washington dispatched L'Enfant to the heights above Georgetown, the
planner could have created an Athenian capital for the United
States. But the American Cincinnatus and his fellow citizens considered themselves republicans, not democrats. To them, Rome,
not Athens, provided the appropriate model. Therefore Washington pointed L'Enfant to the fields and woodlots of the relatively level plain through which the Tiber flowed. L'Enfant knew what had
been accomplished on similar landscapes in France. His long–range
view of a capital of magnificent buildings and landscapes reflected
America's optimistic outlook for the survival of the Union and the
establishment of a republican empire, and his admirer George
Washington became wedded to his vision and the resulting plan.[38]

Publication of the plan stimulated newspaper praise for
L'Enfant's genius, taste and imagination. George Walker, promoting the site as the most beautiful, salubrious and convenient in
America if not in the world, predicted that the federal city would
rise with a rapidity previously unparalleled in urban history. It
would become the delight and admiration of the world and future
generations would consider it one of Washington's greatest accom-
plishments. But unanimity was lacking; at least one writer condemned the plan as overly grand.[39]

At the end of June Washington returned to Georgetown where,
with the aid of L'Enfant's plan, he allayed the proprietors' fears of
financial ruin and obtained the deeds. Washington, Jefferson, Madison and L'Enfant met in Philadelphia in August 1791 to consider
what measures should be taken to prepare the capital for Congress
by 1800. Although encouraged to express their own opinions freely

and reach independent conclusions, the next month the commissioners unanimously concurred on every point that had been decided at Philadelphia. In addition, they named the city "Washington" (a suggestion made publicly as early as August 1789) and the district the "District of Columbia."[40]

With the foundation so carefully laid by his own efforts, Washington planned to turn responsibility for the federal city over to the Commission. But his assessment of the politics of the issue, his obsession with the political economy of the Potomac, and his desire to remain informed kept the president busy with the affairs of the city which bore his name. In the few years remaining to him before his death, Washington not only faced, but also contributed to, a variety of threats to the Potomac capital which emanated from both enemies and friends.

In praising L'Enfant's plan to the public, Walker had noted that Congress could repeal its decision to place the capital on the Potomac, but predicted that, as it had refused to alter the funding act when the public creditors of Pennsylvania asked it to do so during the third session of the First Congress, it would not violate public and private faith by altering the seat of government act. Nevertheless, Madison and others showed concern when the Second Congress opened, for rumor persisted that a New York representative planned to introduce a motion to repeal the act before the idea of a Potomac capital sunk deeper roots. It proved to be no more than a rumor, since the Eastern States refused to join in attempted alterations of the Compromise of 1790, well aware of their gains from it.

At the end of 1791 a prominent Boston Federalist informed Washington's secretary Tobias Lear that the capital was the cement of union between the North and South. This helped to convince Washington that the Eastern States had essentially accepted the decision. Indeed, some of the Potomac's most vocal opponents in the First Congress, Gerry foremost among them, had publicly declared their opposition to a repeal of the seat of government act. Rep. Richard Bland Lee concluded in 1793 that his New England colleagues had no intentions of impeding the development of the federal city and that his constituents could expect the value of their property to rise accordingly. A year later he defended his 1790 votes on funding–assumption, asserting that the location had reunited

Virginia's and New England's interests, a result for which he claimed credit.[41]

Although New England's opposition had been neutralized, Washington remained sensitive that some Philadelphians wanted to retain Congress if a way could be found. "There is a current in this city which sets so strongly against everything that relates to the federal district," he complained to Stuart in 1792, "that it is next to impossible to stem it. . . . Danger from them is to be apprehended; and in my opinion, from no other." The president blamed the city's engravers for delaying the publication of L'Enfant's plan and even considered sending it to London. Pennsylvania's decision to erect buildings at Philadelphia for the use of the federal government worried him more. Not even his statement that he probably would not reside in a presidential mansion, if one was built, stopped the state. He refused to move into the building and John Adams followed his example.[42]

Another major threat to the seat of government act at Philadelphia came not from politicians but from pestilence. Yellow fever struck in the summer of 1793. Should the president convene the Third Congress elsewhere? Washington turned to Jefferson and Madison for advice, and they concurred that he must not establish a precedent for future infringement of the seat of government act. Congress should meet and adjourn itself. If the president disagreed, his advisers urged a place in Pennsylvania, such as Germantown, Lancaster, or Reading, as the best political choice. Washington toyed with the idea of calling Congress to Annapolis, but decided against it because of the local motives which would be imputed to him. A few New Yorkers actively sought the return of Congress, a measure opposed by Senator Rufus King, at last reconciled to the Compromise of 1790. In the end the president did nothing, and received criticism for acting out of fear of establishing a precedent for others to violate the seat of government act.[43]

Even before yellow fever hit Philadelphia, Washington had recognized reluctantly that the real threat to the capital came from discord among its friends rather than from the Eastern States and Pennsylvania. The Anacostia and Georgetown proprietors eyed one another jealously. The Commission sparred with both groups, with its employees and with the land speculators who invested in city lots. Washington attended personally to most of the crises which arose among the friends of the federal city, for they delayed construction and threatened to offer Congress good reason, if it sought one, for not moving to the Potomac in 1800. As a result he immersed himself in the details of personnel, building regulations and financing from 1791 until his retirement in 1797.

The first personnel crisis proved devastating. Opposed to a sale of lots before wider dissemination of his plan, L'Enfant refused to make it available to the Commission for the October 1791 sale. He believed plats of the lots for sale to be sufficient, arguing that the absence of data with which to compare the lots to other points in the city would bring higher prices. Only 35 lots sold for a total of $8,756, of which but $2,000 was due immediately.

Although the results of the sale confirmed his opposition to its timing, L'Enfant bore the onus. Secretary of State Jefferson encouraged the president to take the opportunity to assure the Commission that the planner served at its pleasure. This placed Washington in a quandary. He considered L'Enfant to be defensive about his plan, yet he recognized that the commissioners did not pay enough attention to the feelings of either L'Enfant or Ellicott. And he probably knew that Jefferson lacked sympathy for both planner and plan. Jefferson's intense feelings apparently arose from L'Enfant's friendship with Hamilton and a difference of opinion with L'Enfant over how grand the capital of a republic ought to be. Washington chose a middle course. He admonished L'Enfant for withholding the plan, and sent word to the Commission—in a private communication through David Stuart—that he deemed the assistance of L'Enfant and Ellicott essential and that the Commission should honor their feelings, or at least appear to do so. He promised Stuart that he would instruct L'Enfant that he served at the pleasure of the Commission.

L'Enfant next antagonized the Commission when he took an action that threatened its chances of obtaining assistance from the Maryland legislature. The politically influential Daniel Carroll of Duddington had continued to construct a house in the midst of a square set aside by L'Enfant as a focal point for the southeastern sector of the city. Fearful of the precedent and indignant over Carroll's refusal to remove the structure when asked, L'Enfant ordered the walls taken down—but carefully, so that Carroll could use the bricks elsewhere. He left the foundation alone, for it had been dug before the land became public.

The high tone of L'Enfant's letter to the Commission defending himself grew out of pride and unfamiliarity with the subtleties of the English Language. Subject to one master, the infuriated commissioners refused to take orders from an employee, no matter how talented. Consequently Washington finally instructed L'Enfant to consider himself subordinate to the Commission in all matters. At the same time, the president urged the commissioners to gratify L'Enfant's pride by giving him ample powers to carry out their objects, for he was irreplaceable. Tensions between the Commission and L'Enfant seemed to improve, and he restrained himself when he discovered that the newly completed house of Notley Young— another relative of Commissioner Daniel Carroll—sat in the middle of one of his planned streets.[44]

Early in 1792 L'Enfant came to Philadelphia to supervise the engraving of his plan. He submitted to the president an expensive, detailed proposal for the year's work, thus clearly indicating his refusal to act under the supervision of the Commission. Washington ignored the proposal. He pressed L'Enfant to complete the engraving, and, when it was not ready by mid–February, instructed Ellicott to complete it, authorizing him to make certain changes with Jefferson's guidance. Meanwhile, Stuart informed Washington privately that the commissioners had all agreed to resign rather than be subjected any longer to L'Enfant's caprice. The president must either make the planner their servant or render him independent. Stuart warned against the latter course because of the expense of L'Enfant's extravagant plan, citing as an example the extensive park about the presidential mansion. Perhaps such an "immense and gloomy wilderness" within a city was appropriate for despotic governments, but not for the United States. Stuart's view of L'Enfant's plan, which Washington pointedly rejected, indicated a lack of support on the Commission not only for the artist but also for his plan.

Recognizing another crisis at hand, the president sought a solution through the mediation of L'Enfant's supporter and federal city promoter, George Walker. To Walker, L'Enfant poured out his grievances: the commissioners refused to rely on him for matters within the pale of his professional competence, they did not have the cause of the federal city at heart, and they openly sided with the Anacostia proprietors against those about Georgetown. He would not serve under them and later take the blame for the failure of the dream of a Potomac capital. Washington attempted to mollify L'Enfant's suspicions about the commissioners and to find a compromise acceptable to the planner, but L'Enfant's response to him so offended Washington that he fired the planner. In order to minimize the political repercussions, the politically astute president asked L'Enfant's supporter Alexander Hamilton to draft the letter of dismissal for Jefferson's signature.[45]

Deeply hurt, L'Enfant believed he had had at heart only the advancement of the president's favorite object. Washington urged the Commission to pay L'Enfant handsomely for his services. He always regretted the loss of the talented designer, and praised the beauty of his plan whenever the opportunity arose. L'Enfant refused the compensation offered by the Commission as beneath his dignity—just as he had turned down that offered for his work on Federal Hall. He lived out most of his life as the impoverished guest of the Digges Family on its estate directly across the Potomac from Mount Vernon, moving a year before his death in 1825 to the home of the daughter of his former nemesis Daniel Carroll of Duddington.[46]

George Walker publicly defended L'Enfant, but his efforts came to naught. It was one of the last of Walker's many contributions to the creation of Washington, D.C. He had invested $25,000 in a 383-acre tract on the eastern side of the federal city, for he had always argued that early development of nonfederal buildings should be there. When the Commission did not support this, he became disaffected and openly fought with them. In 1793 he went to England in an attempt to save his investment. There he published *A Description of the Situation and Plan of the City of Washington . . .* (London, 1793), a pamphlet based in part on "A Citizen of the World." Walker never received satisfaction from the commissioners and, after Congress arrived on the Potomac in 1800, he returned permanently to Scotland. Forgotten by history, the man who first proposed the site actually selected for the federal city deserves a special place in the history of Washington, D.C.[47]

Who served on the Commission was as important to the early development of the federal city as who planned it. Knowing this, Washington devoted considerable effort to appointing committed replacements as the original members retired in the mid-1790s. Thomas Johnson's seat went to Gustavus Scott, a Potomac Company investor who had served on the Maryland legislative committee which had met with Washington in 1784 and drafted the bill to charter the company. To replace Stuart, Washington turned to another intimate, Tobias Lear, who had become involved with the Potomac Company after retiring as the president's secretary and moving to Georgetown. When Lear declined, William Thornton, the man whose design for the Capitol had so captivated Washington, accepted Stuart's seat.

Former Massachusetts Senator Tristram Dalton, who had joined Lear in a Georgetown mercantile partnership, applied for Daniel Carroll's place, but, with two Marylanders already on the Commission, Washington felt obliged to appoint a Virginian. He chose Alexander White, a Potomac Company investor and former congressman, whose vote, like that of the man he replaced, had been essential to the Compromise of 1790. Dalton, who like others saw the federal city as the favorite object of Washington's heart, finally became a commissioner in 1801 as one of President John Adams's "midnight appointments." President Thomas Jefferson and Secretary of State James Madison, recognizing Dalton's deep commitment to the Potomac capital following his critical Senate votes on the seat of government bill in 1790, saw no reason to withhold his commission as they did so many of Adams's other last minute appointments.[48]

Other personnel problems at the federal city required less of Washington's time; nevertheless, they proved worrisome. Not long after assuming L'Enfant's duties, Andrew Ellicott fought with the Commission and the scenario of a year earlier repeated itself. The proprietors generally backed Ellicott, and Washington, while publicly supporting the commissioners, privately urged them to compromise. After Ellicott resigned, the Commission relied on Samuel Blodget of Massachusetts as a superintendent to expedite construction. Blodget, a man consumed by the idea of a Potomac capital and the establishment of a national university there, survived only briefly in the job. Several years after his dismissal, he published a defense which averred that he had heard Washington advocate the Potomac for the American capital when he was encamped with the Continental Army outside of Boston in 1775. L'Enfant, Ellicott and Blodget were only the most prominent among those who left the employ of the federal government after disputes with the Commission.[49]

Washington's concern over the physical development of the city led him to intervene in design details as important as the Capitol and as mundane as the street railings. In 1794 he determined that a fort to protect the city should be built opposite Mount Vernon. Then, against the advice of two secretaries of war, he decided to build only one federal armory and to place it at Harpers Ferry on the Potomac, a site he considered to be of immense strength, inaccessible to the enemy and open to inland navigation in all directions. Perhaps the most short-sighted decision he made occurred in 1796 when, in order to expedite construction, he waived, until after the arrival of Congress, the regulation that all buildings be either stone or brick.[50]

A final major problem Washington faced was funding: the vast project needed more than the $192,000 provided by Virginia and Maryland. The promoters of the capital had long expected the federal city lots to be their major source of money; in April 1791 they estimated that the public would realize $800,000 from their sale. The 1792 auction raised little more than the 1791 sale, and Washington gave his blessing to a land speculation scheme to provide funds, speed construction and tie more closely New England to the site. James Greenleaf of Massachusetts agreed to purchase 3,000 lots from the public at $66.50 each, to build 70 houses prior to 1800 and to lend the commissioners $2,200 a month until the arrival of Congress. A consortium he formed with former Senator Robert Morris and John Nicholson of Pennsylvania sold 500 lots to Thomas Law at four times what they had paid the Commission for them a year earlier. Furious, Washington privately censured the Commission for not finding such buyers itself. Greenleaf got into a dispute with the Commission and withdrew from the consortium. By 1795 Morris and Nicholson owed the federal government thousands of dollars and the president personally asked his friend Morris to pay the debt. Instead, the partners went to jail for bankruptcy, leaving un-finished houses in the federal city and tarnishing its name as a place for investment. Law proved to be a more able manager of his lots, and in 1796 Washington consented to his marriage to Martha Washington's granddaughter.[51]

When the sale of lots failed to provide the money needed to carry on the public works and foreign loans proved unattainable, Washington realized reluctantly that he would have to turn to Congress and the state legislatures. Virginia showed no interest, for its concern with the future capital waned as its opposition to federal measures waxed. The president urged the Commission to approach Maryland, despite expected opposition from the Upper Chesapeake Interest. Maryland refused to lend any money without guarantees, and in January 1796 Washington turned to Congress for permission to use the public lots for that purpose.[52]

Congress took the opportunity to launch an investigation into what Washington called "all the faupaus which have been committed—all the neglects, inattentions, and want of the close and constant scrutiny of those to whom the business was intrusted." Opposition to the request centered in Pennsylvania, New York and Connecticut, and was led by the Philadelphians, one of whom declared it a violation of a verbal agreement in 1790 that public funds would not be employed in constructing the capital.

Sectionally based party strife focused on the Jay Treaty with Great Britain tore at the Fourth Congress. Senator Rufus King and other northerners let it be known that they would not support the loan guarantee bill unless southerners in the House gave up their opposition to the appropriation necessary to implement the Jay Treaty. King deemed it foolish to adopt a bill which the South considered essential to the survival of the Union, while refusing appropriations for a treaty which the North believed equally vital to the same goal. Soon after the treaty appropriations passed the House, the bill to guarantee the Maryland loan with the federal city lots passed the Senate by a substantial majority. Only two of the twenty-four members who had served in the First Congress voted against it; included in the majority were such avid former opponents of the Potomac site as Ames, Goodhue, Sedgwick and William L. Smith. Sedgwick, in fact, gave one of the strongest speeches in support of what had been accomplished at the federal city. Once again the Compromise of 1790 had been reaffirmed. Beginning with a direct appeal from Washington, Maryland lent the Commission $250,000 between 1797 and 1799. Once committed to borrowing money, the federal government assumed the full cost of the development of its capital.[53]

Distant from the federal city and obsessed with dreams for its success, Washington had not always made wise decisions. Nevertheless, by the time he retired to Mount Vernon in March 1797, the only opposition to a removal to the Potomac in 1800 centered at Philadelphia. Its residents called the federal city a forest with no access to commercial information and contrasted Philadelphia's civic improvements to the City of Washington. Some Philadelphians still asserted that the Northern States would refuse to go to the Potomac and that, if the South insisted, the Union would be severed. In reporting these opinions, an English visitor concluded that the transfer would occur on schedule not only because a large majority of Americans favored it, but also because a refusal would destroy the harmony of the Union, if not the Union itself.[54]

Friends and neighbors at Alexandria joined to welcome Washington into retirement and he offered them his vow of support for the town's prosperity. To keep this vow and to satisfy his own dreams, Washington violated his commitment to keep out of federal city concerns. Just as his very existence overshadowed President John Adams's efforts in military and foreign policy, it operated in the affairs of the federal city. Adams declined to participate in routine decision making for the capital and even refused Washington's suggestion that he make a symbolic visit. He yielded, however, when the former president disagreed strongly with Adams's proposal to place the executive offices near the Capitol instead of the presidential mansion as originally planned. This disagreement did not relate to the city plan but to a difference of opinion over the role of the executive branch. Adams more than Washington viewed the executive as a servant of the legislative branch. Washington maintained a correspondence with the Commission and individual commissioners, and relied on Commissioner Thornton to oversee the construction of his houses in the federal city.[55]

Although retirement had not completely separated Washington from federal affairs, it did allow him more time to think about the inland navigation of the Potomac. "I do not hesitate to pronounce," he informed an English correspondent just before leaving the presidency, that "the lands on the waters of the Potomac will, in a few years, be in greater demand, and in higher estimation than in any other part of the United States . . . an immensity of produce will be water borne, thereby making the Federal City the great emporium of the United States." He attributed the commercial growth of Alexandria during the 1790s to the opening of the upper Potomac. Besides attending meetings of the Potomac Company, he vigorously denied rumors that his interest in—and expectations for—the river had declined. He declared himself more sanguine than ever, encouraging the Commission and friends in Maryland to push the inland navigation of the river whenever possible.[56]

The year 1800, at whose end the federal government would move to the Potomac, was a presidential election. Deeply split, the Federalist Party had good reason to fear Jefferson and the Democratic–Republican Party. The Federalists' best hope, argued the manipulative Gouverneur Morris, lay in Washington's once again coming out of retirement to accept the presidency. After all, he urged the former president, the proximity of the capital to Mount Vernon would allow for relaxation there. And, he wondered, "may not your acceptance be the needful means of fixing the Government in that Seat?" The proprietor of Mount Vernon did not receive the letter. Washington would live, a eulogist proclaimed, "cherished in the remembrance of all faithful Americans while their empire shall continue."[57]

Epilogue

Potomac Fever Revisited

PRESIDENT JOHN ADAMS NEVER SUFFERED FROM Potomac Fever, but he understood the susceptibility of Virginians to it, concluding in 1806 that "Virginian geese are all Swans. . . . The Philadelphians and New Yorkers, who are local and partial enough to themselves, are meek and modest in comparison with Virginian Old Dominionism." But if anyone hoped in 1800 that he would seize upon lingering opposition to the seat of government act at Philadelphia to keep Congress there, they misjudged the man. Adams had worked closely with the Virginians to bring about the Revolution three decades earlier. He understood the necessity of a removal to the Potomac for the preservation of the Union, and he respected George Washington's belief that a Potomac capital would bind North to South and East to West.

Adams thought he knew where Washington had found the guiding principles of his political life: Charles Rollin had observed in his popular *Ancient History* that there was nothing nobler for a person of eminent merit and virtue, who modestly preferred a life of retirement, than to "refuse the offer made to him of reigning over a whole nation, and at last consent to undergo the toil of government, upon no other motive than that of being serviceable to his fellow citizens." The leader whom Rollin described became so powerful that he commanded "his subjects to build a city, marking out himself the place and circumference of the walls."[1]

Ironically, Adams, not Washington, got blamed when the federal city became a minor subject of bickering between Democratic–Republicans and Federalists in the late 1790s. Some of the former believed the expensive and grand city on the Potomac formed part

235

of a repressive Federalist program including assumption, the bank, the Jay Treaty and the Alien and Sedition Acts. That it did not become more of a partisan issue stemmed from the well known involvement of James Madison and Thomas Jefferson in the 1790 decision and the continued support it received from most southern Democratic–Republicans. Nevertheless, Thomas Paine later pointed to Adams as the culprit, and pictured him strutting before the presidential mansion in Washington, declaring in the pomp of his imagination, "Is not this great Babylon that I have builded?" But Adams bore the criticism and carried out the terms of the Compromise of 1790. No evidence exists for claims that Adams was an enemy of the seat of government act, or that he and his divided party agreed to move to the Potomac only because they hoped thereby to gain votes for his reelection in 1800.[2]

The Commission for the Federal City informed President Adams in the fall of 1799 that the capital was ready, and when the Sixth Congress met in December, Adams called its attention to the impending transfer of the government. In April 1800 Congress passed a removal act—the funds for which had been appropriated in 1790—and in May ordered its next meeting to be at Washington in November. Adams directed the executive departments to move in June and traveled to the Potomac for a personal inspection. To the residents of Georgetown, who gave him a grand welcome, he expressed his hope that all opposition to removal would soon vanish. At a special ceremony in the Capitol, his old friend Tristram Dalton welcomed him on behalf of the inhabitants of the federal city. From there Adams rode down to Mount Vernon to pay respects to the widow Washington, and at a banquet in Alexandria, he toasted the town's delusions of grandeur: "May it become intimate in commerce with its namesake in Egypt." In November Adams returned to the Potomac with the federal government. He congratulated Congress on assembling at last at its permanent seat. The House recognized the importance of the event to the political affairs of the nation, and both houses acknowledged Adams's reference to the intimate relationship between the federal city and its recently deceased namesake.[3]

In the spring of 1801 the House appropriated money for a one hundred square foot pyramid mausoleum at the federal city for the body of Washington, but eight decades would pass before a monument to Washington, first proposed in 1783 and included in the L'Enfant plan, was dedicated at the nation's capital. The early problems encountered by advocates of the monument amused Timothy Pickering of Philadelphia, who believed "that a monument, which would be more durable than a few pieces of brass or marble, was already founded by the city, established for the seat of national government, and called by his name."[4]

Early Washington, D.C., is popularly believed to have been a swamp. Dozens of observers of the young town, Europeans as well as Americans from all sections of the country, indicate otherwise. Almost all agreed that "New Jerusalem on the Potomac," as William L. Smith called it, had a stunning natural setting, or echoed and expanded on First Lady Abigail Adams's simple assessment that it was "beautiful."[5]

The City of Washington was laid out on three river terraces, seamed with stream valleys, which rose gradually from tidewater at the White House grounds northward to an elevation of one hundred feet at what became Florida Avenue, the boundary of the amphitheatrical city. To the north and east of the city stood two more eroding terraces, 400 feet at their highest elevation. To the west across the mile wide, eighteen foot deep Potomac River, rose the Arlington hills and the estate of George Washington Parke Custis. On the northwest the Georgetown heights dominated the horizon, while to the south rose the hills of the Anacostia River terraces. Tobacco and grain fields, pastures, woods of maple, tulip poplar, black cherry, and oak, and a few roads quilted the landscape. Scattered homes and outbuildings sheltered small planters and farmers who had first settled the area in the second quarter of the eighteenth century. A majority of these farmers and planters owned no slaves and only a few owned more than ten.

Navigable water—the Potomac, the Anacostia and Rock Creek—bounded the federal city on three sides while Tiber Creek cut deeply into it. Cattail and reed tidal marshes, home to kingfishers, herons, muskrats and turtles, lined the Upper Anacostia and the smaller inlets and creeks, but were less common on the more rapidly flowing Potomac, where sturgeon and wintering canvasbacks offered good hunting and fishing. Forests of sycamore, tulip poplar and river birch lined the Potomac River bottoms above Georgetown. Along the Upper Anacostia grew extensive patches of wild rice. Springs were abundant, particularly in the city's eastern sector.

No part of the well-drained city supported a swamp, a wetland where trees stand in water all or most of the time. The lowland between the White House and the Capitol south to the Anacostia, an area virtually synonymous with southwest Washington, was the most likely part of the nine and one-half square mile federal city to support a swamp. Even given the loose definition of the word "swamp" in the late eighteenth century—it could mean swamp, marsh, fen, bog, brushy area or just river bottom land—only a few of the dozens of descriptions of the early federal city mention swamps in this area: one between the base of Capitol Hill and the present site of the East Wing of the National Gallery and another at the Justice Department. These two small, low lying areas between Tiber Creek and Pennsylvania Avenue were subject to periodic flooding, but the most descriptive source clearly used "swamp" in the sense of an area overgrown with bushes, briars and thorns, not trees in standing water. Andrew Ellicott's 1793 topographic map of the District of Columbia clearly delineated sizeable marshes where they occurred. None were within the federal city.

Historic land usage in southwest Washington does not support the existence of a swamp either. Notley Young's plantation home stood at what became G and 10th Streets, S.W., and his family's graveyard and gardens lay even closer to the river, lower than the thirty-foot elevation of the house. Daniel Carroll of Duddington had platted the town of Carrollsburg there, and prominent Maryland families purchased lots. Thomas Law chose that part of the federal city for his successful investments. Most importantly, George Washington, whose eye for good land had few rivals, would never have selected swampy lowlands for the seat of an empire which he expected to perpetuate his name and reputation in history. The swamp myth simply lacks credibility whether one reads the landscape or the documents.[6]

The effects of a decade of man's hand on the land proved a contrast to the natural setting. By 1800 over half a million dollars had been spent on the development of the capital. The population and number of houses had grown dramatically. An imposing mansion for the president and the first wing of a magnificent Capitol rose dramatically above the landscape. Despite these achievements the city left most visitors with a sense of incompletion. Clumps of houses sat scattered here and there, a few left unfinished by the Morris and Nicholson Consortium and already in decay. Broad muddy streets, often lined with tree stumps, connected the widely separated buildings. The distance between the presidential mansion and the Capitol struck many observers: it was greater than that from one side of the settled portion of Philadelphia to the other. Although the two buildings required much additional work, the latter housed Congress, the Supreme Court and the Library of Congress, which had been created by the 1800 removal act. Despite a newspaper, taverns, a theater and such other amenities of urban life as outdoor concerts by the marine band, the cultural deprivation of the federal city in comparison with Philadelphia was striking. Abigail Adams, stunned that after so many years in preparation the city could be so unimproved and inconvenient, concluded that New Englanders would have done better.[7]

Nothing better symbolizes the triumph of the Democratic–Republican Party in 1800 than the movement of the United States capital from Philadelphia to underdeveloped Washington, D.C. Once again, as from 1790 to 1792, the urbane Thomas Jefferson became deeply involved in the development of the capital. His efforts proved more fruitful than Washington's in part because he resided in the city he nurtured. In his farewell to federal city residents, he expressed his hope for the achievement of the compromises necessary to preserve the Union, and his conviction that Washington, D.C., would grow with sure and steady steps until it became the fairest seat of science and wealth in the world. Despite Jefferson's belief that a constitutional Amendment would be needed before Congress could establish a museum at Washington, the capital became a seat of science with the creation of the Smithsonian Institution in 1846. Only in the late twentieth century has it become a seat of wealth.[8]

Adams's treasury secretary had considered himself in the company of madmen when he arrived at Washington in 1800 and observed the proprietors' visions with respect to their own prospects.

Thus did a son of Connecticut encounter Potomac Fever, just two years before the completion of a canal around Great Falls. Dreams of the federal city as a commercial emporium, including wharves, canals, a deepened river channel, a port on the Anacostia and, finally, railroads, continued until after the Civil War. As late as 1873 support existed for a manufacturing city at Great Falls. Long before the dreams faded, the reality of Washington's commercial destiny was starkly evident to the unbiased eye. The total absence of all sights, sounds and smells of commerce struck Frances Trollope in 1830.

The exclusive jurisdiction of Congress over the affairs of the city provided the primary obstacle to commercial development. Other, more pressing problems confronted the legislature of an aggressive, westward–expanding nation. Neglect and delay governed its approach to the city's needs, not to mention its desires. Congressmen opposed appropriations for commercial facilities which might draw trade from the states they represented. Away from Congress, Baltimore and the Erie Canal destroyed Washington's commercial dreams. To capture the trade of the Ohio Valley, Baltimore's merchants turned their backs on the Susquehanna and reached for the Potomac route. In 1828, as President John Quincy Adams turned the first spadeful of earth at Georgetown for the Chesapeake and Ohio Canal, former Senator Charles Carroll broke ground at Baltimore for the Baltimore and Ohio Railroad. It was this railroad, and not the navigational scheme of George Washington or even a full–scale canal, that penetrated the valleys and bold ridges separating the coastal plain from the fertile Ohio Valley. Three years earlier, the completion of the Erie Canal had connected the Upper Midwest to the Atlantic along the Mohawk, the route which had always been the Potomac's true rival.[9]

Even before the unfortunate relationship between commercial growth and congressional government dawned on the Potomac's residents, calls arose for Congress to divest itself of exclusive jurisdiction. The pressure started within a Congress burdened by debates over the proper forms of government for the District of Columbia and the City of Washington, the rights and needs of its politically disenfranchised citizens and the expenses involved. For years residents of Georgetown and Alexandria opposed all efforts at partial or complete retrocession of the District to Maryland and Virginia. Finally, in 1846, complaining about the denial of their political rights and the premature commercial death of their town, Alexandrians secured the retrocession of one-third of the District to Virginia. Even George Washington Parke Custis, who for years had opposed the measure as counter to the wishes of George Washington, supported retrocession. In the 1980s some residents of the District of Columbia support retrocession of much of the remainder of the capital to Maryland as a means of escaping from the exclusive jurisdiction of Congress and regaining representation in that body. In 1990 legislation was introduced in Congress which would provide District residents with the right to vote in Maryland federal elections, but which would retain Congress's jurisdiction over the District. Its advocates argued that the denial of voting rights after 1800 arose from a wrong judicial ruling in 1805 (*Riley vs. Lamar*, 6US344) which overlooked the intent of the 1801 District Organic Act.[10]

One argument local residents used against retrocession was their fear that it might give ammunition to those who advocated removing the capital from the Potomac, a threat which haunted Washington, D.C., until after the Civil War. In 1804 a senator proposed that Congress reside temporarily at Baltimore. A New Jersey senator offered the public buildings at Trenton as an alternative. Both motions met with defeat, but in debate on them northern and southern senators had an opportunity to confirm the Compromise of 1790. John Quincy Adams of Massachusetts denied that Congress had the power to leave the Potomac. James Jackson of Georgia declared that public faith, including the assumption of $21,500,000 in state debts, had been pledged to the location. Further, he pointed out, the federal city "might be called the hobby-horse of, perhaps, the most illustrious man that ever lived," and he hoped that his grandchildren would not see that predestined day, perhaps centuries in the future, when the capital would move to the newly acquired Louisiana Territory west of the Mississippi River.[11]

A far more serious threat arose when the Philadelphians sprang back into action in 1807. A series of anonymous letters denied that the federal city was a heart pumping blood throughout the Union, describing it instead as an unhealthy, expensive, rickety infant which drained the vital fluids, particularly of the commercial North. Congress should return to Philadelphia, the home of the real Father of the Revolution, Benjamin Franklin. The thinly populated federal city was easy prey for anyone intent on overthrowing the government by another revolution; had not Aaron Burr claimed he could drive Congress and President Jefferson into the Potomac with just 300 men? Not surprisingly, Benjamin Rush told John Adams that he approved of a removal to Philadelphia. Adams savored the irony of Pennsylvania's complaint, and insisted to Rush that his state must accept not only responsibility for the location but also the domination of the federal government which it had given the South.

In February 1808 the House debated and turned back a temporary move to Philadelphia. Supporters of the resolution, led by New Jersey and Pennsylvania representatives, argued that it was despotic to deny the citizens of the district their political rights, wrong to surround the capital of a republic with slavery and absurd to build a navy yard so far from the ocean. George Washington's predilection for the Potomac, they argued, marked the solitary blot on his character. Opponents of a removal appealed to the memory of Washington, reminded members of the harassment former congressmen had received from anti–slavery Quakers in Philadelphia, and insisted that if the seat of government act of 1790 were repealed, the funding act of 1790 should also be repealed. The Virginian who suggested the double repeal declared Washington, D.C., to be a Federalist plot intended to perpetuate the name of their favorite idol.[12]

The burning of the Capitol and the presidential mansion in 1814 attracted votes from many who otherwise would not have supported a temporary move, much as had the 1783 military demonstration at Philadelphia. Opponents of the effort pictured a move in response to British predation as a disgrace, and urged Congress not to break the strongest link in the federal chain. The Democratic-Republican press, asserting that President James Madison would veto any removal, reminded readers that Washington had placed the federal government on the Potomac, that Madison had played a prominent role in the compromise and that to go elsewhere would be a breach of the public faith equivalent to a repudiation of the public debt. Support for removal dwindled away as Madison exerted pressure on his party and the motion failed.[13]

After the failure of these three attempts, the question did not arise again in Congress for half a century. Nevertheless, several factors led to occasional public discussion about transferring the seat of empire from the Potomac. One was the southern atmosphere of the capital, enhanced not only by slavery but also by the disproportionately large number of civil and military offices filled by Virginians and Marylanders. Also, the rapid westward expansion of the nation combined with tensions between the North-South spurred talk of removal. At first Cincinnati or some other spot on the Ohio River seemed to merit attention, but by mid-century most eyes had turned to St. Louis on the Mississippi River. The West's demand for a more centrally located capital united residents of the Atlantic States in opposition, except for some vocal abolitionists. The same states which had fought so bitterly over a proper central location during the Revolution now joined to dismiss calls for a more central site as irrelevant in an age of steam and telegraph.

With the advent of the Civil War—an event perhaps delayed by placing the capital on the Potomac—the United States acted quickly to reassume control over that part of the District of Columbia which had been returned to Virginia. On George Washington Parke Custis's estate across the Potomac, then the property of his daughter and her husband, General Robert E. Lee, the United States buried its dead soldiers. Immediately after the war Senator Benjamin Wade of Ohio unsuccessfully sought repeal of retrocession. He argued that the 1846 act had been an unconstitutional secessionist plot and a slap both at George Washington and the greatest political compromise in American history. It, in his opinion, had prevented the dissoluation of the Union and ended debate on the most controversial issue of its day, the location of the American capital. All efforts to move the capital had failed, he concluded, because of the sanctity of that compromise which had *permanently* placed the capital on the Potomac River.[14]

The late 1860s saw a flood of petitions from the Mississippi Valley seeking a new centrally located national capital. Many suggested St. Louis. Logan U. Reavis, evangelist for the "St. Louis, the Future Great City of the World" Movement, called upon the federal government to leave ugly, effete Washington, D.C. Congress took up the subject once again in 1870. An Ohio representative who supported removal to the Mississippi Valley discounted both the investment of federal funds in Washington and the cost of leaving. In eighty years, he claimed, the United States had spent only thirty-eight million dollars for the buildings, grounds and works of art at Washington. Not only the archives and art treasures of the government, but also the buildings themselves, could be relocated. Certainly Americans had a reverence for their capital and the tomb of Washington nearby, but about them had existed for years a society based on slavery, which advocated rebellion against the Union. When the future grandeur of the nation was surveyed, when Canada and all of the lands south to the Isthmus of Panama would be part of the nation, who but maiden ladies and widows who kept boarding houses at the capital could oppose a transfer?

Rep. John Logan of Illinois, leader of the removal campaign, agreed. The location of the capital on the Potomac had given Virginia excessive influence and slavery excessive protection. A Pennsylvania capital, the wish of the majority in 1790, might have meant an earlier abolition of slavery. Only after Abraham Lincoln came out of the West was slavery's stronghold on the Potomac taken away. Let the ashes of George Washington, Father of the Old Republic, remain on the Potomac, and let the capital follow the ashes of Lincoln, Father of the New Republic, to the Mississippi Valley, the center of population and transportation as well as agricultural, commercial and mineral wealth. (Logan's body, incidentally, did not follow Lincoln's home to Illinois; it, like those of many other politicians who have served on the Potomac, lies buried near its banks.)

Not all midwesterners supported removal. A Wisconsin representative believed the capital should remain where the Father of the Country placed it. California, he argued, was no farther from Washington, D.C., in 1870 than New York had been in 1790. Most importantly, President Ulysses Grant of Illinois declared that the removal of the capital required a process similar to amending the Constitution. Grant's suggestion that a two-thirds vote of Congress was necessary and the implication of a presidential veto otherwise soon sounded the death knell of the campaign. Logan U.

Reavis attacked Grant in a letter to the *New York Tribune,* which drew a rejoinder from the editors, who commented that New York City was the proper site for the United States capital since it was so corrupt that it need have no fears of the corrupting influence of Congress. New Orleans, or a city in Panama, not St. Louis, it added, might be a better choice for a future capital, since these locations reflected the possible annexation of more of the waning Spanish Empire.[15]

The 1870 discussion settled the question: Washington was the permanent capital of the United States. From time to time since, there have been calls to transfer the capital to the Mississippi Valley, or to establish a second, summer residence near the Rockies. Nevertheless, as the implications of permanence began to dawn on Congress, the aesthetic possibilities of a truly monumental city crept toward realization. In 1901 Congress declared its intention to adhere to Pierre L'Enfant's design wherever possible. This proved a false start, for the open spaces of the mall were too tempting, particularly in wartime. Much of the credit for the revival of concern with the aesthetics of the United States capital belongs to the executive branch where John and Jacqueline Kennedy and Lady Bird and Lyndon Johnson provided leadership during the 1960s.

George Washington, Thomas Jefferson, James Madison, George Walker and Pierre L'Enfant would today easily recognize the core of the city they founded. The Great Falls of the Potomac would be even more familiar to Washington. Its turbulent waters, sycamores, spring beauties and pileated woodpeckers remain a natural monument to the failure of his dream of commercial empire on the Potomac. On the other hand, Big Government has brought to that ancient river a tide of economic growth which not even Washington pictured in his most fevered dreams. Many new, and presumably temporary, residents of Washington, D.C., drawn there by its political and economic importance, succumb to something called Potomac Fever. That powerful affliction is neither new nor particularly different from that which infected George Washington when he sought immortality in the creation of the United States and the capital named after him.

... about the conclusion of the eighteenth century, a due attention to the interests and preservation of the western and southern country obliged them [Congress] to remove to the banks of the Potomac; near to what was formerly esteemed the head of the navigation of that fine river; a river, which ... has become the grand canal and never–failing inlet and medium of conveyance, to and from some of the most beautiful and fertile countries in America. There they have erected a city, which like Rome in her glory, may be called the strength of nations, the delight of the universe, the birth place of sages, and, if not* the abode of gods, *yet truly the nurse of heroes, statesmen, and philosophers.*

[Philip Freneau], *"Description of* NEW YORK *One Hundred and Fifty Years Hence,"* Daily Advertiser (New York), 14 June 1790.

The establishment of the federal city was one of the offsprings of that revolutionary enthusiasm, which elevated the american mind. . . . It has been said that the idea of creating a new city, better arranged in its local distribution of houses and streets, more magnificent in its public buildings, and superior in the advantages of its site to any other in the world, was the favorite folly of General Washington. Its existence at last was due to a compromise of interests between the Eastern and Southern States. . . . The site itself is upon a river noble in its extent and depth of water below the city, but above of difficult navigation. . . . On the map the Potomac appears a mighty river, but in fact it is, with the exception of the Shenandoah and few other branches, the drain of mountains and barren country. . . . I have not indeed said one half of what belongs to the history of this Gigantic Abortion.

Capitol Architect Benjamin H. Latrobe to Italian Patriot Phillip Mazzei, Washington, 29 May 1806, John C. Van Horne, ed. *Papers of Benjamin Henry Latrobe* 2:227–28

Abbreviations Used in Notes

AFMT	Adams Family Manuscript Trust, Massachusetts Historical Society, Boston
AH	Harold C. Syrett, Jacob E. Cooke, eds., *The Papers of Alexander Hamilton* (36 vols., New York, 1961–79)
BG	Benjamin to Stephen Goodhue Letters, Essex Institute, Salem, Massachusetts
BR	Lyman H. Butterfield, ed., *Letters of Benjamin Rush* (2 vols., Princeton, 1951)
CC	*Connecticut Courant* (Hartford)
CP–EU	Correspondence–Politique, Etats–Unis, Archives Nationales, France; microfilm at Library of Congress
CT	Eugene R. Sheridan and John M. Murrin, eds., *Congress at Princeton, Being the Letters of Charles to Hannah Thomson, June–October 1783* (Princeton, 1985)
CtHi	Connecticut Historical Society, Hartford
DLC	Library of Congress, Washington
EIHC	Essex Institute *Historical Collections* (Salem, 1859–)
FA	Seth Ames, ed., *Works of Fisher Ames* (2 vols., Boston, 1854), Vol. 1
FE	Gordon DenBoer, Lucy T. Brown, Merrill Jensen, and Robert A. Becker, eds., *The Documentary History of the First Federal Elections, 1788–1790,* (4 vols., Madison, 1976–90)
FG	*Federal Gazette* (Philadelphia)
GC	Gratz Collection, Historical Society of Pennsylvania
GUS	*Gazette of the United States* (New York and Philadelphia)
GWC	"The Writings of George Washington Relating to the National Capital 1791–1799," *Records* of the Columbia Historical Society, 17 (1914)
GWD	Donald Jackson and Dorothy Twohig, eds., *Diaries of George Washington* (6 vols., Charlottesville, 1976–79)
GWP	George Washington Papers, Library of Congress

GWW   John C. Fitzpatrick, ed., *Writings of George Washington* (39 vols., Washington, 1931–44)

IG   *Independent Gazetteer* (Philadelphia)

JCC   W.C. Ford, *et al.*, eds., *Journals of the Continental Congress, 1774–1789* (34 vols., Washington, 1904–37)

JM   William Hutchinson, Robert A. Rutland, Charles Hobson, *et al.*, eds., *The Papers of James Madison* (16+ vols., Chicago and Charlottesville, 1962–)

LDC   Paul Smith, Gerald Gawalt, Rosemary Fry Plakas, and Eugene R. Sheridan, eds., *Letters of Delegates to Congress, 1774–1789* (16+ vols., Washington, 1976–)

LMCC   Edmund C. Burnett, ed., *Letters of Members of the Continental Congress* (8 vols., Washington, 1921–38)

MB   Chamberlain Collection, Boston Public Library

MD   Kenneth R. Bowling and Helen E. Veit, eds., *The Diary of William Maclay and Other Notes on Senate Debates, Volume 9 of the Documentary History of the First Federal Congress* (Baltimore, 1988)

MdG(B)   *Maryland Gazette* (Baltimore)

MdHi   Maryland Historical Society, Baltimore

MdJ   *Maryland Journal* (Baltimore)

MHi   Massachusetts Historical Society, Boston

MHSC   Massachusetts Historical Society *Collections* (Boston, 1792–)

MHSP   Massachusetts Historical Society *Proceedings* (Boston, 1879–)

NHi   New–York Historical Society, New York

NjHi   New Jersey Historical Society, Newark

NN   Rare Book and Manuscript Division, Astor, Lenox, and Tilden Foundations, New York Public Library, New York

NYDA   *Daily Advertiser* (New York)

NYDG   *New–York Daily Gazette*

NYJ   *New–York Journal*

OFC	Allen C. Clark, "Origin of the Federal City," *Records of the Columbia Historical Society*, 35–36 (1935):1–97
PCC	Papers of the Continental Congress, RG 360, National Archives, Washington
PG	*Pennsylvania Gazette* (Philadelphia)
PHi	Historical Society of Pennsylvania, Philadelphia
PMHB	*Pennsylvania Magazine of History and Biography*
PP	*Pennsylvania Packet* (Philadelphia)
PPAmP	American Philosophical Society, Philadelphia
PPL	Library Company of Philadelphia manuscript collections at the Historical Society of Pennsylvania, Philadelphia
RCHS	*Records* of the Columbia Historical Society (51 vols., Washington, 1897–1984)
RiHi	Rhode Island Historical Society, Providence
RM	Robert to Mary Morris Letters, Henry E. Huntington Library, San Marino, California
ROC	John Kaminski, Gaspare J. Saladino, Richard Leffler, and Merrill Jensen, eds., *The Documentary History of the Ratification of the Constitution* (8+ vols., Madison, 1976–)
RPJCB	Brown Papers, John Carter Brown Library, Providence, Rhode Island
TC	Tench Coxe Papers, Historical Society of Pennsylvania, Philadelphia
TJ	Julian Boyd and Ruth Lester, eds., *The Papers of Thomas Jefferson* (22+ vols., Princeton, 1950–)
TJC	Saul K. Padover, ed., *Thomas Jefferson and the National Capital, 1783–1818* (Washington, 1946)
TS	Theodore Sedgwick Papers, Massachusetts Historical Society, Boston
TPP	*Times, and Patowmack Packet* (Georgetown, Maryland)
ViU	University of Virginia, Charlottesville
ViW	The College of William and Mary, Williamsburg, Virginia

VMHB	*Virginia Magazine of History and Biography*
WHi	State Historical Society of Wisconsin, Madison
WLS	George C. Rogers, Jr., "Letters of William Loughton Smith," *South Carolina Historical Magazine,* 69 (1965)
WMQ	*William and Mary Quarterly,* third series
WS	*Washington Spy* (Elizabethtown [Hagerstown], Maryland)

Introduction

1. The role of the idea of empire in America prior to 1790 has not been adequately studied. Several works have proven useful as background for the relationship between that idea and the location of the United States capital: Richard Koebner, *Empire* (Cambridge, Eng., 1961); Durand Echeverria, *Mirage in the West* (Princeton, 1957); Marc Egnal, *Mighty Empire, The Origins of the American Revolution* (Ithaca, 1988); Richard Van Alystyne, *Rising American Empire* (New York, 1960); and Henry Nash Smith, *Virgin Land* (Cambridge, Mass., 1950).

2. Gerald Stourzh, *Benjamin Franklin* (Chicago, 1954), 43–82; John A. Schutz and Douglass Adair, eds., *Spur of Fame* (San Marino, Ca. 1966), 81; David Ramsay, *Oration on the Advantages of American Independence* (Charleston, S.C., 1778), 20.

3. Morse, v, 469; *New Jersey Journal*, 2 Dec. 1789; WMQ 16:410; Dale Van Every, *Ark of Empire* (New York, 1963), viii.

4. MD, 332. *See also* MdG(B), 17 March 1789.

5. Henry Jackson to Henry Knox, 23 Aug. 1789, Knox, MHi; Philip Lewis to Joseph Nicholson, n.d., Nicholson, DLC; James Fairlye to Philip Schuyler, 16 Aug. 1789, Schuyler, NN; AH 3:408, 5:208, 6:503; TJ 6:365, 16:385; JM 12:393, 13:93–94; MHSC(5) 2:229; Boudinot to William Bradford, Jr., 28 Sept. 1787, Wallace, PHi; "Centinel Revived," IG, 10 Sept. 1789; John Berney and Co. to Nicholas Low, 12 Feb. 1791, Low, DLC; GWW 28:165; Thomas Burke, Comments in the North Carolina House of Commons, 12 Aug. 1788, Burke, University of N.C.; N.C. Senators to Governor, 22 Feb. 1791, Executive Letterbooks, N.C. Department of Archives and History; *Annals of Congress* 1:739, 1094; "Thomas Sumter Letter," *City Gazette*, 13 Oct. 1789; Samuel Meredith to Henry Hill, 19 April 1790, John Jay Smith, PPL; Charles to John Mortimer, 27 July 1788, Minor Family, Virginia Hist. Soc.; Samuel Chessman to Stephen Collins, 9 June 1790, Collins, DLC.

6. Boudinot to Rush, 25 July 1783, Boudinot, DLC; LMCC 7:266; "Memnon," MdG(B), 11 July 1788; Fitzsimons to [Miers Fisher], 15 July 1790, Fisher, PHi; JM 12:375.

7. *See* Joseph Davis, *Sectionalism in American Politics, 1774–1787* (Madison, 1977).

8. NYDA, 7 and 8 Sept. 1789 (quoted); GUS, 11 Feb. 1795; Marbois to Vergennes, 26 Dec. 1784, CP–EU, 28; Ephraim Blaine to James Wilson, 15 Feb. 1785, Wilson, PHi; R. Morris to Horatio Gates, 12 June 1788, Emmet, NN; Solomon Drowne to Theodore Foster, 25 July 1790, Drowne, Brown University; [J. Dickinson], Ten Queries, [Jan. 1791?], Dickinson, PHi; Christopher Gore to Tobias Lear, 28 Dec. 1791, Lear, DLC; "True Federalist," PP, 5 Jan. 1789; [George Lux, Jr.?], "True American," MdJ, 29 July 1783; FE 1:72–73, 97–100; "Citizen of America" [John O'Connor], *Political Opinions*, ([Georgetown], 1789); MHSC(5) 2:416, 3:229; TJ 16:385; ROC 3:134; JM 12:398–99.

9. George Clymer thought it pretentious for residents of New York City to refer to their town as the federal capital (To Rush, [June] 1789, *American Scene*, [Paul C. Richards, c. 1983], item 80). For rare, early use of "capital" to refer to the seat of Congress *see* LDC 10:39 and GWW 6:424. For use of "imperial" *see* Holder Slocum to Goodhue, 10 April 1789, Goodhue, New York Society Library, and JM 12:389.

10. MHSC(5) 3:281 (quoted), 330; John Churchman to Washington, [7 May 1789], Baron Poelnitz to Washington, 20 March 1790, Charles Willson Peale to Washington, 27 June 1790, GWP; "C.W. Peale to the Citizens," PP, 3 Feb. 1790; GWC,

115, 167; GWW 35:316–17; PJM 16:401–03, 425–26, 436–37; David Madsen, *National University*. . . (Detroit, 1966), 25–37; Max Farrand, ed., *Records of the Federal Convention* (4 vols., New Haven, 1911–37), 2:616.

11.   PCC, item 78, 14:605; 11 Sept. 1789, GWP.

12.   For more on American republicanism in the revolutionary era *see* Robert E. Shalhope, "Republicanism and Early American Historiography," WMQ 39:334–58. For the clash between republicanism and eighteenth century fiscal and commercial policy *see* Joyce Appleby, *Capitalism and a New Social Order* (New York, 1984), Lance Banning, *Jeffersonian Persuasion* (Ithaca, 1978), and especially Drew R. McCoy, *Elusive Republic* (Chapel Hill, 1980).

13.   For pre– and post–ratification comment on the dangers to republicanism posed by the capital *see* MHSC 73:306; R.R. Livingston, Instructions, [c. Jan. 1782], Livingston, NHi; JM 7:151, 363; LMCC 8:71n; FE 1:121; TJ 16:385. Arthur Campbell to Archibald Stuart, [25–29] July 1789, Draper, WHi; P. Henry to R.H. Lee, 29 Jan. 1790, Franklin, Yale; Mercy to [James Warren?], 27 March 1790, Mercy Warren, MHi; William to Charlotte Vans Murray, 27 Nov. 1790, Vans Murrary, DLC; and [J. Dickinson], Ten Queries, [Jan. 1791?], Dickinson, PHi. *See also* Lawrence D. Cress, "Whither Columbia? Congressional Residence and the Politics of the New Nation, 1776–1787," WMQ 32:581–600.

14.   *Columbian Magazine* 1:6; *Massachusetts Centinel,* 12 Sept. 1789.

15.   Boudinot to [John Caldwell?], 17 May 1790, Boudinot, Special Collections, Rutgers; "Connecticut," CC, 28 June 1790; George to Sarah Thatcher, 29 Sept. 1788, Thatcher, MHi; FG, 10 Sept. 1788; NYDA: 7 Sept., "X," 8 Sept. 1789; R.R. Livingston, [Draft of a Speech, Sept. 1789], Livingston, NHi; FE 1:74.

16.   Farrand, *Convention Records* 1:533, 542, 584, 2:3, 442, 452; Clymer to Rush, 7 Aug. 1789, photocopy, courtesy of George M. Curtis, III, and Richard H. Kohn, PHi. For more on ambivalence toward the West during the 1780s *see* Peter S. Onuf, *Statehood and Union* (Bloomington and Indianapolis, 1987).

17.   White to Horatio Gates, 1 June 1789, Gates, NHi; GWD 6:72–73; JM 12:279–80, 398–99, 426–27; TJ 19:429–518.

18.   PP, 26 May 1789 (quoted); "Farmer," NYDG, 5 June 1789; NYDA, 1 June, 2 July 1789.

19.   GUS, 17 July 1790; JM 11:242; P. Muhlenberg to Rush, 18 March 1789, GC. Especially articulate on this are "Citizen of the World," [George Walker], MdJ, 23 Jan. 1789; [Walker?] "Conference between the Patapsco and Patowmack Rivers," MdJ, 24 March 1789; and "Friend to Good Government," NYDA, 26 June 1790. *See* the debate over moving the capital of Maryland to Baltimore: Alexander C. Hanson, *Considerations on the Proposed Removal* (Annapolis, 1786), and Charles Carroll, Reasons Against Moving the Seat of Government, Ms. 215, MdHi.

20.   J. Dickinson, Ten Queries, [Jan. 1791?], Dickinson, PHi; FG, 28 Sept. 1789; PG, 5 Nov. 1783.

21.   EIHC 25:24; Adams to Rush, 9 June 1789, AFMT; MdJ, 17 Feb. 1789; "Friend to Good Government," NYDA, 25 June 1790; R.R. Livingston, [Draft of a Speech, Sept. 1789], Livingston, NHi; "Citizen of the Union," FG, 24 Sept. 1789; William Bradford, Jr., to Boudinot, 20 Sept. 1789, Wallace, PHi.

22.   MdJ, 17 Feb. 1789; IG, 2 March 1789.

23. "Gallio," [Simeon Baldwin], *Connecticut Journal,* 1 Sept. 1790; LMCC 7:293; Manasseh Cutler, *Explanation of the Map.* . . (Salem, 1787); "Quid Pro Quo," FG, 15 Aug. 1789; "X," NYJ, 3 Sept. 1789; NYDA, 2 June 1790.

24. GWW 30:203 and 36:113 (quoted); Schutz and Adair, *Spur of Fame,* 98; Edmund S. Morgan, *Genius of Washington* (Washington, 1980) and *Meaning of Independence* (Charlottesville, 1976), 30.

Chapter 1

1. Hampton L. Carson, *History of the 100th Anniversary of the Constitution* (2 vols., Philadelphia, 1889), 2:450–75; Stephen R. Boyd, "a supreme continental legislature" (M.A., Wisconsin, 1970); Stourzh, *Franklin,* chapter 2; *Pennylvania Evening Post,* 5 March 1776.

2. Arthur Jensen, "Origin of the First Continental Congress, 1773–1774" (M.A., Wisconsin, 1949); GWW 3:235; "Aratus" [George Lux, Jr.], *To the General Assembly of Maryland* (Baltimore, 1782).

3. Jonathan Boucher, *Reminiscences of an American Loyalist* (New York, 1925), 101 (quoted); David Hawke, *In the Midst of Revolution* (Philadelphia, 1961), chapter 2, pp. 112–14; LDC 1:25–27, 92; JM 1:126; Robert L. Brunhouse, *Counter-Revolution in Pennsylvania* (Harrisburg, 1942), chapters 1–2; BR, 153n.

4. LDC 1:271, 365, 433, 494, 531, 600, 645, 2:44, 491 (quoted), 4:227; PCC, item 65, 1:55.

5. LDC 5:615, 654, 660, 669, 689, 6:14, 53 and 398 (quoted), 7:31, 57, 64, 100, 129, 139, 184, 193–94, 210, 213, 294–95; BR, 130–34; Hawke, *Revolution,* 114.

6. LDC 6:87, 453, 596, 599–603, 611–17, 631–92, 7:303 and 625 (quoted), 12:167–73; Brunhouse, *Counter-Revolution,* chapter 2; Gordon S. Wood, *Creation of the American Republic* (Chapel Hill, 1969), 83–90, 233–37.

7. LDC 6:581–82, 7:195, 623, 655–56, 661, 8:3, 27; Brunhouse, *loc. cit.;* BR, 186.

8. LDC 8:34–35, 9:4, 40 (quoted), 85, 129, 264, 327, 726, 792, 10:34, 143, 151, 167, 268–70, 283–84; JCC 10:325, 626, 662; TJ 2:202.

9. LDC 10:57–59, 11:342, 359, 388–90, 516–17, 523, 525–26, 12:3, 26, 90–91, 95–96, 117, 139–40, 143, 157, 167–73, 178–80, 187, 218–22, 248–52, 259–61, 280, 283, 297n, 315–22, 329–30, 373–75, 384–85, 400, 538, 13:110n, 286, 320n, 379, 14:19, 290, 15:443–45; JCC 10:325, 626, 662; TJ 2:202; LMCC 7:217n; G. Morris to Jay, 25 Sept. 1783, Jay, Columbia; Hawke, *Revolution,* 231–37; Brunhouse, *Counter-Revolution,* chapter 3; BR, 241n, 244; Robert East, *Business Enterprise in the American Revolutionary Era* (New York, 1938), 199–201; Samuel Hazard, ed., *Pennsylvania Archives* (138 vols., Philadelphia and Harrisburg, 1852–1949), ser. I, 7:347; PCC, item 69, 2:23; Harry Tinkcom, *Republicans and Federalists in Pennsylvania* (Philadelphia, 1950), 32.

10. LDC 14:247n, 259, 285, 353, 371, 376, 448–49n, 463–65, 15:56 (quoted); Brunhouse, *Counter-Revolution,* 62–63; BR, 245; PMHB 2:153–56; LaLuzerne to Vergennes, 6 Aug. 1780, CP-EU, 3.

11. Alexander McDougall to Nathanael Greene, 8 Aug. 1780, McDougall, NHi (quoted); Brunhouse, *Counter-Revolution,* chapter 4; LDC 16:114, 409.

12. LDC 6:410 (quoted); ROC 1:78–137. James L. Cooper, "Interests, Ideas, and Empires: The Roots of American Foreign Policy, 1763–1779" (Ph.D., Wisconsin, 1964), details the struggle over the nature of the American Empire. The term "na-

tionalist," as used by eighteenth century American historians, can be properly applied only to those few centralists who advocated a consolidated or unitary central government.

13. Davis, *Sectionalism,* chapter 2; ROC 1:140–45; JM 6:251.

14. LDC 5:609.

15. E. James Ferguson, *Power of the Purse* (Chapel Hill, 1961), chapter 6 (120 and 122 quoted).

16. LMCC 6:368n, 378, 384, 505 (quoted); JM 7:81; Davis, *Sectionalism,* 40.

17. Ferguson, *Purse,* chapter 8 (154 quoted); Davis, *Sectionalism,* 31–32; A. Lee to St. George Tucker, 21 July 1783, Tucker–Coleman, ViW; MHSP 63:483; J. Dickinson to Thomson, 12 June 1783, Thomson, DLC; JM 6:286; LMCC 7:7–10.

18. To Jay, 12 April 1783, Jay, Columbia (quoted); LMCC 7:220, 233; AH 3:426–29.

19. LMCC 7:28; Richard H. Kohn, *Eagle and Sword* (New York, 1975), chapter 2.

20. GWW 26:227, 298, MHSP 63:488, Ferguson, *Purse,* 121, and G. Morris to Nathanael Greene, 18 May 1783, Greene, DLC (quoted); GWW 26:324; JCC 24:309; AH 3:330.

21. MHSP 63:469–70 (quoted), 489, 497.

22. Clymer to Fitzsimons, 24 May 1783, GC, and Thadeuz Kosciuszko to Otho Williams, 2 July 1783, Ms. 908, MdHi (quoted); La Luzerne to Vergennes, 29 Oct. 1782, CP-EU, 22; LMCC 7:180, 182, 187; Nathaniel Gorham to Caleb Davis, 4 June 1783, Davis, MHi; Nathanael Greene to Alexander McDougall, 11 Feb. 1779, McDougall, NHi; James McHenry to John Armstrong, 1 May 1783, McHenry, DLC; Jay to G. Morris, 24 Sept. 1783, Morris, Columbia.

23. LMCC 7:156 and 378 (quoted), 6:379.

24. AH 3:401–02 (quoted). For details on the mutiny and the relevant source material *see* my "New Light on the Philadelphia Mutiny of 1783," PMHB 101:419–50 (432 quoted). On the role of Dickinson's pride *see* CT, 10, 31–32. For the assertion that Congress was surrounded by the soldiers and the legal assumption that this event was the basis for Article I, § 8, Paragraph 17, *see* Joseph Story, *Commentaries on the Constitution* (Boston, 1833), 3:1212–22.

25. LMCC 7:201, 251n; CT, 19.

26. William D. McCracken, ed., *Huntington Letters* (New York, 1905), 56–59, and James McHenry to William Hindham, 19 July 1783, Ms. 647, MdHi (quoted); JM 7:378n; Mary to [Isaac] Norris, 26 Aug. 1783, Norris Letterbook, PHi; PCC, item 38:127, 135, 143, item 46:51–85; George A. Boyd, *Elias Boudinot* (Princeton, 1952), p. 128, chapter 12; LMCC 8:841; GWW 27:148; CT, 5–6, 16, 34–35, 46; Varnum L. Collins, *Continental Congress at Princeton* (Princeton, 1908), chapters 4, 7.

27. William Clark, ed., *State Records of North Carolina* (16 vols., Winston and Goldsboro, 1895–1905), 16:970, and John Scott to A. Lee, 20 Aug. 1783, Lee, Harvard (quoted by permission of the Houghton Library); Howell to Nicholas Brown, 30 July 1783, RPJCB; R.R. Livingston to Boudinot, 3 July 1783, Livingston, NHi; JM 7:218, 235–36; LMCC 7:210n, 342n; William Whipple to A. Lee, 15 Sept. 1783, Emmet, NN; Alexander Gillon to A. Lee, 29 Nov. 1783, Lee, ViU.

28. LMCC 7:200n (quoted), 201n, 205–06n, 215, 217; IG, 28 June (quoted), 9 Aug. 1783; Winslow Warren to Samuel Holten, 2 July 1783, Holten, DLC; BR, 302,

307–09; Rush to John Montgomery, 7 July 1783, Rush, PPL; PP, 28 June, 5, 17 July 1783; *Pennsylvania Journal*, 5, 19 July 1783; PG, 9 July 1783; Collins, *Princeton*, 33–35.

29. James to John Mercer, 15 July 1783, Mercer, Virginia Hist. Soc. (quoted); AH 3:412; LMCC 7:195; Boudinot to William Livingston, 23 June 1783, Boudinot, DLC; James McHenry to Thomas S. Lee, 28 [26] June 1783, McHenry, DLC; AH 3:408–10; JM 7:222–24n, 382–83; LaLuzerne to Vergennes, 1 Nov. 1783, CP-EU, 26; *American Register*, 5:379; CT, 29.

30. LMCC 7:233–34 (quoted), 236, 344–45; Thomson to William White, 8 July 1783, Society, PHi; Diary, 9 July 1783, R. Morris, DLC; Peter S. DuPonceau to R.R. Livingston, 15 July 1783, Livingston, NHi; LaLuzerne to Vergennes, 15 July 1783, CP-EU, 25; Boudinot to Rush, 25 July 1783, Boudinot, DLC; Thomson to [J. Dickinson], Dickinson to Thomson, 11 July 1783, Dickinson, PHi; Brunhouse, *Counter-Revolution*, 138–39; JCC 24:452; CT, 27–28, 33–34.

31. LMCC 7:220, 233, 390; AH 3:420–30, 459–60; JM 7:407n; CT, 8–9, 14, 19–20, 25–26.

32. CT, 94; JCC 24:412; LMCC 7:235–36, 256–57, 266, 299; Ebenezer Hazard to Jeremy Belknap, 9 Aug. 1783, Belknap, MHi; R.R. Livingston to Marbois, 9 Oct. 1783, Livingston, NHi; *Henkels Catalog* 896:item 481.

33. CT, 19, 29–30, 66.

34. LMCC 7:252, 263, 8:840–41 (quoted); A. Lee to St. George Tucker, 21 July 1783, Tucker-Coleman, ViW; Ferguson, *Purse*, 172–74; MHSC(2) 8:179; JM 7:380; Howell to Nicholas Brown, 20 July 1783, RPJCB.

35. F. Muhlenberg to Peters, 30 Aug. 1783, Peters, PHi, and BR, 308 (quoted); LMCC 7:234, 241, 266–67, 329–31 (this is Peters's motion to adjourn, [26–30 July 1783]); JM 7:307–08; Brunhouse, *Counter-Revolution*, 139; James Wilson to J. Dickinson, 4 Aug. 1783, Dickinson, PHi.

36. AH 3:408; JCC 24:424–25, 484–85, 506–09, 25:530, 537; LMCC 7:254, 260, 296; PCC, item 46:113, item 69, 2:451–57; Samuel Holten to [John?] Avery, 11 Sept. 1783, Holten, DLC; CT, 54.

37. William Ellery to Benjamin Stelle, 1 Sept. 1783, Ellery, Brown University (quoted); William R. Staples, *Rhode Island in the Confederation Congress* (Providence, 1870), 456; Rush to John Montgomery, 27 Sept. 1783, Rush, PPL; Thomas Willing to Bingham, 12 Sept. 1783, Balch, PHi.

38. JM 7:207–08, 230, 232, 256–57, 263, 281, 352, 380.

Chapter 2

1. The offers Congress received in 1783 and 1784 and the documents related to them can be found in PCC, item 46. For detailed citations and additional information about the various offers *see* my "'A Place to Which Tribute Is Brought': The Contest for the Federal Capital in 1783," *Prologue: The Journal of the National Archives* 8:129–39.

2. George Dangerfield, *Chancellor Robert R. Livingston* (New York, 1960), chapters 3–5; LMCC 4:530, 5:161; James Duane to R.R. Livingston, 30 Nov. 1781, Livingston to Egbert Benson, 21 Dec. 1781, Instructions to New York Delegates, [c. Jan. 1782], Benson to Livingston, Feb. 1782, Livingston, NHi; JCC 24:376; AH 3:349.

3. TJ 6:353.

4. M.J. to Walter Stone, 29 May 1783, *Argosy . . . Catalog* 479:item 1182 (quoted); Daniel Carroll to Thomas S. Lee, 20 May 1783, Ms. 1974, MdHi. On Lux and exclusive jurisdiction *see* Chapter 3.

5. JM 7:219n.

6. *New Jersey Gazette,* 23 Dec. 1783.

7. GWW 27:148.

8. LMCC 7:272, 280, 285, 286–87 (quoted), 324, 8:840–41; JCC 25:647–60; PCC, item 73:307; JM 7:374, 379; TJ 6:345, 352; Clark, *N.C. Records* 16:730; Connecticut Historical Society *Collections* 20:176–77; Howell to Nicholas Brown, 20 July 1783, RPJCB; Boudinot to R.R. Livingston, 29 Aug. 1783, Livingston, NHi; G. Morris to Jay, 25 Sept. 1783, Morris, Columbia; A. Lee to St. George Tucker, 21 July 1783, Tucker–Coleman, ViW; F. Michaelis to George Beckwith, 4 Oct. 1783, Bancroft 1783 II, NN; Grayson to unknown, 11 Sept. 1783, Etting, PHi; James to John Mercer, 23 Sept. 1783, Mercer, Virginia Hist. Soc.; Christopher Richmond to Horatio Gates, 18 Oct. 1783, Gates, NN.

9. PCC, item 46:123–24, item 78, 22:285–86; JCC 25:659–60, 664–67; JM 7:353, 374–82; Rush to John Montgomery, 9 Oct. 1783, Rush, PPL; Fitzsimons to G. Morris, 11 Oct. 1783, Morris, Columbia; R. Morris to Washington, 15 Oct. 1783, GC; LMCC 7:328; Samuel Holten to John Hancock, 9 Oct. 1783, Members of Congress, Clements; Stephen Higginson to Gerry, 30 Oct. 1783, Dreer, PHi.

10. James McHenry to Peggy Caldwell, 10, 12 (quoted), 23, [n.d.] Oct. 1783, Ms. 647, MdHi; LMCC 7:731–32; JCC 25:666–72, 675–76; JM 7:374–75, 380; 7:331–32; CT, 62, 65.

11. LMCC 7:332, 353, 354 (quoted), 378; JM 7:379; TJ 6:349, 352.

12. LMCC 7:327, 339, 349–50, 378–79, 397 (quoted), 422, 430–32; Samuel Osgood to John Adams, 7 Dec. 1783, Samuel Adams, NN; Gerry to Adams, 23 Nov. 1783, William Ellery to Adams, 3 Dec. 1783, AFMT.

13. Clymer to Fitzsimons, 18 Oct, 1783, GC; Peters to Jacob Read, 23 Feb. 1784, Read, DLC; Joseph Jones to Monroe, 15 May 1784, Monroe, DLC; LaLuzerne to Vergennes, 1 Nov. 1783, CP–EU, 26; CT, 72; LMCC 7:346–48.

14. Daniel Carroll and James McHenry to [Maryland Governor], 3 Nov. 1783, The John Work Garrett Library of Johns Hopkins University; JCC 25:697–714, 767–71, 799, 802, 807; LMCC 7:350–51, 367; CT, 74–86; LaLuzerne to Vergennes, 1 Nov. 1783, CP–EU, 26.

15. MHSC 73:229–30, 233 (quoted); LMCC 7:350; Stephen Higginson to Gerry, 5 Nov. 1783, Miscellaneous, NHi; Adams to Gerry, 9 April 1784, AFMT; Samuel Holten to Gerry, 2 Dec. 1783, Stephen Higginson to Gerry, [Dec.–Jan. 1783–84], Gerry, MHi.

16. R.R. Livingston to Boudinot, Livingston to LaLuzerne, 1 Nov. 1783, Livingston, NHi; IG, 1, 12, 29 Nov. 1783; PG, 5 Nov. 1783; PP, 18 Nov. 1783.

17. Cadwalader Morris to Thomson, 12 Feb. 1784 (quoted), Peters to Thomson, 22 Feb. 1784, Thomson, DLC; Peters to Jacob Read, 22 Feb. 1784, Read, DLC; PP, 14 Feb. 1784; Henry P. Johnston, *Letters and Public Papers of John Jay* (4 vols., New York, 1890–93), 3:109; PG, 5 Nov. 1783; Samuel Osgood to Benjamin Lincoln, 24 Nov. 1783, Lincoln, MHi; TJ 6:375–76; CT, 72; Bingham to Rush, 1 Jan. 1784, Dickinson College; R. Morris to Willink and Co., 12 Dec. 1783, Morris, DLC.

18. "Intelligence Extraordinary," PG, 29 Oct. 1783; "Summary of Some Late Pro-
     ceedings in a Certain Great Assembly," *Freeman's Journal*, 26 Nov. 1783. For
     later comment on the dual residence *see* TJ 14:291; Abigail Adams to Cotton
     Tufts, 1 Sept. [1789], Miscellaneous, NHi; and NYDA, 7 Sept. 1789.

19. MdJ: "Sojourner," 14 Nov., "Hiram," 16 Dec. 1783 (quoted); PCC, item 78,
     6:219; "Publicus," PP, 18 Nov. 1783; Joseph Jones to Monroe, [1783–1784] and 6
     Dec. 1783, Monroe, DLC.

20. TJ 6:349, 352, 358, 371; JM 7:386, 388.

21. PCC, item 60:169; JCC 25:841; *New Jersey Gazette*, 9 Dec. 1783.

22. JCC 25:770, 27:444–45; TJ 7:275, 290; LMCC 7:550.

23. Mary Lazenby, "Amos Cloud's House," Vertical File, Palisades Branch, Washing-
     ton, D.C., Public Library; *American Motorist* (Washington Edition), June 1930,
     58–59, 76.

24. PCC, item 46:27–29; TJ 6:367–68, 391–92.

25. LMCC 7:438, 472 (quoted), 498; John Montgomery to Thomson, 2 Aug. 1784,
     Thomson to Clymer, 3 April 1784, Thomson, DLC; Alice Keith, ed., *John Gray
     Blount Papers* (3 vols., Raleigh, 1952–65), 1:134, 136; PMHB 44:237; Howell to
     Nicholas Brown, 18 Sept. [Dec.] 1783, RPJCB; Staples, *Rhode Island*, 463; Henry
     to Levi Hollingsworth, 25 Nov. 1783, Hollingsworth, PHi; Edward C. Papenfuse,
     In Pursuit of Profit: The Annapolis Merchants (Baltimore, 1975), 155, 250–54.

26. LMCC 7:406, 421–22 and 439 (quoted), 533–34; JCC 27:469; Campbell, *Bland,*
     2:113; William Gordon to Adams, 7 Jan. 1784, AFMT; TJ 7:130.

27. JCC 26:221–26, 287–96; LMCC 7:426, 451, 486; John Montgomery to Cad-
     walader Morris, 5 March 1784, Strettell, PHi.

28. TJ 6:546 (quoted), 7:35, 275–76, 278; LMCC 7:461 and 524 (quoted), 550;
     Joseph Jones to Monroe, 28(?) April 1784, Monroe, DLC; Thomson to Peters, 19
     Jan. 1784, Peters, PHi; Abiel Foster to William Whipple, 25 March 1784,
     Langdon–Elwyn Family, New Hampshire Hist. Soc.; JCC 26:411–18, 444.

29. JCC 26:446–509; TJ 6:516–29, 547; LMCC 7:538–40; MdG(B), 11 June 1784;
     Beverly Randolph to Monroe, 14 May 1784, Monroe, DLC.

30. LMCC 7:549, 554–56, 583 (quoted), 586, 8:859–60, 862; JCC 27:550–56,
     561–79; Thomson to John Montgomery, 22 Aug. 1784, Montgomery to Thom-
     son, 2 Aug. 1784, Thomson, DLC; Richard D. Spaight to Thomson, 9 Sept. 1784,
     GC; Edward Hand to Mrs. Hand, 28 Aug. 1784, Hand, PHi.

31. LMCC 7:610–12, 615.

32. James C. Ballagh, *Letters of Richard Henry Lee* (2 vols., New York, 1914), 2:293,
     296; PP, 29 Dec. 1784; Robert A. Fortenbaugh, *Nine Capitals of the United States*
     (York, Pa., 1973), 67–70; Joseph Jones to Monroe, 4 Dec. 1784, Monroe, DLC;
     TJ 7:534–35; JM 8:141–42, 176; *New Jersey Gazette*, 30 Aug. 1784; Edwin
     Walker, *History of Trenton* (2 vols., Princeton, 1929), 1:191–92; JCC 27:649;
     Samuel Holten to James Warren, 11 Nov. 1784, Holten, DLC; Francis Dana to
     Adams, 12 Dec. 1784, AFMT; NYJ, 9 Dec. 1784; *Boston Gazette*, 20 Dec. 1784;
     BR, 345; Sarah to John Jay, 10 Dec. 1784, Jay, Columbia; PCC, item 78, 13:313,
     item 67, 2:477, item 46:133, item 18, Letterbook A:47.

33. LMCC 7:637, 639, 8:1, 15–16, 28–33, 46; JCC 27:678–81, 696, 699–704,
     707–10; Thomson to Jay, 18 Sept. 1784, Jay to Thomson, 20 Oct. 1784, Thom-
     son, DLC; Gerry to A. Lee, 25 Dec. 1784, Signers, Indiana University; MHSC(5)
     2:416; Marbois to Vergennes, 26 Dec. 1784, CP–EU, 28.

34. JCC 27:704; LMCC 7:637, 8:28–29, 34 (quoted); King to Daniel Kilham, 12 Dec. 1784, King, Columbia; Samuel Holten to Thomas Cushing, 24 Jan. 1785, Holten, DLC; GWW 28:172–73; Walter Rutherford to John Stevens, Jr., 14 Feb. 1785, NjHi.

35. Marbois to Vergennes, 26 Dec. 1784, CP–EU, 28; Samuel Osgood to Gerry, 3 Jan. 1785, James Warren to Gerry, 11 Jan. 1785, Gerry, MHi; Thomas Cushing to Samuel Holten, 12 Jan. 1785, MB; Francis Dana to Adams, 30 Jan, 1785, AFMT.

36. GWW 28:70–71; TJ 8:228–29; Thomas Stone to Monroe, 18 March 1785, Monroe, DLC; David J. Mays, ed., *Letters and Papers of Edmund Pendleton* (2 vols., Charlottesville, 1967), 2:475–76, 478.

37. "New York, December 29," PP, 1 Jan. 1785 (quoted); James Duane to John Livingston, 6 Jan. 1785, Livingston–Redmond, FDR Library; IG, 5 Feb. 1785; Marbois to Vergennes, 26 Dec. 1784, CP–EU, 28; PCC, item 78:451, 478; Moore Furman to William Coxe, 10 Jan. 1784 [1785], TC; Walker, *Trenton,* 1:194.

38. JM 8:510; Harold T. Pinkett, "New York as the Temporary National Capital," *National Archives Accessions* 60:1–4; *New York Independent Journal,* 12, 22 Jan., 5 Feb. 1785; PCC, item 43:343, 351; PP, 28 Dec. 1784; Walter Rutherford to John Stevens, 14 Feb. 1785, Stevens, NjHi; LMCC 8:8–9n, 15, 24–25, 69n, 264; Samuel Holten to Col. Hutchinson, 7 Feb. 1785, Holten, DLC; James to Peggy McHenry, 6 Feb. 1785, Ms. 647, MdHi; PMHB 14:29; King to Daniel Kilham, 8 Dec. 1785, King, Columbia; Marbois to Vergennes, 23 Aug. 1785, CP–EU, 30.

39. JCC 27:4n, 35n, 614–15, 28:45; MHSC(5) 2:418; David Jackson to George Bryan, 4 June 1785, Bryan, PHi; JM 8:360.

40. Marbois to Vergennes, 26 Dec. 1784, CP–EU, 28; LMCC 8:16, 27, 29, 35–36, 46–47, 69n, 81; JCC 28:48–53; R.H. Lee to Adams, 23 Oct. 1785, Adams to John Sullivan, 11 March 1785, AFMT; Jay to Lafayette, 19 Jan. 1785, Johnston, *Jay,* 3:137–38; Walter to R.R. Livingston, 3 Jan. 1784 [1785], Livingston–Redmond, FDR Library.

41. JCC 28:10n, 16–18, 37n, 52n, 54–58; LMCC 8:74–75n, 105–08, 149; PCC, item 78, 14:477, 605, item 137, appendix, 379, item 153, 3:637; Philip Schuyler to Walter Livingston, 3 March 1785, Livingston, NHi.

42. GWW 28:172–73; LMCC 8:17–18, 48, 71n, 85, 91, 110–11, 119, 195, 225–26, 263; JCC 28:86, 232–33, 237–38, 333n, 734; PCC, item 137, appendix, 389; Joseph Jones to Monroe, 15 April 1785, Monroe, DLC; Samuel Hodgdon to Timothy Pickering, 13 April 1785, Pickering, MHi; Pierce Long to John Langdon, 21 Aug. 1785, Long, NHi; Samuel Holten to George Partridge, 8 Oct. 1785, Holten, DLC; "South Carolina Letter," PP, 8 April 1785.

43. JM 7:380, 9:386 (quoted), 397–99; JCC 32:74; LMCC 8:218, 333; "Baltimore Letter," PP, 20 Dec. 1787; Liste des Membres et Officers du Congress, Sketch of Jay, [Sept. 1788], CP–EU, Supplement, 26; Henry to Levi Hollingsworth, 16 Feb. 1788, Hollingsworth, PHi.

44. Nathaniel Hazard to Matthew Carey, 16 Feb. 1787, Gardiner, PHi (quoted); LMCC 8:537–38, 558, 585; Charles Willson Peale to David Ramsay, 22 Feb. 1787, Peale Letterbooks, PPAmP; Mary Norris to Hannah Thomson, 25 Feb. 1787, Norris Family, PHi; Thomas Willing to James Wilson, 6 March 1787, Carson, PHi; Arthur St. Clair to John Nicholson, 19 March 1787, Dreer, PHi; Noah Webster to Rush, 24 Feb. 1789, Rush, PPL; BR, 450; William to Thomas Lee Shippen, 24 Feb.–1 March, 7–15 May, 29 Nov. 1787, Shippen, DLC; JM 9:372,

386, 391; Erastus Wolcott to Governor and Assembly of Connecticut, 5 May 1787, Revolutionary Series 2:37, Connecticut State Library.

45. Lambert Cadwalader to Samuel Meredith, 27 March 1787, Dreer, PHi; John Rutherford to Gen. Robertson, 29 April 1787, Eastburn, NjHi; Clymer to Samuel Meredith, 5, 28 May [1787], Clymer–Meredith–Read, NN; NYJ, 12 April 1787; JM 9:371–72, 375, 379–80; LMCC 8:573–74, 585, 596–97; ROC 15:374; Leonard Gansevoort to Stephen(?) Van Rensselaer, 6 April 1788, New York State Library; JCC 32:157, 167–69, 251, 258, 279–90 (several events which occurred on 11 April are entered in JCC on the 10th).

46. JM 9:417 (quoted); LMCC 8:596n.

Chapter 3

1. Maunsell Van Rensselaer, *Annals of the Van Rensselaers* (Albany, 1888), 83–84; Grayson to Monroe, 29 May 1787, Monroe, DLC; Farrand, *Convention Records* 2:127–28, 261–62; JM 9:5–23; "Jersey Farmer," NYDG, 5 Sept. 1789; FG, 7 April 1790.

2. BR, 245; LaLazurne to Vergennes, 10 Sept. 1782, CP-EU, 22.

3. Charles Campbell, ed., *Bland Papers* (2 vols., Petersburg, Va., 1843), 2:95–97 and PP, 17 July 1783 (quoted); George Lux, Jr., to Nathanael Greene, 23 Nov. 1782, Greene, DLC; G. Morris to Jay, 25 Sept. 1783, Jay, Columbia; Benjamin Lincoln, Sr., to Jr., 23 July 1783, and reply, 21 August 1783, Lincoln, MHi; LMCC 7:302n; JM 7:218–19n, 254–55n, 257, 300, 305–06n, 354. Jefferson's resolutions (TJ 6:368–70) have been given various dates; the most probable is October 1783 after Madison asked (TJ 6:33) him to consider the issues.

4. LMCC 7:183n, PP, 17 July 1783, and *Pennsylvania Journal*, 5 July 1783 (quoted); PG, 9 July 1783; "True American," [George Lux, Jr.?], MdJ, 29 July 1783.

5. JCC 25:548 (quoted), 603–04, 616–17, 654; Howell to Nicholas Brown, 25 Sept. 1783, RPJCB; LMCC 7:250, 271n, 302n; Boudinot to Rush, 25 July 1783, Boudinot, DLC; JM 7:357–58.

6. Farrand, *Convention Records* 2:324–25, 508–10.

7. ROC 1:chapter 9, 2:152, 154; Ebenezer Dibblee to Samuel Peters, 16 Nov. 1787, Peters, Archives of the Episcopal Church, USA, Austin; Jonathan Elliot, ed., *Debates in the Several State Conventions on the Adoption of the Federal Constitution* (5 vols., Philadelphia, 1861), 2:401; TJ 13:157; R.H. Lee to John Lamb, 27 June 1788, Aedanus Burke to Lamb, 23 June 1788, Lamb, NHi; *Brunswick Gazette*, 24 March 1789.

8. ROC 15:266–67 and Elliot, *Debates* 2:402 (quoted). Jackson Main, *Antifederalists* (New York, 1961), 151–52, Cecilia Kenyon, *Antifederalists* (New York, 1966), lxix, and others generally dismiss Antifederal concern about the federal city.

9. "Brutus," NYJ, 10 April 1788 (quoted); Elliot, *Debates* 2:287–88, 402 (quoted), 3:291–92, 354–55, 430–39, 4:203; ROC 2:156, 3:240, 13:407, 482, 14:9, 27, 48, 112, 182, 217, 15:264, 266–67, 299, 16:285, 287; A Federal Farmer, *Additional Number of Letters* (New York, 1788), 174–79; "Agrippa," [James Winthrop], *Massachusetts Gazette*, 23, 30 Nov. 1787, 5 Feb. 1788; "Consider Arms," *Hampshire Gazette*, 9 April 1788; *New Hampshire Spy*, 21 June 1788.

10. *New Hampshire Spy*, 13 May 1788; FE 4:30; *United States Chronicle*, 5 June 1788. *See* NYJ, 23 April 1788, for an example of Antifederal ridicule of Federalists. I

have not found any contemporary references to the alleged Antifederal concern that the Pope or a member of the British royal family would take up residence in the federal city.

11. ROC 2:168, 416, 455; 13:340, 15:439–40; Elliot, *Debates* 2:98–99, 292, 3:89, 432–40, 454–55, 4:209, 219–20; [Monroe], *Some Observations on the Constitution* (New York, 1788), 31–32; Federalist Essay No. 84.

12. Edward Dumbauld, *Bill of Rights* (Norman, 1957), 187 (quoted), 195, 203; AH 5:189 (quoted); Records of the Danville Political Club, [1788], Filson Club; ROC 3:240, 15:267; Joshua Atherton to Federal Republican Committee, 23 June 1788, Lamb, NHi; Elliot, *Debates* 3:431, 602; Federal Farmer, Additional Letters, 174–79; FE 1:263; *Annals of Congress* 1:761–63; [Nicholas Collin], "Foreign Spectator," NYDA, 17 June 1789.

13. PP, 9 July 1788.

14. GWW 30:9; William Brown to William Cullen, 19 July 1788, Miscellaneous, PPAmP.

15. FE 1:27–33, 38, 41–44, 49, 58, 94, 106, 124; Sidney I. Pomerantz, *New York, An American City, 1783–1803* (Port Washington, N.Y., 1938), 103.

16. FE 1:35–44, 94, 100; Jeremiah Wadsworth to [Oliver Wolcott, Sr.?], 15 July 1788, Oliver Wolcott Sr. to Jr., 23 July 1788, Wolcott, CtHi; Richard Penn Hicks to J. Dickinson, 15 July 1788, Dickinson, PHi; Jedidiah Morse, Sr., to Jr., 22 July 1788, Morse, Yale; "Poughkeepsie Letter," NYDA, 14 July 1788; AH 5:160; Notes on Ratification Debate, 12 July 1788, McKesson, NHi; JM 11:191; Linda G. DePauw, *Eleventh Pillar* (Ithaca, 1966), 246–50, 270; Elliot, *Debates* 2:412; LMCC 8:772; NYJ: 7 Aug., "Sidney," 4 Dec. 1788; "Philadelphia Letter," *New York Packet*, 7, 12 Aug. 1788; *Independent Journal*, 28 July 1788 extra; *New York Weekly Museum*, 29 July 1788.

17. LMCC 8:696, 707, 712, 722, 772; FE 1:34, 36, 91.

18. FE 1:27, 31, 38, 41, 43, 50–54, 75, 89, 107, 121 (quoted), 122; BR, 469, 478; J. Dickinson to Coxe, 14 July 1788, Dickinson College; Mathew Carey to Ebenezer Hazard, 14 Aug. 1788, Carey Letterbook, PHi; Description of Congress, [Nov. 1788], CP–EU, Memoirs et Documents, 4; "Letter from Amelia County," MdG(B), 30 Jan. 1789.

19. FE 1:41, 53–57 (55 quoted), 60–72, 76–87, 96–97, 103, 106–07, 110, 121–22, 126, 135–36, 413, 4:45, 49, 76, 453; Charles Nisbet to Earl of Buchan, 16 Sept. 1788, Dickinson College; AH 5:225; Lambert Cadwalader to Samuel Meredith, 6 Aug. 1788, Read, DLC; *Historical Magazine* 16:350; Jay to James Duane, 4 Jan. 1788, Duane, NHi; NYJ, 15 April 1788; Brissot De Warville, *New Travels,* 142.

20. FE 1:72–75 (quoted), 97–100.

21. FE 1:57, 82–83, 96, 100, 101 (quoted), 137–38; LMCC 8:784, 796.

22. FE 1:76, 81, 89–129 (94, 95, 123, 126, and 129 quoted), 134, 140, 4:48; PP, 25 Aug. 1788; *Independent Journal*, 13 Sept. 1788; Ephraim Harris to Richard Smith, 12 July 1788, Samuel Smith, Rutgers; Lucy to Henry Knox, 1 Sept. 1788, Knox, MHi; John Langdon to Nicholas Gilman, 25 Aug. 1788, Miscellaneous, DLC.

23. FE 1:129–33, 137–38.

24. FE 1:126, 135, 139–40.

25. LMCC 8:596n (quoted), 801; Mays, *Pendleton* 2:546–47; JM 10:263–64; FE 1:59–60, 90–91, 135, 138–39, 141; JM 11:310; GWW 30:95.

26. James Duane to New York Delegates, 29 Sept. 1788, PCC, item 78, 18:237; AH 5:240n; TJ 14:416–17; NYJ, 26 March 1789; *Massachusetts Magazine,* 1:331–33; *Laws of New York* (New York, 1790), 7; William to Euphemia Paterson, 24 March 1789, Paterson, Rutgers; Henry Sewall to William Heath, 6 Jan. 1789, Heath, MHi.

27. F. Muhlenberg to Rush, 5 March 1789, GC (quoted); George to Sarah Thatcher, 29 Sept. 1788, Thatcher, MHi; Benjamin Contee to Levi Hollingsworth, 8 Oct. 1788, Hollingsworth, PHi; Maclay to Rush, 19 March 1789, Rush, DLC; Ebenezer Hazard to Mathew Carey, 16 Oct. 1788, Lea–Febiger, PHi; RM, 4 March 1789; White to Mrs. Wood, 8 March 1789, Morristown National Military Park; AH 5:282; FG, 14 Feb., 18 March 1789.

28. FE 1:143; *New York Packet,* 7 Feb. 1789; *New York Historical Society Quarterly* 9:40; FG, 3, 6 Nov. 1788, 31 Jan., 17 Feb. 1789; PP, 20 Feb. 1789; AH 5:247; *American Herald,* 19 March 1789; Coxe to Thatcher, 8 April 1789, "Historic Structures Report," Independence National Historical Park; GUS, 15 April 1789; Coxe to William Irvine, 13 March 1789, Irvine, PHi; Coxe to Rush, 2 Feb. 1789, TC.

29. *New York Packet,* 10 Feb. 1789 (quoted); FG, 10 Dec. 1788, 7, 9, 16, 31 Jan. 1789; IG, 5 Jan., 3 Feb. 1789; NYJ, 1, 15 Jan. 1789; NYDA, 21 Jan. 1789; NYDG, 16 Jan. 1789.

30. Kenneth R. Bowling, "Federalists and Antifederalists After Ratification: The First Congressional Election" (M.A., Wisconsin, 1964), chapter 3; John Armstrong to Horatio Gates, 7 April 1789, Emmet, NN; FE 1:316.

31. BR, 478; J. Dickinson to Coxe, 14 July 1788, Dickinson College; Bowling, "First Election," chapter 1, pp. 78–79; FE 3:28, 45, 89, 95, 98, 128, 140, 4:467, Papenfuse, *Annapolis Merchants,* 183.

32. Bowling, "First Election," 119–28, 132–39; FE 3:223–24, 314, 317, 326–27, 341–42, 369, 409–10, 426, 465–69, 476–77, 479, 481–82, 553–55, 4:168, 200; AH 5:273, 286–87, 298–99; NYDA, 4, 13 March, 7 April 1789; NYJ, 2 April 1789.

33. MD, 87–88 (quoted); FE 1:31, 76; JM 11:432.

34. William S. Smith to Adams, 6 April 1789, AFMT (quoted); FE 4:71, 173, 281–82, 285; BR, 501 and 508 (quoted), 506–08, 513, 517.

35. FG, 3 Feb. 1789 and "Williamsburg Letter," IG, 3 Feb. 1789 (quoted); PP, 29 Jan. 1789; MdJ, 17 March. "True Federalist," which appeared in PP on 5 Jan. and again on 16 April 1789, was a skillful weaving of Bingham's "Member of the Federal Club" and his undelivered congressional resolution of August 1788 (FE 1:72–75, 97–100).

36. George to Sarah Thatcher, 4 March 1789, Thatcher, MHi; IG, 9 March 1789; FA, 31–32; Maclay to Rush, 6 March 1789, Rush, DLC; Bingham to Coxe, 23 Feb. 1789, Hartley to Coxe, 16 March 1789, TC; PMHB 38:47; I.N.P. Stokes, *Iconography of Manhattan Island* (6 vols., New York, 1895–1928), 5:1166; AH 5:251, 282. *See* also notes 37 and 38.

37. FE 4:190–91, 200–201, 204, 207–208, 232; Hartley to Coxe, 16, 30 March 1789, TC; P. Muhlenberg to Rush, 2 April 1789, Society, PHi; Rush to Timothy Pickering, 25 March 1789, Pickering to Paine Wingate, 15 April 1789, Pickering, MHi; Maclay to Rush, 6 March 1789, Rush, DLC. For anti–New York propaganda *see* FG, 9, 10, 14, 18, 31 March, 3 April 1789.

38. FE 4:217, 219, 226–27; IG, 24 March 1789; P. Muhlenberg to John Hubley, 4
     April 1789, Valley Forge Hist. Soc.; Hartley to Coxe, 9 April 1789, TC; Maclay to
     Richard Willing, 2 April 1789, Maclay Diary, DLC.

Chapter 4

1. Charles O. Paullin, "Early Landmarks between Great Hunting Creek and the
    Falls," RCHS 31–32:53–79 (57 quoted); Robert Humphrey and Mary E. Cham-
    bers, "Ancient Washington: American Indian Cultures of the Potomac Valley,"
    George Washington [University] Studies, No. 6; Frederick Gutheim, *Potomac* (New
    York, 1961), chapters 2–3; Fairfax Harrison, *Landmarks of Old Prince William*
    (Berryville, Va., 1964), pt. I, and 607–17; Guy Castle, "Washington Area between
    1608 and 1708," RCHS 1963–65:1–18; Charles W. Stetson, *Four Mile Run Land
    Grants* (Washington, 1935), 1–35; Bessie Gahn, *Original Patentees of Land at
    Washington Prior to 1700* (Silver Spring, Md., 1936), 65–100; Cornelia B. Rose,
    Jr., *Arlington County Virginia* (Arlington, 1976), chapters 1–2; Nelson R. Burr,
    "Federal City Depicted, 1612–1801," *Quarterly Journal of the Library of Congress*
    8:64–77.

2. Harrison, *Prince William,* chapters 11, 23; Richard H. Lee, Jr., *Memoir of the Life
    of Richard Henry Lee* (2 vols., Philadelphia, 1825), 1:7.

3. John W. Reps, *Town Planning in Frontier America* (Princeton, 1965), chapter 4;
    Virginia Gazette (Richmond: Purdie and Dixon), 22 March 1770; John Rainbolt,
    "Absence of Towns in Seventeenth Century Virginia," *Journal of Southern History*
    25:343–60; Carville Earle and Ronald Hoffman, "Urban Development in the
    Eighteenth Century South," *Perspectives in American History* 10:7–80, esp. 14, 27.

4. Alfred P. James, *Ohio Company* (Pittsburgh, 1958), chapters 2–4.

5. Ronald E. Grim, "Origins and Early Development of the Virginia Fall Line
    Towns," (M.A., Maryland, 1971), chapter 5; Gay Moore, *Seaport in Virginia*
    (Richmond, 1949), pt. I; Douglas S. Freeman, *George Washington* (7 vols., New
    York, 1948–57), 1:21, 77, 236; Harrison, *Prince William,* chapter 25; Gaspare
    Saladino, "Maryland and Virginia Wheat Trade," (M.A., Wisconsin, 1960).

6. Lawrence H. Gipson, *Lewis Evans* (Philadelphia, 1939), 23, 40, 179; Marcus Cun-
    liffe, *George Washington* (London, 1959), 41–48; Lawrence C. Wroth, *American
    Bookshelf* (New York, 1969), chapter 2; GWW 1:116.

7. Gutheim, *Potomac,* chapter 5; *American Historical Review* 16:311–19; Mary Gei-
    ger, *Daniel Carroll* (Washington, 1943), chapters 1–2; Eugene Prussing, *Estate of
    George Washington, Deceased* (Boston, 1927), chapters. 7, 19–27; Roy Bird Clark,
    Washington's Western Lands (Strasburg, Va., 1930); Alice Desmond, *Martha Wash-
    ington* (New York, 1924), 73; Freeman, *Washington* 2:300–01, 6:388, 392; James
    T. Flexner, *Washington, the Indispensable Man* (Boston, 1974), chapter 6;
    Elizabeth Cometti, ed., *American Journals of Lt. John Enys* (Syracuse, 1976), 246;
    MHSP 51:63.

8. GWW 3:20; Grace L. Nute, "Washington and the Potomac," *American Historical
    Review* 28:497–519 (esp. 502), 705–22; Edward S. Delaplaine, *Life of Thomas
    Johnson* (New York, 1927), chapter 7; *Maryland Gazette,* 11 Feb. 1762.

9. Delaplaine, *Johnson,* 72–83; TJ 7:49–52; Bessie Gahn, *George Washington's
    Headquarters . . . Rock Creek to the Falls* (Silver Spring, Md., 1940), 65–100;
    Richard K. McMaster, "Georgetown and the Tobacco Trade, 1751–83," RCHS
    11:120–224; Harrison, *Prince William,* 149; [DLC], *District of Columbia: Sesqui-
    centennial . . . Exhibition* (Washington, 1950), 3–6.

10. Alexandria Address, 31 Dec. 1783, GWP, and GWW 27:288; Delaplaine, *Johnson*, 77–84; GWD 3:291; Moore, *Alexandria*, pt. I; GWW 28:321, 356; TJ 14:304; Pamela C. Copeland, *Five George Masons* (Charlottesville, 1975), 217–18.

11. GWW 30:133 and "Alexandria Letter," *Freeman's Journal*, 23 Aug. 1786 (quoted); TJ 6:365, 7:215, 260–61, 380, 562 (quoted), 11:385–91; JM 7:401, 8:64–65, 93, 127; Daniel and Isaac McPherson to Adam Stephen, 25 Feb. 1789, Stephen, DLC; A. Lee to Thomas Lee Shippen, 25 April 1790, Shippen, DLC; East, *Business Enterprise*, 235; Brissot de Warville, *New Travels in the United States* (Durand Echeverria, ed., Cambridge, Mass., 1964), 341–42; Drew R. McCoy, "Virginia Port Bill of 1784," VMHB 83:288–303.

12. East, *Business Enterprise*, 164–65, 234–35 (quoted); MdJ, 1 July 1783, 24 July 1787; Saladino, "Wheat Trade," 75–76; James W. Livengood, *Philadelphia–Baltimore Trade Rivalry* (Harrisburg, 1947), chapter 1.

13. JM 7:425–26, 8:9–10, 20.

14. TJ 7:16, 25–27, 49–50.

15. Lambert to John Cadwalader, 13 April 1785, Cadwalader, PHi (quoted); *Virginia Journal*, 25 Nov. 1784, 27 Oct. 1785 (quoted); GWD 4:1–71, esp. 58–59; TJ 7:592; GWW 27:471–80, 495, 504–05, 28:3–4, 11–12, 18–22, 24, 214, 267; JM 8:160, 205, 223–26, 12:478–79; IG, 20 Nov., 18 Dec. 1784; Ballagh, *Lee* 2:390–91.

16. JM 8:215–16, 223–26; Proceedings of the Potomac Company, 17 May 1785, RG 79, National Archives; Peter Albert, "George Washington and the Improvement of the Potomac, 1754–85" (M.A., Wisconsin, 1969), 60–61.

17. TJ 13:554–55; W.P. Palmer, *et al.*, eds., *Calendar of Virginia State Papers* (11 vols., Richmond, 1875–93), 5:99–100; *New Jersey Journal*, 4 April 1787; MdJ, 16 Dec. 1788; NYDA, 19 May, 16 June, 14 July, 10 Sept. 1789.

18. JM 11:321–22, 349–51, 356 (quoted), 371–72, 387, 399–400, 420–23, 12:213–14, 13:58, 14:183–85; NYJ, 22 Nov. 1790; *Virginia Centinel*, 29 July 1789; *Hampshire Gazette*, 12 Aug. 1789; TJ 14:619–21, 15:415–16; H. Lee to Washington, 9, 14 Feb. 1789, GWP; GWW 30:199–203; Thomas Boyd, *Lighthorse Harry Lee* (New York, 1931), chapter 11.

19. GWW 28:48–55, 73–75 (51–52, 55, and 75 quoted), 79–80, 289–91; Elkanah Watson, *Memoirs* (New York, 1856), 242–46, 277; TJ 8:36–37, 119; JM 8:10–11, 24, 89–90, 206–07; Thomas Stone to Washington, 28 Jan. 1785, GC; Robert A. Rutland, ed., *Papers of George Mason* (3 vols., Chapel Hill, 1970), 812–23.

20. GWW 27:475, 483, 28:4 (quoted), 207, 214, 218, 231, 460–61, 29:4, 35, 204–05; GWD 4:65–68; TJ 10:531–32, 11:385–87; Davis, *Sectionalism*, chapters 6–7; MdJ, 24 July 1787; *Virginia Journal*, 21 May 1789; Thomas Johnson to Washington, 11 Dec. 1787, GWP.

21. MdJ, 24 March 1789 (reprinted in *Maryland Historical Magazine* 71:310–21).

22. An article in the *Maryland Journal* of 8 April 1791 stated that the proprietors of land in the federal city had donated several lots to George Walker because he was "the first projector of the magnificent plan now in contemplation." Louis Dow Sisco concluded (RCHS 1957–59:136) that this statement referred to Walker's role in resolving the differences between the proprietors and Washington in 1791. Allen C. Clark (OFC, 49) hits closer to the mark by suggesting that Walker may have projected the plan of acquisition. I believe that the article referred to Walk-

er's having been the first to propose the idea of the Anacostia to Rock Creek area for the capital, the engraved plat and the sale of the lots. *The Georgetown Weekly Ledger,* 9 April 1791, states that Mayor Thomas Beall presented Walker with a Georgetown lot. (Walker to Huie, Reid and Co, 17 March 1788, Biographical Sketches, Huie, Reid and Co., DLC; OFC, 95.)

23. MdJ, 23 Jan. 1789. Using the signature "Civis," Walker regularly used the *Maryland Journal* to publish his thoughts on a variety of matters.

24. William Smith to Otho Williams, 31 Aug. 1789, Ms. 908, MdHi; Henry R. Evans, *Old Georgetown* (Washington, 1933), 1–30.

25. Otho Williams to David Ross, 1 Sept. 1788, Ms. 908, MdHi; MdJ, 3 March 1789.

26. Robert Mitchell, "Upper Shenandoah Valley of Virginia" (Ph. D., Wisconsin, 1969); *Maryland Historical Magazine* 32:293–300; Thomas Williams, *History of Washington County, Maryland* (2 vols., Hagerstown, 1906), chapters 1–6; GWW 31:439; JM 12:7, 389.

27. Elliot, *Debates* 3:611; "American," [Tench Coxe], PG, 28 May 1788; *Virginia Independent Chronicle,* 2 July 1788; "Citizen of America" [John O'Connor], *Political Opinions Particularly Respecting the Seat of Federal Empire* ([Georgetown], 1789), 43–44.

28. *Journal of the House of Delegates . . . 1788* (Richmond, 1828), 125; "C.H.," MdG(B), 27 Jan. 1789; "Edenton Letter," MdG(B), 23 Jan. 1789; William Smith to Otho Williams, 31 Aug. 1789, Ms. 908, MdHi; David Galloway to R.H. Lee, 28 April 1789, Lee, ViU; NYDG, 9 July 1790.

29. JM 11:253, 255, 258, 265; "Friend to the Union," *Virginia Gazette* (Winchester), 4 March 1789; White to Adam Stephen, 24 March 1789, Stephen, DLC; P. Muhlenberg to Rush, 2 April 1789, Society, PHi; NYDA, 7 Sept. 1789.

30. GWD 5:437; TJ 11:446, 450.

31. Thomas and Samuel to Levi Hollingsworth, 21 May 1787, Hollingsworth, PHi; Alexandria Address, 16 April 1789, GWP; GWW 30:287; TPP, 23 April 1789; GUS, 29 April 1789.

Chapter 5

All dates are 1789 unless otherwise noted. House debates and official actions by the House and Senate are from Linda DePauw, Charlene Bickford, Kenneth Bowling and Helen Veit, eds., *Documentary History of the First Federal Congress* (7+ vols., Baltimore, 1972–), under the appropriate date; *see especially* vols. 6:1850–70 and 11: to be published. The August–September residence negotiations would be better understood if Fitzsimons' letters to Rush dated 21 August, 4, 8, 12, 13, and 28 September, presently in private collections, were available (*Manuscripts* 24:172–81).

1. FG, 6 March.

2. *New York Morning Post,* 4 Aug.; EIHC 25:23; White to Horatio Gates, 1 June, Gates, NHi; WLS, 4; R.B. Lee to David Stuart, 4 June, McGregor Library Mss., ViU; Paine Wingate to Jeremy Belknap, 6 July, Belknap, MHi; JM 12:280.

3. FE 4:2, 274, 277; A. to Francis L. Lee, 29 Aug., Lee, Harvard. For Pennsylvania's concern about the residence question prior to August *see* PMHB 38:56 and Clymer to Samuel Meredith, 15 June, to Rush, 3 July, Clymer–Meredith–Read, NN. For New York's attempts to retain Congress *see* FA, 31–32; F. Muhlenberg to

Coxe, 5 May, TC; George Partridge to Samuel Holten, 20 May, GC; *Rhode Island History* 7:57–59; IG, 22 July; Austin Keep, *History of the New York Society Library* (New York, 1908), 207; NYDA, 15 April, 17 July; NYDG, 22 May, 19 Aug., 5 Sept.; NYJ, 2 April; GUS, 15 Aug.; FG, 11 April, 11 May, 8, 20 June, 30 July, 22, 24, 25, 26 Aug., 2, 16 Sept.; and IG, 4 Aug. For awareness of the relationship between the location of the capital and other issues before Congress *see* White to Horatio Gates, 1 June, Gates, NHi; MD, 75; FA, 63; Abigail to John Quincy Adams, 5 Sept. 1790, AFMT; and F. Muhlenberg to Rush, 18 Aug., Society, PHi.

4. JM 12:329 (quoted); FE 4:274; R. Morris to Peters, 9 Aug., Peters, PHi; Daniel Hiester to James Hamilton, 3 Aug., Cumberland Co. Hist. Soc.; Hiester Journal, 31 July, 5 Aug., Berks County Hist. Soc.; P. Muhlenberg to Rush, 10 Aug., GC; F. Muhlenberg to Rush, 18 Aug., Society, PHi; EIHC 83:216.

5. P. Muhlenberg to Rush, 10 Aug., GC; PMHB 38:60–61; MD, 144–45; Fitzsimons to Coxe, 6 Sept., TC; RM, 28 Aug.; NYDA, 22 Aug.; JM 12:353; William Smith to Otho Williams, 23 Aug., Ms. 908, MdHi.

6. Additional detail and annotation on sites proposed for the capital can be found in my "Neither in a Wigwam nor the Wilderness: Competitors for the Federal Capital, 1787–1790," *Prologue, The Journal of the National Archives* 20:163–79.

7. JM 9:63, 417; "Common Sense," *American Herald*, 8 May 1788; Elliot, *Debates* 3:158.

8. P. 332 (quoted). I am indebted to Betty Huber of Morrisville and Tee Loftin of Washington, D.C., for calling to my attention a recorded deed documenting Morris's 1787 land transaction in the Morrisville area.

9. "Citizen of Philadelphia" [Pelatiah Webster], *Essay on the Seat of the Federal Government and the Exclusive Jurisdiction of Congress Over a Ten Miles District* (Philadelphia, 1789), 15–29.

10. ROC 15:267.

11. MdJ, 24 July 1787; PP, 28 July 1787; BR, 449; JM 12:397; Fitzsimons to Coxe, 6 Sept., TC; Livengood, *Philadelphia–Baltimore*, 1–3, 27–34, 81–84, 100–02.

12. Hartley's pamphlet was printed at New York shortly after his arrival; part of it came directly from "True American," [George Lux, Jr.?], MdJ, 29 July 1783.

13. FE 4:152.

14. Pp. 353–54. On Elkton *see* "Citizen of the World," [George Walker], MdJ, 23 Jan. 1789.

15. PMHB 38:61; *Perkiomen Region Past and Present* 1:163; Robert Lewis Diary, 27 Aug., Mount Vernon; Fitzsimons to Rush, 28 Aug., Miscellaneous, PPAmP; MD, 138; "Thomas Sumter Letter," *City Gazette*, 13 Oct.

16. MD, 135, 138, 144–45; RM, 28 Aug.

17. MD, 140–41; Arthur to Francis L. Lee, 29 Aug., Lee, Harvard; FA, 71; BG, 6 Sept.; P. Muhlenberg to Rush, 9 Sept., Society, PHi; JM 12:402–03.

18. King, Summary of Bargaining, [c. 26 Sept.], King, NHi; MD, 144–46; Hartley to Coxe, 2 Sept., TC; PMHB 38:62; R. Morris to James Wilson, 23 Aug., Morris, Willing and Swanwick, Pennsylvania Historical and Museum Commission; RM, 28 Aug., 6 Sept.; R. Morris to Peters, 13 Sept., Peters, PHi.

19. MD, 145–46, 152–53; P. Muhlenberg to Rush, 9 Sept., Society, PHi; Fitzsimons to Coxe, 6 Sept., TC; FG, 9, 10 Sept.; Clymer to Peters, 6 Sept., Peters, PHi.

20. Hartley to Coxe, 23 Aug., TC; William Smith to Otho Williams, Ms. 908, MdHi. Some of Hartley's lands are listed in *Pennsylvania Herald*, 4 March.

21. On Clymer's lands *see Freeman's Journal*, 15 Dec. 1790, Supplement #6, and Norman B. Wilkinson, *Land Policy and Speculation in Pennsylvania, 1779-1800* (New York, 1979), 9.

22. James Hart, *American Presidency in Action, 1789* (New York, 1948), 150.

23. "Letters," *Salem Mercury*, 15 Sept. and Thomas Dwight to Sedgwick, 3 Sept., TS (quoted); Hartley to Jasper Yeates, 6 Sept., Yeates, PHi; EIHC 83:216.

24. Fitzsimons to Coxe, 6 Sept., TC, and WLS, 14-15 (quoted); FA, 35-36 (quoted), 48-49; Sedgwick to Benjamin Lincoln, 19 July, Lincoln, MHi; MHSC(2) 8:322; Ames to Sedgwick, 6 Oct., TS.

25. JM 12:400.

26. JM 12:395-96 (quoted), 409-10; "Brutus," CC, 26 April 1790.

27. MD, 145-48; Elias to Elisha Boudinot, 2 Sept., Miscellaneous, New York State Library; Hartley to Jasper Yeates, 31 Aug., Yeates, PHi.

28. Fitzsimons to Samuel Meredith, 7 Sept., Dreer, PHi.

29. P. Muhlenberg to Rush, 9 Sept., Society, PHi; Hartley to Jasper Yeates, 20 Sept., Yeates, PHi.

30. William Smith to Otho Williams, 14 Sept., Ms. 908, MdHi; Ames to Sedgwick, 8 Sept., 6 Oct., TS; Ames to John Lowell, 13 Sept., E.L. Diedrich, Clements; Hartley to Coxe, 13 Sept., Fitzsimons to Coxe, 13 Sept., TC; R. Morris to Peters, 13 Sept., Peters, PHi.

31. Clymer to Peters, 9 Sept., Peters, PHi, Clymer to Coxe, 13 Sept., TC, and R.B. to Charles Lee, 16 Sept., Roberts, Haverford (quoted); IG, 14 Sept.; "Aminidae," PP, 17 Sept.; *New York Packet*, 10 Sept.; NYJ, 17 Sept.; NYDA, 8 Sept.; RM, 11 Sept.

32. RM, 9 Sept. (HM 13538); R.B. to Theodorick Lee, 12 Sept., R.B. Lee, DLC; GWW 30:147; VMHB 87:81-82; David Stuart to Washington, 12 Sept., GWP.

33. Goodhue to Salem Insurance Officers, 13 Sept., Goodhue, New York Society Library; Fitzsimons to Coxe, 16 Sept., TC; Clymer to Peters, 15 Sept., Peters, PHi; MD, 148-49, 152-53, 406-10; NYDA, 17 Sept.

34. Hartley to Jasper Yeates, 20 Sept., Yeates, PHi.

35. Ames to Sedgwick, 6 Oct., TS; MD, 152-55; William Smith to Otho Williams, 18 Sept., Ms. 908, MdHi; PMHB 38:185; Hartley to Jasper Yeates, 20 Sept., Yeates, PHi; EIHC 83:217.

36. Ames to Sedgwick, 6 Oct., TS; JM 12:419.

37. RM, 25 Sept. (HM 13534); MD, 156; R. Morris to Peters, 13 Sept., Peters, PHi; PMHB 1:443.

38. MD, 156-59, 449-50 (quoted), 468-69, 491.

39. King, Summary of Bargaining, [c. 26 Sept.], King, NHi.

40. MD, 161-68, 449-50, 491-92; Schutz and Adair, *Spur of Fame*, 251.

41. BG, 27 Sept.; Hartley to Coxe, 27 Sept., TC; Boudinot to William Bradford, Jr., 27 Sept., Wallace, PHi; Ames to Sedgwick, 6 Oct., TS.

42. Ames to Sedgwick, 6 Oct., TS; DeWitt to Charles Clinton, 20 July 1790, extra-illustrated *Old New York*, NHi.

43. NYDA, 29 Sept.; Boudinot to William Bradford, Jr., 27 Sept., Wallace, PHi; IG, 3 Oct.; Richard Butler to William Irvine, 3 Nov., Draper, WHi; Ames to Sedgwick, 6 Oct., TS.

44. MD, 159, 170, 179, 196, 199, 208; John Armstrong, Jr., to Baron von Steuben, 4 Oct., Miscellaneous, NHi; Fitzsimons to Coxe, 28 Feb. 1790, TC; *Carlisle Gazette,* 28 Oct; IG: "Citizen," 2 Oct., "Taxpayer," 23 Nov.; R. Morris to Thomas S. Lee, 1 July 1784, 19 Oct., Ms. 1974, MdHi.

Chapter 6

All dates are 1790 unless otherwise noted. House debates and official actions by the House and Senate are from Linda DePauw, Charlene Bickford, Kenneth Bowling and Helen Veit, eds., *Documentary History of the First Federal Congress* (7 + vols., Baltimore, 1972-), under the appropriate date; *see especially* 5:713-937, 6:1767-91.

1. Grayson to P. Henry, 29 Sept. 1789, Henry, DLC; Ames to Sedgwick, 6 Oct., TS; Ames to Caleb Strong, 15 Sept., Thompson, Hartford Seminary Foundation.

2. [Pelatiah Webster], *Seat of Federal Government,* 3-15; John Witherspoon, "Few Reflections on the Federal City," [Oct. 1789-May 1790], *Miscellaneous Works* (Philadelphia, 1803), 232-37; R.R. Livingston, [Draft of a Speech, Sept. 1789], Livingston, NHi.

3. TPP, 14 April; JM 12:128, 343, 389. 398-99, 410, 418, 425-27, 431-32, 452-53.

4. J.F.D. Smyth, *Tour in the United States* (2 vols., London, 1784), 2:144-45 (quoted); George Burtchaell, ed., *Alumni Dublinenses* (Dublin, 1935), 630; MHSC(5) 2:477; *Virginia Herald,* 22 April 1789; PCC, item 78, 17:497; John Murray to Horatio Gates, 20 Sept. 1789, Gates, NN; TPP, 14 Oct. 1789; *Virginia Gazette* (Alexandria), 19 Nov. 1789; MdG(B), 16 April. *Political Opinions,* the earliest known non-newspaper imprint from Georgetown, achieved some circulation because a short extract appeared in the *Massachusetts Centinel* on 10 March.

5. David Stuart to Washington, 3 Dec. 1789, GWP; *David Stuart et al. to Gentlemen, 7 Dec. 1789* [Alexandria, 1789]. The Force Collection (Series 9, Box 34), DLC, contains draft versions of the broadside. Newspaper reprints include *Massachusetts Centinel,* 2 Jan., *Massachusetts Spy,* 7 Jan., *Federal Herald,* 1 Feb., and GUS, 13 Jan. Texts of the final and draft versions are in Donald Sweig, "Capital on the Potomac," VMHB 87:74-104.

6. TJ 19:14-15; St. George Tucker, *Notes of Reference. . . ,* I(pt. 1, Appendix):139; JM 12:461-62; *Calendar of Virginia State Papers* 5:99-100; White to Gov. Beverly Randolph, 24 Feb., Resolution of Maryland House of Delegates, 25 Dec. 1789, Executive Papers, Virginia State Library.

7. 8, 22 Jan.

8. Daniel and Isaac McPherson to Adam Stephen, 28 Dec. 1789, Stephen, DLC; JM 13:83, 176. *Expostulations of Potowmac* was published at Martinsburg, [West] Virginia, in 1790; it has often been cited as a 1789 Georgetown imprint. Among the newspapers which printed it were the *Virginia Gazette* (Alexandria), 6 May, *Massachusetts Centinel,* 22 May, *American Mercury,* 24 May, *Herald of Freedom,* 25 May, and *Cumberland Gazette,* 31 May.

9. R.B. to Charles Lee, 10 Jan., Miscellaneous, NN; "Familiar Epistle," CC, 14 Jan.; "X," *Massachusetts Centinel,* 6 Jan.

10. WMQ 21:415.

11. JM 12:466; MD, 187-91; William Smith to Otho Williams, 24 Jan., Ms. 908, MdHi; Hartley to Jasper Yeates, 24 Jan., Yeates, PHi. *See* WLS, 101-02; for another reason one member favored the *de novo* procedure.

12. Ferguson, *Purse*, chapters 13–14; William G. Anderson, *Price of Liberty: The Public Debt of the American Revolution* (Charlottesville, 1983), pt. I; JM 13:87–90, 102–03, 136–37, 142, 154–57; Irving Brant, *James Madison, The Nationalist* (Indianapolis, 1948), chapter 16.

13. WLS, 109.

14. Theodore to Pamela Sedgwick, 4 March, TS; George Cabot to Goodhue, 5 May, Goodhue, New York Society Library; Abigail Adams to Cotton Tufts, 7 March, Miscellaneous, DLC; MD, 240; Maclay to Rush, 12 April, Rush, DLC; Maclay to John Nicholson, received 2 Feb., Miscellaneous, DLC. For the changing votes on assumption *see* my "Dinner at Jefferson's: A Note on Jacob E. Cooke's 'The Compromise of 1790,'" WMQ 28:629–48.

15. Fitzsimons to Coxe, 28 Feb., TC; Theodore to Pamela Sedgwick, 3–[4], 7 April, TS; MD, 214–15, 230, 241, 250; Philip Schuyler to Stephen Van Rensselaer, 30 May, Morristown National Military Park.

16. MD, 268, 271, 304; Pennsylvania Abolition Society Memorial, 3 Feb., RG 46, National Archives; Adams to James Sullivan, 18 June 1789, AFMT; Philip Schuyler to Jeremiah Olney, 7 June, Shepley, RHi; Richard Bassett to George Read, 1 March, Rodney, Hist. Soc. of Delaware.

17. John Brown to Harry Innes, 8 June, Innes, DLC; David Stuart to R.B. Lee, 23 May, R.B. Lee, DLC; Maclay to Rush, 7 May, DLC; Abigail Adams to Mary Cranch, 30 May, American Antiquarian; Samuel Ogden to Henry Knox, 22 May, Knox, MHi.

18. John Dawson to Coxe (quoted), 26 Oct. 1789, TC; JM 13:87–90, 102–03, 136–37 (quoted), 147–48; Grayson to P. Henry, 28 Sept. 1789, Henry, DLC; John Murray to Horatio Gates, 20 Sept. 1789, Gates, NN; H. Lee to Henry Knox, 10 Oct. 1789, Knox, MHi; R.B. to Theodorick Lee, 9 April, R.B. Lee, DLC.

19. To Washington, 15 March, 2 June, GWP; GWW 31:28–30.

20. JM 13:181, 230; Mays, *Pendleton* 2:564–67; David Stuart to R.B. Lee, 23 May, R.B. Lee, DLC; John Dawson to Coxe, 28 May, TC; Alexander Martin to Hugh Williamson, 29 June, Governor's Letterbooks, N.C. Dept. of Archives and History; Pierce to William Butler, 22 May, Butler, British Museum; Griffith McRee, *Life and Correspondence of James Iredell* (2 vols., New York, 1857–58), 2:285; White to Horatio Gates, 16 April, Gates, NN.

21. Henry Jackson to Henry Knox, 25 April, Knox, MHi and Christopher Gore to King, 30 May, King, NHi (quoted); FA, 77; Oliver Wolcott, Sr., to Jr., 26 April, Wolcott, CtHi; "Brutus," CC, 26 April; Cotton Tufts to Abigail Adams, 17 April, AFMT; Nathaniel Gorham to Henry Knox, 17 April, Knox, MHi; Henry Van Schaack to Sedgwick, 23 May, TS.

22. Oliver Wolcott, Sr., to Jr., 23 April, Wolcott, CtHi; Thomas Cushing to Goodhue, 17 April, Goodhue, New York Society Library; Adams to Stephen Higginson, 14 March, AFMT.

23. Maclay to Rush, 7 March, Rush, DLC; Fitzsimons to Coxe, 28 Feb., TC; William Irvine to [John Nicholson], 18 March, Miscellaneous, WHi; Hartley to Jasper Yeates, 11 April, Yeates, PHi; Samuel Meredith to Henry Hill, 19 April, John Jay Smith, PPL; MD, 235–36, 238.

24. John Fenno to Joseph Ward, 11 April, Ward, Chicago Hist. Soc.; BG, 11 April; Thatcher to David Sewall, 11 April, Thatcher, MHi.

25. William L. Smith to Coxe, 14 April, 2 May, TC; Goodhue to Samuel Phillips, 17 April, Phillips, MHi; Philip Schuyler to Stephen Van Renssellaer, 16 May, Schuyler Mansion, New York State Library.

26. WLS, 115 (quoted); John Steele to Gov. Alexander Martin, 17 May, Steele, University of N.C.; John Fenno to Joseph Ward, 23 May, Ward, Chicago Hist. Soc.; Hartley to Jasper Yeates, 11 May, Yeates, PHi; F. Muhlenberg to Coxe, 2 May, TC; JM 13:239.

27. RM, 23 May; F. Muhlenberg to Coxe, 2 May, Coxe, PHi; MD, 269–74; Maclay to Rush, 23 May, Rush, DLC.

28. MD, 271, 275–77; Hartley to Jasper Yeates, 24 Jan., Yeates, PHi; Samuel to Margaret Meredith, 15 April, Meredith, PPL; "Cassius," CC, 12 July; TJ 16:449; F. Muhlenberg to Rush, 30 May, Society, PHi.

29. MD, 276–79, 282–83, 459–60 (quoted); Goodhue to Samuel Phillips, 1 June, Phillips, MHi; PMHB 38:198; Thatcher to Nathaniel Wells, 25 May, Thatcher, MHi; JM 13:233–34; Ballagh, Lee 2:521–22; Paine Wingate to Samuel Hodgdon, 2 June, Pickering, MHi.

30. MD, 285–87, 470; Fitzsimons to Rush, 10 June, Parke-Bernet Catalog 499:item 118.

31. Hartley to Jasper Yeates, 9 June, Yeates, PHi; FA, 79–80.

32. MD, 292–93, 497; Thatcher to Nathaniel Wells, 13 June, Thatcher, MHi.

33. MD, 291; IG, 29 May; Stokes, Iconography 5:1262–69; WMQ 28:638; EIHC 84:157; WLS, 117.

34. MD, 293 (quoted); FE 4:417, 432.

35. WLS, 116; TJ 17:206; Theodore to Pamela Sedgwick, 29 May, TS.

Chapter 7

(All dates are 1790 unless otherwise noted. House debates and official actions by the House and Senate are from Linda DePauw, Charlene Bickford, Kenneth Bowling and Helen Veit, eds., Documentary History of the First Federal Congress (7+ vols., Baltimore, 1972–), under the appropriate date; see especially 6:1767–91, 13: to be published. Certain details of the Compromise of 1790 and the events leading to it are contained in letters Fitzsimons sent to Rush which are privately owned and unavailable; they are dated 6, 10, 15, 19, 25 June, 2, 4, and 11 July (Manuscripts 24:172–81).

1. MD, 293–94; TJ 17:206; Theodore to Pamela Sedgwick, 29 May, TS; PMHB 70:101.

2. JM 13:246; BG, June.

3. PMHB 70:101–02 (quoted); MD, 179, 184, 196, 249; P. Muhlenberg to Rush, 10 July, GC; RM, 19–21 June.

4. MD, 297. On Jefferson's role see the comments of Senator William Samuel Johnson in Lord Dorchester to Lord Grenville, 25 Sept., Report on Canadian Archives . . . 1890 (Ottawa, 1891), 146. Jefferson's earliest account of the dinner can be found in TJ 17:205–07. It is self-serving and sometimes inaccurate, but less so than his 1818 statement in Franklin B. Sawvel, ed., Complete Anas of Thomas Jefferson (New York, 1903). The precise date of the dinner cannot be determined; the evidence points to Sunday, 20 June (see my "Politics in the First Congress,

1789–91," Ph.D., Wisconsin, 1968, 183–85). A dinner on 6 June attended by Jefferson, Madison, and Hamilton's colleague Tench Coxe may have been related to the Pennsylvania–Virginia agreement to push for a removal of Congress to Philadelphia without mention of the permanent residence, one of the precursors of the Compromise of 1790. (*See* Norman Risjord, "Compromise of 1790: New Evidence on the Dinner Table Bargain," WMQ 33:309–14.)

5. R.B. to Theodorick Lee, 23 Feb., 9 April (quoted), 26 June, R.B. Lee, DLC; WMQ 28:635–38; TJ 17:207; R.B. to Charles Lee, 10 Jan., Miscellaneous, NN; GWW 31:50n; White to Horatio Gates, 13 March, Emmet, 17 April, Gates, NN; Sawvel, *Anas*, 34.

6. [Daniel Carroll], "To the Inhabitants," WS, 26 Aug.; "B.L.," IG, 7 Aug.; "To B.L.," *New York Morning Post,* 29 July; M.J. Stone to unknown, 24 June, Stone, DLC.

7. William Davies to Gov. Randolph, 29 June, Executive Papers, Virginia State Library; BG, 22 June; Theodore to Pamela Sedgwick, 22, 27 June, TS; FA, 84; James Sullivan to Gerry, 18 [July], Gerry, DLC; WLS, 125–26, 130–32.

8. MD, 301–04; TJ 17:207.

9. King to Caleb Strong, 26 June, Natick Hist. Soc.; Memorandum for Strong, [26 June], "Residence, 2d Session," 30 June (quoted), King, NHi; William L. Smith to Pierce Butler, 25 June, Butler, British Museum; M.J. to Walter Stone, 2 Aug., Stone, DLC; Hartley to Jasper Yeates, 25 June, Yeates, PHi; *Canadian Archives . . . 1890,* 152; "New York Letter," *American Mercury,* 12 July. For a different interpretation of Hamilton's role, which argues that the dinner bargain was never consummated, and that the final compromise involved only financial issues not the location of the capital, *see* Jacob E. Cooke, "Compromise of 1790," WMQ 27:523–45.

10. John Fenno to Joseph Ward, 27 June, Ward, Chicago Hist. Soc.; Theodore to Pamela Sedgwick, 27 June, TS; FA, 84; R.B. to Theodorick Lee, 26 June, R.B. Lee, DLC.

11. MD, 305–10.

12. MD, 308; M. J. Stone to "Dear Brother," 2 July, Stone, Duke; JM 13:262; *Virginia Journal,* 8 July; Thatcher to David Sewall, 4 July, Thatcher, MHi; Philip Schuyler to Stephen Van Renssellaer, 4 July, Morristown National Military Park; Samuel to Margaret Meredith, 1 July, Meredith, PPL.

13. Ballagh, Lee 2:532.

14. [William L. Smith], *Politicks of a Certain Party Displayed* (n.p., 1792), 14.

15. MD, 321 (quoted); Fitzsimons to Rush, 11 July, *Parke–Bernet Catalog* 499:item 119; P. Muhlenberg to Rush, 10 July, GC; Maclay to Rush, 10 July, DLC; RM, 2 July; PMHB 38:200–01.

16. Joseph Stanton to George Christopher, 29 June, RHi; BG, [c. 2 July]; Jonathan Trumbulll to William Williams, 12 July, Series 7E, Force, DLC; "Jack Forecastle," NYJ, 29 June; *Boston Gazette,* 5 July; *Columbian Centinel,* 3 July; NYDG, 30 June; NYJ, 13 July; IG, 17 July; Theodore to Pamela Sedgwick, 13 July, TS; Thatcher to David Sewall, 20 July, Thatcher, MHi.

17. To Daniel Parker, 5 May, 8 July (quoted), Craigie, American Antiquarian Society.

18. "Civis," NYJ, 13 July; Samuel to Margaret Meredith, 14 July, Meredith, PPL; WMQ 3:541. Julian Boyd's excellent account of the incident (TJ 17:163–208)

contains the documents mentioned here. "Junius Americanus" was reprinted in the *Columbian Herald* at Charleston, S.C., on 10 August. This and the fact that a 10 July NYDG article predicted that Smith would have more to say on the subject points to him as the author.

19. DeWitt to Charles Clinton, 20 July, extra-illustrated *Old New York*, NHi (quoted); WMQ 21:441; Walter Rutherford to Mathew Clarkson, 27 July, Jay Family, Yale; *Georgia Gazette*, 5 Aug.; NYJ: 16 July, "Z," "Sketches of Congressional Biography," 23 July, "Citizen of America," 27 July, "S," "T," 6 Aug., "Vox Res Publica," 20 Aug.; NYDA: 11 Aug., "Truth," [William L. Smith?], 12 Aug; "New York Farmer," *New York Magazine* 2:30.

20. Ferguson, *Purse,* 321; "B.K.," NYJ, 27 July.

21. WLS, 125–26; John to James Brown, 11 Aug., Liberty Hall, Frankfort, Kentucky; Ballagh, *Lee* 2:535; Henry Wagstaff, ed., *Papers of John Steele* (2 vols., Raleigh, N.C., 1924), 1:74; "B.K.," NYJ, 27 July.

22. "X," FG, 31 July; WLS, 128.

23. Thatcher to David Sewall, 20 July, Thatcher, MHi; MD, 331–32.

24. Ferguson, *Purse,* chapter 14, esp. 322–24; JM 13:284–85.

25. GWW 31:84; TJ 17:390–91.

26. Freneau's 14 June *"Description of NEW YORK One Hundred and Fifty Years Hence"* predicted success for the Potomac's dreams of commercial glory and the rise of a magnificent capital. The widely reprinted "Nanny" and "Nabby" poems, letters betweeen New York and Philadelphia housekeepers, appeared on 1 and 15 July. His "Bergen Planter," which argued that the removal of Congress held no interest for the average American, appeared on 12 July. "The Departure," published as "The Removal" in the *New York Journal* of 10 August, attacked Senator Morris. These are printed in F.L. Pattee, ed., *Poems of Freneau* (3 vols., Princeton, 1902–07), 3:42–50. From the bouncy metre, the romantic imagery, the format of a conversation and the place of publication, I surmise that he also wrote "River Delaware to the River Hudson" printed in NYDA on 5 July.

27. John Pintard to Elisha Boudinot, 12 June, Boudinot–Pintard, NHi; Clymer to Coxe, 1 May, TC; *New York Packet*, 12, 17 June; FG, 29 May, 16 June (Rush); IG, 22 June; *Pennsylvania Mercury,* 19 June; NYJ: 4 June, "Citizen," 6 July; NYDA: 3 June (quoted), "X," 29 June; NYDG: "George," 14 June, "Aristippis," 22 June, "Fixed Star," 2 July.

28. *New York Weekly Museum:* 10 July, "T.C.," 31 July; NYJ: 10 Aug., "Connecticut U," 6 July, 9 July, "Citizen," 20 July; *New York Morning Post,* 5 July; "Jamaica, N.Y., Letter," MdJ, 27 Aug.; DeWitt to Charles Clinton, 20 July, extra-illustrated *Old New York,* NHi; "Minority's Farewell," TPP, 15 Sept.; NYDG: 3 July, "Friend to the Union," 10 July.

29. Hartley to Jasper Yeates, 10 July, Miscellaneous, NN; *New York Morning Post,* 2 July; Fitzsimons to Rush, 4 July, *Collector* 59:item 1402; PMHB 38:204; Theodore to Pamela Sedgwick, 4 July, TS; "New York Letter," FG, 14 July; "New Song," *New York Morning Post,* 4 Aug.; NYJ, 22 June, 2, 23 July.

30. RM, 19–21 June, 2 July; Fitzsimons to Rush, 18 July, ARA Foundation, Philadelphia; PMHB 38:201; WLS, 130; "Valedictory," *New York Morning Post,* 21 Aug.; TJ 17:207; East, *Business Enterprise,* 140, 146; MD, 272.

31. "Tycho Brache" [sic], *New York Packet,* 15 July; NYJ: 9 July, "Citizen," 20 July, "Sketches of Congressional Biography," 23 July, 3 Aug., "W_____," 31 Aug.; NYDG, 17, 18 Aug.; *New York Morning Post,* 26 July; IG, 7 Aug.

32. "New York Farmer," *New York Magazine* 2:26–29 (quoted); NYDA, "Happy Dick," 12 July, "Traveller," 22 Sept.

33. MD, 312; TJ 17:xxxiv–vii; *New York Morning Post,* 8 July; James Burrill to Theodore Foster, 24 July, Foster, RHi; *Columbian Centinel,* 14 July; *New Hampshire Recorder,* 26 August.

34. Theodore to Pamela Sedgwick, 4 July, TS. William A. Duer described the cartoon in 1847 (*Reminiscences,* 76–77). Rufus Griswold saw it or a reference to it (*Republican Court,* New York, 1855, 234). DeWitt to Charles Clinton, 20 July (extra-illustrated *Old New York,* NHi) implies that there are two, not one, nonextant versions of this cartoon.

35. Stephen Collins and Son to Samuel Breck, 15 July, Collins, DLC (quoted); William, Jr., to Tench Coxe, 14 June, 1 Nov., TC; Thomas Duncan to William Irvine, 7 June, Irvine, PHi; William Bradford, Jr., to Boudinot, 1 July, Wallace, PHi; Samuel Hodgdon to Goodhue, 23 June, Goodhue, New York Society Library; Samuel W. Stockton to Boudinot, 1, 12 July, Boudinot, Princeton; *American Historical Magazine* 3:22; "Another Citizen," FG, 30 July; Maclay to Rush, 30 July, Rush, DLC.

36. "Cassius," CC, 12 July (quoted); "Republican," *Connecticut Journal,* 2, 16 June; *Boston Gazette,* 21 June, 12 July; "Junius," *Independent Chronicle,* 15 July; "Connecticut," CC, 28 June; [George Champlain?] to Joseph Stanton, 5 July, Champlain, RHi; Thomas Dwight to Sedgwick, 24 June, Henry Van Schaack to Sedgwick, 9 July, TS; William Ellery to Benjamin Huntington, 7 June, Ellery, Rhode Island State Archives; Oliver Wolcott, Sr., to Jr., 11 June, Wolcott, CtHi; Joseph Barrell to Samuel B. Webb, 13 June, Barrell, Yale; Joseph Whipple to John Langdon, 23 July, Sturgis, Harvard; John Trumbull to Adams, 5 June, AFMT; Henry Jackson to Henry Knox, 27 June, 4 July, Knox, MHi; MHSC(5) 3:225; *Columbian Centinel,* 7 July.

37. "Republican," *Connecticut Journal,* 21 July and John Trumbull to Adams, 5 Feb. 1791, AFMT (quoted); Thomas Dwight to Sedgwick, 19 July, TS; Christopher Gore to King, 11 July, King, NHi; James Sullivan to Gerry, 18 [July], Gerry, DLC; "Junius," *Independent Chronicle,* 19 Aug.; *Western Star,* 27 July; NYJ, 27 July; "Hop, Skip, and Jump," NYDA, 15 July; WS, 2, 9 Dec.

38. Lemuel Hopkins to Oliver Wolcott, Jr., 3 Aug., Wolcott, CtHi and *Columbian Centinel,* 28 Aug. (quoted); John Hobby to Thatcher, 31 July, MB; "Friend to Humanity," *United States Chronicle,* 26 Aug.; Gov. Arthur Fenner to R.I. Senators, 28 Feb. 1791, James Burrill to Theodore Foster, 24 July, Foster, RHi.

39. JM 13:261–63, 270–71, 276–77, 283–84, 292, 337–40 (quoted); TJ 17:277, 296, 332–33; "N.C. Letter," *New York Packet,* 31 July; Arthur to James Iredell, 23 July, Charles Johnson, N.C. Department of Archives and History; William to Henry Knox, 14 July, Knox, MHi; Mays, *Pendleton* 2:570; John Dawson to Coxe, 6 Aug., TC; MdJ, 30 July.

40. John Murray to Horatio Gates, 19 Aug., Gates, NN; TJ 17:345; R.B. Lee to Freeholders, 21 Aug., A. Lee to Freeholders, 18 Sept., Joseph Lyons Miller, Richmond Academy of Medicine.

41. Richard Terrell to Col. Minor, 27 Oct., Watson Family, ViU; House of Delegates Papers, 3–4 Nov., Virginia State Library; John Harvie to George Nicholas, 10

NOTES 273

Dec., Thomas Clay, DLC; AH 7:149–50; McRee, *Iredell,* 2:300–04, 311–13; Wagstaff, *Steele,* 1:72–77; *Augusta Chronicle,* 18 Sept. 1790–15 Jan. 1791; MdJ, 31 Dec., 4, 11 Jan. 1791.

42. "Memnon," MdJ, 11 June; "Baltimore Letter," **NYDG**, 22 June; M.J. to Walter Stone, 2 Aug., Stone, DLC; Charles Carroll to Mary Caton, 11 July, Ms. 220, MdHi; MdG(B): "Marylander," 20 July, 23 July, "Plain Truth," 31 Aug.; Samuel Smith to Wilson C. Nicholas, 20 July, Smith, ViU; *A Citizen to the Voters of Maryland* (Baltimore, 1790).

43. "One of the People," *Maryland Herald,* 21 Sept.; M.J. to Walter Stone, 2, 22 Aug., Stone, DLC; Charles Carroll to Mary Caton, 11 July, Ms. 220, MdHi; Lee L. Verstanding, "Emergence of the Two Party System in Maryland" (Ph.D., Brown, 1970), 118; Benjamin Stoddert to Thomas S. Lee, 26 Sept., Ms. 1974, MdHi.

44. MdJ, 8, 26 Oct.; *Maryland Herald,* 18 Jan. 1791; JM 13:307; TJ 19:63, 67–68; William Deakins *et al.* to Delegates, 23 Aug., WS, 2 Sept.

45. G. to R. Morris, 31 Aug., G. Morris, DLC; William Short to John B. Cutting, 14 Jan. 1791, Cutting to Short, 1 Sept., 24 Jan 1791 (quoted), Short, DLC; David Humphreys to Lear, n.d., *Charles Hamilton Catalog* 19:item 325.

46. To William Short, 7 Oct., Short, DLC.

47. James Sullivan to Gerry, 18 [July], Gerry, DLC; JM 13:337–38.

48. Edward Bangs to Thatcher, [c. Jan. 1791], MB.

Chapter 8

House debates and official actions by the House and Senate are from Linda DePauw, Charlene Bickford, Kenneth Bowling and Helen Veit, eds., *Documentary History of the First Federal Congress* (7 + vols., Baltimore, 1972–), under the appropriate date; *see especially* 4:164–215, 6:1793–97, 14:to be published.

1. MdJ, 4 Feb. 1791.

2. An adequate history and historical geography of Washington and the District of Columbia in the 1790s remains to be written. Source materials are abundant, particularly in RCHS and at the National Archives, DLC and PHi. Julian Boyd covers 1791 and early 1792 in detail in TJ 19:3–58 and 20:3–72. Several works present an overview. The classic study is Wilhelmus Bryan, *A History of the National Capital* (2 vols., New York, 1914–16). Renewed interest on the part of historians followed Constance Green's *Washington: Village and Capital, 1800–1878* (Princeton, 1962), the physical and cultural renaissance of Washington, and the support of Princeton University Press and the Smithsonian Institution. John W. Reps' *Monumental Washington* (Princeton, 1967), like Green's work, gives limited attention to the 1790s. Two works were published in connection with a bicentennial exhibition at the Smithsonian: Frederick Gutheim and Wilcomb E. Washburn, *Federal City: Plans and Realities* (Washington, 1976) and Frederick Gutheim, *Worth of a Nation* (Washington, 1977). Both gave some attention to the 1790s and the latter contains an excellent bibliographic essay.

3. Charles Nisbet to the Earl of Buchan, 10 Jan. 1792, Dickinson College; Thomas Johnson to Washington, 25 Feb. 1795, GC; Uriah Forrest to James McHenry, 6 Dec. 1797, *Publications of the Southern History Association* 10:33; John Carroll and Mary Ashworth, *George Washington, First in Peace: Volume Seven of the Biography of Douglas Southall Freeman* (New York, 1957), 433.

4. TJ 17:460–61, 19:58–60 (Madison).

5. TJ 16:536, 17:25, 278; M.J. Stone to "Dear Brother," 2 July 1790, Stone, Duke; R.B. to Theodorick Lee, 26 June, R.B. Lee, DLC. Two widely reprinted reports which name Georgetown as the site are "New York Letter," MdJ, 25 June 1790, and "New York Letter," *Columbian Centinel,* 10 July 1790. For a more detailed treatment and a somewhat different interpretation *see* Julian Boyd's "Locating the Federal District," TJ 19:3–58.

6. TJ 17:461–68, 19:60 (quoted); NYDG, 17 Aug. 1790; John Carroll to Charles Plowden, 2 Sept. 1790, Thomas Hanley, ed., *John Carroll Papers* (3 vols., Notre Dame, 1976), 1:454; Keith, *Blount Papers,* 2:102; Stokes, *Iconography,* 5:1273; MdJ, 7 Sept.; TPP, 15 Sept. 1790; MdJ, 28 Sept. 1790.

7. TJ 17:469–71; TPP, 20 Oct. 1790; William Deakins to Washington, 3 Nov. 1790, GWP. The plat of property north and east of Georgetown was made by Charles Beatty and Archibald Orme (GWC, 33); it is at DLC.

8. John Darnall to Francis Deakins, 1 Nov. 1790, Deakins to Washington, 12 Nov. 1790, William Good, *et al.,* to Washington, 1, 4, 5 Dec. 1790, GWP; GUS, 27 Nov., 25 Dec. 1790; TJ 19:348 (the Sharpsburg plat).

9. Thomas Sprigg and Citizens of Elizabethtown [Hagerstown] to Washington, [Oct. 1790], Otho Williams to Washington, 1 Nov. 1790, Williams to Francis Deakins, 8 Nov. 1790, GWP; William Smith to Otho Williams, 15 July 1790, Ms. 908, MdHi; GWW 31:135; "Inhabitant" [Williams], *Residence Law* [Hagerstown(?), 1790]; MdJ, 24, 28 Sept., 1, 5, 8, 15, 29 Oct., 2 Nov. 1790; TJ 19:348 (the Williamsport plat).

10. "Georgetown, 10 Nov.," *New Jersey Journal,* 24 Nov. 1790; *Connecticut Gazette,* 26 Nov. 1790; Samuel Davidson to Robert Dunlop, 28 Nov. 1790, Davidson, DLC; Horace Johnson to Andrew Craigie, 6 Jan. 1791, Craigie, American Antiquarian Society; R.H. Lee and John Walker to Speaker, 9 Aug. 1790, Maryland Resolution, 16 Nov. 1790, Legislative Papers, Virginia State Library; TJ 17:468, 644, 19:62–63; William to Charlotte Vans Murray, 27 Nov. 1790, Vans Murray, DLC; Gov. John E. Howard to Washington, 22 Jan. 1791, William Deakins and Benjamin Stoddert to Washington, 9 Dec. 1790, GWP; *Maryland Herald,* 4 Jan. 1791; JM 13:306–08.

11. *American Mercury,* 17 Feb. 1791; *American Daily Advertiser,* 4 Feb. 1791; MdJ, 28 Jan. 1791; *City Gazette,* 24 March 1791; Jonathan Trumbull to William Williams, 18 Dec. 1790, Trumbull, CtHi; FA, 93–94; Henry Marchant to Adams, 19 Feb. 1791, AFMT; George Gibbs, *Memoirs of the Administrations of Washington and Adams* (2 vols., New York, 1846), 1:62–63; Otto to Montmorin, 15 Nov. 1790, CP-EU, 35; William North to Benjamin Walker, 15 Jan.–4 Feb. 1791, Miscellaneous, NHi; "Civis," FG, 1 Feb. 1791.

12. Gibbs, *Memoirs,* 1:62; James Pemberton to Coxe, 1 Aug. 1790, TC; Theodore to Pamela Sedgwick, 26 Dec. 1790, 9 Jan. 1791, TS; John Rutledge, Jr., to William Short, 30 March 1791, Short, DLC; IG, 29 Jan. 1791; "Philadelphia Letter," NYDA, 8 Dec. 1790; Tobias Lear to Washington, 24 April, 5 June 1791, GWP.

13. Samuel Meredith to Henry Hill, 12 July 1790, John Jay Smith, PPL; *American Historical Magazine* 3:22; Fitzsimons to Miers Fisher, 15, 16 July 1790, Fisher, PHi; J.T. Mitchell, ed., *Statutes at Large of Pennsylvania* (17 vols., Harrisburg, 1896–1908), 14:181–83; MdJ, 19, 20 July 1790; Pennsylvania Delegation to Mayor Samuel Miles, 19 July 1790, Common Council Minutes, PHi; Francis Bailey to Coxe, 7 Sept. 1790, Miers Fisher to Coxe, 4 Sept. 1790, Thomas Affleck

to Coxe, 16 Sept. 1790, TC; Coxe to New York Mayor, 7 Sept. 1790, Miscellaneous American Autographs, Pierpont Morgan Library; "Citizen," FG, 26 July 1790; FA, 1:89; "A.B.," [Francis Hopkinson], PG, 2 Sept. 1790; Report of the Committee to Accommodate the President, 22 Nov. 1790, Etting, PHi; "Philadelphia, 4 Sept.," NYDA, 7 Sept. 1790. *See also* "Historical Structures Report," Independence National Historical Park.

14. Samuel Davidson to Robert Dunlop, 28 Nov. 1790, Davidson, DLC; TJ 19:61–62, 64–66.

15. Thatcher to Jeremiah Hill, 24 Jan. 1791, Thatcher, MHi; MD, 368; Benjamin Bourne to William Channing, 25 Jan. 1791, Channing–Ellery, RHi.

16. William Smith to Otho Williams, 24 Jan., 3 Feb. 1791 (quoted), Ms. 908, MdHi; William to Catherine Few, 25 Jan. 1791, Miscellaneous, DLC; Sedgwick to Ephraim Williams, 24 Jan. 1791, TS; Donald A. Wise, "George Washington's Four Mile Run Tract," *Arlington Historical Magazine* 5(1975).

17. Charles Nisbet to the Earl of Buchan, 10 Jan. 1792, Dickinson College; C.W. Janson, ed., *Stranger in America* (London, 1807), 206; Schutz and Adair, *Spur of Fame*, 174, 185, 251. *See* the anecdote about Washington and the location in Joseph Jones, *Life of Ashabel Green* (New York, 1849), 179.

18. GWW 30:408, 31:24–26, 35, 38, 33:175–76, 34:410; W. W. Hening, ed., *Statutes at Large . . . of Virginia* (13 vols., Richmond, 1809–23), 13:99–100.

19. GWW 31:438, 32:19 (quoted). On George Beck *see Proceedings of the American Antiquarian Society* 52:187–342; on the other artist, William Winstanley, *see* James T. Flexner, *George Washington, Anguish and Farewell* (Boston, 1972), 368–69.

20. Samuel Davidson to Crawford and Co., 24 March 1791, Davidson, DLC (quoted); [J. Dickinson], Ten Queries, [Jan. 1791?], Dickinson, PHi; "Georgetown, 2 April," WS, 13 April 1791; *John Branch Historical Papers* 1:229; Huie, Reid and Co. to George Walker, 20 Jan. 1791, Huie, Reid and Co., DLC; Rutland, *Mason Papers* 3:1226–27.

21. TJ 18:484; Theodore to Pamela Sedgwick, 26 Dec. 1790, 17 Feb. 1791, TS; William Symmes to Thatcher, 10 Feb. 1791, MB; Otto to Montmorin, 15 Nov. 1790, CP–EU, 35; MdJ, 23 Nov. 1790.

22. Bray Hammond, *Banks and Politics in America from the Revolution to the Civil War* (Princeton, 1957), 54; MHSC(2) 8:322; William Few to Edward Telfair, 15 Jan. 1791, University of Georgia; Otto to Montmorin, 15 Nov. 1790, CP–EU, 35; Pierce Butler to James Jackson, 24 Jan. 1791, Butler Letterbooks, University of South Carolina; Thatcher to Jeremiah Hill, 24 Jan. 1791, Thatcher, MHi.

23. MD, 364; FA, 93, 95–96; Ames to Andrew Craigie, 2 Feb. 1791, Society, PHi; [Smith], *Politicks*, 17–18; Paine Wingate to Nathaniel Peabody, 4 Feb. 1791, C.F. Jenkins, PHi; FA, 95; FG, 26 Jan. 1791.

24. JM 14:396.

25. GUS, 9 Feb. 1791; FA, 96; AH 8:50, 134–35.

26. Paine Wingate to Josiah Bartlett, 21 Feb. 1791, MB; Theodore to Pamela Sedgwick, 17 Feb. 1791, TS; MD, 368, 386; TJ 19:35; William Smith to Otho Williams, 21 Feb. 1791, Ms. 908, MdHi; "Philadelphia Letter," *Cumberland Gazette*, 14 March 1791; White to Charles Simms, 20 Feb. 1791, Simms, DLC.

27. [Smith], *Politicks*, 28; WMQ 3:542–43; *American Daily Advertiser*, 16 Feb. 1791; William Smith to Otho Williams, 23 Feb. 1791, Ms. 908, MdHi, 25 Feb. 1791,

Dreer, PHi; Paine Wingate to Josiah Bartlett, 21 Feb. 1791, MB; JM 13:395, 14:14–18; Sedgwick to Ephraim Williams, 23 Feb. 1791, TS; "Philadelphia Letter," MdJ, 1 March 1791.

28. John Rutledge, Jr., to William Short, 30 March 1791, Short, DLC and FA, 96 (quoted); WMQ 3:543; Henry B. Adams, *Life and Writings of Jared Sparks* (2 vols., Boston, 1893), 1:557; H. S. Randall, *Life of Thomas Jefferson* (3 vols., New York, 1858), 1:631; GUS, 26 Feb. 1791. For a somewhat different interpretation of these events *see* Benjamin B. Klubes, "The First Federal Congress and the First National Bank," *Journal of the Early Republic* 10:19–41.

29. TJ 19:59; Charles Carter to R.B. Lee, 2 Dec. 1790, Mathew Clarkson to Washington, 2 Jan. 1790 [1791], GWP; GWW 31:176–77, 200; TJC, 85; GWC, 32.

30. Bryan, *Capital*, 1:122–23; GWC, 140; Elizabeth S. Kite, *L'Enfant and Washington, 1791–92* (Baltimore, 1929), 81n.

31. TJ 19:44, 68–71; Catharine Mathews, *Andrew Ellicott, His Life and Letters* (New York, 1908), 83–84, 89, 95–96; MdJ: "Citizen of the World," [George Walker], 23 Jan. 1789, [Walker?], "Conference...," 24 March 1789. On Banneker *see* Silvio A. Bedini, *Life of Benjamin Banneker* (New York, 1972), and TJ 19:41–43n.

32. A.C. Hanson to Washington, 2 Aug., 10 Nov. 1790, William Gordon to Washington, 31 Jan. 1791, Washington, DLC; Joseph Clark to Washington, 5 Dec. 1790, Digges–L'Enfant–Morgan, DLC; W.S. Smith to Adams, 3 Dec. 1790, AFMT; Samuel Blodget, *Economica* (Washington, 1806), 23–24; John Macpherson to Washington, 9 March 1791, RG 59, National Archives; MHSP 63:561–62; John B. Cutting to William Short, 19 March 1791, Short, DLC; [Coxe], "Remarks on the laying out of the federal city," [c. Feb. 1791], Jefferson, DLC; GWC, 31; J.J. Jusserand, "Introduction," Kite, *L'Enfant;* Fitzsimons to [Miers Fisher], 16 July 1790, Fisher, PHi.

33. Dick Dabney, "George Washington Reconsidered," *Washingtonian,* 17 (Feb. 1982):83–89.

34. OFC, 21; TJ 19:63, 67–68, 20:14–15; GWC, 8–9, 11–12; AH 8:254; TJC, 42–44, 51, 126; William North to Benjamin Walker, 15 Jan.–4 Feb. 1791, Miscellaneous, NHi.

35. GWC, 7–15; OFC, 44–46, 58; Louis Dow Sisco, "Site for the Federal City," RCHS 1957–59:133; RCHS 1973–74:1; Kite, *L'Enfant,* 44–48; GWD 6:103–06; MdJ, 8 April 1791; AH 8:254; TJC, 47–50; *Public Documents Printed by Order of the Senate, 2nd Session, 23rd Congress* (4 vols., Washington, 1834), 3(doc. 97):17. On financing the capital *see* Paine Wingate to Timothy Pickering, 29 April 1789, Pickering, MHi; "Citizen of the World," [George Walker], MdJ, 23 Jan. 1789; "Observer," FG, 18 Jan. 1790. In 1988 Priscilla McNeil produced the first accurate plat of the holdings of the proprietors at the time they signed the agreement with Washington; a copy is in the Cartographic Division, DLC.

36. GWC, 22–23; MdJ, 8 April 1791; OFC, 54–58; Jabez Bowen to Benjamin Bourne, 7 Feb. 1791, Peck, RHi; Tobias Lear to David Humphreys, 12 April 1791, Rosenbach Foundation; Lear to Washington, 24 April 1791, GWP; "George Walker," Biographical Sketches, Huie, Reid and Co., DLC

37. MHSP 51:62 (quoted); AH 8:253–56; JM 14:11–13.

38. GWD 6:164–65; Kite, *L'Enfant,* 35–37, 43–48, 52–58; OFC, 89, and plate 5; "Essay on the City of Washington," GUS, 11 Feb. 1795. L'Enfant and his plan are aspects of early Washington history which have been treated frequently. H. Paul

Caemmerer, *Life of Pierre Charles L'Enfant* (Washington, 1950), and Kite, *L'Enfant*, are rich in source materials. Analyses of the plan can be found in William T. Partridge, "L'Enfant's Methods and Features," *Annual Report of the National Capital Park and Planning Commission, Supplement* (Washington, 1930), 20–38; John W. Reps, *Monumental Washington* (Princeton, 1967); Paul O. Spreiregen, *On the Art of Designing Cities* (Cambridge, Mass., 1968); and J.P. Dougherty, "Baroque and Picturesque Motifs in L'Enfant's Design," *American Quarterly* 26:23–36. Richard W. Stephenson and J.L. Sibley Jennings discuss the plan in the *Quarterly Journal of the Library of Congress* 36:207–78. Julian Boyd downplays L'Enfant's role in TJ 20:3–72.

39. OFC, 57–58, 75–76; GWD 6:164–66; *American State Papers, Miscellaneous* 2:483; *Georgetown Weekly Ledger*, 2 July 1791; "Amicus," *General Advertiser*, 12 July 1791; "Spectator," [George Walker], MdJ, 30 Sept. 1791, *New York Magazine*, Nov. 1791, GUS, 8 Oct. 1791 (attributed to Francis Cabot in TJ 20:54).

40. TJC, 65–74; *Newport Herald*, 27 Aug. 1789.

41. MdJ, 30 Sept. 1791; JM 14:172–73, 177–78, 200–01, 16:402, 421; George Walker to the Commissioners, 21 Jan. 1792, RG 42, National Archives; EIHC 73:352–61; TJC, 164–65; GWC, 33, 60, 64, 65, 72; Elbridge to Ann Gerry, [Oct.–Dec. 1791], Sang, Southern Illinois University; Christopher Gore to Tobias Lear, 28 Dec. 1791, Lear, DLC; R.B. to Theodorick Lee, [1793], *This Month at Goodspeed's* (Feb.–March, 1951), 118; "R.B. Lee Letter," *American Daily Advertiser*, 12 Feb. 1795.

42. GWC, 22, 51–52 (quoted); TJC, 60, 103; Tobias Lear to Washington, 24 April, 21 Sept. 1791, GWP; Lear to Samuel Powell, 20 Sept. 1791, Fisher, PHi; Bryan, *Capital* 1:141.

43. TJC, 187–88; GWW 33:117; JM 15:129–32; Germantown to Washington, 6 Nov. 1793, GWP; James Wilkinson to Anthony Wayne, 11 Dec. 1793, *Henkels Catalog* 694:item 350; King to Jeremiah Wadsworth, 3 Nov. 1793, Joseph Trumbull, Connecticut State Library; Tobias Lear to John Langdon, 5 Nov. 1793, Langdon–Elwyn Family, New Hampshire Hist. Soc.; Mathew Carey, *A Short Account of the Malignant Fever* (Philadelphia, 1793), 14–15; A.J. Dallas to Albert Gallatin, 8 Nov. 1793, Gallatin, NHi; Martin S. Pernich, "Politics, Parties and Pestilence," WMQ 29:559–86.

44. Kite, *L'Enfant*, 67–102; James T. Flexner, *George Washington and the New Nation, 1783–93* (Boston, 1970), 336; AH 8:355; TJC, 76, 78; GWC, 30–42; TJ 17:463, 20:3–72; JM 14:130–31.

45. Kite, *L'Enfant*, 105–51; TJC, 90–131; GWC, 48, 52; David Stuart to Washington, 26 Feb. 1792, GWP; TJ 19:89, 20:63–69; AH 11:50; Samuel Davidson to Isaac Roberdeau, 13 April 1792, George Walker to L'Enfant, 6 June 1792, Huie, Reid and Co., DLC.

46. TJC, 137–38; GWC, 50, 64; GWW 37:218–19; Kite, *L'Enfant*, 152–53; Caemmerer, *L'Enfant*, 367–410; TJC 233–39, 265–67.

47. "George Walker," Biographical Sketches, Huie, Reid and Co., DLC.

48. GWC, 106, 123–26, 164, 173, 190; Horace E. Hayden, *Virginia Genealogies* (Wilkes-Barre, Pa., 1891), 624–28; Allen C. Clark, *Greenleaf and Law in the Federal City* (Washington, 1901), 255; Tobias Lear to Washington, 3 Nov. 1793, GWP; GWW 33:151, 34:132–33; Bryan, *Capital* 1:197–201; Thomas J. Pettigrew, *Memoirs of the Late John Coakley Lettsom* (3 vols., London, 1817), 2:547; Dalton to Adams, 26 March 1797, AFMT.

49. GWC, 64–80, 95, 96, 99, 103; TJC, 169–80; Bryan, *Capital* 1:241, 314; Mathews, *Ellicott,* 99–100; Blodget, *Economica,* 22–23.

50. GWC, 57, 70, 72, 105, 147, 160, 201; RCHS 7:4; VMHB 81:415–36.

51. Bryan, *Capital* 1:204–05; RCHS 7:87–88; GWC, 114, 141–42, 150.

52. GWC, 76, 103, 143–46, 149; JM 14:351–52.

53. GWC, 154, 158 (quoted), 176–77; JM 16:247, 286; *Annals of Congress* 5:79, 363–75, 447, 825–39; Bryan, *Capital* 1:265–72, 299, 329; White to the Commissioners, 6 Dec. 1795, 8, 13, 18 Jan., 8, 18, 24 April, 2 May 1796, RG 42, National Archives.

54. GWW 35:219; GWC, 188; TJC, 193; Janson, *Stranger,* 214; Isaac Weld, *Travels . . . 1795–1797* (2 vols., London, 1799), Letter IV (1795); John C. Van Horne and Lee W. Formwalt, eds., *Correspondence and Miscellaneous Papers of Benjamin Henry Latrobe* (3 vols., New Haven, 1984–88), 1:122.

55. GWW 35:422, 37:217–18; GWC, 198–232; *American State Papers, Miscellaneous* 2:482; Prussing, *Estate of Washington,* 247, chapter 21.

56. GWW 34:54, 35:328–29 (quoted), 36:116, 37:310–11, 330; GWC, 55, 196–98, 202, 216; GWD 6:250, 280–81, 312, 359; Bryan, *Capital* 1:96n.

57. 9 Dec. 1799, GWP; Freeman, *Washington* 7:650.

Epilogue

1. Schutz and Adair, *Spur of Fame,* 94–95 and 98 (quoted); TJC, 193; William Craik to James M. Lingan *et al.,* 15 March 1799, Miscellaneous, PPAmP; RCHS 1973–74:55; Dalton to Adams, 26 March, 28 June, Adams to Dalton, 1 July 1797, AFMT.

2. *National Intelligencer,* 22 Nov. 1802 (quoted); AH 25:350n, 357–58; Schutz and Adair, *Spur of Fame,* 95; RCHS 1971–72:139; *Publications of the Southern History Association* 10:33.

3. RCHS 3:201 (quoted); Commissioners to Adams, 21 Nov. 1799, D.C. Miscellany, DLC; *Annals of Congress* 10:190, 195, 723, 726, 790, 1493–95; *Centinel of Liberty,* 6 June 1800; Clark, *Greenleaf,* 149.

4. *Annals of Congress* 10:711–12; 51:156, Pickering, MHi.

5. George C. Rogers, *Evolution of a Federalist, William Loughton Smith* (Columbia, 1962), 216–17; Stewart Mitchell, *New Letters of Abigail Adams* (Boston, 1947), 257–58; W. P. and J. P. Cutler, *Life, Journals, and Correspondence of Rev. Manasseh Cutler* (2 vols., Cincinnati, 1888), 2:50–51; MHSP 81:191; Alexander Wilson to Samuel Miller, 24 Dec. 1808, McGregor Library Mss., ViU.

6. WMQ 8:77; Christian Hines, *Early Recollections of Washington* (Washington, 1866), 45; Martha S. Carr, *District of Columbia . . . Geologic History* (Geological Survey Bulletin No. 967, Washington, 1950); Allan Kulikoff, *Tobacco and Slaves* (Chapel Hill, 1986); Lester F. Ward, *Guide to the Flora of Washington* (National Museum Bulletin No. 26, Washington, 1881); W.L. McAtee, *A Sketch of the Natural History of the District of Columbia* (Biological Society of Washington Bulletin No. 1, Washington, 1918). James Sterling Young, *Washington Community, 1800–1828* (New York, 1966), 42, is a good example of the swamp myth.

7. TJC, 252, 366; MHSP 81:191; H. Cushing to Margaret Bowers, 29 Jan. 1801, Emmet, NN; Clark, *Greenleaf,* 180; Green, *Washington,* 17–22; Bryan, *Capital*

1:chapter 14; Charles F. Adams, ed., *Letters of Mrs. Adams* (Boston, 1848), 383; RCHS 1971–72:60–71. For a bird's eye view *see* Tee Loftin's excellent "City of Washington, 1800," Cartographic Division, DLC.

8. RCHS 1971–72:71, 138–39; TJC, 460.

9. Jefferson to Charles Willson Peale, 16 Jan. 1802, Jefferson, DLC; Green, *Washington*, 116; Clark, *Greenleaf*, 180; Frances Trollope, *Domestic Manners of the Americans* (New York, 1960), 217; H. Roy Merrens, "Location of the Federal Capital of the United States" (M.A., Maryland, 1957), 55–58. Both Green, *Washington*, and Bryan, *Capital*, describe the attempts at establishing commercial ventures at some length.

10. Linda Arnold, "Congressional Government in D.C., 1800–1846" (Ph.D., Georgetown, 1974); Rose, *Arlington*, 71, 79–82; OFC, 82; William Tindall, *Origin and Government of the District of Columbia* (Washington, 1909), 77–91; *Washington Post*, 13 Jan. 1983. I am indebted to Mark Robertson, minority staff director of the House Committee on the District of Columbia, for background information on the proposed 1990 legislation.

11. *Annals of Congress* 13:282–87 (285 quoted); Walker, *Trenton* 1:196.

12. *Crito's Letters* (Philadelphia, 1807); Schutz and Adair, *Spur of Fame*, 99–100, 103–05, 169; *Annals of Congress* 18:1532–79, 1648; WMQ 8:93.

13. William Barlow, "Jonathan Fisk's Attempt to Relocate the National Capital," *New York Historical Society Quarterly* 53:69–77; *Annals of Congress* 28:357–76.

14. MHSP 65:46; PMHB 73:368; Green, *Washington,* 109; *National Era* (Washington), 9 Dec. 1852; *Congressional Globe* 39(pt. 4):3578, 3705;

15. Logan U. Reavis, *A Change of National Empire* (St. Louis, 1869); Reavis, *Saint Louis, The Future Great City of the World* (St. Louis, 1875); *Congressional Globe* 42(pt. 1):671–74, 679–85, 692–93; Bryan, *Capital* 2:565; Reavis, *National Capital Movable* (St. Louis, 1871).

Index

Adams, Abigail, 17, 18, 237, 239
Adams, John, 1, 16, 19, 29, 173, 202; on capital, 11, 22, 55, 242; on civil war, 173; elected vice president, 102–03, 105; and Philadelphia, 17, 18, 102; president, 226, 230, 233, 235–36; role in 1789, 156–57, 158, 162, 177, 178; on George Washington, 13, 213
Adams, John Q., 241
Adams, Samuel, 16, 17
Agricultural economy, 5, 22–23, 82, 206, 244; sectional implications of, 139–40, 144–45, 157, 165–66
Albany, N.Y., 14, 17, 21, 44
Albany Plan of Union, 14
Alexander, John, 107
Alexandria, Va., 8, 87, 112, 117, 126, 151, 164, 165; capital at, 50, 136, 185, 192, 209, 213–19 *passim*; commercial growth, 109–19 *passim*, 125, 234, 236, 240–41
Alien and Sedition Acts (1798), 204, 236
Allegheny River, 114, 120
American Revolution, 20–21, 206, 242; constitutional aspects, 26, 27, 34, 74, 76; ideas behind, 1, 14; New England–South axis, 53, 91, 164, 235; "second revolution" of 1787–1790, 80–81, 83, 87, 95–96, 161, 164, 171, 206. *See also* Revolutionary War

Ames, Fisher, 147, 194, 212, 219, 232; and Bank Act, 216; role in 1789, 142, 144–45, 150, 152–53, 158, 160, 161; role in 1790, 178, 188, 197
Anacostia River, 106, 112, 188, 190, 209, 210, 213, 217; described, 164, 221, 237, 238
Annapolis, Md., 67, 112, 118, 136, 192; capital at, 29, 41, 45, 49, 77, 103, 129; described, 45, 58–59; temporary seat at, 15, 51–52, 54–55, 63, 94, 226
Antifederalists, 80–81, 87–88, 95, 98, 101, 145, 147, 169; on constitutional provision for capital, 81–87, 97; viewed as prophets, 97, 161, 172
Archives of the United States. *See* Federal records
Aristocracy, 53, 82, 86, 88–89
Arlington, Va., 107, 213, 237, 243
Armstrong, John, Sr., 135
Army. *See* Military; Revolutionary War
Army Corps of Engineers, 6
Arnold, Benedict, 20, 21, 22
Articles of Confederation, 5, 29, 39, 56, 61, 68; amendments, 25, 26–27, 71, 80; and constitutionality of a capital, 24, 66, 68, 77–78; provisions, 23–24
Assumption: constitutionality, 168–69, 203, 209–10, 218; of federal debt by states, 31; of state debt, 75, 168–75 *passim*, 178–81, 184–85, 194, 195–98, 202–06. *See also* Compromise of 1790

280

Athens, 130, 224
Atlantic Ocean. *See* Capital city, types: inland vs. tidewater

Baldwin, Abraham, 91, 94–95
Baltimore, 17, 136, 190; capital at, 49, 100, 122, 135, 139, 187–88, 190–93, 204–05; commercial growth, 112, 113–14, 132–33, 135, 150, 153, 205, 240; as Potomac rival, 45, 112, 114, 122, 126, 165; temporary seat at, 17–18, 19, 89, 96, 178, 180, 191–92, 241. *See also* Chesapeake Interest, Upper
Bank Act (1791), 169, 215–19, 236
Bank of North America, 29, 31, 36, 41
Banks, 22, 26, 74–75. *See also* Capital city, functions: financial; Capitalism
Banneker, Benjamin, 220
Bassett, Richard, 156, 157, 176, 177, 178, 219
Beatty, Charles, 57
Beck, George, 214
Belknap, Jeremy, 5
Bethlehem, Pa., 19, 21
Bill of Rights, 80, 82, 84, 86, 161
Bingham, William, 91–92, 95, 103, 104
Bland, Theodorick, 169, 170
Blodget, Samuel, 230–31
Bloodworth, Timothy, 169, 196
Bordentown, N.J., 47, 65, 130
Boston, Mass., 29, 173
Boudinot, Elias, 9, 24, 40, 46, 100; and Elizabethtown, N.J., 47, 78–79; in First Congress, 149, 158, 159, 175; and Philadelphia Mutiny, 31, 33–34, 37, 38
Brissot de Warville, 114
Brooklyn, N.Y., 130
Broome, John, 102
Brown, John (R.I.), 69
Bucks Co., Pa., 132, 157
Burke, Aedanus, 169, 190–91, 192, 193
Burlington, N.J., 21
Burr, Aaron, 242
Butler, Pierce, 154, 155, 157, 158, 176, 177–78, 188–89

Cadwalader, Lambert, 101
California, 121, 244
Calvert, Leonard, 107
Canada, 121, 134, 141–42; admission to Union, 2, 8, 151, 167, 244
Capital city. *See also* Washington, D.C.
—benefits: economic, 3–4, 7; political, 3–4, 12–13, 43, 44, 144; local and sectional, 3–4 (*See also* names of places)
—development: name for, 5, 7; plan, 6, 66 (*See also* Walker, George); public buildings, 3, 21–22, 45–48 passim, 61–66 passim, 77, 85, 92, 93, 138, 145, 153, 156, 159, 166, 185, 190, 192, 221, 222
—effect on extremities of Union, 24, 70, 83, 84, 92 (*See also* Capital city, functions: financial; Capital city, site qualities: centrality)
—financing: appropriations, federal, 6, 22, 53, 55, 56, 66, 69–70, 91, 94, 136, 145, 154, 159, 162, 222; appropriations, state, 7, 45, 46, 47, 61, 63, 72, 160, 166, 222; donations, 47, 154, 157, 158, 190; loans, 150, 153, 222; lot sales, 222
—functions: commercial, 3, 4, 6, 7, 11, 15, 75, 82–83, 85, 93, 121–22, 122–23, 135–36, 144, 159, 167; cultural, 4, 5–6, 83, 94, 155, 230; financial, 3, 14, 27, 65, 83, 93, 185, 192; manufacturing, 3, 4, 125, 215; Society, 4, 11–12, 16, 67, 82–83, 83, 198, 200, 202, 211–12
—importance as political issue, 43, 88, 97, 104, 127, 146, 168, 198, 203, 205, 244
—residents: home rule, 79, 84; mentioned, 77–86 passim, 131; representation in Congress, 81, 85–86, 241
—site qualities: access (*See* Capital city, types: inland vs. tidewater; West, The: access to); centrality, 8, 45, 49, 50, 53, 63, 67, 70, 71, 89, 93, 104, 136–44 passim, 148, 150, 162, 165, 167, 172, 175, 176, 177; climate, 8,

Capital city (Continued)
49, 52, 60, 64, 89, 94, 104, 124, 164, 165, 198; defense, 3, 8, 11, 48, 49, 75, 93, 122, 123, 135, 141, 164, 165, 210; health, 8, 17, 57, 60, 62, 67, 98, 103, 144, 165, 198, 210; labor, 8, 198; natural resources, 8, 17, 57, 98, 123–24, 135, 155, 165, 177; scenery, 8, 57
—types: inland vs. tidewater, 8, 10, 123, 123–26, 137, 139–40, 144 (See also West, The: access to); multiple (See transient); rural vs. urban, 7, 8, 11, 84, 136, 191, 193, 201; separate executive and legislative, 17, 39, 58; size, 5, 44–48, 65, 76, 79–82 passim, 86; state (See States); transient, 14, 15, 23, 29, 52–57, 63, 64, 75–76, 205

Capitalism, 7, 24, 75, 168, 204

Capitol, The, 97, 223–24, 228, 231, 236, 238–39, 241–42

Carbery, Henry, 58

Carlisle, Pa., 124, 134

Carpenter's Hall, 16

Carroll, Charles, 240; Potomac promoter, 100, 125, 217; role in 1789, 155, 157, 158; role in 1790, 176, 177, 185, 187, 188, 189, 195, 205, 210

Carroll, Daniel, 44, 54, 100, 106, 125, 209–10, 216; commissioner, 219, 228, 229; role in 1789, 139, 153, 163; role in 1790, 185–86, 196, 197, 205

Carroll, Daniel, of Duddington, 106, 112, 209–10, 220, 227, 238

Carroll, John, 164

Carrollsburg, Md., 112, 123, 210, 220, 238

Cartoons, 200–01

Centralists, 24–25, 59, 68, 80–81, 169; and capital, 5, 33, 56, 77, 78–79; and Philadelphia, 29, 54–55; program, 26–29, 31, 39–40, 73, 74. See also Federalists

Centralization, 7, 24

Charleston, S.C., 22, 52

Charlestown, Md., 57, 129

Chesapeake and Delaware Canal, 133, 155

Chesapeake and Ohio Canal, 240

Chesapeake Bay, 60–61, 107, 114, 120, 133, 152; capital on, 56, 58, 129, 149, 156 (See also names of towns)

Chesapeake Interest, Upper, 44–45, 56, 58, 72–73, 112, 114–15, 122, 129, 135–36, 166, 204–05, 211, 232

Chester Co., Pa., 58, 135, 157

Chestertown, Md., 103

Cincinnati, Ohio, 243

Cities: benefit of, 24; bad as capital, 10–11, 15, 21, 37–38, 43, 48, 75, 91; good as capital, 11–12; fear of, 7, 23, 81, 131; size of, 81–82. See also Virginia, commercial city in

Civil war, 39, 166, 171, 172, 173, 192, 207, 240, 243

Clark, Abraham, 90, 101

Clinton, George, 81, 88, 98

Clymer, George, 9, 24, 29; and capital, 99, 150, 152, 170, 179

Columbia, Pa. See Wrights Ferry, Pa.

Commerce, 7, 10, 23, 25, 49, 104, 161, 206. See also Capital city, functions; names of places; Ch. 4

Commissioners, 65, 68–69. See also Presidential commission; Washington, D.C.: commissioners

Committee of the States, 61–62, 63

Compromise of 1790, 128, 214, 219, 225, 226, 230, 233, 236, 241, 244; failed attempts at, 174–81. See also Ch. 7

Compromise of 1820, 206–07

Compromise of 1850, 206–07

Congress
—Continental: First (1774), 14–15, 16, 93, 112; Second (1775–1781), 16–25, 112–13
—Confederation (1781–89): breakdown of, 52, 62, 167–68; mentioned, 25–42, Ch. 2, 77–80, 87–97, 161, 191

Congress (Continued)
— First Federal (1789–91): first session (1789), 104–05, *Ch. 5*, 161, 162, 163, 167; second session (1790), 161, 163, 167–81, *Ch. 7*, 203, 218–19; third session (1790–91), 211–19, 225; breakdown of, 180–81, 188, 197–98; filibuster, 154; House and Senate as institutions, 158; mentioned, 10, 76, 81, 86, 88, 92–93, 94–95, 97–98, 98–99, 101–02, 103–04; place of meeting (*See* Seat of government in Confederation Congress: 1788 Ordinance); power to adjourn, 75–76, 152–53, 183, 194–95, 226; rules, 168; significance, 1, 74, 87
— Later Federal (1791–1990), 225–26, 227, 232, 236, 237, 241, 244–45
— Library of, 239
Congress Hall, 212
Connecticut, 3; delegation, 88–89, 90, 92, 153, 170, 187, 192, 218, 232
Conococheague Creek, Md., 108, 110; capital on, 125, 135, 177, 188, 190, 192, 211; described, 123–24, 191–92, 202
Constitution, 92, 114, 140, 142, 170, 173; amendment, 12, 74, 99, 102, 105, 127, 147, 161, 244, 250 (*See also* Bill of Rights); balance and separation of powers, 74; interpretation, 152–53, 169, 172, 194–95, 198, 216–19; ratification, 7, 74, 79–88, 92, 96–97, 114, 124, 127, 130, 131, 142, 147, 165, 172 (*See also* New York; North Carolina; Rhode Island). *See also* American Revolution, "second revolution"
Contee, Benjamin, 100
Continental Army. *See* Revolutionary War
Coxe, Tench, 24, 124, 147; and capital, 93, 100, 102–03, 179, 180
Craigie, Andrew, 194
Crevecoeur, Hector St. John de, 206
Cumberland, Md., 111, 119, 129, 166

Custis, George W.P., 208, 213, 214, 241, 243
Cutler, Manasseh, 12
Cutting, John Browne, 206

Dalton, Tristram, 11, 157, 230, 236
Dayton, Jonathan, 101
Debt, public, 66, 74; funding to pay, 24–28 *passim*, 75, 168, 201–02; importance as issue in 1790, 162, 297, 203–04, 206; land sales to pay, 12, 23, 169. *See also* Assumption; Funding Act
Decentralists, 22–23, 24, 68, 79–80, 80–81, 143, 169, 170; and capital, 51–57 *passim*, 60, 76; and Philadelphia, 30, 33–37 *passim*, 41, 53, 55; revival of, 26–27, 28–29, 38, 39, 59, 79–80. *See also* Antifederalists
Delaware, 15, 44, 100, 103, 130; capital in, 46, 47, 100, 130; delegation, 49, 50, 65, 68, 69, 91, 96, 153, 170, 187, 189, 218
Delaware River, 10, 12, 15, 47, 64, 141; capital on, 46, 93, 99, 102, 130–32, 140, 149, 153, 154, 165, 176, 192, 193 (*See also names of towns*); Falls, capital at, 49–58, 65–66, 68, 69, 72, 95, 129, 130, 137, 138, 140, 154, 158, 175, 176, 183
Democracy, 18, 30, 45
Democratic–Republican Party, 234, 235–36, 239, 242
Dickinson, John, 7, 23, 38, 102, 120, 215; and Philadelphia Mutiny, 32–33, 33–34, 37–38, 40–41
Dickinson, Philemon, 68–69
Disunion, 3–4, 22, 27, 39, 84, 127, 163, 197, 206; northern threats, 162, 173, 184, 185, 191, 202; relation to capital location, 103, 137, 139–40, 142–43, 144–45, 146, 162, 166, 168, 191–92, 233, 235; southern threats, 92, 104–05, 151, 157, 158, 167, 171–72, 197, 203. *See also* West, The: loss of
Dual Residence. *See* Seat of government in Confederation Congress: 1783 resolutions

Eastern States, 62, 151, 161, 162, 163, 192, 197, 199; defined, 3; delegation (*See* Seat of government). *See also* New England; New York State
Easton, Pa., 19
Elizabethtown, N.J., 47, 78–79
Elkton, Md., 129, 135
Ellery, William, 41
Ellicott, Andrew, 220, 227, 228, 230, 238
Ellsworth, Oliver, 77, 157, 180, 188
Elmer, Jonathan, 154, 176, 177, 187, 189
Embassies, 51, 78, 84, 86, 153, 164
Empire, American, 1-2, 4, 7, 22, 24, 224; contemporary references to, 6, 10, 12, 22, 27, 28, 29, 87, 111, 115, 122, 172, 234; relationship with capital, 6, 10, 29, 53, 69, 73, 75, 92, 131, 203, 208, 223
Europe, 10, 22, 24, 55, 60, 63, 163; news from, 11, 29, 49; respect for U.S., 4, 197. *See also* History, use of
Evans, Lewis, 117
Excise Act (1791), 197, 206, 211, 219
Exclusive jurisdiction. *See* Jurisdiction, exclusive federal
Executive "branch," 6, 17, 23, 51, 105, 128, 143, 161, 245; increased influence for, 24, 25, 63, 79–80, 105, 204, 233; officials, 3, 10, 25–26, 28, 34, 39, 59, 64, 70, 82, 158, 197, 205, 236, 242; role in 1790, 174, 179, 182, 197, 206 (*See also* Hamilton; Jefferson; Washington). *See also* Federal officials; President
Extradition, 82

Federal aid, 119
Federal Convention, 9, 74–75, 92, 126; calls for, 27, 36–37, 38, 63, 71; and capital, 5, 75–76, 79–80, 125, 152; second, 88, 95
Federal elections, 82, 95, 99–103, 149, 162, 165, 203–04, 205, 241

Federal Hall, 97, 102, 105, 159, 200, 221, 229
Federal records, 19, 56, 58, 62, 83, 153, 164, 244
Federal revenues, 23–28 *passim*, 80, 82–83, 85, 92, 105, 127, 142, 161. *See also* Excise Act
Federal supremacy, 23, 27, 28, 79
Federalism, 9, 14, 24, 27, 34, 80, 81, 84, 173, 216; as issue in revolutionary Philadelphia, 18–19, 20, 31, 74. *See also* Antifederalists; Centralists; Decentralists; Federalists
Federalist No. 10, 2, 143
Federalists, 80–81, 87, 88, 95, 97, 101–02, 147; on constitutional provision for capital, 83–85; in First Congress, 127–28, 143, 146; post–1791 party, 234, 235–36, 241
Fenno, John, 188
Few, William, 88, 90, 94, 176, 177, 178, 186, 187, 188
Filibuster, 154
Fitzsimons, Thomas, 24, 50, 99, 221; role in 1789, 145, 146, 152, 154; role in 1790, 176–79 *passim*, 199, 221
Fleete, Henry, 107
Food, 29, 35, 45
Fort Frederick, Md., 129
Fort Pitt. *See* Pittsburgh, Pa.
Four Mile Run, Va., 212
France, 4, 10, 66, 110, 124, 147, 224; reports from diplomats in America, 37–38, 39, 61, 66, 77, 89, 96, 167, 215, 216
Franklin, Benjamin, 1, 14, 15, 242
Frederick, Md., 129, 185, 210
Fredericksburg, Va., 21
Freneau, Philip, 198
Funding Act (1790), 175, 176, 178, 187, 191, 192, 194, 196, 202, 204, 225, 242. *See also* Assumption
Funkstown, Md. *See* Hamburg, Md.

Gale, George, 100, 150, 152; role in 1790, 186, 196, 197, 205
Galloway, Joseph, 15
Gates, Horatio, 69
Georgetown, Md. 8, 119, 139, 236, 240; as Baltimore rival, 112, 136; capital at, 44, 49, 54–57, 61, 64, 66, 70, 72, 73, 75, 123, 129, 136, 177, 182, 186, 188–89; commerce, 114, 123, 164, 165, 230; described, 112, 210, 237; and siting of Federal City, 209–10, 220, 221–22, 224
Georgia, 43, 196, 204; delegation, 18, 63–64, 88, 94, 153, 170, 171, 190
Germantown, Pa., 47, 91, 132, 155, 156–60, 166, 182, 193, 226
Gerry, Elbridge, 17, 22, 225; in Confederation Congress, 43, 53, 54, 60, 64, 70; at Federal Convention, 9, 74, 80; in First Congress, 158, 169, 176, 178, 191, 192
Goodhue, Benjamin, 138, 139, 146, 152, 175, 232
Gordon, William, 28–29
Grant, Ulysses, 244–45
Grayson, William, 22, 49, 67; and 1785 appropriation fight, 69–70; Potomac promoter, 75, 118, 125, 163; role in 1789, 154–58 passim, 161
Great Britain, 14, 98, 108, 110, 114, 146; Great Lakes forts, 114, 115; Parliament, 36, 51, 76. See also Canada; Revolutionary War
Great Falls. See Potomac River
Great Hunting Creek, Va., 106, 107, 109
Great Kanawha River, 111, 114, 116, 117
Great Lakes, 75, 107, 114, 115, 124, 200
Great Valley, The, 119, 124, 132, 134, 211
Greenleaf, James, 231
Gunn, James, 157, 176, 177, 186–89 passim

Hagerstown, Md., 211
Hamburg, Md., 57–58, 112, 123
Hamilton, Alexander, 19, 83, 86, 102, 104; and capital location prior to 1790, 36–38, 44, 89–91, 95, 101, 137, 138; role in 1790, 178–87 passim, 193, 196, 197, 201; and L'Enfant, 223, 227, 229; and Philadelphia Mutiny, 31–34, 36–41 passim; political philosophy, 24, 28, 204, 217, 218–19; and ratification of Constitution, 83, 86; Report on Public Credit, 128, 168–69, 170, 215–216
Hamilton, William, 134
Hancock, Md., 136, 166, 188
Harmar, Josiah, 202
Harpers Ferry, (West) Va., 125, 139, 185, 214, 231
Harrisburg, Pa., 131, 135
Harrison, Benjamin, 36, 57, 117, 121
Hartford, Conn., 17, 20, 21
Hartley, Thomas, 134, 141, 146, 152, 154, 168, 170, 179, 192
Havre de Grace, Md., 56–57, 129
Hawkins, Benjamin, 176, 177, 186–88 passim
Henry, John, 100, 155, 157, 158, 176, 177, 178, 188, 189, 205
Henry, Patrick, 7, 22, 116, 130, 147, 161, 172, 204
Hiester, Daniel, 99–100, 135, 170
History, use of, 2, 31, 117; ancient, 2, 4, 53, 56, 76, 83, 91, 122, 125, 148, 220, 235, 236 (See also Athens; Rome); European, 2, 10, 148, 155; George Washington's, 13, 125, 208, 209, 214, 218–19, 238–39, 245
Hopkinson, Francis, 56, 69, 86
Howard, John E., 136
Howell, David, 12, 22, 26, 53, 79; and Ordinance of 1784, 64, 69, 70; and Philadelphia, 39–40, 41, 52, 54
Howell's Ferry, N.J., 57, 130
Hudson River, 29, 40, 44, 49; Mohawk route west, 12, 64, 75, 114, 115, 124, 165, 200, 240

Hume, David, 2
Humphreys, David, 206
Hutchins, Thomas, 57, 117

Illinois River, 12
Immigration, 9, 121, 128
Implied powers, 169, 172, 198, 216–18
Independence Hall. *See* Pennsylvania,
    public buildings
Indians, 12, 106–07, 108, 110, 124,
    202, 204
Izard, Ralph, 186, 187, 188

Jackson, James, 140, 241
Jackson, William, 174, 175, 179
James River, 114–17 *passim*, 166
Jay, John, 63, 64, 71, 138, 201
Jay, Sarah, 63
Jay Treaty, 232, 236
Jefferson, Thomas, 3, 22, 65–66, 78, 92,
    217, 234, 242; on commerce, 7,
    115–16; analysis of Compromise of
    1790, 185, 197, 199; development
    of D.C., 209–10, 219, 224–30 *pas-
    sim*, 231, 239, 245; Potomac pro-
    moter, 7, 46, 57, 58, 60–61, 66, 70,
    72, 113, 115–17, 118, 120, 165;
    role in 1790, 180–85 *passim*, 189,
    194, 201, 203, 236
Johnson, Lyndon and Lady Bird, 245
Johnson, Thomas, 106, 111, 112, 119,
    121, 209; commissioner, 209,
    219–20, 230
Johnson, William S., 157
Johnston, Samuel, 176, 177, 178,
    186–88 *passim*
Judiciary, 80, 82, 105, 144, 153, 239
Judiciary Act (1789), 127, 128, 137, 161
Juniata River, 133
Jurisdiction, federal, 5, 56, 57, 68; prob-
    lems at Philadelphia, 18–19,
    20–21, 30–34, 61–62, 68, 76; in
    state offers, 43–48, 77, 77–78
Jurisdiction, exclusive federal, 4, 24, 45,
    48, 74, 76–80, 131; over public
    buildings only, 85; ratification issue,
    81–86; and state law, 159, 190; un-
    desirables attracted to, 45, 78, 82,
    85

Kearney, Dyre, 88
Kennedy, John and Jacqueline, 245
Kentucky, 9, 85, 111, 154
King, Rufus, 67, 75–76, 226, 232; role
    in 1787, 72, 102; role in 1789, 138,
    156, 157, 159; role in 1790, 176,
    187, 189, 191, 196
Kings Co., N.Y., 130
Kingston, N.Y., 29, 43–44, 45, 48, 49
Knox, Henry, 121, 201

LaFayette, Marquis de, 120
Lamberton, N.J., 46–47, 50, 57, 101
Lancaster, Pa., 15, 31; capital at,
    134–35; temporary seat at, 18, 19,
    89, 94, 131, 133, 134, 226
Langdon, John, 175, 177, 189, 219
Laurance, John, 102, 138, 142, 150,
    187, 191, 193
Law, Thomas, 231, 238
Lear, Tobias, 225, 230
Lee, Arthur, 22, 26, 28, 79, 109, 128,
    203–04; and resolutions of 1783,
    54, 203–04; and Philadelphia, 29,
    30, 36, 39, 52, 72, 97
Lee, Henry, 139, 166; and New York
    City, 72–73, 90–91, 93, 96, 97; Po-
    tomac promoter, 13, 109, 113, 119,
    124; as southern spokesman,
    171–72, 204, 207
Lee, Richard Bland, 109; role in 1789,
    139, 140, 142, 145, 148, 149, 151;
    role in 1790, 185, 188, 192, 196,
    197, 203, 225
Lee, Richard Henry, 22, 63, 68, 80; Po-
    tomac promoter, 66, 72, 109, 111,
    118, 125; role in 1789, 155, 157,
    158; role in 1790, 176, 177, 178,
    187, 188, 189
Lee, Robert E., 207, 243
Lee, Thomas, 108, 109, 110, 118, 119
Lee, Thomas Sim, 44
Lee family, 27, 72, 97, 106, 109, 139,
    207

Legislative branch, 79–80, 82, 143, 158; supremacy, 6, 23, 25, 145. *See also* Jurisdiction, federal: exclusive

L'Enfant, Pierre, 69, 97, 208, 227–29, 230–31, 245; plan, 6, 221–29 *passim*, 237, 245

Liberty, idea of, 4, 5, 6, 11, 14, 22, 26–27, 46, 164, 211

Lincoln, Abraham, 244

Lincoln, Benjamin, 30, 78

Livingston, Margaret Beekman, 27

Livingston, Robert R., 21, 24, 29, 36, 39, 43–44, 55

Livingston, William, 69

Localism, 13, 60, 62, 77, 143, 147, 170

Logan, John, 244

London, 1, 5, 7, 11, 76, 81, 164, 226; as American capital, 14, 16, 27

Loyalists, 18, 24

Lux, George, Jr., 45, 77

Luxury. *See* Republicanism

McHenry, James, 37, 51–52, 68, 69

Maclay, William, 99, 105, 216, 217; analysis of Compromise of 1790, 170, 189, 193, 197, 199; role in 1789, 135, 138, 151, 152, 154, 156–60 *passim*; role in 1790, 168, 174–79 *passim*, 189

Madison, James, 3, 16, 27, 35, 36, 48, 50, 60, 67, 70, 103, 125, 126; adoption of Constitution, 71, 76, 83, 87, 88; analysis of 1789 and 1790 decisions, 162–63, 189–90, 197; criticism of, 146–47, 170, 199; development of D.C., 209–10, 219, 224–25, 226, 230, 245; evolution of political philosophy, 2, 24, 128, 143–44, 146–47, 169–70, 171, 216–18; jurisdiction over capital, 77, 78, 79, 83, 85; Philadelphia Mutiny, 32, 37, 41; Potomac promoter, 46, 113–19 *passim*; president, 146–47, 242–43; role in 1788, 92, 94, 96, 97; role in 1789, 105, 138–45 *passim*, 150, 152, 153, 158, 159, 160, 189–90; role in 1790, 168, 177, 181, 182–86, 189–95 *passim*, 197, 201, 203, 236, 242

Madrid, 10

Manufacturing, 7, 119, 139, 144, 161, 166, 167, 206, 240. *See also* Capital city: functions

Maps, 58, 117, 210

Marietta, Ohio, 12, 119, 167, 176

Marshall, John, 204

Martinsburg, (West) Va., 167

Maryland
—mentioned, 3, 15, 56–57, 66, 106, 107, 110, 120, 220, 243
—capital in: appropriations for, 45–46, 61, 66, 166, 211, 221, 232–33; cession act (1788), 135; mentioned, 29, 43–48 *passim*, 56–57, 58, 72, 77, 122–25, 129, 135–36, 149–50, 152, 156, 163–66, 178, 189, 199, 205, 215, 221
—delegation: in Confederation Congress, 50, 51, 55, 63, 68, 69, 91, 96; in 1789, 149, 153, 159; in 1790, 170, 174, 177, 178, 185, 187, 190, 199, 204–05
—federal elections, 100, 103, 205, 241
—navigational improvements: Potomac River, 112, 118–22 *passim*, 126, 234; Susquehanna River, 132–34, 150, 152, 153, 155
—public opinion, 56–57, 66, 199, 215
—rival of Virginia, 41, 44–46, 121–22, 124, 149, 191, 204–05

Mason, George, 22, 75, 80, 81, 82, 123, 209, 215; Potomac promoter, 108, 112

Massachusetts, 7, 17, 164, 173, 219; delegation, 20, 21, 62, 73, 90–91, 153, 218; delegation in 1790, 169–70, 174, 183–88 *passim*, 193, 230

Mathews, George, 183

Middle States, 21, 39, 60–61, 75, 99, 151, 162; centralist power base, 24, 25, 29, 55; defined, 3, 18; delegation (*See* Seat of government). *See also* Union

Middletown, Pa., 133, 135
Military, 80, 82, 86, 92, 168; civilian control, 28, 31, 32. *See also* Navy; Revolutionary War
Militia, 82, 86
Mississippi River, 2, 115, 124, 134; capital on, 96, 241, 242-45; and Spain, 70, 71, 114, 121
Missouri River, 111, 134
Mobs, 7, 10, 20, 48, 82, 92, 192, 198
Mohawk River, 111. *See also* Hudson River
Monarchy, 7, 39, 53, 82, 86, 88
Monongahela River, 109, 114, 117
Monopolies, 83, 85
Monroe, James, 66, 75, 84, 114, 189, 203
Montesquieu, 141
Montgomery Co., Pa., 132
Moravians, 21
Morgantown, (West) Va., 119
Morris, Gouverneur, 9, 19, 24, 28, 31, 37, 48; and capital, 20-21, 75, 205-06, 234
Morris, Lewis, 48
Morris, Mary, 153, 175
Morris, Robert, 13, 18, 68-69, 75, 90-91, 95-96, 99, 120, 212, 219; constitutional ideas, 24, 25-27; D.C. speculator, 231, 239; Philadelphia advocate, 18, 37, 39-40, 50; role in 1789, 105, 129, 130, 138-39, 149, 151, 153-60, 163; role in 1790, 168, 175-82 *passim*, 186, 189, 190, 199, 200-01; Superintendant of Finance, 28, 36, 39-40, 52, 55, 59
Morrisania, N.Y., 48
Morrisville, Pa., 130. *See also* Delaware River, Falls
Morse, Jedidiah, 1-2, 130, 136
Mount Vernon, 110, 126, 209, 231, 236; described, 109, 110-11; and location of capital, 13, 213, 214, 234
Mount Vernon Conference, 120
Muhlenberg, Frederick, 40, 100, 134, 170
Muhlenberg, Peter, 100, 134, 170, 183

Naturalization, 82
Navy, 48, 75, 93, 242
Netherlands, ambassador from, 55, 92
Newark, N.J., 47
New Brunswick, N.J., 47
Newburgh, N.Y., 8, 75
Newburgh Conspiracy, 28-29, 31
New Castle, Del., 47
New England, 15, 22, 60, 102-04 *passim*, 141, 164-65, 223, 239; commercial ties to Potomac, 164, 1665-66, 167, 170, 173, 201-03; defined, 3; delegation (*See* Seat of government); public opinion, 54-55, 66, 146, 167. *See also* Disunion; Eastern States; North, The; Sectionalism; Union
New Hampshire, 43, 153; delegation, 18, 62, 69, 88-89, 90, 170, 193, 217
New Haven, Conn., 17
New Jersey, 15, 35, 63, 64-65, 95, 129-30, 241, 242; capital in, 46-50 *passim*, 57-58, 65, 68-70, 72, 89, 93, 95, 129-30; delegation in Confederation Congress, 51, 62, 70, 72, 90, 95; delegation in First Congress, 138, 149, 153, 159, 170, 190, 193, 218; federal elections, 100-01, 103, 149; internal division, 15, 72, 95, 100-01, 154, 176, 190, 193
New Orleans, 121, 245
Newport, R.I., 60, 72, 167
New Windsor, N.Y., 75
New York City, 14; accommodations for Congress, 67, 130, 175, 191, 198, 199-200; Battery, The, 87, 179; capital at, 29, 44, 75, 130, 170; commercial future, 114, 174, 199-200; described, 16, 48, 67, 71, 81, 87, 88, 89, 93, 96, 98, 104; public opinion, 67, 147, 150, 198-202, 218; residents, 67, 75, 104, 137, 159, 175, 199, 209, 211, 235; temporary seat at, 15, 37, 40, 41, 55, 63-68, 70-73, 87-105 *passim*, 128-29, 130, 138, 139, 149-59 *passim*, 167, 176-81, 183, 186-89, 195, 226. *See also* Federal Hall

New York State, 3, 14, 101-02, 105, 133; capital in, 29, 43-48 *passim*, 63, 77, 130, 170; delegation in 1789, 137, 145, 153, 156, 192; delegation in 1790-91, 170, 175, 178, 180, 193, 196, 218; delegation in other congresses, 49, 73, 90, 225, 232; ratification, 81, 85-88 *passim*, 91, 94, 95, 192, 193, 199. *See also* Eastern States
Nicholas, George, 203
Nicholson, John, 231, 239
Nisbet, Charles, 134, 213
Norfolk, Va., 8, 108-09, 111, 113, 125
North, The, 14, 29, 103, 147; commercial interests, 142, 215-16, 242; defined, 3; delegation (*See* Seat of government); public opinion, 147, 173; and The West, 9-10. *See also* Disunion; Sectionalism; Union
North Carolina, 153, 196, 204; delegation, 49, 63, 64, 170, 190; out of the Union, 104, 137, 151, 154; ratification, 85, 87, 90, 95, 160
North, Lord, as symbol, 27, 160
Northwest Territory, 9, 12, 108, 110, 113, 121, 202
Nottingham Township, N.J., 46-47

O'Connor, John, 163-64
Ohio Companies, 12, 109, 110, 124
Ohio Country. *See* Northwest Territory
Ohio delegation, 244
Ohio River, 111, 119, 120, 167, 185; capital on, 8, 12, 96, 103, 243; land speculation on, 106, 117; transportation links to, 114, 115, 133, 141, 215. *See also* Northwest Territory
"Ohioisms," 8
Ordinances of 1784 and 1788. *See* Seat of government in Confederation Congress: 1784 and 1788 ordinances
Osgood, Samuel, 81, 87, 132

Pacific Ocean, 134
Page, John, 193
Paine, Thomas, 15, 37, 236
Panama, 2, 244, 245
Paris, 10, 11, 20
Paterson, William, 154, 157, 176
"Patapsco River," 122
Peach Bottom, Pa., 135
Peale, Charles Willson, 5-6
Penn, William, 14, 15, 122, 132, 133, 212
Pennsylvania
—capital in, 46, 47, 50, 51-52, 57, 63-65, 68-69, 99, 100, 105, 128-29, 130-35, 137, 152, 156, 160, 166, 168, 177, 178, 180, 189, 244
—Congress and: state politics, 16, 17-19, 31-42 *passim*, 51-52; state jurisdiction (*See* Jurisdiction, federal)
—delegation: in Confederation Congress, 21, 49, 60, 63, 64-65, 72, 87, 91-92; in 1789, 105, 128, 137-38, 139, 146, 149-56 *passim*, 160; in 1790, 170, 174-86, 189, 193, 199, 205; mentioned, 125, 218, 232, 242
—federal elections, 98, 102, 162
—government of: executive council, 18-20 *passim*, 30-37 *passim*, 41; political parties, 18-19, 21, 29, 132; public buildings, 16, 17, 30-33, 63-65, 92, 98, 105, 212, 214, 226
—influence of, 18, 29, 44, 159, 174-75, 191, 224
—internal division, 132-34, 138-39, 160; ratification, 85, 130, 131
—mentioned, 3, 18, 45, 159, 163, 171, 191, 197-212
—rival of Virginia for access to The West, 110, 113-14, 117, 120, 124
—and Susquehanna Proviso, 132-34, 150-51, 152, 153, 155, 156
Pendleton, Edmund, 85

Peters, Richard, 24, 38, 40
Philadelphia, 14, 58, 110, 117, 220, 224
—anti-slavery sentiment, 89, 176, 191, 198, 203, 212, 242
—capital at: attempts to leave, 21, 29, 43, 226–27; leaves, 17, 19, 34, 236; mentioned 75, 131–32, 157, 176; suburbs as, 91, 132 (See also Germantown, Pa.); disliked as, 15–21 passim, 25, 29–30, 33, 35–36, 40–49 passim, 51–52, 53, 63, 64, 67, 89, 90–91, 104, 158, 159, 167, 176, 191, 198, 241–42; temporary, 34, 41, 50–51, 54, 55, 59–73 passim, 88–105 passim, 128–29, 131–32, 137–38, 149, 162, 163, 174–83, 186–91 passim, 196, 241–42; would not move in 1800, 191, 193, 194, 198, 201, 215, 216–18, 226, 233 (See also Seat of Government in First Congress, Act (1790): attempts to thwart)
—commercial hinterland, 15, 57, 93, 97, 113, 133–36 passim, 149, 150, 155, 165
—County, 132, 157
—described, 15–21 passim, 29–30, 35, 62, 71, 81, 86, 93, 98–99, 104, 130–31, 134, 198, 202, 211
—Mutiny of 1783, 30–35, 39, 40, 58, 67, 77, 78, 84, 98, 104, 198, 242
—public opinion, 55, 67, 147, 150, 175, 198, 201, 218
—residents, 16, 17, 19, 190, 209, 235
Pickering, Timothy, 237
Pittsburgh, Pa., 12, 49, 53, 177, 178
Political parties, 81, 128, 137, 143, 146, 170. See also Pennsylvania: government
Potomac Company, 118, 122, 125, 144, 164–66, 209, 215, 219–20, 230, 234, 240. See also Potomac River, navigation
Potomac Fever, 13, 109, 163, 214, 219, 235, 240
Potomac Interest, 44, 49, 100, 122, 130, 136, 150, 163–167, 205, 215

Potomac River, 8, 70, 171; capital on, 10, 42, 44–61 passim, 66, 71, 72, 89, 93, 95, 97, 103, 104, 106, 108, 123–26, 136–50 passim, 162–67, 172, 174; capital upriver, 123–26, 144, 178, 188, 192, 210–11, 213; commercial potential, Ch. 4, 188–93 passim, 214, 215, 225; described, 12, 103, 106–07, 142, 163–65, 202, 210, 237–38; Eastern Branch (See Anacostia River); falls, 57, 107, 109, 111, 119; Great Falls, 119, 125, 214, 240, 245; healthiness of, 103, 165, 192; navigation, 12, 64, 110–22, 125, 144, 150, 192–93, 214, 231, 234, 240; pre-Revolutionary history, 106–13; removal of capital from, 240–45; temporary seat on, 96
President: adjourning and convening of Congress, 75–76, 183, 194–95, 225–26; aides, 137, 174, 175, 179; as institution, 74, 82–83, 126, 195, 201; mansion for, 179, 212, 214, 226 (See also White House); as monarch, 82, 158; and proviso of 1789, 150, 152, 153, 156, 158
Presidential commission, 145, 152, 153, 190, 208. See also Washington, D.C.: commissioners
Princeton, N.J.: capital at, 44, 76; described, 35, 67; temporary seat at, 21, 33, 50–51, 96
Progress, idea of, 2
Proprietors. See Washington, D.C.
Prostitution, 200
Public creditors, 25, 26, 28, 168, 225

Quakers, 18, 19, 33, 38, 198; and slavery, 89, 191, 242

Randolph, Edmund, 217
Read, George, 156, 157, 176, 177, 179, 185, 189, 219
Reading, Pa., 18, 19, 132, 226
Reason, idea of, 164, 206
Reavis, Logan V., 243, 244–45

Removal Act (1800), 236, 239
Republican Court. *See* Capital city,
    functions: Society
Republicanism, 14, 22, 23, 143, 203,
    215; and capitals, 7, 34, 53, 148,
    215, 242; and federal jurisdiction,
    56, 80–83; and luxury, 7, 10, 23, 30,
    43, 46, 49, 50, 59, 116, 123, 212;
    changing definition of, 6–7, 11, 24,
    75. *See also* Cities
Republics, 56, 79, 195; political deals
    bad for, 193, 199, 202, 203, 206;
    empires as, 1, 4, 224; military
    threats to, 32–33; size of, 2, 23, 143
Residence. *See* Seat of government
Revenue. *See* Federal revenues
Revolutionary War, 2, 3–4, 5, 17–22,
    49, 55, 67, 98, 113; Continental
    Army, 6, 17, 22, 26, 28, 30–35, 36,
    55, 112, 220, 221, 231; peace, 20,
    27, 60, 113
Rhode Island, 16, 26, 164, 203; delega-
    tion, 21, 54, 60, 64, 72, 218; ratifi-
    cation, 87, 90, 104, 137, 151, 154,
    171, 177; senators, 177, 180, 185,
    187
Richmond, Va., 46, 104, 114, 125
Rock Creek, Md., 58, 107, 123, 237
Rome, 4, 5, 30, 36, 81, 212, 224. *See
    also* History, use of
Rush, Benjamin, 9, 51, 100, 175; sup-
    ports Philadelphia, 18, 36, 37, 38,
    40, 41, 102–03, 242

St. Louis, Mo., 243
St. Petersburg, Russia, 10, 148, 155
Savage, Edward, 208
Savannah, Ga., 52
Schureman, James, 72, 100
Schuyler, Philip, 44, 68–69, 102; in First
    Congress, 156, 157, 159, 170, 171,
    189, 219
Schuylkill River, 129, 132, 133
Scott, Gustavus, 230
Scott, Thomas, 99, 129, 136, 170

Seat of government in Confederation
    Congress
– 1783 resolutions: debate, 41–42, 43,
    48–55, 60–61, 79–80; public opin-
    ion, 55–57
– 1784 ordinance: debate, 63–65,
    68–70, 79, 94; public opinion,
    66–67
– 1787 and 1788 motions, 71–77, 102,
    187
– 1788 ordinance: debate, 87–97; men-
    tioned, 102–03, 125, 139–40, 171,
    182; public opinion, 93, 96, 97
Seat of government in First Congress
– Seat of Government Bill (1789):
    House action, 128, 136–53,
    158–59, 168; as issue before intro-
    duced, 73, 89, 102–03, 104, 128;
    mentioned, 182, 185–86, 189, 191,
    192, 194, 213; public opinion, 147,
    150–51, 160–63, 171; Senate ac-
    tion, 152, 153–58, 159–60, 168;
    proposed veto, 152
– Seat of Government Act (1790): at-
    tempts to thwart, 203, 208, 212,
    215, 225–26, 236; House action,
    190–93; implementation, *Ch. 8;* as
    issue before introduced, 168,
    173–81; mentioned, 89, 102–03;
    politics of Compromise of 1790,
    182–85; public opinion, 198–206;
    Senate action, 176–79, 186–87,
    188–89; proposed veto, 194
– Seat of Government Act (1791), 206,
    213, 217–19
Sectionalism, 6, 17, 18, 21–22, 60, 88,
    223; and First Congress, 73, 105,
    127–28, 136–37, 146; importance
    of, 3–4, 8–9, 12–13, 70, 206–07.
    See also Disunion; Seat of govern-
    ment; Union
Sedgwick, Theodore, 90, 141, 146,
    160–70, 213, 215, 218, 232; analy-
    sis of Compromise of 1790,
    187–88, 197–98; role in 1790, 181,
    193, 194, 201

Seney, Joshua, 204, 217; supports Susquehanna River, 100, 135, 138, 148, 149, 150, 152, 190, 193
Sexuality, 30, 35, 89, 131, 200
Sharpsburg, Md., 211
Shenandoah River, 119, 163
Shepherdstown, (West) Va., 125, 210
Siberia, 163–64
Sinnickson, Thomas, 101
Slavery, 58–59, 82, 128, 141, 144, 237; First Congress issue, 170–71, 172, 173; institution of, 4, 128, 161, 244; and Potomac capital, 7, 103, 215, 243; and George Washington, 110–11, 212. *See also* Philadelphia: anti–slavery sentiment
Smallpox, 16, 17, 58, 71
Smith, John, 106
Smith, William (Md.), 204, 213, 217; supports Susquehanna River, 100, 138, 148, 149, 150, 152, 187, 190, 193
Smith, William L. (S.C.), 146, 216, 232; and constitutionality of 1790 act, 194–95; describes Federal City, 223, 237; role in 1790, 175, 178, 180, 193
South, The, 41–42, 93, 215, 216, 222; defined, 3, 4; delegation (*See* Seat of government); lower, 22, 39, 64, 183; minority status, 4, 52, 61, 70, 92, 140, 142, 161, 171–72, 173, 192; upper, 106; and The West, 4, 9, 9–10, 104, 121, 141–42, 242. *See also* Disunion; Sectionalism; Union; West, The
South Carolina, 143, 171, 204; favors assumption, 169, 170, 174, 175, 178; delegation, 20, 49, 52, 54, 64, 89, 145, 153, 186, 190; and Philadelphia, 51, 89, 90–91, 102, 139, 177, 177–78, 191
Spanish Empire, 10, 70, 71, 107, 114, 121, 134, 245
Speculation: land, 3, 69, 91, 106, 107, 110–111, 116, 117, 119–20, 133–34, 134–35, 215; securities, 3, 169, 218. *See also* Washington, D.C.: lot speculation

Stamp Act Congress, 14–15
States: abolition of, 24, 169; capitals, 2, 5, 15, 19, 45, 46, 47, 52, 53, 59, 75, 131, 143, 212; debts (*See* Assumption); new, 9, 154, 162, 171 (*See also* West, The); rights, 28, 128, 143, 169 (*See also* Federalism); supremacy, 13, 22–23, 23–24
Stephen, Adam, 167
Steuben, Baron von, 69
Stock Market, 218
Stone, Michael Jenifer, 100, 125, 141–42, 149, 152, 186, 189, 205
Strong, Caleb, 194
Stuart, David, 151, 164–65, 168, 172; commissioner, 214, 219, 226, 227, 228, 230
Sumter, Thomas, 145, 169
Susquehanna Canal Company, 133, 155
Susquehanna River, 8, 120; capital on, 100, 125, 128, 132–68 *passim*, 176, 191, 193, 197, 204 (*See also names of towns*); navigation, 12, 114, 124, 133–34, 140–41, 141, 150–56 *passim*, 205, 240
Sussex Courthouse, N.J., 10
Swarta Creek, Pa., 133, 135

Taxes. *See* Excise Act (1791); Federal revenues
Tennessee, 9
Thatcher, George, 98, 174, 179, 189–90, 196–97, 216
Thatcher, Sarah, 98
Theater, 67, 98, 200, 212, 239
Thomson, Charles, 16, 20, 24, 35, 38, 39, 59, 68, 126; and capital, 37, 47, 52, 61, 62, 63, 68
Thomson, Hannah, 59, 67
Thornton, William, 230, 233
Tiber Creek, Md., 112, 215, 221, 237, 238; capital at, 164, 166, 209, 210, 221. *See also* Washington, D.C., natural setting
Transvestites, 200

Trenton, N.J., 66, 67; capital at, 103 (*See also* Delaware River, Falls); temporary seat at, 21, 33, 34, 47, 49–55 *passim*, 60, 61, 241
Trollope, Frances, 240
Tucker, Thomas Tudor, 90, 140, 145, 169, 171, 193
Tulpehocken Creek, Pa., 132, 133

Union, 14–15, 68, 121; preservation, 4, 50, 52–54, 55, 61, 65, 68, 71, 73, 95, 128, 137–44 *passim*, 147, 165, 168, 177, 214, 224, 225, 232, 235, 239 (*See also* Civil war; Disunion); sense of, 13, 27, 31, 171; need to strengthen, 25–28, 33, 39, 59, 62, 68, 73, 208 (*See also* Constitution)

Vermont, 154, 171
Vetoes, 151, 194–95, 203, 217–18, 244
Vining, John, 140
Virginia
—capital in: appropriations for, 46, 61, 72, 108, 210–11, 231; cession act (1789), 166, 213; mentioned, 44–45, 48, 58, 121–26, 129, 136, 154, 163–66, 177, 178, 199
—protests assumption, 203–04
—commercial city in, 108–09, 113–14, 115, 119–120, 182
—delegation: in Confederation Congress, 18, 52, 54, 60–61, 64, 65, 89, 90–91; in 1789, 125, 128, 142, 150, 152, 153, 160; in 1790, 169, 170, 174–77 *passim*, 182–86, 189–90, 199
—federal elections, 103, 203–04
—finances, 185, 186, 195–96
—rival of Maryland (*See* Maryland)
—mentioned, 3, 15, 27, 29, 214, 225–26, 243, 244
—rival of Pennsylvania for access to The West (*See* Pennsylvania)
—Philadelphia influence over, 15, 57, 97, 113
—public opinion, 57, 66, 97, 151, 171–72, 219
—ratification, 81, 85, 87, 124–25, 130, 142, 147, 244
Virginia and Kentucky Resolutions, 204

Wabash River, 12
Wade, Benjamin, 243
Wadsworth, Jeremiah, 69, 144, 169
Walker, George, 122–23, 164, 166, 245; ideas for capital, 123, 220, 222; proprietor and promoter, 223, 224; supports L'Enfant, 228, 229
Walker, John, 176, 177, 187, 188, 189
Warren, Mercy, 7, 22, 81
Washington, George, 62, 87, 88, 92, 97, 105, 125, 135, 164, 165, 172, 196–197; and Alexandria, 87, 112–13, 126, 151, 212, 217–19, 233–34; capital site chosen by, 209–11, 212–13, 217, 242; character, 6, 13, 140, 151, 156, 172, 182, 211, 213–14, 235; Commander in Chief, 17, 28, 33, 231; criticism of, 118, 126, 194–95, 201, 214, 218–19; death, 171, 173, 234, 236, 244; land speculations, 110–11, 114, 116, 117, 120, 213–14, 221, 238; monument for, 56, 236–37; motives, 13, 148, 201, 213–14, 217–18; and Mount Vernon, 70, 109, 110–11, 129, 209; political philosophy, 24, 28, 29; Potomac-bias, 106, 139, 150, 152, 162–63, 186, 214, 231, 242, 245; and Potomac navigation, 111–12, 113–26 *passim*, 214, 234, 240; role in 1790, 182, 189, 194–95, 197, 205; on capital location prior to 1789, 15, 48, 66, 69–70, 126, 231; Seat of Government Act (1790) implementation, *Ch. 8, esp.* 233; slavery, 110–11, 212; use of veto, 156, 194–95, 217–18; and The West, 103, *Ch. 4, esp.* 111, 114, 117, 121. *See also* History, use of; President
Washington, Lawrence, 109
Washington, Martha, 111, 213, 214, 232, 236
Washington Crossing, N.J. and Pa., 57, 65, 130

Washington, D.C.: commercial center,
221, 234, 239, 240, 245, 246; commissioners, 209, 217, 219–20,
222–23, 225, 226–31, 233; cost of
developing, 208, 209, 211, 221,
222, 227, 231–32, 238, 241, 244;
cultural center, 239, 244; defense,
231, 242; and exclusive jurisdiction,
240–41; federal buildings at, 210,
217, 222, 231, 233, 244 (*See also*
Capitol; White House); land patents, 57–58, 107, 223; lot speculation, 58, 220, 226–27, 229,
231–32, 239; named, 225; natural
setting, 109, 221, 223, 237–38;
plan, 220–24; proclamation locating, 212; proprietors, 209, 221–22,
223–24, 226, 229, 230, 239; removal of capital from, 241–44; residents, 237, 238–39, 240–41;
retrocession, 240–41, 243; southern character, 242, 243; survey,
220; swamps, 237–38
Washington Family, 208
Wealth, influence of, 22, 53, 141, 173.
   See also Republicanism
Webster, Noah, 202
Webster, Pelatiah, 131
West, The: access to, 8, 10, 12, 49, 64,
75, 108, 110, 129, 132–42 *passim,*
149, 155, 159, 165; fear of, 9–10,
11, 162; importance of, 9, 52, 92,
103, 121, 123–24, 143–44, 144,
177, 235; lands, 9, 12, 23, 24, 70,
169, 223; loss of, 9–10, 40, 114,
121, 123, 134, 144, 151, 162, 163;
new states, 4, 9, 61, 66, 70, 128,
154, 162; as southern ally, 4, 9,
9–10, 104, 121, 141–42. *See also*
Potomac River: removal of capital
from
Westchester Co., N.Y., 48
White, Alexander, 125, 150, 152, 218,
230; role in 1790, 172, 185,
192–93, 196, 197
White House (presidential mansion),
223, 228, 236, 238, 239, 242

Wilderness, 12, 128, 191. *See also* West,
   The
Williams, Otho H., 123, 211
Williamsburg, Va., 46, 49, 52, 125, 176
Williamson, Hugh, 51, 75, 89
Williamsport (Williams Ferry), Md.,
   123, 125, 136, 166, 211
Willing, Thomas, 41
Wilmington, Del., 47, 50, 58, 88, 94,
   130
Wilson, James, 77, 84, 212
Wingate, Paine, 157, 175–76, 177, 217
Wisconsin delegation, 244
Wolcott, Oliver, Jr., 239
Women, 30, 63, 67, 89, 98, 99, 104, 190,
   200, 202
Wrights Ferry, Pa., 133, 135, 151
Wynkoop, Henry, 99

Yellow Fever, 226
York, Pa., 19–20, 133, 134, 135
Young, Notley, 220, 228, 238